10/93

SURVIVING
and Other Essays

SURVIVING
and Other Essays

Bruno Bettelheim

VINTAGE BOOKS

A Division of Random House
New York

First Vintage Books Edition, April 1980
Copyright 1952, © 1960, 1962, 1963, 1969, 1976, 1979
by Bruno Bettelheim
All rights reserved under International and Pan-American Copyright
Conventions. Published in the United States by Random House, Inc.,
New York, and simultaneously in Canada by Random House of
Canada Limited, Toronto. Originally published by Alfred A. Knopf,
Inc., New York in April 1979.

Owing to limitations of space, all acknowledgments for permission to
reprint previously published material appear in the back of the book,
following the index.

Library of Congress Cataloging in Publication Data
Bettelheim, Bruno.
    Surviving and other essays.
    Includes index.
    1. Personality change—Addresses, essays, lectures.   2. Psychic
trauma—Addresses, essays, lectures.   3. Concentration camps—
Germany—Psychological aspects—Addresses, essays, lectures.
4. Holocaust, Jewish (1939-1945)—Psychological aspects—Addresses,
essays, lectures.   5. Oppression (Psychology)—Addresses, essays,
lectures.   6. Social psychology—Addresses, essays, lectures.   I. Title.
[BF698.2.B47   1979b]   150'.8   79-22029
ISBN 0-394-74264-8

Manufactured in the United States of America
987654

To Trude, Ruth, Naomi, Eric

Contents

Preface

The essays forming this book were written over the last thirty-seven years. Some have been previously published in response to requests that various lectures given by me should be made available to a wider audience; others were written for specific occasions. Still others, comprising about a fifth of this book, were written specifically for it, and have not been published before.

Many of the articles reprinted here originally appeared in publications with limited circulation. In going over these old papers, it seemed best to eliminate repetitions caused by subject matter overlapping from one essay to another. However, by a natural process, some subjects originally dealt with in these essays became the basis of, or were incorporated into, some of my books published over the years. Thus the reader may recognize some parts or themes in these essays, or even whole essays, as being already familiar to him. For this type of repetition I must apologize and ask his indulgence.

It was not possible to avoid repeating myself, particularly in those papers that deal with the German concentration camps. After their original publication, large segments of some of these essays became part of my book *The Informed Heart*; similarly, much of "Schizophrenia as a Reaction to Extreme Situations" was later worked into *The Empty Fortress*.

The decision to republish these papers, forming about a fifth of the book, when they had been contained in previous books, was made only after much consideration, and with some misgivings. Respect for the readers of my earlier books demanded that they not be expected to read again that with which they are familiar. But respect for the readers of this book required that I should submit to their critical evaluation the most basic, important influences in shaping my thoughts over these many years, and explicate why and how I had reacted to them. This meant approaching these issues both in the form in which I had first struggled with it all, and also in the way I later elaborated on this work.

But more important, respect for the readers of this book demanded also that this book should not contain important lacunae that could be filled in only by referring to my other books. So it seemed best to repeat that which seemed essential in the context of this book.

Reprinting old papers permitted alterations to make them more comprehensible, more readable, and—without changing anything essential—to eliminate errors. I only hope that in trying to correct old errors I have not committed too many new ones. Previously published papers are indicated by a footnote which tells where they originally appeared and what alterations have been made in preparing them for republication here. These occasionally quite extensive additions, eliminations, and other changes are not indicated in the text in order not to break it up. But when a paper was given a new introduction this is shown by its being printed in italics.

Many contributed to what is contained in this book. Some did so by their willingness to listen to what occupied my mind, thus encouraging me to put it into words. Others helped by asking questions and by making suggestions. Again others, with their acid criticisms, induced me to write down my thoughts to be able to scrutinize and correct them.

One's writings are amalgams of what one has learned from others and from one's life experience. I learned so much from so many that it is impossible to name them here; and acknowledging my debt to some and not to others would be arbitrary. But I can express my gratitude at least to those who directly helped to bring this book about.

Theron Raines and Robert Gottlieb encouraged me to collect some of my old papers; it was their kind insistence that overcame my hesitations. Joyce Jack, who helped me to put this book together, again and again quenched my doubts and gave me the courage to go on. She immersed herself in many more papers than are included here, and with unfailing good judgment, superb integrity, and greatest consideration for my feelings helped me to choose the papers to be excluded and those to be included in this selection—the one as difficult a decision as the other. Most of the previously published articles had been originally edited by others, who much improved what I had written. I owe them a debt of gratitude which I am happy to restate here. Finally, both old and new writings needed considerable reworking before they could be included here. All this difficult work was done by Ms. Jack, and it was she who suggested how the various papers should be arranged in this book. For all this and much more I am deeply grateful to her.

At various places in the book I suggest that how survivors fare later on in life depends in large measure on the support they receive from those closest to them. I was very lucky in this respect, much more so than most, thanks to my wife and children. They have asked me to write my history since they thought I had participated in a sufficient variety of events to give it some interest. Being reticent, due either to my nature or to my upbringing, I feel unable to do so any more than is implied in this book. Since this is the best I can do to comply with their request, as a small token of my love this book is dedicated to them.

PART ONE

The Ultimate Limit

Death is the ultimate limit of all things.
(*Mors ultima linea rerum est.*)
—HORACE, *Epistles*, I

Unless philosophically inclined, people are content to take life as it comes when things go reasonably well, preferring to evade the troublesome question of life's purpose or meaning. While we are quite ready to accept intellectually that man in general is but the chance product of a long and complex evolutionary process, and that we in particular came into being as the consequence of our parents' procreative instinct and—so we hope—also their desire to have *us* for a child, I doubt that this rational explanation is ever truly convincing to our emotions. From time to time we cannot help wondering what life's purpose for human beings might be, if any. But it is not a problem that oppresses us greatly in the normal course of events.

In times of trouble, however, the problem of life's purpose, or meaning, forces itself on our awareness. The greater the hardship we experience, the more pressing the question becomes for us. It makes good sense psychologically that we begin to worry about life's meaning when we already suffer from serious trials and tribulations, because then our search for answers has a purpose. It seems that if we could just grasp life's deeper significance, then we would also comprehend the true meaning of our agony—and incidentally that of others—and this would answer the burning question of why we have to bear it, why it was inflicted on us. If in the light of our understanding of life's design our suffering is needed to achieve its purpose, or is at least an essential part of it, then as an integral element of life's great design our affliction becomes meaningful, and thus more bearable.

Great as one's pain may be, it becomes more tolerable when one

THE ULTIMATE LIMIT: Incorporated in this chapter are the first three pages of a different essay with the same title in which the fate of survivors of Hiroshima is discussed. It appeared in *Midway* 9 (Autumn 1968), pp. 3–25.

is certain that one will survive the sickness that caused it and eventually be cured. The worst calamity becomes bearable if one believes its end is in sight. The worst agony is mitigated as soon as one believes the state of distress is reversible and will be reversed. Only death is absolute, irreversible, final; first and foremost our own, but equally that of others. That is why death anxiety, when not relieved by a firm belief in an afterlife, surpasses all other anxieties in depth. Death, life's ultimate denial, poses most acutely the problem of life's meaning.

So intricately, so inextricably interwoven are death and life's meaning that when life seems to have lost all meaning, suicide seems the inescapable consequence. Suicidal attempts further elucidate this connection. Very few suicides are due to the wish to end insufferable pain which prevents any further enjoyment of life, when the condition causing the pain is definitely irreversible. More frequently suicides are the consequence of an unalterable conviction that the person's life has completely and irremediably lost all meaning. From my experience with persons who tried to commit suicide, I believe that the majority of suicides are accidents in attempts which are expected to be aborted, but unfortunately are not.

The vast majority of suicide attempts are desperate cries for help to become able to continue living. Such suicide attempts are serious, because if the help is not forthcoming, then the person may indeed end his life. What the suicidal person needs to be able to continue living, and the response which he tries to evoke, is the restoration of meaning to his existence.

A suicide attempt is thus most often an utterly desperate demand directed at some real or imaginary, but always emotionally significant person. This very special person's response to the suicidal action should demonstrate clearly, tellingly, beyond any possible doubt, that —contrary to the suicidal person's fear—there is meaning to his life. The more or less specific demand inherent in the suicide attempt is usually that this other person, through his action, should show that he is willing to go to extreme lengths—not to prevent suicide, as is all too often the inadequate response—but to give meaning to the afflicted person's life by convincingly showing that his existence is of singular importance to the intended rescuer. The suicidal person believes that only through his being important on the deepest level to this uniquely significant person can meaning be restored to his life. By virtue of being so meaningful to this all-important person, the suicidal individual's life becomes also meaningful to himself, and death is no longer an acceptable alternative to life.

To have found meaning in life is thus the only certain antidote to the deliberate seeking of death. But at the same time, in a strange dialectical way, it is death that endows life with its deepest, most unique meaning.

We cannot really imagine what life would be like, had it no end; how it would feel, how we would live it, what would give it importance. Those cultures which believe in successive reincarnations desire most that their chain should end; not only is the final goal of all reincarnations their cessation, but each separate existence also has its definite conclusion. If there have been civilizations which believed in the desirability of an unending life, it seems they could imagine it only as the eternal repetition of the same well-known daily events, or as an existence without any problems, challenges, change.

Even the poets have found it difficult to visualize a paradisal existence with any other content besides eternal bliss. Whatever the experience of life may have been for those who believed it to be without end, and whatever their ideas about the continuation of life after death, to us an existence in which nothing ever changes seems devoid of interest. Thus it is the finiteness of life—much as we may dislike contemplating it and dread life's end—which gives life its unique quality and makes us wish to savor every one of its moments to the fullest.

It is man's struggle to find the significance of life, and of its finiteness, and through his search master his fear of death, which defines not only his religion, but also much of what he considers best in his culture and the personal style of his life. Essentially man has dealt with the inescapability of death in three ways: through acceptance or resignation, making all of life a mere preparation for death and what supposedly comes after it; through denial; and through efforts at temporary mastery.

During the centuries when Christianity shaped life for Western man, he tried to both accept death and deny it. It was largely the denial that made the acceptance possible, because only the belief in a life eternal in the hereafter enabled man to face the knowledge that on this earth even "in the midst of life we are in death."

Later, when a rational-scientific view of the world began to emerge, belief in the hereafter crumbled. Acceptance and resignation became less possible, because from the start these had been based on denial. In the mood of this new age of reason, with its commitment to this world here and now rather than to the next, a good life on earth was thought to be assured through social, economic, and scientific progress.

With this, the widely held faith in life's definite goal of gaining salvation and, with it, life eternal, underwent a radical change: it became the struggle to achieve progress—which was thought to be limitless—which was to give life its ultimate meaning. This is the Faustian solution to the enigma of life's significance, and it found its most beautiful and concise expression at the end of Goethe's poem, when Faust had overcome his dread of death through his efforts to reshape the world for the better. Because of the improvements he had worked, Faust, the archetypical modern Western man, felt sure that

> *The imprints of my earthly days,*
> *In aeons shall not disappear.*

But the monumental improvement which Faust believed he bequeathed to the world, and which he trusted would guarantee the permanent continuation, if not of himself as a person, then of his life's achievement, is but a mirage.

By putting his trust in what progress could achieve, man sought to free himself ever more from the terror of death. Science would conquer disease, extend the span of life, make it ever safer, less painful, more satisfying. Because of decline in faith, the denial of death through the religious promise of life eternal wore thin, and came to be replaced by a concentration on postponing death. Man cannot worry about too many things at once; one anxiety easily replaces another. By concentrating his attention, as well as his anxieties, for example, on cancer and on cancer-causing agents, pollution, etc., man manages to push death anxiety so much into the background of his mind that for all practical purposes it is denied.

Since it is reasonable to assume that a solution to the cancer problem will be found, belief in progress seems to have proven its capacity to combat death anxiety, since with all the emphasis on fighting cancer the question is hardly considered of what will then cause the death of those who now die of cancer. Innumerable health fads serve the same purpose of trying to repress death anxiety by devoting one's mental—and often also one's physical—energies to prolonging life, so that thoughts about its end will not permit death anxiety to come to awareness.

For the rest, Western man has relied on hiding stark death anxiety behind soothingly scientific and less threatening euphemisms. Since anxiety is a psychological phenomenon, death anxiety came to be viewed as but a special form of "separation anxiety" or "fear of abandonment." Such terms, born of trust in unlimited progress, suggest that remedies for the fear of abandonment will eventually be forthcoming. And they can indeed be found for temporary desertion —although not, of course, for the ultimate one. Still, by using the same concept—anxiety—to refer to reversible and to irreversible events, to the feelings which both a temporary and the ultimate, eternal abandonment evoke, the irreversible event is made to seem similar to the reversible one.

But whatever man's psychological defenses against death anxiety, they have always broken down whenever catastrophe struck and vast numbers of people were suddenly and unexpectedly killed in a very short time. Probably the first such disaster for which we have ample records was the Black Death in the fourteenth century. This event resulted in an image of life as being nothing but a dance with death, a visual and poetic expression of the death anxiety then sweeping the Western world.

The earthquake which destroyed Lisbon in 1755 and caused great loss of life was widely experienced as a cataclysmic event which called the wisdom and benevolence of God seriously into question. With this doubt, men were deprived of the belief which until then had served them well to ward off death anxiety and had given meaning to their temporary existence on earth. This was also true for the boy Goethe, as he described in his autobiography a lifetime later;[1] it may very well have been this shattering experience at the beginning of his conscious existence which led Goethe to embrace the Faustian solution quoted above.

In the past it was mainly natural catastrophes: plagues, earthquakes, floods, devastating conflagrations—all of which came to be known as holocausts—which shook man's trust in those of his beliefs which gave deeper meaning to his life and at the same time served as

---

[1] *Dichtung und Wahrheit*, part one, book one.

his defense against death anxiety. When a war wiped out cities and countries, it was regarded as the scourge of God, as were natural disasters. As such, they led in religious times to renewed efforts to do God's will, to pacify His wrath through greater devotion.

All this changed with this century. In the twentieth century, man's mastery over natural catastrophes became more effective than ever. But at the same time it seemed he became the hapless victim of man-made cataclysms even more devastating than the natural disasters which had thrown him into panic death anxiety in the preceding centuries. Worse, progress in the sciences and in the rational organization of society, into which man had put his faith as the best defense against death anxiety and as that which would give meaning to his life, turned out to provide the tools for a much more radical destruction of life than man had imagined possible.

The modern defense against death anxiety—belief in the unlimited blessings of progress—was severely undermined by World War I and its aftermath. That war led Freud to recognize that death is as powerful a force in our mind and in shaping our actions as is our love of life. Unfortunately he cast this important insight into theories that paralleled his earlier concept of the libido (the sex instinct, or the life drives) and proposed a theoretical death drive. Actually it is not the battle between the life and the death drives that governs man's life, but a struggle of the life drives against being overwhelmed by death anxiety. In short, there is an omnipresent fear of extinction which threatens to run destructively rampant when not successfully kept under safe control by our conviction of the positive value of life.

The full impact of this recognition came much less from World War II (which was essentially a continuation of the first World War) than from the concentration camps with their gas chambers and from the first atomic bomb. These confronted us with the stark reality of overwhelming death, not so much one's own—this each of us has to face sooner or later, and, however uneasily, most of us manage not to be overpowered by our fear of it—but the unnecessary and untimely death of millions. Senseless mass murder in the gas chambers, genocide, the leveling of an entire city by the dropping of one single bomb—these became the indicators of the ineffectiveness of our civilization's defenses against the reality of death. Progress not only failed to preserve life, but it deprived millions of their lives more effectively than had been possible ever before.

Years ago Freud wrote of the three great blows dealt to our narcissism by the discoveries of science. The first was the Copernican revolution, which revealed that man's home, the earth, was not the center of the universe. The second was the Darwinian, since it removed man from his unique position and placed him squarely in the animal world. Finally, the Freudian revolution showed that man is not even fully aware of his motives, so that often they drive him to act in ways he does not understand.[2]

It seems that in addition to these basic blows to man's self-oriented world, he has sustained three additional shattering blows in this century alone. The first crisis was World War I, which destroyed the belief that in and of itself progress would solve our problems, provide meaning to our life, and help us master our existential anxiety —the human fear of death. It forced us to realize that despite great scientific, technological, and intellectual progress, man is still prey to irrational forces which push him to engage in violence and wreak destruction.

In World War II Auschwitz and Hiroshima showed that progress through technology has escalated man's destructive impulses into more precise and incredibly more devastating form. It was progress toward an all-powerful social organization that made Auschwitz— which epitomizes man's organized cruelty to man—possible. The atomic bomb demonstrated the destructive potentials of science and called the very benefits of scientific progress into question.

When the holocausts of past times were viewed as God's will, they had to be accepted as such. Inscrutable as His decisions were, men believed a catastrophe was a warning from Him to mend their ways while there was still time, so that they would not end in Hell, but gain eternal salvation. Thus while what happened was terrible, it neither undermined belief in the purpose and meaning of life nor disintegrated the individual man's personal system of beliefs, and with it his personality. Although the event was horrible, it was in harmony with the existing image of things. To accept without flinching the suffering God inflicted on man was a demonstration of the strength of man's faith, and with it of the solidity of his integration. It changed neither

---

[2] "A Difficulty in the Path of Psychoanalysis," *The Standard Edition of the Complete Psychological Works of Sigmund Freud*, vol. 17 (London: The Hogarth Press, 1955).

life's goal: salvation; nor its purpose: to do God's will; nor the way to achieve both: religious piety. Far from leading man to doubt his defenses against death anxiety, it strengthened them through religious fervor. With this, it also increased the resilience of an integration which was based on a system of religious beliefs.

Exactly the opposite holds true for the impact of modern holocausts. Far from fitting into our world picture, or the image of man which we would like to hold on to, they are utterly destructive to both. Since we realize that these mass murders are man-made, we can no longer ascribe some deeper meaning to them which potentially could benefit the survivor.

To our dismay we have been forced to realize that what rational man felt confident was life-enhancing stood revealed to be also life-destroying. Despite all the advantages which scientific and technological progress has brought us, it has also led to atomic fission and the holocaust of Hiroshima. Social organization which we believed would bring about ever greater security and well-being was used in Auschwitz to murder millions more efficiently. The reorganization of Russian society for the purpose of achieving a more beneficial social system resulted in the death of untold millions of citizens.

It is most destructive to a person—and when it happens to many at the same time and in the same way, to an entire culture—when the beliefs which gave direction to life are revealed as unreliable, and when the psychological defenses which were depended upon to secure physical and psychological well-being and protect against death anxiety—psychological structures which in their entirety form our personality—turn out to be untrustworthy. That experience is sufficient to disintegrate a personality built up on the basis of these beliefs.

It can become completely shattering to a person's integration when the system of beliefs on which he relied for his integration, and for offering protection against death anxiety, not only lets him down, but worse, is about to destroy him psychologically and physically. Then nothing seems left that can offer protection. Furthermore, we now no longer can feel confident that we will be able ever again to know reliably what to trust, and what to defend against.

Thus modern man's Faustian defense against death anxiety, and the system of beliefs which gave meaning to his life—striving to work for progress, although with no specific goal—have become shaky even under normal circumstances. The sheer prospect of death is not all that haunts us; there is also the anxiety we feel when the social structures we created to protect us from abandonment collapse, or when the personality structure we built up for the same purpose disintegrates.

While either source of protection, the personal or social, can easily crumble in moments of great stress, if normal life continues around us, it permits us to soon reestablish our protective stances, unless insanity or senility occurs. Matters are different when not only does the trust we put in man and society suddenly turn out to have been an illusion, but also our personality structure no longer protects us from a fear of abandonment. The only worse situation occurs when we really are abandoned and immediate death is possible and likely, although we feel our time is not yet ripe. Then the effects are catastrophic. The combined and sudden breakdown of all these defenses against death anxiety projects us into what I called some thirty-five years ago, for want of available terms, an *extreme situation*.

EXTREME SITUATIONS

We find ourselves in an extreme situation when we are suddenly catapulted into a set of conditions where our old adaptive mechanisms and values do not apply any more and when some of them may even endanger the life they were meant to protect. Then we are, so to say, stripped of our whole defensive system and thrown back to rock bottom—whence we must carve out a new set of attitudes, values, and way of living as required by the new situation.

This is what happened to me, as it did to thousands of others, when in the spring of 1938, immediately after the annexation of Austria, I was first arrested in my home and deprived of my passport, making orderly emigration impossible, and a few weeks later imprisoned for a few days and then transported into the concentration camp at Dachau. It happened to tens of thousands in November of the same year as part of the huge pogrom in the wake of the murder of vom Rath,[3] and in an even more horrible form to the millions

---

[3] On November 7, 1938, Herschel Grynszpan, a young Polish Jew, deeply upset by the Nazi persecution of Jews, went to the German embassy in Paris and there shot Ernst vom Rath, the third secretary, who died two days later. This served as the excuse for a terrible pogrom in Germany in which thousands of Jews were murdered and tens of thousands put into concentration camps.

who were shipped into the extermination camps during the war.

In some ways I was better prepared for the immediate shock of this "extreme experience" than many of my fellow prisoners, because out of political interest I had become familiar with the few reports which had trickled out of the Third Reich, telling what life in these camps was like. In addition, through the teachings of psychoanalysis I had become cognizant of the dark sides of man—his hatreds and destructive potentials, the power of those forces which Freud had named the death drive.

In a way, I also was lucky. During the transport I had been hurt badly enough to be looked at by an SS physician on the morning following my arrival at Dachau. He permitted me three days of complete rest, to be followed by a week of preferred treatment (*Schonung*).[4] This gave me a chance to recuperate to some measure. What may have been more beneficial in the long run, it was also an opportunity to attempt taking stock of my experience, to sort out first impressions of what being in this horrible predicament was doing to my comrades and to me, and of how those prisoners who had been in the camps for some years seemed to cope.

---

[4] On the train ride from Vienna to Dachau, which had lasted a night and the better part of a day, all the prisoners were severely mistreated. Of the approximately 700 to 800 prisoners who were part of this particular transport, at least twenty were killed during the night. Hardly anybody escaped unharmed, and many were wounded severely. Compared to them I was relatively lucky to suffer no permanent damage, although I received a few severe blows on the head and some other minor wounds. The horn-rimmed glasses I happened to be wearing when I was imprisoned marked me as an intellectual in the eyes of the SS, and this particularly aroused their antagonism, which may explain the blows on the head, the first of which smashed my glasses.

On my arrival at Dachau, my state was sufficiently bad—mainly due to loss of blood—that on the next morning the prisoner in command of the barrack (the so-called *Blockältester*) included me among the few whom he took to the camp clinic. There the SS orderly chose me as one of those to be looked at by the SS physician, who granted me a few days of rest. Since my glasses had been broken, and since without them I am near-blind, the physician also permitted me to write home for a replacement. Having learned my lesson, I requested—and a while later received—glasses of the simplest and cheapest kind. Even so, I found it best to hide my glasses and do without them whenever the SS went on a rampage; I was much safer this way. This was but one of the many precautions a prisoner had to learn to take if he wanted to increase his chances for survival.

This demonstrated the validity of what I had learned during my psychoanalysis: how psychologically reconstructive it is to try to comprehend one's mental responses to an experience, and how helpful it is to fathom what goes on in the minds of others who are subjected to the same experience. This effort to gain at least some limited awareness probably convinced me that something of my old system of mastery might be salvaged, that some aspects of the belief in the value of rational examination—such as in what could be learned from psychoanalysis—might be of some use, even under these radically changed conditions of living. Had I been projected immediately into the dreadfully destructive grind of deadly mistreatments and utterly exhausting labor, as were my comrades, I do not know whether I would have succeeded equally well in reestablishing some parts of my psychological protective system.

Of course, at the time nothing was further from my mind than salvaging something of my old defensive system. All my thoughts, all my energies went into the desperate struggle to survive the day, to fight off depressive moods, to keep up the will to resist, to gain some small advantages that might make seemingly impossibly difficult efforts to survive just a bit more likely to succeed, and to frustrate as much as possible the SS's unrelenting efforts to break the spirit of the prisoners. When I was not too exhausted or downhearted to do so, I tried to understand what went on in me and in others because this was of interest to me, and it was one of the rare satisfactions that the SS could not deprive me of.

Only with the passing of months did I very slowly come to realize that without any conscious planning, by doing only what came naturally, I had unconsciously hit on what would "protect this individual against a disintegration of his personality" (as I put it in the fourth of these essays). Stating it so confidently was possible only in hindsight; while still a prisoner in the camps, it was whistling in the dark on my part to view it so positively. I did view it thus, however, to fight off the lurking anxiety that the SS might succeed in their efforts to disintegrate my personality further, as they tried to do to all prisoners.

I began writing "Individual and Mass Behavior in Extreme Situations" in 1940, about a year after I had been set free and moved to the United States.[5] From the moment I arrived in this country, within weeks after liberation, I spoke of the camps to everybody willing to listen, and to many more unwilling to do so. Painful as this was because of what it brought back to mind, I did it because I was so full of the experience that it would not be contained. I did it also because I was anxious to force on the awareness of as many people as possible what was going on in Nazi Germany, and out of a feeling of obligation to those who still suffered in the camps. But I met with little success.

At that time, nothing was known in the U.S. about the camps, and my story was met with utter disbelief. Before the U.S. was drawn into the war, people did not wish to believe Germans could do such horrendous things. I was accused of being carried away by my hatred of the Nazis, of engaging in paranoid distortions. I was warned not to

---

[5] As will be discussed further, the terror the concentration camps created was made even more effective by the utterly arbitrary manner in which the gestapo imprisoned some people and set others free. There was no way to guess why one prisoner was let go after a few months, when another just like him was released only after several years, and yet again another was doomed to remain forever in the camps. So I have no idea why I was among the lucky ones who were released. It may have helped that one of the most prominent American public figures intervened personally and also through the American legation in my behalf. This interest in my fate was due to the fact that I had for many years taken care of in my home, and attempted to treat, an autistic child, the offspring of an old, prominent American family. On the other hand, this may have postponed my release, since some who in many respects were like me had been released sooner. How interventions could have the opposite from the desired effect may be illustrated by the fate of a very good friend of mine. A member of a royal family most determinedly and repeatedly requested his liberation. But he remained in Buchenwald all through the war and gained his freedom only when the American army liberated the camp. The danger of an intervention on the part of very prominent persons in favor of a particular prisoner was that the gestapo might conclude that he would be useful as a hostage, enough reason to keep him imprisoned until he might be used in that way.

Up to the time of the war, practically every week—at times every weekday— a few prisoners were released. During 1938/39 quite a number of Jewish prisoners were among them, in their case if all their possessions—often including also some large sums paid by their relatives—had been turned over to the Nazis and they could show that they would leave Germany immediately upon release. These conditions were met by me, and had been for many months before my release, and this may have been the reason I was finally let go. During this year

spread such lies. I was taken to task for opposite reasons at the same time: that I painted the SS much too black; and that I gave them much too much credit for being intelligent enough to devise and systematically execute such a diabolic system, when everybody knew that they were but stupid madmen.[6]

Such reactions only convinced me more of the need to make people aware of the reality of the camps, of what went on in them, and the nefarious purposes they served. My hope was that publishing a paper, written as objectively as possible to forestall the accusation that I distorted facts out of personal hatred, might make people listen to what I had to tell. That was my conscious reason for writing "Individual and Mass Behavior in Extreme Situations," which I finished in 1942.

Unfortunately, for well over a year, this paper was rejected by one after another of the psychiatric and psychoanalytic journals to which I sent it, thinking that these were most likely to be willing to print it. The reasons for rejection varied. Some editors objected because I had not kept written records while in the camps, implicitly revealing that they had not believed a word of what I had written about conditions in the camps. Others refused it because the data were not verifiable, or because the findings could not be replicated. A

---

so many Jewish prisoners—relatively speaking—were set free on this basis that there was a saying among the gentile prisoners: "There are only two ways to get out of here: feet first [meaning in a coffin], or being a Jew." But the friend I mentioned was Jewish and was not let go, although his family and their royal friend were most anxious to buy his freedom with a large sum, and all had been prepared for his immediate emigration.

To increase uncertainty and with it anxiety about the camps to the highest pitch, the gestapo played a cat-and-mouse game with the prisoners' relatives. For example, twice members of my family, while pleading for my release at gestapo headquarters in Vienna—as they did regularly both there and in Berlin—were told that I had already been set free and that they should hurry home because I probably had by now arrived there. Once they were told to send an emissary (a Nazi lawyer) to Weimar, the town closest to Buchenwald, to receive me there, which they did, to no avail. All this happened several months before I was finally released.

[6] For the deliberate unwillingness of the American government, and of large parts of the population, to believe in Nazi atrocities even as late as 1942 to 1944, see, for example, Arthur D. Morse, *While Six Million Died: A Chronicle of American Apathy* (New York: Random House, 1967).

few came right out and said that both what I claimed were facts and my conclusions were most improbable exaggerations. Some added— probably correctly, as judged by my experience when I tried talking about these matters to professional people—that the article would be too unacceptable to their audiences. But, given my reasons for want- ing to see the essay printed, I could not give up, and eventually it was published.[7]

Writing the essay was difficult intellectually, because at the time psychological thought had not yet developed the conceptual frame- work necessary for dealing adequately with these problems, so I was forced to struggle with it myself. But even harder was trying to deal with the anxiety-provoking and otherwise deeply upsetting memories which constantly intruded, making it arduous to think objectively about the camps. Trying to be objective became my intellectual de- fense against becoming overwhelmed by these perturbing feelings. Consciously I felt a great urge to write about the concentration camps, and in a manner which would make others think about them, make it possible for them to grasp what went on in them. It was a need which, many years later in the literature on survivors, was called their compulsion to "bear witness." My desire to make people under- stand received much impetus from my need to comprehend better what had happened to me while in the camps, so I could gain intellec- tual mastery over the experience.

I did not realize then that unconsciously my efforts were an at- tempt to master this shattering experience not just intellectually but also emotionally, because it continued to keep me in thrall, and much more seriously than I wished to accept consciously. Despite the night- mares about the camp, which at that time still haunted me every night, despite the great anxiety I felt every day about the fate of

---

[7] I am grateful to Gordon Allport who, as editor of the *Journal of Abnormal and Social Psychology*, not only accepted this paper by an unknown author, but found it of sufficient interest to publish it as the lead article of the *Journal*'s October 1943 issue; and to Dwight MacDonald, who reprinted it in *Politics* in August 1944.

How unknown the nature of the concentration camps was even at the end of the war can be seen from the fact that at that time General Eisenhower made this essay obligatory reading for all U.S. military government officers in Germany. Only by then, recognition was of no help to the millions who had been murdered in the camps.

others who faced starvation, torture, and death in the camps (a fact of which I was well aware), I wished to believe that there would be no lasting psychological effects of having been a concentration camp prisoner. This belief was facilitated by the tremendous relief I experienced at being liberated, at knowing that all those dearest to me were safely beyond Germany's frontiers. Unconsciously, I probably hoped that a consequence of getting this paper written and published would be the ability to put the camp experience behind me, so that I could move on to less emotionally loaded issues.

Maybe when I wrote the article it was easier to believe that this would be possible, that being a survivor and all it meant could be laid to rest once and for all, because at that time the extermination camps did not yet exist—the "final solution" of the Jewish question had not yet taken place in the gas chambers.

While we are scarcely able to believe any longer that life has a specific goal, but must be satisfied with striving in what seems the right direction, still we must continue to struggle to integrate our personality and master difficult experiences. We can never hope to achieve these elusive goals once and for all. This is true in general, but it is much more pressingly so for the crucial experiences of our lives, especially an extreme experience. Even more unsolvable are extreme experiences that also pose the central problem of our times: the potentially destructive aspects of progress.

This is speaking theoretically about that which to the survivor of the camps was and to some extent remains an immediately personal predicament. If one has mastered the experience of being a survivor on one level, the problem presents itself on still another level that must be resolved. This was true for me and for many others who attempted to integrate their camp experiences. The process of resolution is what underlies as a common trend the various essays forming this book.

After the article "Individual and Mass Behavior in Extreme Situations" had been published, I felt that I had dealt more or less directly with some aspect of what being a survivor meant. I then turned my attention to some interesting but much more innocuous problems. But after a while, I could not help getting involved once more in thinking, and often also in writing, about survivor problems.

It would have been easy in what follows to isolate those essays addressing themselves to survivorship and its direct consequences from the others, which ostensibly discuss entirely different issues, but such neat organization would not mirror the process of my mental life. Nor would it reveal how I arrived at certain attitudes as a result of my efforts to cope with the problem of survivorship. I hope the presentation of the essays in this book, with their discussion of such disparate topics as education, privacy, or art, will be recognized as different levels of the same effort at striving for integration.[8]

---

[8] If a reader should wish to read those essays dealing directly with the concentration camps and survivorship in sequence, he might do so in the following order: "Trauma and Reintegration"; "German Concentration Camps"; "Individual and Mass Behavior in Extreme Situations"; "Unconscious Contributions to One's Undoing"; "Remarks on the Psychological Appeal of Totalitarianism"; "The Ignored Lesson of Anne Frank"; "Eichmann: The System, The Victims"; "Surviving"; and finally "The Holocaust—One Generation Later."

In addition to these papers and *The Informed Heart*, I published the following articles and reviews of books dealing with the concentration camps and related issues: "The Helpless and the Guilty," *Common Sense* 14 (July 1945), pp. 25–28; "War Trials and German Reeducation," *Politics* 2 (December 1945), pp. 368–69; "The Dynamism of Anti-Semitism in Gentile and Jew," *Journal of Abnormal and Social Behavior* 42 (1947), pp. 153–68; "The Concentration Camp as a Class State," *Modern Review* 1 (October 1947), pp. 628–37; "Exodus, 1947," *Politics* 5 (Winter 1948), pp. 16–18; "The Victim's Image of the Anti-Semite," *Commentary* 5 (February 1948), pp. 173–79; "Doctors of Infamy—The Story of the Nazi Medical Crimes," *American Journal of Sociology* 55 (1949), pp. 214–15; "Returning to Dachau," *Commentary* 21 (February 1956), pp. 144–51; "A Note on the Concentration Camps," *Chicago Review*, August 1959, pp. 113–14; "Foreword" to Dr. Miklos Nyiszli, *Auschwitz—A Doctor's Eyewitness Account* (New York: Frederick Fell, 1960), pp. v–xviii; "Freedom from Ghetto Thinking," *Midstream* 8 (Spring 1962), pp. 16–25; "Survival of the Jews," *New Republic*, July 1967, pp. 23–30.

Trauma and Reintegration

Selecting from one's lifetime published work those essays which seem worth preserving in book form is a hazardous undertaking. Upon reviewing what one wrote some twenty or thirty years ago, one discovers that some articles which once seemed to shed new light on issues, proposing ideas ahead of their time and suggesting improvements, are now revealed as hopelessly antiquated, trivial, and impaired by shortcomings that have become glaringly apparent due to a better understanding gained with the passage of years or revealed by the publications of others.

This is why I was at first quite reluctant to follow the suggestions of others to prepare a book of collected papers. I was not insensitive to the lure of this method of satisfying vanity, but my fear was that far from bolstering my ego, such an enterprise could possibly inflict on it a serious blow. This anxiety found expression in the devious form of thinking that it would be a better use of my time to struggle with new problems instead of squandering it going over old papers, deciding which still had some merit, and bringing them up to date, where this seemed required.

Eventually, however, I had to recognize that thinking it would be preferable to write something new was a subterfuge to avoid the risk that, when reviewing what I had published over the years, I might discover that it had not been worthwhile. In fact, if at least some of my old essays were not still of interest, then the chances were minimal that any new writing I might engage in would have greater merit. When I realized this, the task of looking back on old papers from the perspective of today could no longer be sidestepped.

The incentive for writing on some topic can be external or internal; probably most often it is a combination of the two. As far as I knew then, and know now, the direct motive for my writing the papers forming this book was a personal desire to gain greater clarity about some vexing problem, finding an answer to a question that had become important to me. Since I was at all times fully occupied, and more often than not preoccupied, with directing a psychiatric institution for children, outside stimuli could induce me to devote time and effort to writing only when an inner pressure was present which took advantage of the external motivation to seek expression, and with luck, resolution.

Once my written ruminations had served the purpose of making things more comprehensible to me, the question would arise whither to commit these thoughts—to the wastebasket, which was the final resting place for most of them? This happened because what I had arrived at, although always useful to me, seemed of little interest to other people.

When I wished to promote a similar understanding in others, hoping that this might alter some of their attitudes concerning what seemed important issues, I felt it was permissible to publish such writings. Thus the final cause for my publishing an article was a wish to promote changes in thought or action which seemed desirable at the time.

This book's external causes were two chance events, without which it probably would not have come into being. And this, even though the basic motive for both writing these essays and assembling them now has been at work in me for some forty years, dominating my private thoughts and feelings during all that time. The final cause for this publication is a desire to permit comprehension of the nature of this inner motive which, although it is a highly personal one, may be of some general interest. First, however, a few words about the book's external cause.

Nowadays I go to the movies only rarely. But Lina Wertmüller's *Love and Anarchy* and *The Seduction of Mimi* had interested me sufficiently to see them, because the first deals with the fate of the individual man living under fascism, and the second with man's existence in modern mass society. Despite some parallels in these two films, the destinies of the two heroes (played by the same actor) are quite different: in *Love and Anarchy*, it is moral victory and physical death; in *The Seduction of Mimi*, moral death and physical survival—

but one fate is depicted as being as senseless as the other. In these films Wertmüller poses the problems of meaning in human existence and of what is involved in the struggle to achieve personal autonomy —issues which for many have been and continue to be of greatest concern. But Wertmüller seemed to embrace conclusions opposite from those I could accept.

In *Love and Anarchy* the hero, carried away by his private need to be loved, bungles the opportunity to assassinate Mussolini, which he has avidly sought. Out of guilt and disgust with himself for having missed his chance to carry on successfully the fight of the individual against the fascist state, he provokes an objectively meaningless battle with the police and in consequence is killed. It is thus the story of a man who—at least under fascism—can assert his autonomy only by courting death. The message of this film is ambivalent: the main character is both silly and heroic; his actions both admirable and senseless.

The Seduction of Mimi is also about the problem of individual autonomy in mass society. It is set in modern Italy, long after Mussolini's downfall. Here the film's ending suggests that for the average man, given societal conditions, survival requires the relinquishment of the quest for autonomy. Thus both films captivate by raising the crucial question of how to achieve autonomy, but fail to answer it. They seem to suggest that the problem has no solution; thus the search for autonomy is made to appear as most understandable, possibly inescapable, but utterly pointless.

Soon after seeing these films, I was asked by the editor of a prestigious weekly to write an article about Wertmüller's *Seven Beauties*, which had just opened in New York to rave notices. The reason the editor had thought of me was the fact that scenes taking place in a German concentration camp were central to this new film. Despite my demurral that I was incompetent to judge movies, the editor insisted that since I had been much concerned with the problems of the concentration camps in some of my writings, I was the right person to evaluate this film.

Having read about some other films which used the terror of the camps as a device to titillate, which I had found alarming and disgusting, and having seen the two other Wertmüller films mentioned above, which had intrigued me, I was curious about how she might have handled these scenes. With the understanding that it was not likely I would feel able to write about it, I agreed to attend a screening of *Seven Beauties*.

This film perturbed me deeply, and I told the editor I could not write the article he requested. Nevertheless he asked me to reconsider, and the film's distributor suggested a second screening. Thinking a great deal about the film for a couple of weeks did not dissipate its disturbing impact, and made it more pressing to comprehend the cause and nature of my severe reactions. For this reason I agreed to view the movie once more. Watching it now with much better preparation, I found it, if anything, even more upsetting than the first time; but I gained considerably more clarity as to why this was so.

A small group of sensitive and intelligent critics also attended the second screening, and they were much impressed by the film, although in an entirely different manner than I. Afterwards some of them discussed the film and their impressions of it with me. I was astounded by the degree to which these critics took the film's utterly distorted picture of the German concentration camp to be true to fact; and how ready they were to accept Wertmüller's interpretation of the camps, of what was required to survive them, and of the meaning of survival. That this was the film's effect on those who were likely to be among its most perceptive viewers concerned me much more than the film itself, particularly since most of the reviews of it which I had read suggested a similar general reaction.

By then it had become clear that it would take me considerable time to sort out my reactions—longer than the magazine editor could afford to wait for the contemplated article—and that the amount of space he could devote to this article would be insufficient to express my opinion. So I suggested that he ask someone else to write the article, which he did, and it appeared shortly thereafter.

But this did not end my having to struggle with what the film, and even more the reactions to it, had aroused in me. I continued to read what was published on the film, which was more than appears in print on most movies. The opinions expressed were mainly similar to those I had encountered in my conversation with the critics who had viewed the film with me. This made it all the more important to comprehend in detail why I had been convinced that the film was utterly wrong, when so many praised it highly.

To get hold of my feelings and clarify my thoughts, I began to put the latter down on paper, essentially for my own benefit. As I was in the process of doing so, articles on survivors and survivorship began to appear which seemed to express views paralleling those I believed I had detected in the film. These gave me more stimulation to figure it all out. So the essay became longer and longer, as I spent more and more time writing it. Eventually I felt I had met my need to come to grips with what the film and its reactions meant to me. But I doubted that the essay was publishable, given that opposite views on the matters it dealt with had found such wide acceptance. To my great surprise and satisfaction, however, *The New Yorker* was willing to publish it.

Equally surprising and unexpected were the several hundred letters I received in spontaneous response to the article. Nearly all were commendatory and gave expression to deeply felt reactions. Among the very few critical letters only a couple were angry; the rest were polite and thoughtful, showing that despite their writers' rejection of my ideas, the issues the article had dealt with were obviously of great importance to them.

The content of practically all the letters suggested that coming to terms with what the concentration camps and the extermination of European Jewry aroused was very troublesome, if not impossible, for many people. This was even more true in regard to the problem of the camps' aftermath: survivorship. These letters led to the suggestion, mentioned initially, to publish the essay on survivors as part of a book of collected papers. But another experience was required to overcome my hesitation to do so.

Half a year after the publication of "Surviving" in *The New Yorker,* I participated in a conference on the Nazi holocaust, attended by some three hundred persons, self-selected on the basis of their personal concern with this event. They were people well above average in intelligence, education, and social awareness. Talking with them and observing their reactions to what was presented made me shockingly aware how little these serious and well-meaning persons really understood what it had been all about, and what it ought to mean today; or so it seemed to me. While giving verbal expression to how horrendous, to what an abomination it had been, these people nevertheless seemed most eager to repress and deny it all by making it appear ordinary, robbing it of any present importance.

Probably they were induced to act thus because the Nazi horror had been a cataclysmic event which defied imagination, arousing so much anxiety that people needed to deny it any bearing on them as persons. Thinking about it seemed to raise the most perturbing questions about the nature of man if—without any hesitation and even with some satisfaction—he could spontaneously participate in the vilest and most systematic mass murder, not only of defenseless men, but also of millions of women and small children. Watching this with their own eyes on a documentary film, and listening to reports of it, seemed to create unmanageable feelings of revulsion and helplessness in the conference participants. This may explain why persons who had voluntarily chosen to watch this truly terrifying film showing scenes of the worst debasement possible of innocent men, women, and children, of torture, starvation, and mass killings, and then participate in a discussion of it, reacted to this experience by distancing themselves from it emotionally, and by denying it emotional and intellectual relevance to themselves in the here and now. They could not seem to deal with what it would otherwise have aroused in them.

It took the combination of these two events—the reactions to the article on survivors, and my experience at the conference—to convince me that it was worthwhile to attempt, as best I could, to suggest how one may try to cope with the two connected phenomena of genocide and survivorship. Coping with these requires, first, an understanding of what the holocaust was all about, how it could and did happen; second—and, since the holocaust is past history, more important today—some constructive way of dealing with what it evokes emotionally. Survivors are not alone in that they must learn to integrate an experience which, when not integrated, is either completely overwhelming, or forces one to deny in self-defense what it means to one personally in the present.

And so this book came about: its external causes were two chance events. But the personal involvement which took advantage of them to express itself could be called life-long, since by now it goes back over forty years.

SURVIVORSHIP

Survivorship consists of two closely related, but separate, issues. First is the original trauma—in this context, the personality-disintegrating impact of being imprisoned in a German concentration camp which completely destroyed one's social existence by depriving one of all previous support systems such as family, friends, position in life, while at the same time subjecting one to utter terrorization and degradation through the severest mistreatment and the omnipresent, inescapable, immediate threat to one's very life. Second, there are the life-long aftereffects of such a trauma, which seem to require very special forms of mastery if one is not to succumb to them.

In some of my past publications on the German concentration camps and related issues, I tried to do as much justice as I could to the first of these two problems. But these writings did not attempt to shed light on the second crucial problem, that of survivorship: on how to live with an existential predicament which does not permit of any solution. That question is one of maintaining integration in the face of the effects of past disintegration; and my efforts at helping others achieve their integration, as in my work with children at the University of Chicago's Orthogenic School, came to bear some relevance to it. So I hope that this collection of various essays may in its entirety offer some implicit suggestions about the nature of what may be involved in coping with these problems of trauma and integration.

Maybe I can best adumbrate the efficient cause for putting them all together by quoting the essential content of one of the letters I received in reaction to the article on survivors. It came, like all the others, from a stranger.

I have just finished reading "Surviving" in *The New Yorker* and am so impressed that I want to write you a letter. . . . I grew up in Berlin, Christian with some Jewish grandparents. When the Nazis gained power, I went to Holland. When there the Jews were rounded up, friends got fake papers for me. Another friend removed my papers from the files in the Hague, so I practically did not exist. A parsonage—until then unknown to me—took me in "for one night." But I then stayed there from January of 1942 until May of 1945. Nobody but the minister and his wife knew that I was not really their cook "Cathrine."

The reason I am writing you all this, is to confirm (as if you needed a confirmation!) that all you say about feelings of guilt are true. You probably know how many perished in Holland under the Nazi occupation, even if they had good faked papers. I was among the lucky ones, but again and again I have asked myself "Why was *I* saved?" . . . "Why did I get all this help?"

After the war I met Eva Hermann, a German gentile who had been imprisoned for years because she had helped Jews.[1] When I put the question of "Why?" to her, she answered, "So that you prove for the rest of your life that it was worth you being saved."

So this brings up the question, "Have we survivors a responsibility?" Maybe you can write on this subject.

As this letter shows, I am not a psychologist (I am a librarian) and more than once in my life I felt that there are problems which one cannot solve, but with which one must live.

The lady also wrote: "I know your book on Buchenwald. Quite some years ago I gave a talk on it at a meeting of the Quaker fellowship in ——. I still remember the very vivid discussion. . . ." Since quite a few other letters also expressed the wish that I should write more about how to cope with survivorship, I was encouraged to publish this book.

As this letter shows, struggling with the problem of survivorship does not require that one have been subjected to starvation, torture, or direct degradation—nor that one have stood helplessly by watching others like oneself murdered daily, as did those who were survivors of the camps. Having to live for years under the immediate and continuous threat of being killed for no other reason than that one is a member of a group destined to be exterminated, and knowing that one's closest friends and relatives are indeed being killed—this is sufficient to leave one for the rest of one's life struggling with the unsolvable riddle of "Why was I spared?," and also with completely irrational guilt about having been spared.

Being one of the very few who were saved when millions like oneself perished seems to entail a special obligation to justify one's luck and very existence, since it was permitted to continue when that of so many others exactly like oneself was not.

Survivorship also seems to entail a vague but very special responsibility. It is due to the fact that what should have been one's birth-

---

[1] Eva Hermann and her husband Karl had sheltered some Jews, which, at the time, was a crime in Germany. They were both imprisoned. He was sentenced to death, but reprieved because his scientific knowledge was needed, and he was made to serve as a slave laborer. Eva Hermann's pamphlet *In Prison Yet Free*, describing her experience, was published by the Tract Association for Friends (Philadelphia, 1948).

right: to live one's life in relative peace and security—not to be wantonly murdered by the state, whose obligation it should be to protect one's life—is actually experienced as a stroke of unmerited and unexplainable luck. It was a miracle that the survivor was saved when millions just like him perished, so it seems that it must have happened for some unfathomable purpose.

One voice, that of reason, tries to answer the question "Why was I saved?" with "It was pure luck, simple chance; there is no other answer to the question"; while the voice of the conscience replies: "True, but the reason you had the chance to survive was that some other prisoner died in your stead." And behind this in a whisper might be heard an even more severe, critical accusation: "Some of them died because you pushed them out of an easier place of work; others because you did not give them some help, such as food, that you might possibly have been able to do without." And there is always the ultimate accusation to which there is no acceptable answer: "You rejoiced that it was some other who had died rather than you."

These feelings of guilt and of owing a special obligation are irrational, but this does not reduce their power to dominate a life; in more ways than one, it is this irrationality which makes them so very difficult to cope with. Feelings which have a rational basis can be met with rational measures, but irrational feelings, more often than not, are impervious to our reason; they must be dealt with on a deeper emotional level.

I object particularly to the idea that anybody, including the survivor, has an obligation to prove that he was worth saving, if for no other reason than that this somehow implies that those who perished were not worth saving. But while to be a survivor does not entail a special obligation, it is nevertheless an extremely unusual and heavy burden—it is, as the letter says, a problem "which one cannot solve, but with which one must live."

The emotional aftermaths of the miracle that the survivor was saved were not infrequently psychological liabilities so serious that some survivors found them too difficult to master, while others succeeded in coping with them only to a limited degree. When discussing the unfortunate consequences of having been a concentration camp prisoner, it must at all times be borne in mind that the experience was of such an extremely traumatic nature that it shattered personal integration either entirely or to a very considerable degree.

Any trauma proves that in some respect the integration one has achieved fails to offer adequate protection. If the trauma is utterly destructive—as was true of the concentration camp experience—then it demonstrates that the integration of one's personality has failed the crucial test of its validity.

The psychological reaction of a survivor to this failure of his integration was never entirely a conscious one; on the contrary, it was largely conditioned by unconscious factors, such as unconscious responses to his concentration camp experience and to his pre-camp existence. Basically only three different psychological responses are possible to the experience that one's integration has failed one more or less completely. Which of these dominated the life of the survivor largely determined his post-camp existence. If one wishes to sum up —all too glibly—the three different responses to being traumatized to the most extreme degree, one might say that one group of survivors allowed their experience to destroy them; another tried to deny it any lasting impact; and a third engaged in a lifelong struggle to remain aware and try to cope with the most terrible, but nevertheless occasionally realized, dimensions of man's existence.

THE CONCENTRATION CAMP SURVIVOR SYNDROME

The most destructive of these three possible responses was to unconsciously conclude that the reintegration of one's personality was impossible, or pointless, or both. Consciously the survivor was aware of his inability to manage life, because it had become so fragmented that he felt unable to piece it together again. But this was because unconsciously he had decided that he could not rebuild his old personality because too much, or all, that gave it meaning was gone: those closest to him had been murdered; he had done things that could never be forgiven; he had lost what gave meaning to his life and it could not be recovered; and anyway there was no point in trying to build up a new integration since it could turn out to be as untrustworthy as the old one, which had let him down completely when he needed it most.

These survivors remain debilitated by the conviction that they cannot achieve a viable integration, which is true as long as they feel certain that to attempt the task of reintegration is hopeless or pointless. Unable to embark on the strenuous and hazardous task of integrating their personalities, such survivors suffer from a psychiatric disorder which has been named the *concentration camp survivor syndrome*.

Their state of mind is similar to that of an individual suffering from a depressive or paranoid psychiatric disturbance. But a basic difference between a psychotic individual and a survivor suffering from the concentration camp syndrome is that the first breaks largely due to inner pressures, not under those inflicted by an utterly destructive environment. The psychotic person breaks because he has invested significant figures in his environment with the power to destroy him and his integration. Thus while the psychotic person only delusionally believes that there are all-powerful figures who control his life and who plan to destroy him, the concentration camp prisoner observed correctly that those in whose absolute power he was actually had destroyed others like him, and were bent on destroying him, too. Thus the crucial difference between the prisoner and the psychotic is that the first assessed his situation realistically, the second, delusionally. But both experienced that their integration failed to protect them—and they are unable to reintegrate themselves effectively.

The person suffering from the concentration camp survivor syndrome usually made some effort to reintegrate himself in a viable way, but to no avail. Part of the tragedy leading to this syndrome was that the survivor tried to reintegrate himself too soon, at a moment when he was still utterly depleted of all psychological energy because of his camp experience—energy he needed to rebuild his integration. His failure at early reintegration gave him the conviction that he would never be able to do it by himself. To protect himself against another experience of painful defeat, he gave up trying.

Then, unable to accept that his survivorship posed an intractable problem with which, nevertheless, only he himself could cope, the survivor tried to find a solution to his predicament in what seemed the most readily available way: by having his spouse and his children solve his problems for him. He hoped and wished that they could relieve him of the burden of the haunting question "Why me?" and of his guilt, either directly through what they did for him, or indirectly, by permitting him to escape his burdensome life by living through his children.

As for the feeling of obligation, he tried to free himself of it by the primitive psychological mechanism of projection: it should be the special obligation of his family (or of the community) to take care of him, because he had suffered incredibly, and was unable to do it himself. It is the tacit request, and expectation, that others ought to solve his problems for him—to prove, for example, that he is *not* guilty, that he *was worthy* to be the one elected to be saved—which perpetuates the survivor syndrome, because unfortunately such efforts to have others solve one's problems always remain fruitless. Even more unfortunately, often the families of such survivors also came to suffer from the same syndrome, albeit in reduced intensity.[2]

It is so unjust, so unreasonable, that of all people the survivor should have to struggle, all by himself, with some of the greatest psychological difficulties imaginable—with psychological hardships everybody else is spared. He who has suffered so much: unrelieved death anxiety, and this often for years on end; extreme physical, moral, psychological pain; he who even after his miraculous liberation continues to suffer most severe deprivation because many or all of his family have been exterminated, he has lost all his possessions, has been uprooted also in all other respects, forced to live in a new land, learn a new occupation, etc.—why should he in addition be obliged to feel a special responsibility, be persecuted by guilt, tortured by obviously unanswerable questions? Why should he have to cope

---

[2] There is by now quite a literature on the survivor syndrome. To mention only some references: P. Matussek, *Internment in Concentration Camps and Its Consequences* (Berlin and New York: Springer Verlag, 1975); H. Krystal, *Massive Psychic Trauma* (New York: International Universities Press, 1969); R. J. Lifton, *Death in Life: Survivors of Hiroshima* (New York: Random House, 1967); Chodoff, "Psychiatric Aspects of Nazi Persecution," in S. Arieti, *American Handbook of Psychiatry*, vol. 6 (New York: Basic Books, 1975), and "Depression and Guilt Among Concentration Camp Survivors," *Existential Psychiatry* 7 (1970); Samai Davidson in "Psychiatric Disturbances of Holocaust (Shoa) Survivors. Symposium of the Israel Psychoanalytic Society," *Israel Annals of Psychiatry and Related Disciplines* 5:1 (1967). The survivor syndrome among the children of survivors is discussed in Helen Epstein, "Heirs of the Holocaust," *New York Times Magazine*, June 19, 1977, and in a personal communication to the author from Samai Davidson; Mr. Davidson's findings on this subject will eventually be published.

with it all, and worse, all by himself? The unfairness of all of this is not lost on the survivor; and if he has any tendency to give up in a state of complete emotional exhaustion, he eventually does so.

LIFE AS BEFORE

There were other survivors—and they may very well be the majority —who drew entirely different conclusions from the experience of having their integration give way under the impact of the concentration camp trauma. Their response was based on the correct realization that after liberation one had to rebuild one's personality. Therefore it seemed to them that a reasonable way to cope with the aftermath of the camp experience was to reintegrate oneself essentially the same way one had been before imprisonment.

In order to be able to do this, they had to use some devious psychological methods for evading the feelings of guilt, or the question "Why was I saved?" and the special obligations it seems to imply. The defenses they used were mainly repression and denial. In consequence, their integration is somewhat shaky and incomplete— because a most important group of feelings is denied access to awareness—and their personalities are to some degree depleted of energy for coping realistically with life, since they must expend it on keeping repression and denial going. But by and large their reintegration is quite viable, at least as long as it is not once again put to a serious test.

What happened in the camps was so horrible, and one's behavior while there open to so many perturbing questions, that the desire to forget it all, as if it had never happened, is most understandable. To be incarcerated in a camp meant to be cut off from all aspects of one's previous life. The SS and the Nazi state made it amply clear that the life the person had been living was ended; they denied one's former life all validity, now and forever. Most survivors, in counter-reaction, tried to deny validity to their camp experience after their liberation; to pretend it all hadn't happened.

Since they could not forget that it had happened, the closest they could come to negating its validity was not permitting it to change either their way of life or their personality. As a matter of fact, to be able to return to life after liberation the same person one had been before was a wish fervently held by many prisoners; to believe that

that could happen made the utter degradation to which prisoners were subjected more bearable psychologically.

The Nazis had destroyed the world the prisoner had been living in, had tried to destroy his very life. If so, the greatest defeat he could hand them was to demonstrate that they had utterly failed in their design by taking up life after liberation as closely as possible to the way it had been before imprisonment. Such return to a previous existence was greatly facilitated if the survivor was able to take up living with his wife, children, or parents, those with whom he had been living before, since they expected this of him. In view of these and many more facts—such as that the prisoner, emotionally utterly depleted by his experience, did not trust on liberation that he would have the strength and ability to commence a new and different life—most prisoners chose to make things as simple as possible for themselves, by continuing with the life they had known best. This, incidentally, was my plan at first: to take up my life in most important respects where it had been so cruelly interrupted.

Only doing this was not as easy as the prisoner had imagined in the wish-fulfilling daydreams which had sustained him in his distress. On liberation the elation that one had been saved overshadowed all other emotions, and regaining one's physical strength commanded all of one's attention. But soon the question "Why me?" cropped up, and with it the feeling of special obligation because one was one of the very few who had survived. Haunting nightmares do not permit the survivor to forget his camp experiences even if he manages not to think of them during the day—which is also difficult to avoid, especially for the first few years. As he becomes physically stronger, many half-forgotten events come back to memory which evoke guilt feelings, unjustified as these may be when viewed objectively. Understandably, many tried to ban these painfully upsetting thoughts from consciousness.

Once one has begun to deny validity to what one has experienced in the camps by not permitting one's vague feelings of guilt to come to conscious awareness, ever larger denials and further repression of memories become necessary to keep up the original denials. Thus every denial requires further denials to be able to maintain the original one, and every repression, to be continued, demands further repression.

Here one must remember that the simplest, most primitive, and most radical psychological defense against the impact of a shattering experience is to repress and deny it, while the most difficult is to work it slowly through, step by step, and adjust one's personality accordingly. So if most survivors try to deal with the trauma of the concentration camp experience through repression and denial, this is only what one should expect.

Engaging in denial and repression in order to save oneself the difficult task of integrating an experience into one's personality is of course by no means restricted to survivors. On the contrary, it is the most common reaction to the holocaust—to remember it as a historical fact, but to deny or repress its psychological impact which would require a restructuring of one's personality and a different world view from that which one has heretofore embraced. This, as mentioned, was the typical reaction of the participants in the conference on the holocaust.

The difference is that while such repression does not interfere with coping in the case of persons who were not directly and immediately afflicted by the holocaust, the same is not true for the survivor. First, his guilt is more direct and personal. Second, he has experienced what the non-prisoner has not: his old integration has been shattered; and so he can never fully trust it again, even if he can rebuild it.

Survivors who deny that their camp experience has demolished their integration, who repress guilt and the sense that they ought to live up to some special obligation, often do quite well in life, as far as appearances go. But emotionally they are depleted because much of their vital energy goes into keeping denial and repression going, and because they can no longer trust their inner integration to offer them security, should it again be put to the test, for it failed once before.

So while these survivors are relatively symptom-free, their life is in some essential respects, deep down, full of inner insecurity. They usually manage to hide this fact quite well from others, and to some degree also from themselves. But theirs is a house-of-cards existence. If all goes well, they have nothing to fear. But any strong wind of serious trouble may collapse their integration, which they themselves semi-consciously know is questionable, although they do not admit this to full awareness.

In order to continue with their integration as before, they must protect themselves against some of what could be their most meaningful experiences. Not because these would necessarily shatter them, but because they fear they might, since they cannot trust their integration to be maintained under severe strain. They fear that any deep experience might reveal the relatively empty existence they are living, which is due to the fact that they deny meaning and impact to what has been the most horrendous experience of their lives—the most terrible experience anybody can live through.

REINTEGRATION

Finally, there is the group of survivors who concluded from their experience that only a better integration would permit them to live as well as they could with the aftereffects of their concentration camp experience. Their reintegration had to permit them to cope with the feeling of guilt, and the unanswerable question of "Why me?" It had to be an integration which, by including in its makeup the aftermath of the camp experience, seemed to promise to be more resistant to severe traumatization than had been the old one.

These are survivors who tried to salvage something positive from their camp experience—horrible as it had been. This often made their lives more difficult than their old ones had been, also in some ways more complex, but possibly even more meaningful. This is the advantage they derived from restructuring their integration in a way which gave full cognizance to the most tragic experience of their lives.

A survivor has every right to choose his very own way of trying to cope. The experience of being a concentration camp prisoner is so abominable, the trauma so horrendous, that one must respect every survivor's privilege to try to master it as best he knows and can. The foregoing discussions of the "survivor syndrome," and of some of the aftereffects of choosing "life as before," suggest why I believe that these most understandable solutions are not also the most constructive ones. I think the letter quoted implies a more viable solution than do projections or the denial or repression of guilt. It suggests a working-through of the original trauma and of its consequences which is more effective and satisfying than despairing of achieving a new integration, or of maintaining to oneself that no new integration is needed.

A precondition for a new integration is acceptance of how severely one has been traumatized, and of what the nature of the trauma has been. With that, it becomes easier to accept and cope with one's guilt. As for the question "Why was I saved?" it is as unanswerable as "Why was I born?"

But since one was saved, one might as well try to live in such a way that without either pride or arrogance one can say to oneself, "Since I was saved, I am trying to make the best of my life, limited as it must be by my shortcomings."

The nature of the new integration which can be achieved by the survivor who—like the writer of the letter—has become able to accept and to live constructively with the feelings of guilt, and with the knowledge that the question "Why me?" while haunting, must not be repressed, will be different for each person since, like any true integration, it has to be built up out of unique life experiences. That the author of the letter has achieved reintegration can be seen not only from how open she is about the deepest problems of survivorship, but even more clearly by her stating her feelings of guilt, without any need to justify herself and her surviving.

The survivor, then, has no special obligation. The prison number tattooed on his arm is neither a mark of Cain nor a special distinction. I do not think it is particularly laudable to spend one's life bearing witness to the inhumanity of man to man. Even mass murder on the scale of Nazi genocide is unfortunately not unique in the history of man, although the mechanistic and systematic way it was carried out by the Nazi Reich is unique.

But to have come face to face with such mass murder, to have come so close to being one of its victims, is a relatively unique, psychologically and morally most difficult, experience. It follows that the survivor's new integration will be more difficult—and, one may hope, also more meaningful—than that of many a person who has been spared subjection to an extreme experience, because the survivor will have to have integrated into his personality one of the most trying experiences a person can be subjected to.

The essays of this book intimate one person's highly idiosyncratic efforts at reintegration. Some attempt to understand the nature of the trauma, others suggest responses to it. Several papers reflect a very specific approach to the unanswerable question "Why me?" and to the assuaging of a vague, non-specific guilt. By promoting the personality integration of others, one may try to promote also one's own; and by serving the living one may come to feel that one has met one's obligation to the dead as much as this is possible. Again, other essays suggest that no integration will be complete that does not also encompass highly personal interests; that while integration requires some depth of experience, it also demands openness to a variety of experiences.

Personal integration, and with it achievement of meaning, is a highly individual, lifelong struggle. A collection of essays mirroring one man's efforts to approach this goal, reflecting his thinking over nearly forty years, will by necessity have some characteristics of a confession, however much he may have tried to conform in his writings to the requirements of an academically acceptable objectivity— the consequence of his having lived his life in academe, and of having in large part embraced its values. When the underlying motif of one's writings is to give words to one man's struggle against the destructive tendencies in society and in individual man—which very much includes himself—and to express his very personal efforts to extract meaning from life, in particular from his activities in his professional life as an educator and as a therapist, personal emotions will often intrude.

As a student of psychoanalysis and a follower of Freud, deeply impressed by his critical skepticism in regard to man and his nature, which nevertheless did not interfere with Freud's battle to gain for man the freedom to be truly himself, I know that all attempts to extract meaning from life are to a very large measure actually a projecting of meaning into life. This can occur only when and to the degree that a person is able to find meaning within himself, which he can then project outward.

One must invest life with meaning, so that one may be able to extract insight from it. This is not quite the circular or solipsistic process it sounds, because in order to derive meaning from life one has to arrange and organize it in a personal way. This organization then permits one to obtain personal knowledge from one's relation to the world which goes beyond that which one originally projected into it.

Despite the diversity of topics discussed in the essays which follow, there should be an inner consistency in the way the subjects were selected, approached, and dealt with. While the search for personal knowledge may entail many detours, even some dead ends, the struggle to attain it ought to reflect the manner in which one individual feels compelled to seek clarity in regard to some problems rather than others, because struggling with these issues seems particularly meaningful to him. This is the reflection of a mind working on those issues which involve it and that serve as steps toward the better integration of his person.

German Concentration Camps

It is difficult to remember today, when thinking of the German concentration camps, that there were a variety of camps, with quite different purposes. The unfathomable horror of the death camps, with their gas chambers in which millions were asphyxiated, overshadows the memory of the other camps and the innumerable murders committed in them as well. According to the best estimates, between 5.5 and 6 million Jews were killed by the Germans, most of them in the gas chambers of the death camps, in addition to vast numbers of Poles, Gypsies, and others considered undesirable by the Nazis.[1] When the death camps were organized in December of 1941, the gas chambers had not yet been used, but there had been precursors— mobile vans in which people were killed by the exhaust from the engines. The concentration camps as an institution by this time already had quite an abominable history of their own.

The first concentration camps were established immediately after the Nazis came to power in 1933; these were not yet for the purpose of killing those whom the Nazis considered undesirables—although quite a few of them were murdered in somewhat haphazard fashion all along—but mainly to terrorize those who might try to oppose the Nazis, and also to spread terror of retribution for opposition among the rest of the German population. The Nazis hoped to force all Germans to turn themselves into willing and obedient subjects of the Nazi Reich. So they maintained all along to some degree the fiction

GERMAN CONCENTRATION CAMPS: The first half of this essay has not been published before.

[1] There is considerable literature on this. Two books may be mentioned which state the facts concerning the extermination of European Jewry: Raul Hilberg, *The Destruction of the European Jews* (Chicago: Quadrangle Books, 1961), and Lucy S. Dawidowicz, *The War Against the Jews, 1933–1945* (New York: Holt, Rinehart and Winston, 1975).

that the purpose of these camps was to reeducate opponents of the regime, and to destroy those who resisted such reeducation. A third, large group of camps came into being during the war, for the purpose of providing German industry with extremely cheap, readily expendable, and practically unpaid foreign slave labor.[2]

Possibly because my own concentration camp experience antedates the inception of the "Final Solution of the Jewish Problem," with its carefully planned and systematically executed murder of all persons of Jewish descent, I have been concerned in my writings mainly with the meaning of the concentration camp phenomenon and its consequences rather than with the incredibly greater abomination of the death camps. But something else also contributed to this choice.

Of the three types of camps, the slave labor camps—terrible as they were—present the least interesting problems. They were not all that different from the worst of other slave labor situations known throughout history. Given the totalitarian nature of the Nazi state, and the ruthless and near-absolute power of the SS, conditions in the slave labor camps were much worse than those prevalent in even very bad prison labor camps, because the inmates did not enjoy even those small human considerations and the significant protections of the law which are the prerogatives of common criminals. But dreadful as life in the slave labor camps was, these camps did not present new or unique theoretical or psychological problems. Quite the opposite is true for the Nazi death camps, and for the concentration camps.

The death camps were established for the one purpose of perpetrating the "Final Solution of the Jewish Problem," that is, killing all Jews within reach in the most efficient manner possible. The de-

---

[2] From the ample literature on the concentration camps for so-called political prisoners again two books may be cited: Eugen Kogon, *The Theory and Practice of Hell: The Concentration Camps and the System Behind Them* (New York: Farrar, Straus, 1950), whose original German title, *The SS State*, indicates more accurately its scope, and my *The Informed Heart* (New York: The Free Press, 1960). The most complete accounts of all concentration camps, including the death and slave labor camps, are contained in International Military Tribunal, *Trial of the Major War Criminals Before the International Military Tribunal: Official Text*, 42 vols. (Nuremberg, 1947–49). Further, see Office of the United States Chief of Counsel for the Prosecution of Axis Criminality, *Nazi Conspiracy and Aggression*, 11 vols. (Washington, D.C., 1946–48). (Both publications include incidentally my depositions as a witness.)

struction of the Jews, of the Gypsies—of whom about 100,000 were murdered—and of some other groups also considered racially inferior and thus dangerous to the superiority and purity of the German race, was the consequence of paranoic delusions peculiar to Hitler with which he infected his followers—although this could not so easily have led to the destruction of millions had it not drawn support from centuries-old prejudices, discrimination, and hatred, and had not masses of Hitler's followers made this delusion their own, as expressed, among many other ways, in the often-chanted slogan "Awake, Germany! Exterminate the Jews!" (*Deutschland erwache! Juda verrecke!*) In any event, terrible as it was that those given to fantasies about a pure Aryan race had the absolute power to act them out by destroying millions of hapless victims over much of Europe, I am optimistic enough to believe that there is little likelihood of a similar concatenation of circumstances ever again conspiring so that a parallel delusion will lead to an analogous destruction of millions.

I am not equally sanguine in regard to the possible use of the concentration camps as a means to establish total control in a mass society because of the fact that very similar concentration camp systems were spontaneously created for the same purpose by the two otherwise radically different totalitarian mass societies: Leninist and Stalinist Russia, and Hitler's Germany. In both countries these institutions were administered along very similar lines by a secret police.

Although the concentration camps were sometimes located in the same places as the death camps, and although they incidentally provided slave labor (including Jews) for the SS, their purpose was to terrorize, and through the anxiety thus created, permit the state to control all that its subjects did and thought. The specific method used to make the concentration camp an instrument for controlling the entire population was this terror shrouded in secrecy, which vastly increases its power to create incapacitating anxiety. Thus, the existence of concentration camps as the places where opponents of the regime were severely punished was widely and frequently advertised, but what went on in the camps was only suggested through fear-creating innuendos. (Quite the opposite was true for the death camps; more serious—albeit mostly ineffective—efforts were made to keep secret and covert their existence and purpose.)

When before the war sizable numbers of Jews were imprisoned in the concentration camps, this was done to terrorize all Jews so that they would emigrate immediately and leave all their possessions behind—which nearly all did who were psychologically able to contemplate leaving everything behind and starting life anew in a foreign land, and who had the strength to arrange for their move, or to induce others to help them do so—even though in many cases the only places which would accept them were those they would not have chosen, had they had a choice.[3] The large number of Jews who did leave Germany after they, their relatives, or their friends had been imprisoned in the camps illustrates once more the effectiveness of the concentration camp as an instrument of total control not only over the prisoners, but also over the rest of the population. The terror of the concentration camps as a means of altering behavior, and with it attitudes and even personality, is an inherent potential of a technologically oriented totalitarian mass society when its anti-humanistic tendencies are no longer tempered by moral or religious scruples.

Self-interest demands that each person try to reduce his anxiety as much as possible; the best way to do so in a mass state is to become a willing and obedient subject of the state, which means doing the state's bidding all on one's own. Just because this method of control through terror and secrecy was so effective in Nazi Germany, there is danger that it may be used again.

I have devoted a book to the discussion of this danger inherent in the totalitarian mass state (*The Informed Heart*). Its subtitle, *Autonomy in a Mass Age,* suggests what I believe is the antidote to this danger. Because this problem area was treated at length there, albeit in somewhat different form, I hesitated to republish here "Individual and Mass Behavior in Extreme Situations," to be followed by some other articles dealing directly or indirectly with related issues.

The justification for doing so was that it seemed of some interest to review first attempts at understanding the psychological purposes and the broad impact of this modern method of complete coercion which, encompassing both body and mind, induces or forces the individual to change aspects of his personality to conform to the will of the totalitarian state.

---

[3] During various periods it was quite possible to enter some Central American countries, at least for a limited time; and up to the beginning of the war it was fairly easy to go to Shanghai, although for penniless newcomers it was very difficult to earn a living there.

With the exception of some minor editorial changes, "Individual and Mass Behavior in Extreme Situations" is therefore reproduced in its original form. What now seem like awkward efforts to state matters objectively were retained because these reflect both my desire to convince my original audience that what I wrote was not the distorted outpourings of a person carried away by his emotional reactions to his experience—as I had been accused of being—and also my own wish to gain distance from the experience, and to master it.

The forced objectivity of diction is also retained because it was an expression of a first attempt at working through and integrating through distancing and intellectual comprehension; in short, of trying to put a difficult experience behind me without having truly built it into my life and personality with all of its consequences and meanings. It now seems to me that my unconscious hope was that, having dealt with my experience in this intellectual manner, I would then be able to go on with "life as before."

It did not turn out this way. Only a couple of years after publishing the essay, I was to return to writing about the German concentration camps—as I have done repeatedly since then—this time for a much wider audience, in an article for some special volumes of the *Encyclopaedia Britannica*. Some of the facts presented in that article are reprinted below, since they may serve as background for the psychological analyses in the papers which follow.

SOME FACTS ABOUT GERMAN
CONCENTRATION CAMPS[*]

Until 1933, concentration camps had never been deliberately employed by a government to intimidate its own subjects except by Stalinist Russia. The German National Socialist government was therefore the first Western regime to use them as a major instrument for establishing control and ensuring its continuation in power. Because the camps were new inventions of the regime, no rules or regulations inherited from the German republic interfered with their organization. Moreover, the camps were entirely under the control of

---

[*] What follows are selected and updated parts of an article, "Concentration Camps, German," which appeared in *10 Eventful Years*, Vol. 2 (Chicago: Encyclopaedia Britannica, Inc., 1947), pp. 1–12.

the secret state police, removed from any interference by any other governmental institutions such as the courts, which might have exercised a mitigating influence.

The history of the camps, as central institutions of the government, followed closely that of the National Socialist state, and changes reflected developments in the dictatorship itself. Whenever the regime felt threatened, the tools safeguarding it were used more viciously and extensively. As the regime expanded and encompassed all of Germany's life, the concentration camps increased also in size and purpose. The camps then became used for goals not contemplated when they were first established. As time passed, the old types of concentration camps could no longer fulfill the various purposes assigned to them, and new types were developed. During the regime's decline, the camps reflected the disintegration and chaos of a government which was no longer able to control even its central institutions of power.

At least three factors combined in influencing the history of the concentration camp: the history of the regime itself and the various needs it tried to meet by means of the concentration camps; the independent development of the concentration camps as institutions; and, finally, the counter-actions of the prisoners in the camps.

Legally, the creation of the concentration camps was indirectly based on the German constitution, which in its article 48, paragraph 2, gave the president far-reaching emergency powers. These were used by Paul von Hindenburg in 1933 to promulgate a law permitting protective custody (*Schutzhaft*) to protect the state's security. An edict from the Ministry of the Interior of April 12, 1934, introduced into the rules governing protective custody legal grounds for establishment of the camps. It also decreed that persons sent to a concentration camp came under the jurisdiction of the gestapo and that their release was at its discretion. Later, courts ruled that such prisoners could have no access to the courts.

The administration of the law for protecting people and state was entrusted to the secret state police, *Geheime Staats Polizei*, whose name was shortened to the use of the first letters of each word so that it became known as the gestapo. The gestapo never gave any public account of its activities, did not tell why anybody had been imprisoned, never told for how long; and did not even inform prisoners' relations as to whether their kin were still alive—all to increase terrorization through secrecy and uncertainty. It was staffed by the most trusted and fanatic followers of Hitler, the SS troops. Later, when the SS expanded, elite formations were created whose officers administered and ruled the concentration camps while the soldiers served as guards. These specially selected and trained soldiers of the secret state police (*Schutz Staffeln*, hence SS) wore as a distinctive insignia a skull (death's-head) and from this were known as the death's-head (*Totenkopf*) units. The insignia signified both their inhumanity and their commitment to kill and die unhesitatingly for the Reich.

At first only the regime's political enemies were brought into the camps, and from among them, only those who could not be prosecuted successfully in the courts of law. But soon others were included, when it seemed undesirable for the government to make public their imprisonment or any specific grounds for it.

As soon as the Nazi party was securely entrenched in power the situation changed, because then former left-wing opponents were no longer the most dangerous foes of the government. In 1934, the radical element within the party, including followers of Ernst Roehm, became the first party members to enter the concentration camps which some of them had helped create.

The next group considered troublesome included those who opposed what was then the party's main task—preparation for war. Therefore, pacifists, conscientious objectors, and so-called "work-shy" persons were sent to the concentration camps.

The ideology of the Germans as *the* superior race, which became a central concept of the party, was soon reflected in the constituency of the camps. Persons of so-called non-Aryan race who had sexual relations with members of the German "race" were either prosecuted in the courts or sent to the concentration camps. Later, when the party decided to prosecute them, homosexual prisoners were added since these persons had all committed so-called racial crimes, and were considered race polluters.

Defection and disobedience among the SS and within the party were even more dangerous to the regime than opposition outside it. Therefore, the concentration camps came into more use against restive party members themselves.

At the beginning of 1938, there were less than 30,000 prisoners in the German concentration camps. At that time the two main camps were at Dachau, near Munich, with about 6,000 prisoners, and at

Sachsenhausen, near Berlin, with about 8,000 inmates. To them had been recently added the camp at Buchenwald, near Weimar, which at that time had about 2,000 inmates. There were also a few quite small camps, one of them at Ravensbrück for women. There was also a probably equally large number of political prisoners in the regular jails, where they were treated much better, pretty much as prisoners are treated in jails in the rest of the world.

Up to 1938 most prisoners in the concentration camps were political opponents of the Nazis. The rest consisted of several hundred persons charged with being "work-shy"; a few hundred conscientious objectors, most of them Jehovah's Witnesses; less than 500 Jewish prisoners, many of them "race polluters"; a few so-called incorrigible criminals; and a miscellaneous group of less than 100 which included such persons as former members of the French Foreign Legion who had returned to Germany and were considered traitors because they had accepted service under a foreign power.

Within months of the annexation of Austria, in the spring of 1938, the population of the camp at Dachau, for example, increased from not quite 6,000 to well over 9,000. All in all, during 1938 some 60,000 prisoners were added to the camp population. From 1939 on, the number of concentration camp prisoners grew steadily at an ever-increasing rate. More and more Jews were brought into the camps to force all of them to get out of Germany. In an obvious preparation for war, the gestapo tried to incarcerate or intimidate all those inhabitants of Germany who might oppose or impede the war effort. From then on, the character of the camps' populations changed; the number of Jewish, asocial, and criminal prisoners increased much faster than that of political prisoners.

The racial and eugenic notions of National Socialist ideology exercised their influence on the camps as early as 1937. At that time, a few prisoners, mostly so-called sex offenders (homosexuals, rapists, Jews who had had sexual relations with gentile women without being married to them), were sterilized. Later, beginning in 1940, prisoners who were deemed incurably sick, or insane, were killed. Thereafter, the policy intended to improve the race was implemented in the camps by exterminating persons who were considered to carry undesirable genes. While all exterminations were the result of racial dogmas, the use of the extermination camps on a large scale was probably not envisaged when such doctrines were first developed.

The first racial "problem" attacked on a large scale was that of the Jews, culminating in the huge pogroms in the fall of 1938 and the transportation of tens of thousands of Jews into the then-existing concentration camps. During the war, both the desire to execute the racial policy and the fear of having Jews living in German cities spread. So the Jews were first forced to live in ghettos, and later sent to the camps, mainly to the extermination camps built in what had been Poland.

From the beginning of the war in September of 1939, a policy of decimation was inaugurated, mainly for the Jews as "the enemies of the German people," for the Gypsies as carriers of particularly undesirable genes, and for the Polish and Russian elite who might possibly threaten Germany's hegemony on conquered lands. The tools used in the camps were inadequate food and shelter, exhaustingly hard labor, absence of medical care, and so on; but during the first years of the war actual murder, although frequent, was partly selective and partly unsystematic.

The last step was inaugurated with the establishment of the extermination camps. Experiments with the gas chamber had started at the Oswiecim (Auschwitz) camp near Cracow. Extermination was in full swing in July 1942; it was finally stopped in September 1944, on orders from Berlin in the hope of thus gaining more favorable peace terms. Nobody knows how many had died by then in the camps. The estimates vary from 11,000,000 (which official East German sources consider the lowest reasonable estimate) to well over 18,000,000; according to the most reliable estimates, between 5.5 and 6 million of these were Jews. Aside from the extermination camps, in which practically everybody died, the best guess is that from 1933 until 1945 1,600,000 were sent to the non-extermination concentration camps, of whom at least 1,180,000 died. At best 530,000 survived the various camps, and many of these died after liberation from the aftereffects of what had happened to them while in the camps.[4]

---

[4] Since the extermination camps and most of the concentration camps were located either in Poland or in what is now East Germany, and since many of the surviving archives are located there, East German sources seem most reliable. As mentioned above, according to them the lowest reasonable estimate of the number of prisoners murdered in the concentration and extermination camps is 11,000,000. (*Meyers Neues Lexikon* [Leipzig: Bibliographisches Institut, 1974].)

Each of the concentration camps had its separate history, with better and worse periods, with emphasis on one rather than another of the manifold purposes for which the camps were created and used by the gestapo. Thus, for instance, conditions in Dachau in 1938 were typical for the then-existing concentration camps. Buchenwald, from its founding late in 1937 until 1939, was the worst of all the camps. But from 1942 until its total disintegration during 1944/45 (due to Allied bombings), Buchenwald was one of the best, and so was Dachau from about 1943 on. In general, the concentration camps located in Germany proper and in Czechoslovakia (at Theresienstadt, for example) fared better during the later war years, while conditions were worst in those camps located in occupied Polish territory.

According to West German sources, while there were 60,000 prisoners in the concentration camps at the end of 1938 and 100,000 in 1942, their number had swollen to 715,000 in 1945, at which time 40,000 SS were assigned to rule the various camps. In 1945 there were about 20 concentration camps, and, either connected with them or separate from them, some 165 slave labor camps. Auschwitz was all three: an extermination, a concentration, and a slave labor camp. So it might be of interest that according to the commander of this camp, from its inception until December 1, 1943 (that is, long before it was abandoned) 2,500,000 were murdered there—mainly in the gas chambers— while an additional 500,000 died of starvation, exhaustion, or sickness. (*Meyers Enzyklopädisches Lexikon*, 1975.) The German estimates are close to the French, since according to the *Encyclopedia Universalis* (Paris, 1968) at least 12,000,000 died in the concentration and extermination camps.

According to the *Encyclopaedia Britannica* (15th ed., 1974), "It is estimated that in all the camps of Germany and its occupied territories, 18,000,000 to 26,000,000 persons—prisoners of war, political prisoners, and nationals of occupied and invaded countries—were put to death through hunger, cold, pestilence, torture, medical experimentation, and other means of extermination such as gas chambers."

Individual and Mass Behavior
in Extreme Situations

The author spent approximately one year in 1938/39 in what were then the two biggest German concentration camps for political prisoners, Dachau and Buchenwald. During this time he made observations, part of which will be presented here. It is not the intention of this paper to recount once more the horror story of the German concentration camp for political prisoners, but to explore certain aspects of the far-reaching psychological impact the camps had directly on their inmates, and indirectly on the population under Nazi domination.

It is assumed that the reader is roughly familiar with this fact, but it should be reiterated that the prisoners were deliberately tortured.[1] They were inadequately clothed, but nevertheless exposed to heat, rain, and freezing temperatures for as long as seventeen hours a day, seven days a week. They suffered from extreme malnutrition, but were forced to perform hard labor.[2] Every single moment of their lives was strictly regulated and supervised. They were never permitted to see any visitors or a minister. They were allowed almost no medical care, and when they did receive it, it was rarely administered by medically trained persons.[3] The prisoners did not know exactly why

INDIVIDUAL AND MASS BEHAVIOR IN EXTREME SITUATIONS: Reprinted with some small editorial changes from the *Journal of Abnormal and Social Psychology* 38 (October 1943), pp. 417–52.

[1] For the earliest official report on life in these camps see: *Papers Concerning the Treatment of German Nationals in Germany* (London: His Majesty's Stationery Office, 1939).

[2] The daily food the prisoners received yielded approximately 1,800 calories, whereas for the labor they were forced to perform the average caloric requirement was from 3,000 to 3,300 calories. (Later, during the war years, the rations were much lower than in 1938/39.)

[3] Surgical operations, for instance, were performed by a former printer. There were many M.D.'s in the camp, but no prisoner was permitted to work in the camp in his civilian capacity because that would not have implied a punishment.

they were imprisoned, and never for how long. These conditions explain why the author speaks of the prisoners as persons finding themselves in an "extreme" situation.

Reports of the acts of terror committed in these camps arouse strong and justified emotions in civilized persons, and those emotions sometimes prevent them from understanding that terror was, so far as the gestapo was concerned, only a means for attaining certain ends. By using extravagant means which fully absorb the investigator's interest, the gestapo only too often succeeded in hiding its real purposes. One of the reasons that this happens so frequently in respect to the concentration camps is that the persons most informed and able to discuss them are former prisoners, who obviously are more interested in *what* happened to them than in *why* it happened.

If one wants to understand the purposes of the gestapo, and the ways in which they were attained, emphasis on what happened to particular persons is erroneous. According to the well-known ideology of the Nazi state, the individual as such was either non-existent or of no importance. An investigation of the purposes of the concentration camps must therefore emphasize not individual acts of terror, but the cumulative results of the treatment of prisoners.

It may be said that the results which the gestapo tried to obtain by means of the camps were varied; the author was able to identify the following different, although intimately related, gestapo goals: *to break the prisoners as individuals* and change them into docile masses from which no individual or group act of resistance could arise; *to spread terror among the rest of the population* by using the prisoners as hostages for good behavior, and by demonstrating what happened to those who opposed the Nazi rulers; *to provide the gestapo members with a training ground* in which they were educated to lose all human emotions and attitudes and learn the most effective ways of breaking resistance in a defenseless civilian population; *to provide the gestapo with an experimental laboratory* in which to study effective means for breaking civilian resistance, as well as the minimum nutritional, hygienic, and medical requirements needed to keep prisoners alive and able to perform hard labor when threat of punishment is the sole incentive, and the influence on performance if no time is allowed for anything but hard labor and the prisoners are separated from their families.

In this paper, an effort will be made to deal adequately with at least one aspect of the gestapo's aforementioned aims: *the concentration camp as a means of producing changes in the prisoners which would make them more useful subjects* of the Nazi state.

These changes were produced by exposing the prisoners to extreme situations particularly created for this purpose. These circumstances forced the prisoners to adapt themselves entirely and with the greatest speed. This adaptation produced interesting types of private, individual, and mass behavior.

We shall call "private" behavior that which originated to a large degree in a subject's particular background and personality rather than in the experiences to which the gestapo exposed him, although these experiences were instrumental to bringing about the private behavior. We shall call "individual" behavior that which, although developed by individuals more or less independently of one another, was clearly the result of experiences common to all prisoners. The pattern of these behaviors was similar in nearly all prisoners with only slight deviations from the average, these deviations originating in the prisoner's particular background and personality.

We shall call "mass" behavior those phenomena which could be observed *only* in a group of prisoners when functioning as a more or less unified mass. Although these three types of behavior were somewhat overlapping and a sharp discrimination between them seems difficult, making these distinctions seems advisable here. This discussion will be restricted mainly to individual and mass behavior, as the title indicates. Only one example of private behavior will be mentioned on the following pages.

In analyzing the development of prisoners from the moment they had their first experience with the gestapo up to the time when the process of adaptation to the camp situation was practically concluded, different stages can be recognized. The first of these stages centered around *the initial shock of finding oneself unlawfully imprisoned*. The main event of the second stage was *the transportation into the camp and the first experiences in it*. The next stage was characterized by a slow process of changing the prisoner's personality. It occurred step by step but continuously as *the adaptation to the camp situation*.

During this process it was difficult to recognize the impact of what was going on. One way to make it more obvious was to compare two groups of prisoners, one in which the process had only started—the "new" prisoners—with another group, in which the process was already far advanced. This other group consisted of the "old" prisoners. The final stage was reached when *the prisoner had adapted himself to the life in the camp.* This last stage seemed to be characterized by, among other features, a definitely changed attitude toward, and evaluation of, the gestapo.

AN EXAMPLE OF PRIVATE BEHAVIOR

Before discussing these different stages of a prisoner's development, a few remarks on why and how the observations presented in this paper were collected seem advisable. At this moment it seems easy to say why the observations were collected, because these are of such sociological and psychological interest and contain observations which, to the author's knowledge, have rarely been published in scientific fashion. But to accept this as an answer for the "why" would constitute a flagrant example of *logificatio post eventum.*

The academic training of the writer and his psychological interests were helpful in making observations and in conducting the investigation; but he did not study his behavior, and that of his fellow prisoners, as a contribution to pure scientific research. Rather, the study of these behaviors was a mechanism developed by him *ad hoc* in order that he might have at least some intellectual interest and thus be better equipped to endure life in the camp. His observations and collection of data should thus be considered as a particular type of defense developed in the extreme situation. It was behavior individually developed, not enforced by the gestapo, and based on this particular prisoner's background, training, and interests. It was developed to protect this individual against a disintegration of his personality. It is, therefore, a characteristic example of a private behavior. These private behaviors seem always to follow the path of least resistance; that is, they follow the individual's former life interests closely.

Since it is the only example of a private behavior presented in this paper, a few words on why and how it was developed may be of interest. The writer had studied and was familiar with the pathological picture presented by certain types of abnormal behavior. During the first days in prison, and particularly during the first days in the camps, he realized that he behaved differently from the way he used to. At first he rationalized that these changes in behavior were only surface phenomena, the logical result of his peculiar situation. But soon he realized that the split of his person into one who observed and one to whom things happened could not be called normal, but was a typical psychopathological phenomenon. So he asked himself, "Am I going insane, or am I already insane?"

To find an answer to this urgent question was obviously of prime importance. Moreover, the author saw his fellow prisoners acting in most peculiar ways, although he had every reason to assume that they, too, had been normal persons before being imprisoned. Now they suddenly appeared to be pathological liars, to be unable to restrain their emotional outbursts, be they of anger or despair, to be unable to make objective evaluations, etc. So another question arose, namely, "How can I protect myself against becoming as they are?"

The way to answer both questions was comparatively simple: to find out what had happened in them, and to me. If I did not change any more than all other normal persons, then what happened in me and to me was a process of adaptation and not an occurrence of insanity. So I set out to find what changes had occurred and were occurring in the prisoners. By doing so I suddenly realized that I had found a solution to my second problem: by occupying myself during my spare time with interesting problems, by talking with my fellow prisoners with a particular purpose in mind, by pondering my findings for the hours without end during which I was forced to perform exhausting labor which did not ask for any mental concentration, I succeeded in killing the time in a way which seemed constructive. To forget for a time that I was in the camp seemed at first the greatest advantage of this occupation. As time went on, the enhancement of my self-respect due to my ability to continue to do meaningful work despite the contrary efforts of the gestapo became even more important than the pastime.

It was impossible to keep any records, because there was no time to make them, no place to keep them, and no way to take them out of the camp. The only way to overcome this difficulty was to make every effort to remember what happened. Here the author was handicapped by extreme malnutrition, which caused his memory to deteriorate, so that he sometimes doubted whether he would be able to remember what he collected and studied. He tried to concentrate on the characteristic and otherwise outstanding phenomena, repeating his findings to himself again and again—time was abundant and had to be killed anyway—and made it a habit when at work to go over all the observations he could remember so as to impress them all better on his memory. This method seemed to work, because when his health improved after he had left the camp and Germany, much seemingly forgotten material came back.

The prisoners were willing to talk about themselves because finding someone interested in them and their problems added to their self-esteem. To speak when at work was not permitted; but since practically everything was forbidden and punished severely, and since, owing to the arbitrariness of the guards, the prisoners who conformed to the rules did not fare any better than those who transgressed them, all rules were broken whenever there seemed a chance to get away with it. Every prisoner was confronted with the problem of how to endure performing stupid tasks for from twelve to eighteen hours. One relief was to talk, when the guards did not prevent it. During the hours of early morning and late evening twilight, the guards could not see whether the prisoners talked. That provided them with at least two hours a day for conversation while at work. They were permitted to talk during the short lunch-time and when in the barracks during the night. Although most of this time had to be spent sleeping, usually one hour was available for conversation.

The prisoners were frequently changed from one labor group to another, and quite often from the barracks in which they were sleeping, because the gestapo wanted to prevent them from becoming too intimate with one another. Thus, every prisoner came in contact with many others. The writer worked in at least twenty different labor groups, the number of workers in which varied from twenty or thirty all the way up to a few hundred. He slept in five different barracks, in each of which from 200 to 300 prisoners lived. In this way he came to know personally at least 600 prisoners at Dachau (out of approximately 6,000) and at least 900 at Buchenwald (out of approximately 8,000).

Although only prisoners of the same category lived together in a given barracks, all categories were mixed at work, so that the author was able to contact prisoners of all categories. The main categories—enumerated according to their respective sizes, starting with the largest group—were: political prisoners, mostly former German Social Democrats and Communists, but also former members of such

Nazi formations as the followers of Roehm who were still alive; persons supposedly "work-shy," that is, persons who did not agree to work wherever the government wanted them to work, or who had changed workplaces in order to get higher wages, or who had complained about low wages, etc.; former members of the French Foreign Legion, and spies; Jehovah's Witnesses (*Bibelforscher*) and other conscientious objectors; Jewish prisoners, either simply because they were of Jewish ancestry, or because they were Jews who had been politically active against the Nazis (to which group the author belonged), or as race offenders; criminals; homosexuals and other small groups, e.g., persons put under Nazi pressure to extract money; and individuals on whom some Nazi bigwig wanted to take personal revenge.

After having met and talked with members of all different groups and in this way having secured an adequate sampling, the writer tried to check his findings by comparing them with those of other prisoners. Unfortunately, he found only two others who were trained and interested enough to participate in his investigation. Although they seemed less interested in the problem than the author, these two each spoke to several hundred prisoners. Every day during the morning count of the prisoners, and while waiting for the assignment to labor groups, reports were exchanged and theories discussed. These discussions proved very helpful in clarifying mistakes that were due to taking a one-sided viewpoint.[4]

After coming to the United States, immediately after his release from the camp, the author wrote down his memories as far as the case material was concerned. He hesitated for nearly three years to interpret it, because he felt that his anger about the treatment he had received might endanger his objectivity. After that time, and when there could be hope that the gestapo would be destroyed, the author decided he had attained as objective an attitude as he could ever expect to do, so he presented the material for discussion.

---

[4] One of the participants was Alfred Fischer, M.D., who at the time this article was written was on duty in a military hospital somewhere in England. The other was Ernst Federn, who in 1943 was still at Buchenwald, and whose name I therefore did not dare to mention when the article first appeared.

Despite these precautions, however, the peculiar conditions under which the material was collected make it impossible to give a comprehensive picture of all the types of behavior which might have occurred. The writer has to restrict himself to discussing those behaviors (and their possible psychological interpretation) which he was able to observe. The difficulty of analyzing mass behavior when the investigator is part of the group being analyzed should also be apparent. Moreover, the personal difficulty of observing and reporting objectively on situations which arouse the strongest emotions when experienced ought to be mentioned. The writer is aware of these limitations on his objectivity and only hopes that he has succeeded in overcoming some of them.

THE ORIGINAL TRAUMATIZATION

In presentation, the initial psychological shock of being deprived of their civil rights and unlawfully locked into a prison may be separated from the shock of the first deliberate and extravagant acts of torture to which the prisoners were exposed. These two shocks may be analyzed separately because the author, like most of the prisoners, spent several days in an ordinary prison, administered by the regular police. While in their custody prisoners were not deliberately mistreated. All this changed radically when the prisoners were handed over to the gestapo to be transported into the camp. As soon as their status changed from police to gestapo prisoners, they were subjected to the most severe physical abuse. Thus the transportation into the camp and the "initiation" into it was often the first torture which the prisoner had ever experienced and was, as a rule, physically and psychologically the worst torture to which the majority of prisoners were ever exposed. The initial torture, incidentally, was called the prisoner's "welcome" to the camp by the gestapo.

The prisoners' reactions on being brought into prison can best be analyzed on the basis of two categories: the socio-economic class to which they belonged and their political education. These categories obviously overlap and can be separated only for the purposes of presentation. Another factor of importance in respect to the prisoners' reactions to finding themselves in prison was whether they had previously been acquainted with prisons, due either to criminality or political activities.

Those prisoners who had previously spent time in prisons, or who had expected to be imprisoned because of their political activities, resented their fate, but somehow accepted it as something which happened in accordance with their expectations. It may be said that this type of person's initial shock at finding himself imprisoned expressed itself—if at all—in a change of self-esteem.

Often the self-esteem of the former criminals, as well as that of the politically educated prisoners, was initially rather heightened by the circumstances under which they found themselves in prison. They were, as a matter of fact, full of anxieties about their future, and about what might happen to their families and friends. But, despite this justified anxiety, they did not feel too bad about the fact of imprisonment itself.

Persons who had formerly spent time in prison as *criminals* showed their glee openly at finding themselves on equal terms with political and business leaders, attorneys and judges—some of whom had been instrumental earlier in sending them to prison. This spite, and the feeling of being now equal to men who until then had been their superiors, bolstered their egos considerably.

The *politically educated prisoners* found support for their self-esteem in the fact that the gestapo had singled them out as important enough to take revenge on. The members of different parties relied on different types of rationalizations for this building-up of their egos. Former members of radical leftist groups, for example, found in the fact of their imprisonment a demonstration of how dangerous their former activities had been for the Nazis.

Of the main socio-economic classes, the lower classes were almost wholly represented either by former criminals or by politically educated prisoners. Any estimation of what might have been the reaction of non-criminal and non-political members of the lower classes must remain conjecture and guesswork.

The great majority of the *non-political middle-class prisoners*, who were a small minority among the prisoners of the concentration camps, were least able to withstand the initial shock. They found themselves utterly unable to comprehend what had happened to them. They tried to cling to what, up to then, had given them self-esteem. Again and again they assured the members of the gestapo that they had never opposed Naziism. In their behavior, the dilemma of the politically uneducated German middle classes when confronted with the phenomenon of National Socialism became apparent. They had no consistent philosophy which could protect their integrity as human beings, which could give them the strength to make a stand against the Nazis. They had obeyed the law handed down by the ruling classes, without ever questioning its wisdom. And now this law, or at least the law-enforcing agencies, had turned against them, its staunchest supporters.

Even now they did not dare to oppose the ruling group, although such opposition might have shored up their self-respect. They could not question the wisdom of law and of the police, so they accepted the behavior of the gestapo as just. What was wrong was that *they* were made the objects of a persecution which in itself had to be right, since it was carried out by the authorities. The only way out of this particular dilemma was to be convinced that it must be a "mistake." These prisoners continued to believe this despite the fact that the gestapo, as well as most of their fellow prisoners, derided them for it.

Although the guards ridiculed these middle-class non-political prisoners for their own self-aggrandizement, they were not free from anxieties when doing so. They realized that they, too, belonged to the same socio-economic stratum of society.[5] The insistence on the legality of the official German internal policy was probably intended to dissolve the anxieties of middle-class Nazi followers, who felt that illegal acts could destroy the foundation of their existence. The height of this farce of legality was reached when prisoners in the camp had to sign a document stating that they agreed to their imprisonment and that they were well pleased with the way they had been treated. This did not seem farcical to the gestapo, which put great emphasis on such documents as a demonstration that everything happened in a regular and lawful manner. The SS were, for instance, free to kill prisoners, but not to steal from them; instead they forced prisoners to sell their possessions, and then to make a "gift" of the money they received to some gestapo formation.

The great desire of the middle-class prisoners was that their status as such should be respected in some way. What they resented most was to be treated "like ordinary criminals." After some time they could

---

[5] Most soldiers and non-commissioned officers of the SS were very young—between seventeen and twenty years old—and the sons of farmers, of small shopkeepers, or of the lower class of the civil servants.

not help realizing their actual situation; then they seemed to disintegrate. The several suicides which happened in prisons and during the transportation into camp were primarily confined to members of this group. Later on, members of this group were the prisoners who behaved in the most anti-social way: they cheated their fellow prisoners, a few turned spies in the service of the gestapo. They lost their middle-class characteristics, their sense of propriety, and their self-respect; they became shiftless and seemed to disintegrate as autonomous persons. They no longer seemed able to form a life pattern of their own, but followed the patterns developed by other groups of prisoners.

Members of the *upper classes* segregated themselves as much as possible. They, too, seemed unable to accept as real what was happening to them. They expressed their conviction that they would be released within the shortest time because of their importance. This conviction was absent among the middle-class prisoners, who still harbored the identical hope for a quick release, not as individuals, but as a group. The upper-class prisoners never formed a group; they remained more or less isolated, each of them with a group of middle-class "clients." Their superior position could be upheld by the amount of money they could distribute,[6] and by a hope on the part of their "clients" that they might help them once they had been released. This hope was steadily kindled by the fact that many of the upper-class prisoners really were released from prison, or camp, within a comparatively short time.

A few *upper-upper-class prisoners* remained aloof even from the upper-class behavior. They did not collect "clients," they did not use their money for bribing other prisoners, they did not express any hopes about their release. The number of these prisoners was too small to permit any generalizations.[7] It seemed that they looked

---

[6] Money was very important to the prisoners because at certain times they were permitted to buy cigarettes and some extra food. To be able to buy food meant to avoid starvation. Since most political prisoners, most criminals, and many middle-class prisoners had no money, they were willing to make easier the lives of those wealthy prisoners who were willing to pay for it.

[7] The author actually met only three of them—a Bavarian prince, member of the former royal family, and two Austrian dukes, closely related to the former emperor. It is doubtful whether during his year in the camps there were any more of these prisoners there.

down on all other prisoners nearly as much as they despised the gestapo. In order to endure life in the camp they appeared to have developed such a feeling of superiority that nothing could touch them.

As far as the political prisóners are concerned, another psychological mechanism which became apparent later might already have played some part in their initial adjustment: many middle-class political leaders had some guilt-feeling that they had fallen down on their job, particularly the job of preventing the rise of Nazi power either by fighting the Nazis more effectively or by establishing such watertight democratic or leftist class rule that the Nazis would not have been able to overcome it. It seems that this guilt-feeling was relieved to a considerable degree by the fact that the Nazis found them important enough to bother with them.

It is possible that so many prisoners managed to endure comparatively well living under the conditions imposed on them in the camp because the punishment which they had to suffer freed them from much of their guilt-feeling. Indications of such a process may be found in the frequent remarks with which prisoners responded when criticized for any kind of undesirable behavior. When reprimanded, for instance, for cursing or fighting, or for being unclean, they would nearly always answer: "We cannot behave normally to one another when living under such circumstances." When admonished not to speak too harshly of their friends and relatives who were free, whom they accused of not taking care of their affairs, they would answer: "This is no place to be objective. Once I am again at liberty, I shall again act in a civilized way, and evaluate the behavior of others objectively."

It seems that most, if not all, prisoners reacted against the initial shock of arrest by trying to muster forces which might prove helpful in supporting their badly shaken self-esteem. Those groups which found in their past life some basis for the erection of such a buttress to their endangered egos seemed to succeed. Members of the lower class derived a certain satisfaction from the absence of class differences among the prisoners. Political prisoners found their importance as politicians once more demonstrated by their imprisonment. Members of the upper class could exert at least a certain amount of leadership among the middle-class prisoners. Members of "anointed" families felt as superior to all other human beings in prison as they had felt outside of it. Moreover, the initial shock seemed to relieve guilt-feelings of various kinds, such as those originating in political inactivity, or inefficiency, or in acting badly and casting aspersions on friends and relatives in an unjustified way.

After having spent several days in prison, the prisoners were brought into the camp. During the transportation they were exposed to constant tortures of various kinds. Many of these depended on the fantasy of the particular SS soldier in charge of a group of prisoners. Still, a certain pattern soon became apparent. Corporal punishment, consisting of whipping, kicking, slapping, intermingled with shooting and wounding with the bayonet, alternated with tortures whose obvious goal was extreme exhaustion. For instance, the prisoners were forced to stare for hours into glaring lights, to kneel for hours, and so on. From time to time a prisoner got killed; no prisoner was permitted to take care of his own or another's wounds.

These tortures alternated with efforts on the part of the guards to force the prisoners to hit one another, and to defile what the guards considered the prisoners' most cherished values. For instance, the prisoners were forced to curse their God, to accuse themselves of vile actions, accuse their wives of adultery and of prostitution. This continued for hours and was repeated at various times. According to reliable reports, this kind of initiation never took less than twelve hours and frequently lasted twenty-four hours. If the number of prisoners brought into the camp was too large for this torture to be carried out while they were in transit, or if they came from nearby places, the ceremony took place during the first day in camp.

The purpose of the tortures was to break the resistance of the prisoners, and to assure the guards that they were really superior to the prisoners. This can be seen from the fact that the longer the tortures lasted, the less violent they became. The guards slowly became less excited, and at the end even talked with the prisoners. As soon as a new guard took over, he started with new acts of terror, although not as violent as in the beginning, and he eased up sooner than his predecessor. Sometimes prisoners who had already spent time in camp were brought back with a group of new prisoners. These old prisoners were not tortured if they could furnish evidence that they had already been in the camp. That the timing of these tortures was planned can be seen from the fact that during the author's transportation into the camp, after twelve hours in which several prisoners had died and many had been wounded in tortures, the command "Stop mistreating the prisoners" came and from this moment on, the prisoners were left more or less in peace until they arrived in the camp, when another group of guards took over and started anew to mistreat them.

It is difficult to ascertain what happened in the minds of the prisoners during the time they were exposed to this treatment. Most of them became so exhausted that they were only partly conscious of what happened. In general, prisoners remembered the details and did not mind talking about them, but they did not like to talk about what they had felt and thought during the time of torture. The few who volunteered information made vague statements which sounded like devious rationalizations, invented for the purpose of justifying the fact that they had endured treatment injurious to their self-respect without trying to fight back. The few who had tried to fight back could not be interviewed; they were dead.

The writer can vividly recall his extreme weariness, resulting from a bayonet wound he had received early in the course of transportation and from a heavy blow on the head. Both injuries led to the loss of a considerable amount of blood, and made him groggy. He recalls vividly, nevertheless, his thoughts and emotions during the transportation. He wondered all the time whether man can endure so much without committing suicide or going insane. He wondered if the guards really tortured prisoners in the way described in books on the concentration camps; whether the SS were so simpleminded as to enjoy forcing prisoners to defile themselves or if it expected to break the prisoners' resistance in this way. He noted that the guards were lacking in fantasy when selecting the means to torture the prisoners; that their sadism was without imagination. He was rather amused by the repeated statement that guards do not shoot the prisoners but kill them by beating them to death because a bullet costs six pfennigs, and the prisoners are not worth even so much. Obviously the idea that these men, most of them formerly influential persons, were not worth such a trifle impressed the guards considerably.

On the basis of this introspection it seems that the writer gained emotional strength from the following facts: that things happened according to expectation; that, therefore, his future in the camp was at least partly predictable from what he already was experiencing and from what he had read; and that the SS were less intelligent than he had expected, which eventually provided small satisfaction. Moreover, he felt pleased with himself that the tortures did not change his ability to think or his general point of view. In retrospect these considerations seem futile, but they ought to be mentioned because, if the author should be asked to sum up in one sentence what, during all the time he spent in the camp, was his main problem, he would say: *to safeguard his ego in such a way that, if by any good luck he should regain liberty, he would be approximately the same person he was when deprived of liberty.*

The author has no doubt that he was able to endure the transportation and all that followed because right from the beginning he became convinced that these horrible and degrading experiences somehow were not happening to "him" as a subject, but only to "him" as an object. The importance of this attitude was corroborated by statements of many other prisoners, although none would go so far as to state definitely that an attitude of this type was already clearly developed during the time of the transportation. They couched their feelings usually in more general terms, such as "The main problem is to remain alive and unchanged," without specifying what they meant by "unchanged." From additional remarks it became apparent that what should remain unchanged roughly covered the person's general attitudes and values.

All the thoughts and emotions which the author had during the transportation were extremely detached. It was as if he watched things happening in which he was only vaguely involved. Later he learned that many prisoners had developed this same feeling of detachment, as if what happened did not really matter to oneself. This detachment was strangely mixed with a conviction that "this cannot be true, such things just do not happen." Not only during the transportation but through all the time spent in camp, the prisoners had to convince themselves that this was real, really happening, and not just a nightmare. They were never wholly successful.[8]

---

[8] There were good indications that most guards embraced a similar attitude, although for different reasons. They tortured the prisoners partly because they enjoyed demonstrating their superiority, partly because their superiors expected it of them. But, having been educated in a world which rejected brutality, they felt uneasy about what they were doing. It seems that they, too, had an emotional attitude toward their acts of brutality which might be described as a feel-

This feeling of detachment, rejecting the reality of the situation in which the prisoners found themselves, might be considered a mechanism safeguarding the integrity of their personalities. Many prisoners behaved in the camp as if their life there had no connection with their "real" life; they went so far as to insist that this was the right attitude. Their statements about themselves, and their evaluation of their own and other persons' behavior, differed considerably from what they would have said and thought outside of camp. This separation of behavior patterns and schemes of values inside and outside of camp was so strong that it could hardly be touched in conversation; it was one of the many "taboos" not to be discussed.[9] The prisoners' feelings could be summed up by the following sentence: "What I am doing here, or what is happening to me, does not count at all; here everything is permissible as long and insofar as it contributes to helping me to survive in the camp."

One more observation made during the transportation ought to be mentioned. No prisoners fainted because to faint meant to get killed. In this particular situation fainting was not a device protecting a person against intolerable pain and in this way facilitating his life; it endangered a prisoner's existence because anyone unable to follow orders was killed. Once the prisoners were in the camp the situation changed, and a prisoner who fainted sometimes received some attention or was usually no longer tortured. Therefore the prisoners who did not faint under the more severe strains during the transportation usually fainted in the camp when exposed to great hardships, even though they had endured worse during the transportation.[10]

---

ing of unreality. After having been guards in the camp for some time, they got accustomed to inhuman behavior; they became "conditioned" to it and it then became part of their "real" life.

[9] Some aspects of this behavior seem similar to those described in the literature as "depersonalization." But there seem to be so many differences between the phenomena discussed in this paper and the phenomenon of depersonalization that it seems inadvisable to use that term.

[10] I remember clearly how, during the transport, I wished I would faint to stop suffering; but like the other prisoners I did not. During the year in the camps I also occasionally wished I would faint, but I did not manage it. It was probably the realization of the dangers involved in not being able to observe what went on, and to react appropriately to it, which induced me to prevent myself from losing consciousness.

ADAPTATION

Prisoners seemed to deal with camp experiences which remained within the normal frame of reference of their life experience by means of normal psychological mechanisms. Once an experience transcended this frame of reference, however, the normal mechanisms seemed no longer able to deal adequately with it and new psychological mechanisms were needed. The experience during the transportation was one of those transcending the normal frame of reference and the reaction to it may be described as "unforgettable, but unreal."

The prisoners' dreams were an indication that the extreme experiences were not dealt with by the usual mechanisms. Many dreams expressed aggression against members of the SS, usually combined with wish fulfillment in such a way that the prisoner was taking his revenge on his guards. Interestingly enough, the reason he took revenge on them—if a particular reason could be ascertained in such dreams—was always some comparatively small mistreatment, never an extreme experience.

The author had had some previous experience with a slow working through of a trauma in dreams.[11] He expected that his dreams after the transportation would follow the pattern of repetition of the traumatic event in dreams, the shock becoming less vivid and the dream finally disappearing. He was astonished to find that in his dreams the most shocking events did not appear. He asked many prisoners whether they dreamed about the transportation and he was unable to find a single one who could remember having dreamed about it.

Attitudes similar to those developed toward the transportation could be observed in other extreme situations. On a terribly cold winter night when a snowstorm was blowing, all prisoners were punished by being forced to stand at attention without overcoats—they never wore any—for hours.[12] This was after having worked for more

---

[11] The trauma had been a car accident so severe that at first it was thought he would not survive.

[12] The reason for this punishment was that two prisoners had tried to escape. On such occasions all prisoners were always punished severely, so that in the future they would give away secrets they had learned, because otherwise they would have to suffer. The idea was that every prisoner ought to feel responsible for any act committed by any other prisoner. This was in line with

than twelve hours in the open, and having received hardly any food. The prisoners were threatened with having to stand all through the night.

After about twenty prisoners had died from exposure, the discipline broke down. The threats of the guards became ineffective. To be exposed to the weather was a terrible torture; to see one's friends die without being able to help, and to stand a good chance of dying oneself, created a situation similar to the transportation, except that the prisoners had by now more experience with the SS. Open resistance was impossible, as impossible as it was to do anything definite to safeguard oneself. A feeling of utter indifference swept the prisoners. They did not care whether the SS shot them; they were indifferent to acts of torture committed by the guards. The SS no longer had any authority; the spell of fear and death was broken. It was again as if what was happening did not "really" happen to oneself. There was again a split between the "me" to whom it happened, and the "me" who really did not care and was just a vaguely interested, but essentially detached, observer. Unfortunate as the situation was, the prisoners felt free from fear and therefore were actually happier than at most other times during their camp experiences.

Whereas the extremeness of that situation probably produced the mental split mentioned above, a number of circumstances combined to create the feeling of happiness in the prisoners. Obviously it was easier to withstand unpleasant experiences when all found themselves in "the same boat." Moreover, since everybody was convinced that his chances to survive were slim, each felt more heroic and willing to help others than he would have felt in other situations, when helping others might endanger him. This helping and being helped raised the prisoners' spirits. Another factor was that not only were they free of the fear of the SS, but the SS had actually lost its power over them for the moment, since the guards seemed reluctant to shoot all the prisoners.[13]

---

the SS's principle of forcing the prisoners to feel and act as a group, and not as individuals.

The two escapees were eventually captured and hanged while all prisoners had to stand at attention, watching the hanging.

[13] This was one of the occasions in which the antisocial attitudes of certain middle-class prisoners mentioned earlier became apparent. Some of them did not participate in the spirit of mutual help, and some even tried to take advantage of others for their own benefit.

After more than eighty prisoners had died, and several hundred had their extremities so badly frozen that they later had to be amputated, the prisoners were permitted to return to the barracks. They were completely exhausted, but did not experience the feeling of happiness which some of them had expected. They were relieved that the torture was over, but felt at the same time that they were no longer free from fear and no longer could rely on mutual help. Each prisoner as an individual was now comparatively safer, but he had lost the safety originating in being a member of a unified group. This event was again freely discussed, in a detached way, and again the discussion was restricted to facts; the prisoners' emotions and thoughts during this night were hardly ever mentioned. The event itself and its details were not forgotten, but no particular emotions were attached to them; nor did they appear in dreams.

The psychological reactions to events which were somewhat more within the sphere of the normally comprehensible were decidedly different from those to extreme events. Prisoners tended to deal with less extreme events in the same way as if they had happened outside of the camp. For example, if a prisoner's punishment was not of an unusual kind, he seemed ashamed of it and tried not to speak about it. A slap in one's face was embarrassing, and not to be discussed. The prisoners hated individual guards who had kicked them, slapped them, or verbally abused them much more than the guard who had really wounded a prisoner seriously. In the latter case one eventually hated the SS as such, but not so much the individual inflicting the punishment. Obviously this differentiation was unreasonable, but it seemed to be inescapable. One felt deeper and more violent aggressions against particular SS men who had committed minor vile acts than one felt against those who had acted in a much more terrible fashion.

The following tentative interpretation of this strange phenomenon should be accepted with caution. It seems that all experiences which might have happened during the prisoner's "normal" life history provoked a "normal" reaction. Prisoners seemed, for instance, particularly sensitive to punishments similar to those which a parent might inflict on his child. To punish a child was within their "normal" frame of reference, but becoming the object of such punishment destroyed their adult frame of reference. So they reacted to it not in an adult but in a childish way—with embarrassment and shame, with violent, impotent, and unmanageable emotions directed not against the system, but against the person inflicting the punishment. A contributing factor might have been that the harsher the punishment, the more one could expect to receive friendly support which exerted a soothing influence. Moreover, if the suffering was great, one felt more or less like a martyr suffering for a cause, and the martyr is not supposed to resent his martyrdom.

This, incidentally, raises the question as to which psychological phenomena make it possible to submit to martyrdom, and which lead others to accept it as such. This problem transcends the frame of this presentation, but some observations pertinent to it may be mentioned. Prisoners who died under tortures *qua* prisoners, although martyrs to their political conviction, were not considered martyrs. Those who suffered due to efforts to protect others were accepted as martyrs. The SS was usually successful in preventing the creation of martyrs, due either to insight into the psychological mechanisms involved or to its anti-individualistic ideology. If a prisoner tried to protect a group, he might be killed by a guard, but if his action came to the knowledge of the camp administration, then the whole group was always punished more severely than it would have been in the first place. In this way the group came to resent the actions of a protector because it was made to suffer for them. The protector was thus prevented from becoming a leader, or a martyr, around whom group resistance might have formed.

Let us return to the initial question of why prisoners resented minor vile acts on the part of the guards more than extreme experiences. It seems that if a prisoner was cursed, slapped, pushed around "like a child" and if he was, like a child, unable to defend himself, this revived in him behavior patterns and psychological mechanisms which he had developed when a child. Like a child, he was then unable to see his treatment in the general context of the behavior of the SS and hated the individual SS man. He would swear that he was going "to get even" with him, knowing well that this was impossible. Such a prisoner could develop neither a detached attitude nor an objective evaluation which would have led him to realize his suffering was minor when compared with other experiences.

The prisoners as a group developed the same attitude to minor sufferings; not only did they not offer any help, on the contrary—they blamed the prisoner for having brought about his suffering by his stupidity in not making the right reply, in letting himself get caught, in not being careful enough, in short, accused him of having behaved like a child. So the degradation of the prisoner due to being treated like a child took place not only in his mind, but in the minds of his fellow prisoners too.

This attitude extended to small details. For instance, a prisoner did not resent being cursed by the guards when it occurred during an extreme experience, but he hated the SS for similar cursing, and was ashamed of suffering it without retaliating, when it occurred during some minor mistreatment. It should be emphasized that as time went on, the difference in reactions to minor and major sufferings slowly seemed to disappear. This change in reactions was only one of many differences between old and new prisoners. A few others ought to be mentioned.

OLD AND NEW PRISONERS

In the following discussion we refer by the term "new prisoners" to those who had not yet spent more than one year in the camp; "old" prisoners were those who had spent at least three years in the camp. As far as the old prisoners are concerned, the author can offer only observations but no findings based on introspection.

It has been mentioned that the main concern of the new prisoners seemed to be to retain intact their personality and to return to the outer world as the same person who had left it; all their emotional efforts were directed towards this goal. Old prisoners seemed mainly concerned with the problem of how to live as well as possible within the camp. Once they had reached this attitude, everything that happened to them, even the worst atrocity, was "real" to them. No longer was there a split between one to whom things happened and the one who observed them.

Once the stage was reached of accepting everything that happened in the camp as "real," there was every indication that the prisoners were then afraid of returning to the outer world. They did not admit it directly, but from their talk it was clear that they hardly believed they would ever return to this outer world, because they felt that only a cataclysmic event—a world war and world revolution— could free them, and even then they doubted that they would be able to adapt to this new life. They seemed aware of what had happened to them while growing older in the camp. They realized that they had adapted themselves to the life in the camp and were more or less aware that this process had brought about a basic change in their personality.

The most drastic demonstration of this realization was provided by a very prominent radical German politician, a former leader of the Independent Socialist party in the Reichstag. He declared that according to his experience, nobody could live in the camp longer than five years without changing his attitudes so radically that he could no longer be considered the same person he used to be. This prisoner asserted that he did not see any point in continuing to live once his "real life" consisted in being a prisoner in a concentration camp, and that he could not endure developing those attitudes and behaviors he saw developing in all old prisoners. Therefore, he had decided to commit suicide on the sixth anniversary of his being brought into the camp. His fellow prisoners tried to watch him carefully on this day, but nevertheless he succeeded.

There was, of course, considerable variation among individuals in the time it took them to make their peace with the idea of having to spend the rest of their lives in the camp. Some became part of the camp life rather soon, some probably never. When a new prisoner was brought into the camp, the older ones tried to teach him a few things which might prove helpful in his adjustment. The new prisoners were told that they should try by all means to survive the first days and not to give up the fight for their lives, that it would become easier the longer the time they spent in camp. The older prisoners said, "If you survive the first three months, you will survive the next three years." The yearly mortality rate of close to 20 percent was due mostly to the large number of new prisoners who did not survive the first few weeks in camp, either because they did not care to survive by means of adapting themselves to the life in camp or because they were unable to do so.[14]

How long it took a prisoner to cease to consider life outside the camp as real depended to a great extent on the strength of his emo-

---

[14] The prisoners in charge of a barracks kept track of what happened to the inhabitants of their barracks. In this way it was comparatively easy to ascertain how many died and how many were released. The former were always in the majority.

tional ties to his family and friends. The change to accepting camp life as one's "real" life always required a minimum of two years or so. Even then, the person would still overtly long to regain his freedom. Some of the indications from which one could recognize the changed attitude were: scheming to find oneself a better place in the camp rather than trying to contact the outer world;[15] avoiding speculation about one's family or world affairs; concentrating all interest on events taking place inside the camp.[16]

When the author expressed to some of the old prisoners his astonishment at their apparent lack of interest in discussing their future lives outside the camp, they frequently admitted that they no longer could visualize themselves living outside the camp, making free decisions, or taking care of themselves and their families. And this was not the only change which could be observed in them. Other differences between old and new prisoners could be recognized in their respective hopes for their future lives, in the degree to which they regressed to infantile behavior, and in many other ways. In considering these differences between old and new prisoners, however, one should bear in mind that there were great individual variations and that the categories are interrelated, so that all statements can be only approximations and generalizations.

The new prisoners usually received the most letters, money, and other signs of attention from the outside world. Their families tried all possible means of freeing them; nevertheless, the prisoners consistently accused them of not doing enough—of betraying and cheating them. These prisoners would weep over a letter telling of efforts to liberate them, but curse in the next moment when learning that some

---

[15] New prisoners would spend all their money on efforts to smuggle letters out of the camp or to receive communications without having them censored. Old prisoners did not use their money for such purposes. They used it for securing "soft" jobs for themselves, such as clerical work in the offices of the camp or work in the shops, where they were at least protected against the weather while at work.

[16] It so happened that on the same day news was received of a speech by President Roosevelt denouncing Hitler and Germany, and rumors were spread that one officer of the gestapo would be replaced by another. The new prisoners discussed the speech excitedly, and paid no attention to the rumors; the old prisoners paid no attention to the speech, but devoted all their conversations to the changes in camp officers.

of their property had been sold without their permission. They would swear at their families who "obviously" considered them "already dead." Even the smallest change in their former private world acquired tremendous importance. They might have forgotten the names of some of their best friends,[17] but once they learned that the friends had moved, the prisoners were terribly upset and nothing could console them.

This ambivalence of the new prisoners in relation to their families seemed to be due to a mechanism mentioned before. The prisoners' desire to return to the world as exactly the person they had been was so great that they feared any change, however trifling, in the situation they had left. They wished their worldly possessions to be secure and untouched, although these were of no use to them at this moment.

It is difficult to say whether this desire that everything remain unchanged was due to the prisoners' realization of how difficult it might be to adjust to an entirely changed home situation or whether it finds its explanation in some sort of magical thinking running along the following lines: "If nothing changes in the world in which I used to live, then I shall not change, either." In this way the prisoners might have tried to counteract their fear that they *were* changing.

Violent reactions to changes in their families were then the covert expression of the prisoners' realization that they themselves were changing. What enraged them was probably not only the fact of the change, but also the change in standing within the family which it implied. Their families had been dependent on them for decisions, and now they were the ones to be dependent. The only chance they saw for again becoming the head of the family was for the family structure to remain untouched despite their absence. Also they knew the attitudes of most outside persons toward those who had spent time in prisons of any kind.

As a matter of fact, although most families behaved decently to those family members in a camp, serious problems were created. During the first months, such families would spend a great deal of money in efforts to free the prisoner, quite often more than they could afford. When they pleaded with gestapo officers to set their relatives

---

[17] This tendency to forget names, places, and events was an interesting phenomenon which cannot be explained solely by the prisoners' physical exhaustion.

free—an unpleasant task at best—they were told repeatedly that it was the prisoner's own fault that he was imprisoned. Later on, they would have difficulties in finding employment because a family member was suspect; their children had difficulties at school; they were excluded from public relief. So it was only natural that these families came to resent having one of their number in the camp.

Their friends did not have much compassion for such families, because the German population at large developed certain defense mechanisms against the fact of the concentration camps. The Germans could not stand the idea of living in a world where one was not protected by law and order. They just would not believe that the prisoners in the camps had not committed outrageous crimes, since the way they were being punished permitted only this conclusion. So a slow process of alienation took place between the prisoners and their families, but as far as the new prisoners were concerned, this process was only beginning.

The question arises as to how the prisoners could blame their families for changes which actually occurred in themselves, and whose helpless cause they were. It might be that the prisoners took so much punishment and had to endure such hardship that they could no longer accept any blame. They felt that they had atoned for any past shortcomings in their relations to their families and friends, and for any changes which might occur in them. In this way the prisoners were free from accepting any responsibility for such changes and free from any guilt-feelings; thus they felt freer to hate other people, even their families, for their own defects.

This feeling of having atoned for all guilt had some real foundation. When the concentration camps were first established, the Nazis detained their more prominent foes in them. Pretty soon there were no more prominent enemies available, because they were either dead, in the jails or camps, or had emigrated. Still, an institution was needed to threaten the opponents of the system because too many Germans were dissatisfied with it. To imprison all of them would have interrupted the functioning of industrial production, the upholding of which was a paramount Nazi goal. So if a group of the population got fed up with the Nazi regime, selected members of this group would be brought into the concentration camp. If lawyers became restless, a few hundred lawyers were sent to the camp; the same thing happened to physicians when the medical profession seemed rebellious, etc.

The gestapo called such group punishments "actions," and this new system was first used during the year 1937/38, when Germany was preparing to embark on the annexation of foreign countries. During the first of these "actions," only the leaders of opposition groups were punished. But that led to the feeling that just belonging to a rebellious group was not dangerous, since only the leaders were punished. Soon the gestapo revised its system and selected the persons to be punished so that they represented a cross-section through the different strata of the group. This new procedure had the advantage of spreading terror among all members of the group, and also made it possible to punish and destroy the group without necessarily touching the leader, if that was for some reason inopportune.[18] Though prisoners were never told exactly why they were imprisoned, those imprisoned as representatives of a group came to know it.

Prisoners were interviewed by the gestapo to gain information about their relatives and friends. During these interviews, prisoners sometimes complained that they were imprisoned while more prominent foes of the Nazis were at liberty. They were told that it was just their bad luck that they had to suffer as members of a group, but if their fate did not teach the group to behave better, they would get a chance to meet all the others in the camp. So these prisoners rightly felt that they were atoning for the rest of the group; but the outsiders did not see it this way. Not to receive the special attention to which they felt entitled added to the prisoners' resentment against the outside world. But even when they were complaining about and accusing their relatives and friends, the new prisoners always loved to speak about them, their own position in the outside world, and their hopes about their future in it.

Old prisoners did not like to be reminded of their families and former friends. When they spoke about them, it was in a very detached way. They liked to receive letters, but it was not very important to them, partly because they had lost contact with the events related in the letters. It has been mentioned that they had some realization of

---

[18] At one time a movement of opposition to the Nazis' regimentation of cultural activities centered around the person of the famous conductor Furtwängler who himself was favorably inclined toward Naziism in general, but was critical of its cultural policies. He was never punished, but the group was destroyed by the imprisonment of a cross-section of it. Thus he found himself a leader without followers and the movement subsided.

how difficult it might be for them to find their way back, but there was another contributing factor—namely, the prisoners' hatred of all those living outside of the camp, who "enjoyed life as if we were not rotting away."

This outside world which continued to live as if nothing had happened was represented in the minds of the prisoners by those whom they used to know, that is, their relatives and friends. But even this hatred was very subdued in the old prisoners. It seemed that while they had forgotten to love their kin, they had also lost the ability to hate them. Old prisoners had learned to direct a great amount of aggression against themselves so as not to get into too many conflicts with the SS, while the new prisoners still directed their aggressions against the outer world, and—when not supervised—against the SS. The old prisoners did not show much emotion either way; they seemed unable to feel strongly about anybody.

Old prisoners did not like to mention their former social status or their former activities, whereas new prisoners were rather boastful about them. New prisoners seemed to try to maintain their self-esteem by letting others know how important they had been, with the very obvious implication that they were still important. Old prisoners seemed to have accepted their state of dejection; to compare it with their former splendor—and anything was magnificent when compared with the situation in which they found themselves—was probably too depressing.

Closely connected with the prisoners' beliefs about and attitudes toward their families were their beliefs and hopes concerning their life after release from camp. Here the prisoners embarked a great deal on individual and group daydreams. To indulge in them was one of the favorite pastimes if the general emotional climate in the camp was not too depressed. There was a marked difference between the daydreams of new and of old prisoners. The longer the time a prisoner had spent in camp, the less true to reality were his daydreams. This was so much so that the hopes and expectations of the old prisoners often took the form of eschatological or messianic hopes, in line with their expectation that only an event like the end of the world would liberate them. Old prisoners would daydream of the coming world war and world revolution. They were convinced that out of this great upheaval they would emerge as the future leaders of Germany at least, if not of the world. This was the very least to which their sufferings entitled them. These grandiose expectations were coexistent with great vagueness as to their future private lives. In their daydreams they were certain to emerge as the future secretaries of state, but they were less certain whether they would continue to live with their wives and children. Part of these daydreams may be explained by the fact that prisoners seemed to feel that only a high public position could help them to regain their standing within their families.

The hopes and expectations of new prisoners about their future lives were much more true to reality. Despite their open ambivalence about their families, they never doubted that they were going to continue to live with them just where they had left off. They hoped to continue their public and professional lives in the same way as they used to live them.

Most of the adaptations to the camp situation mentioned so far were more or less individual behaviors, according to our definition. The changes discussed in the next section, especially the regression to infantile behavior, were according to our definition mass phenomena. The writer is of the opinion—based partly on introspection, and partly on discussions with the few other prisoners who realized what was happening—that this regression would not have taken place if it had not happened in all prisoners. Moreover, whereas prisoners did not interfere with another's daydreams or with his attitudes to his family, they asserted their power as a group over those prisoners who objected to deviations from normal adult behavior. They accused those who would not develop a childlike dependency on the guards of threatening the security of the group, an accusation which was not without foundation, since the SS always punished the group for the misbehavior of individual members. This regression into childlike behavior was, therefore, even more inescapable than the other types of behavior imposed on the individual by the impact of conditions in the camp.

REGRESSION

The prisoners developed types of behavior which are characteristic of infancy or early youth. Some of these behaviors developed slowly, others were immediately imposed on the prisoners and grew only in intensity as time went on. Some of these more-or-less infantile behaviors have already been discussed, such as ambivalence toward one's family, despondency, finding satisfaction in daydreaming rather than in action.

Whether some of these behavior patterns were deliberately produced by the gestapo is hard to ascertain. Others were definitely produced by it, but again we do not know whether this was consciously done. It has been mentioned that even during the transportation the prisoners were tortured in the way in which a cruel and domineering father might torture a helpless child; here it should be added that the prisoners were also debased by techniques which went much further into childhood situations. They were forced to soil themselves. In the camp defecation was strictly regulated; it was one of the most important daily events, discussed in great detail. During the day, prisoners who wanted to defecate had to obtain the permission of a guard. It seemed as if education to cleanliness would be once more repeated. It also seemed to give pleasure to the guards to hold the power of granting or withholding the permission to visit the latrines. (Toilets were mostly not available.) The pleasure of the guards found its counterpart in the pleasure the prisoners derived from visiting the latrines, because there they usually could rest for a moment, secure from the whips of the overseers and guards. However, they were not always so secure, because sometimes enterprising young guards enjoyed interfering with the prisoners even at these moments.

In speaking to each other, the prisoners were forced to employ the familiar *du* ("thou")—a form which in Germany is indiscriminately used only among small children; they were not permitted to address one another with the many titles to which middle- and upper-class Germans are accustomed. On the other hand, they had to address the guards in the most deferential manner, giving them all their titles.

The prisoners lived, like children, only in the immediate present; they lost feeling for the sequence of time; they became unable to plan for the future or to give up immediate pleasure satisfactions to gain greater ones in the near future. They were unable to establish durable object-relations. Friendships developed as quickly as they broke up. Prisoners would, like early adolescents, fight one another tooth and nail, declare that they would never again look at one another or speak to one another, and become close friends once more within a few minutes. They were boastful, telling tales about what they had accomplished in their former lives, or how they succeeded in cheating foremen or guards, and how they sabotaged the work. Like children, they felt not at all set back or ashamed when it became known that they had lied about their prowess.

Another factor contributing to the regression into childhood behavior was the work the prisoners were forced to perform. New prisoners particularly were forced to perform nonsensical tasks, such as carrying heavy rocks from one place to another, and after a while back to the place where they had picked them up. On other days they were forced to dig holes in the ground with their bare hands, although tools were available. They resented such nonsensical work, although it ought to have been immaterial to them whether or not their work was useful. They felt debased when forced to perform "childish" and stupid labor, and preferred even harder work when it produced something that might be considered useful. There seems to be no doubt that the tasks they performed, as well as the mistreatment by the gestapo which they had to endure, contributed to their disintegration as adult persons.

The author had a chance to interview several prisoners who before being brought into the camp had spent a few years in prison, some of them in solitary confinement. Although their number was too small to permit valid generalizations, it seems that to spend time in prison does not produce the character changes described in this paper. As far as the regression into childhood behaviors is concerned, the only feature prison and camp seem to have in common is that in both the prisoners are prevented from satisfying their sexual desires in a normal way, which eventually leads them to the fear of losing their virility. In the camp this fear added strength to the other factors detrimental to adult types of behavior and promoted childlike types of behavior.

When a prisoner had reached the final stage of adjustment to the camp situation, he had changed his personality so as to accept various values of the SS as his own. A few examples may illustrate how this acceptance expressed itself.

The SS considered, or pretended to consider, the prisoners to be the scum of the earth. It insisted that none of them was any better than the others. One of the reasons for fostering this attitude was probably to convince the young guards who received their training in the camp that they were superior to even the most outstanding prisoner, and to demonstrate to them that the former foes of the Nazis were now subdued and not worthy of any special attention. If a formerly prominent prisoner had been treated better than the others, the simple guards would have thought that he still had influence; if he had been treated worse, they might have thought that he still was dangerous.

The Nazis wanted to impress on the guards that even a slight degree of opposition to the system led to the complete destruction of the person who dared to oppose, and that the *degree* of opposition made no difference in the punishment. Occasional talks with these guards revealed that they really believed in a Jewish-capitalistic world conspiracy against the German people. Whoever opposed the Nazis was supposed to be participating in it and was therefore to be destroyed, independent of his role in the conspiracy. So it can be understood that the guards' behavior to the prisoners was to treat them as their vilest enemies.

The prisoners found themselves in an impossible situation, due to the steady interference with their privacy on the part of the guards and other prisoners. So a great amount of aggression accumulated. In the new prisoners this aggression vented itself in the way it might have done in the world outside the camp. But slowly prisoners accepted, as the expression of their verbal aggressions, terms which definitely did not originate in their previous vocabularies, but were taken over from the very different vocabulary of the SS. From copying the verbal aggressions of the SS to copying its form of bodily aggressions was one more step, but it took several years to make this step. It was not unusual to find old prisoners, when in charge of others, behaving worse than the SS. In some cases they were trying to win favor with the SS in this way, but more often they considered it the best way to behave toward prisoners in the camp.

Practically all prisoners who had spent a long time in the camp took over the attitude of the SS toward the so-called unfit prisoners. Newcomers presented the old prisoners with difficult problems. Their complaints about the unbearable life in camp added new strain to the life in the barracks, as did their inability to adjust to it. Bad behavior in the labor gang endangered the whole group. So a newcomer who did not stand up well under the strain tended to become a liability for the other prisoners. Moreover, weaklings were those most apt to eventually turn traitor. Weaklings usually died during the first weeks in the camp anyway, so to some it seemed as well to get rid of them sooner. Old prisoners were therefore sometimes instrumental in getting rid of the "unfit"—in this way incorporating Nazi ideology into their own behavior. This was one of many situations in which old prisoners would demonstrate toughness, having molded their treatment of these "unfit" prisoners to the example set by the SS. Self-protection required elimination of the "unfit" prisoners, but the way in which they were sometimes tortured for days by the old prisoners and slowly killed was taken over from the gestapo.

Old prisoners who identified themselves with the SS did so not only in respect to aggressive behavior. They would try to acquire old pieces of SS uniforms. If that was not possible, they tried to sew and mend their uniforms so that they would resemble those of the guards. The length to which prisoners would go in these efforts seemed unbelievable, particularly since the SS punished them for their efforts to copy SS uniforms. When asked why they did it, the old prisoners admitted that they loved to look like the guards.

The old prisoners' identification with the SS did not stop with the copying of their outer appearance and behavior. Old prisoners accepted Nazi goals and values, too, even when these seemed opposed to their own interests. It was appalling to see how far even politically well-educated prisoners would go with this identification. At one time American and English newspapers were full of stories about the cruelties committed in the camps. The SS punished prisoners for the appearance of these stories, true to its policy of punishing the group for whatever a member or a former member did, since the stories must have originated in reports from former prisoners. In discussions of this event, old prisoners would insist that it was not the business of foreign correspondents or newspapers to bother with German institutions, expressing their hatred of the journalists who tried to help them.

This writer asked more than one hundred old political prisoners the following question: "If I am lucky and reach foreign soil, should I tell the story of the camp and arouse the interest of the free world?" He found only two out of this number who would make the unqualified statement that everyone escaping Germany ought to fight the

Nazis to the best of his abilities. All the others were hoping for a German revolution, but did not like the idea of interference on the part of a foreign power.

When old prisoners accepted Nazi values as their own, they usually did not directly admit this; they would explain their behavior by means of rationalizations. For instance, old prisoners would collect scrap in the camp because Germany was low on raw materials. When it was pointed out that they were thus voluntarily helping the Nazis, they rationalized that through the saving of scrap Germany's working classes, too, became richer. Again, when the prisoners were erecting buildings for the gestapo, controversies started over whether one should try to build well. New prisoners were for sabotaging, a majority of the old prisoners for building well. They rationalized that the new Germany would have use for these buildings. When it was pointed out that a revolution would have to destroy the fortresses of the gestapo, old prisoners would retire to the general statement that one ought to do well any job one has to do. It seems that the majority of the old prisoners had realized that they could not continue to work for the gestapo unless they could convince themselves that their work made some sense. Thus they had convinced themselves that it did.

The satisfaction with which some old prisoners enjoyed the fact that, during the twice-daily counting of the prisoners—which often lasted for hours and always seemed interminable—they had stood really well at attention can be explained only by the fact that they had entirely accepted the values of the SS as their own. These prisoners prided themselves on being as tough as the SS. This identification with their torturers went so far as copying their leisure-time activities. One of the games played by the guards was to find out who could stand to be hit longest without uttering a complaint. This game was copied by some of the old prisoners, as though they had not been hit often and long enough not to need to repeat this experience by inflicting pain on fellow prisoners.

Often the SS would enforce nonsensical rules, originating in the whims of one of the guards. These rules were usually forgotten very quickly, but there were always some old prisoners who would continue to follow the rules and try to enforce them on others long after the gestapo had forgotten about them. Once, for instance, a guard inspecting the prisoners' apparel found that the shoes of some of them were dirty on the inside. He ordered all prisoners to wash their shoes inside and out with water and soap. The heavy shoes, when treated this way, became hard as stone. The order was never repeated, and many prisoners did not even execute it when given. Nevertheless there were some old prisoners who not only continued to wash the inside of their shoes every day but cursed all others who did not do so as negligent and dirty. These prisoners firmly believed that the rules set down by the SS were desirable standards of human behavior, at least within the camp situation.

Most old prisoners also made their peace with the values of the SS concerning race, although racial discrimination had been alien to their scheme of values before they were sent to the camp. They accepted as true the claim that Germany needed more space (*Lebensraum*), although they added, "as long as there does not exist a world federation"; and they believed in the superiority of the German race. It should be emphasized that this was not the result of propaganda on the part of the SS. The SS made no such efforts but insisted in its statements that it was not interested in how the prisoners felt as long as they were full of fear of the SS. Moreover, the SS insisted that it would prevent prisoners from expressing their feelings anyway. Surprisingly, especially when viewing the old prisoners' behavior, the SS seemed to think it was impossible to win the prisoners over to its values after having made them subject to its tortures.

Among the old prisoners one could observe other developments which indicated their desire to accept the SS along lines which definitely could not originate in propaganda. It seems that once prisoners adopted a childlike attitude toward the SS, they had a desire for at least some of those whom they accepted as all-powerful father-images to be just and kind. They divided their positive and negative feelings —strange as it may be that they should have had positive feelings, they had them—toward the SS in such a way that all positive emotions were concentrated on a few officers who were rather high up in the hierarchy of camp administrators, although hardly ever on the governor of the camp. The old prisoners insisted that these officers hid behind their rough surfaces a feeling of justice and propriety; he, or they, were supposed to be genuinely interested in the prisoners and even trying, in a small way, to help them. Since nothing of these supposed feelings and efforts ever became apparent, it was explained that the officer in question hid them so effectively because otherwise he would not be able to help the prisoners. The eagerness of these prisoners to find support for their claims was pitiful. A whole legend was woven around the fact that of two non-commissioned officers inspecting a barracks, one had cleaned his shoes of mud before entering. He probably did it automatically, but it was interpreted as a rebuff to the other man and a clear demonstration of how he felt about the concentration camp.

After so much has been said about the old prisoners' tendency to conform and to identify with the SS, it ought to be stressed that this was only part of the picture. The author has tried to concentrate on interesting psychological mechanisms in group behavior rather than on reporting types of behavior which are either well known or could reasonably be expected. These same old prisoners who identified with the SS defied it at other moments, demonstrating extraordinary courage in doing so.

The author feels that the concentration camp has an importance reaching far beyond its being a place where the gestapo took revenge on its enemies. It was the main training ground for young gestapo soldiers who were planning to rule and police Germany and all conquered nations; it was the laboratory where the gestapo developed methods for changing free and upright citizens not into grumbling slaves, but into serfs who in many respects accepted their masters' values.

It seems that what happened in an extreme fashion to the prisoners who spent several years in a concentration camp happened in less exaggerated form to most inhabitants of that large-scale concentration camp called greater Germany. It could have happened to the inhabitants of occupied countries if they had not been able to form organized groups of resistance. The system was too strong for an individual to break its hold over his emotional life, particularly when he found himself within a group which had more or less accepted the Nazi system. It was easier to resist the pressure of the gestapo and the Nazis if one functioned as an individual; the gestapo seemed to know that, and therefore insisted on forcing all individuals into groups which it could supervise.

Some of the methods used to discourage individualism were the hostage system and the punishment of the whole group for whatever a member of it did; not permitting anybody to deviate in his behavior from the group norm, whatever this norm might be; discouraging solitary activities of any kind, etc.

The main goal of the Nazi efforts seemed to be to produce in their subjects childlike attitudes and childlike dependency on the will of the leaders. The most effective way to break this influence seemed to be the formation of democratic resistance groups of independent, mature, and self-reliant persons, in which every member backed up, in all other members, the ability to resist. If such groups were not formed, it was very difficult not to become subject to the slow process of personality disintegration produced by the unrelenting pressure of the gestapo and the Nazi system.

The concentration camp was the gestapo's laboratory for subjecting not only free men, but especially the most ardent foes of the Nazi system, to the process of disintegration from their position as autonomous individuals. It ought to be studied by all persons interested in understanding what happens to a population subject to the methods of the Nazi system.

The Holocaust—
One Generation Later

My business is not with the dead, but with the living. The events of the Nazi holocaust are by now an appropriate subject for historians; my concern is with its significance for the present generation. This generation should not distort the meaning the holocaust carries, not just because of the terrible things done by average people to average persons one short generation ago, but because of the warning it holds for man today.

It is understandable that we wish to avoid coping with the deeply disturbing perspectives on man which the holocaust opens up; man as a wanton destroyer, and as a victim shorn of all defenses. The appalling nature of that which we ought to understand and build into our view of the world as a terrible warning induces us to avoid facing the true nature of the problem by denying some of its most upsetting aspects, and by distorting others.

All this is hardly new; from the very beginning of the long series of events which we now call the Nazi holocaust, the psychological mechanisms used to deal with it have not been recognition of the facts, correct assessments and interpretations of their implications, and mastery of the event on this basis. Instead we have used various distancing devices, false analogies, and forms of outright denial, so as not to have to come to grips with a grim reality.

Denial is the earliest, most primitive, most inappropriate and ineffective of all psychological defenses used by man. When the event is potentially destructive, it is the most pernicious psychological defense, because it does not permit taking appropriate action which might safeguard against the real dangers. Denial therefore leaves the individual most vulnerable to the very perils against which he has tried to defend himself.

One Jewish survivor of the concentration camps reported recently

THE HOLOCAUST—ONE GENERATION LATER: Parts of this essay were presented at a conference on the holocaust in San Jose early in 1977.

on the TV news that she did not know about the camps at the time she was transported there from her native Hungary. This is dubious, because from the very beginning of Naziism in 1933, Hitler and all Nazis declared most publicly, innumerable times, that they would make Germany *Judenrein*—that they would clear all Jews out of Germany and all the other countries to fall under their power. The Nazis further declared that if there was a war, at its end no Jew would remain alive in Europe.

Actual abuse and vilification of the Jews existed from the moment the Nazis came into power, and even before. The Nazis propagandized the concentration camps, using them deliberately as a threat to intimidate and subdue their opponents, and even their followers, when these showed any sign of independent opinion. This was so much the case that an often-quoted saying sprang up: *Lieber Gott, mach mich stumm, dass ich nicht nach Dachau kumm* ("Dear Lord, please make me mute, so that I won't be sent to Dachau").

When after the war, therefore, some Germans claimed that they had not had any knowledge of the concentration camps—about which they had read so often in their daily papers as a warning not to transgress Nazi rules—this was either an outright lie, or due to their wish not to have known what they could easily have known, but which they (unconsciously) chose not to know. In this context it must be remembered that denial, even when it begins as a conscious process, soon becomes an unconscious one; otherwise it could never work so well, and so completely.

While the concentration camps were public knowledge, the extermination camps were treated more like a poorly kept secret. Poorly kept, because it had been publicly announced that no Jew would be left in Europe after the war. Poorly kept, because anybody who wanted to find out about the extermination camps could do so—too many people were involved, and no news was ever received from or about those who were sent there. Neutral embassies, the Vatican, the American and the other Allied governments, and many other official bodies were well informed about them. Thus knowledge about the extermination of the Jews could be gained, and many efforts were made to spread this knowledge among Jews. Still, officially the extermination camps were treated as something to be kept secret, and there is an interesting reason for this.

Actually, the systematic extermination of the Jews began after

U.S. entrance into the war, when it became likely that Germany would be defeated. The Nazis then decided that the very widespread but until then somewhat haphazard killing of Jews would not eliminate them all before the war ended. Had Germany won the war, the extermination would probably have proceeded more slowly, since a program of sterilizing all Jewish men or women or both was very seriously considered, and it included letting those already alive die out slowly through natural death, while taking advantage of them as slave laborers until then. This, too, would have achieved the purpose of making Europe free of Jews. But with German defeat now a serious prospect, the final solution of the Jewish problem was sharply accelerated.

The first use of the gas chambers was not for the elimination of Jews, but in the so-called euthanasia program, the elimination of those the Nazis considered misfits—mental defectives and inmates of psychiatric hospitals. This was the first group to be systematically killed off, quite a few of them in the first mobile gas chambers. Although this program of extermination was camouflaged—initially, it was claimed that some new, potentially dangerous treatment would be tried out on these people, which had some chance of success although it entailed serious risk of death, etc.—it soon became known what was really going on. There was such a strong reaction against this slaughter of mental patients among religious leaders and the common people that despite massive propaganda and much against their desire, the Nazis had to discontinue this important part of their official eugenics program. This demonstrates that when unpleasant facts are not dealt with by means of denial but are faced squarely, even the most ruthless totalitarian regime can be forced to back down by determined public action.

No such public, widespread objection, however, made itself heard about the persecution of the Jews, or about the random killing of large masses of Jews, or even the extermination of all of them; quite the contrary. If anything, the German people seemed in their overwhelming majority either to applaud the persecution of the Jews, or to condone it by a sin of omission, a very few isolated voices raised against it notwithstanding.[1] These few voices could easily be sup-

---

[1] Today, after all these years, it is easily forgotten how many Germans—by no means only Nazis—derived tangible advantages from the persecution of the

pressed and disregarded by the government, since they found no following.

To some extent the absence of opposition was due to the massive anti-Semitic propaganda, and to the fact that the screws cutting off Jewish breathing space were at first tightened slowly. It would be tedious to retrace here the steps by which the Jews first were made second-class citizens, then robbed of all their citizens' rights, prevented from practicing their professions, then prevented from earning anything, banned from public gatherings, their children excluded from school; how Jews were first publicly ridiculed, then beaten up, jailed, and finally put into the camps.

For a time, these measures were differentially applied; for example, those who had served in the First World War were exempted from some of them, etc. At each step, the Jews could delude themselves with the thought that as terrible as the hardships imposed on them were getting, they could somehow live with them. With each regulation they could fool themselves into believing that this was the last step in putting them down. While at first they had thought that the threats were mere propaganda to gain new followers for the Nazi party and satisfy old ones, soon this proved incorrect. As the hardships became more severe, the greater the Jews' need to take protective action became. But unfortunately for many, the protective action they took consisted of engaging in denial, in order not to give up, fall into despair, or commit suicide. With each new and harsher treatment

---

Jews. The vast majority of Jews either owned business enterprises or held lucrative positions; nearly all owned nice homes. They were deprived of these, which were handed over to Germans. During the last year before the war, when Jews emigrated they could take none of their possessions with them, and the same was true during the war when they were sent first to the ghettos in Poland and later into the camps. Rather than see the Nazis acquire all their possessions, on being forced to leave most Jews preferred to give their art objects, jewelry, valuable furniture and clothing, and whatnot to gentile acquaintances, either as presents or for safekeeping. The end results were nearly always the same: the Jews died in the camps, and nobody was left to claim what was left in safekeeping.

With a Jewish family's enterprise or position going to one gentile German family, their home to another, and their possessions to three or four others, easily five or more German families profited greatly from the persecution of a single Jewish family. Enough reason—if not to be happy with—at least not to object to a policy which greatly enriched them without any effort on their part.

—abuse, beatings, deportations—the Jews were pushed into two opposite groups.

Those who did not engage in denial but could see things for what they were became ever more convinced that their only safety resided in escape. While up to a point in their mistreatment they had been willing to suffer rather than give up all they possessed, they came to realize that giving up almost everything dear to them, including all material things, was a small and necessary price to pay for mere survival. Most of them managed to escape, although some were later overtaken by the German occupation of the countries to which they had fled.

By contrast, those who engaged in denial tried to tell themselves that things couldn't, or wouldn't, get any worse; that the bark of the Nazis, bad as it was, was worse than their bite; that while some other Jews were taken to the camps, they themselves would for some reason or other be saved from such a fate. With each new hardship, denial had to be increased and extended over wider areas in order to be kept up. That is why, in the end, these Jews did not know what they could easily have known, had they not blinded themselves to make the insufferable seem sufferable.

For example, some Jews managed to escape and make their way back to Warsaw; they warned others that in the camps Jews were being killed. They were berated for spreading such rumors and told to remain quiet, because what the Jews needed was to be comforted, not additionally worried. The reason for not listening to the warning voices, for disregarding the writing on the wall which was there for all to read, was the wish to continue with the denial of what was taking place.

If such behavior seems strange, consider the well-known fact that terminal cancer patients typically meet their fate with one of two opposite states of mind. Those who face what is in store for them with clarity soon also gain considerable equanimity of mind; they do everything that can and needs to be done, realizing how little time they have left to do so. But the majority, the closer they come to their end, deny ever more insistently that this is so. They claim that they are getting better, making ambitiously large and unrealistic, even delusional plans and arrangements for their future.

If a terminal cancer patient engages in massive denial, this does not change what is going to happen to him, although it makes it easier for him to live through his ordeal, which is his unconscious purpose. But for Jews under Hitler who engaged in denial for the same basic reason—to make their ordeal more bearable—this denial kept them from doing what they might in fact have done, and so cut them off from such possibilities as actually existed to save themselves. Their denial prevented them from trying to arrange for an escape; or going underground; or preparing to fight back, by joining partisan groups, for example.

Such denial was not restricted to the Jews of Europe, who at least had the excuse of terrible straits for using such a desperate and ineffective psychological defense; it was also the characteristic attitude of the West, very much including the U.S. Most nations which engaged in such denial did so mainly out of self-interest. From 1933 until the beginning of the war—for over six years—the Nazis were more than ready to let the Jews go; as a matter of fact, they tried everything to get rid of the Jews, provided they left all their belongings behind. But no country, not excepting the U.S., let more than an entirely insignificant trickle immigrate to it. The justification was again based on denial: things were not all that bad for the Jews; the Nazis did not really mean what they said, etc.

Later, after the extermination policy was in full swing, and after the American government knew about it, the Nazis offered to American Jewish groups a clandestine deal: they would let the Jews go, if they received in payment for them a number of trucks. (First they had asked for war materiel, but accepting that this could not be done, had reduced their request to trucks.) When American negotiators raised the question of how they could trust Germany to keep its promise, the Nazis offered a down payment. Without it being suggested or requested by the Americans, the Nazis delivered, free of charge, a trainload of Jews into Switzerland to prove that Jews were of no value to them, that all they wanted was to get rid of them. After that, when it was obvious that the Nazis meant business, the negotiations were broken off because the American government would not permit the deal.[2]

---

[2] For details of these negotiations as well as for the ship of refugees who were not permitted to land in the U.S., see, for example, Arthur D. Morse, *While Six Million Died: A Chronicle of American Apathy* (New York: Random House, 1967).

It could be argued that the trucks would have helped the Nazi war effort. But even before the war started, a shipload of German Jews had arrived at the American coast, but had not been permitted to land. They were ultimately returned to Europe, where most of them later perished, being again caught by the Nazis in the countries where they had found refuge. In 1939 a bill was introduced in Congress whose aim was to save at least some German Jewish children by permitting 10,000 of them to immigrate in 1939/40 under a special quota.[3] They would not have created a glut on the labor market since they would all have been under fourteen years of age, and would have been taken in by American Jewish families of means who were ready to raise them like their own children, guaranteeing that they would not become an economic liability to anybody. President Roosevelt, however, refused to endorse the bill, despite repeated urging to do so on the part of the American Jewish community. Because of his and Congress's lack of interest the bill died in the judiciary committees. These refusals to save the doomed Jews were greatly facilitated by a widespread denial of what fate had in store for them, although the Nazis had made their intentions amply clear.

The reason for all this is that it is easier to deny reality when facing it would require taking unpleasant, difficult, or expensive actions. Not to take such actions out of self-interest would evoke guilt-feelings. So that one need not feel guilty for not acting, one denies the facts. Thus denial makes life easier, at least for the moment and if one does not care what the consequences of such denial are for oneself or for others.

Denial, as mentioned before, is the most primitive of all psychological defensive mechanisms. The small child, confronted with some unpleasant fact, will insist that it is not so. Usually as we get older, we no longer use this primitive defense when confronted with incontrovertible facts. But when anxiety becomes overwhelming, even normal adults tend to regress to using it. That is why Jews under Nazi domination, in the face of obvious facts but in mortal anxiety, engaged in denial so massive that under other circumstances it would have been considered delusional.

Americans denied the reality of the extermination camps as the simplest way to avoid facing an unpleasant truth. When they could no

---

[3] It was the Wagner-Rogers Child Refugee Bill.

longer blind themselves to what thousands had seen with their own eyes, Americans began to apply more subtle and devious defensive mechanisms to avoid facing what the holocaust had been like. Imagining it would have meant experiencing it to some measure. Better to declare it unimaginable, unspeakable, because only then could one avoid facing the full horror of what had happened in its details, which would be extremely upsetting, guilt-provoking, and anxiety-creating. These more subtle psychological defensive mechanisms still dominate many Americans' present approach to the true significance of the holocaust.

To begin with, it was not the hapless victims of the Nazis who named their incomprehensible and totally unmasterable fate the "holocaust." It was the Americans who applied this artificial and highly technical term to the Nazi extermination of the European Jews. But while the event when named as mass murder most foul evokes the most immediate, most powerful revulsion, when it is designated by a rare technical term, we must first in our minds translate it back into emotionally meaningful language. Using technical or specially created terms instead of words from our common vocabulary is one of the best-known and most widely used distancing devices, separating the intellectual from the emotional experience. Talking about "the holocaust" permits us to manage it intellectually where the raw facts, when given their ordinary names, would overwhelm us emotionally— because it was catastrophe beyond comprehension, beyond the limits of our imagination, unless we force ourselves against our desire to extend it to encompass these terrible events.

This linguistic circumlocution began while it all was only in the planning stage. Even the Nazis—usually given to grossness in language and action—shied away from facing openly what they were up to and called this vile mass murder "the final solution of the Jewish problem." After all, solving a problem can be made to appear like an honorable enterprise, as long as we are not forced to recognize that the solution we are about to embark on consists of the completely unprovoked, vicious murder of millions of helpless men, women, and children. The Nuremberg judges of these Nazi criminals followed their example of circumlocution by coining a neologism out of one Greek and one Latin root: genocide. These artificially created technical terms fail to connect with our strongest feelings. The horror of murder is part of our most common human heritage. From earliest infancy on, it arouses violent abhorrence in us. Therefore in whatever form it appears we should give such an act its true designation and not hide it behind polite, erudite terms created out of classical words.

To call this vile mass murder "the holocaust" is not to give it a special name emphasizing its uniqueness which would permit, over time, the word becoming invested with feelings germane to the event it refers to. The correct definition of "holocaust" is "burnt offering." As such, it is part of the language of the psalmist, a meaningful word to all who have some acquaintance with the Bible, full of the richest emotional connotations. By using the term "holocaust," entirely false associations are established through conscious and unconscious connotations between the most vicious of mass murders and ancient rituals of a deeply religious nature.

Using a word with such strong unconscious religious connotations when speaking of the murder of millions of Jews robs the victims of this abominable mass murder of the only thing left to them: their uniqueness. Calling the most callous, most brutal, most horrid, most heinous mass murder a burnt offering is a sacrilege, a profanation of God and man.

Martyrdom is part of our religious heritage. A martyr, burned at the stake, is a burnt offering to his god. And it is true that after the Jews were asphyxiated, the victims' corpses were burned. But I believe we fool ourselves if we think we are honoring the victims of systematic murder by using this term, which has the highest moral connotations. By doing so, we connect for our own psychological reasons what happened in the extermination camps with historical events we deeply regret, but also greatly admire. We do so because this makes it easier for us to cope; only in doing so we cope with our distorted image of what happened, not with the events the way they did happen.

By calling the victims of the Nazis "martyrs," we falsify their fate. The true meaning of "martyr" is: "one who voluntarily undergoes the penalty of death for refusing to renounce his faith" (*Oxford English Dictionary*). The Nazis made sure that nobody could mistakenly think that their victims were murdered for their religious beliefs. Renouncing their faith would have saved none of them. Those who had converted to Christianity were gassed, as were those who were atheists, and those who were deeply religious Jews. They did not die for any conviction, and certainly not out of choice.

Millions of Jews were systematically slaughtered, as were untold other "undesirables," not for any convictions of theirs, but only because they stood in the way of the realization of an illusion. They neither died for their convictions, nor were they slaughtered because of their convictions, but only in consequence of the Nazis' delusional belief about what was required to protect the purity of their assumed superior racial endowment, and what they thought necessary to guarantee them the living space they believed they needed and were entitled to. Thus while these millions were slaughtered for an idea, they did not die for one.

Millions—men, women, and children—were processed after they had been utterly brutalized, their humanity destroyed, their clothes torn from their bodies. Naked, they were sorted into those who were destined to be murdered immediately, and those others who had a short-term usefulness as slave labor. But after a brief interval they, too, were to be herded into the same gas chambers into which the others were immediately piled, there to be asphyxiated so that, in their last moments, they could not prevent themselves from fighting each other in vain for a last breath of air.

To call these most wretched victims of a murderous delusion, of destructive drives run rampant, martyrs or a burnt offering is a distortion invented for our comfort, small as it may be. It pretends that this most vicious of mass murders had some deeper meaning; that in some fashion the victims either offered themselves or at least became sacrifices to a higher cause. It robs them of the last recognition which could be theirs, denies them the last dignity we could accord them: to face and accept what their death was all about, not embellishing it for the small psychological relief this may give us.

We could feel so much better if the victims had acted out of choice. For our emotional relief, therefore, we dwell on the tiny minority who did exercise some choice: the resistance fighters of the Warsaw ghetto, for example, and others like them. We are ready to overlook the fact that these people fought back only at a time when everything was lost, when the overwhelming majority of those who had been forced into the ghettos had already been exterminated without resisting. Certainly those few who finally fought for their survival and their convictions, risking and losing their lives in doing so, deserve our admiration; their deeds give us a moral lift. But the more we dwell on these few, the more unfair are we to the memory of the millions who were slaughtered—who gave in, did not fight back—because we deny them the only thing which up to the very end remained uniquely their own: their fate.

There are books and other publications which try to present the facts, so that we may know what has happened. There are other writings which search for the meaning of these terrible events; and they have been given poetic form. Others express the guilt of the survivors, the mourning for the deceased. Unfortunately with the passing of time all these receive less and less attention. By now the interest seems to have shifted to books and movies which exploit the fate of these hapless victims. The more serious of them attempt to provide us with some psychological relief. Such efforts take essentially one of three forms: in the first, these most unfortunate victims are elevated into heroes; in another, their fate is reduced to the everyday level; in the last, what happened to them is made to appear insignificant by drawing attention away from them and concentrating it only on the survivors, who also are made into something they were not, and are not now.

There are other, much more obnoxious ways the camps are used in the media. Among these are novels and films which use the corpses of the death camps to arouse and satisfy a morbid curiosity, or as a background for cheap comedy. There are also efforts to deny validity to the extermination camps by claiming that it never happened, or by directing our attention away from the victims to their murderers, who are made to appear in a favorable light as "interesting" characters.

The most serious and prevalent psychological device used today to distract us from the death camps is to view what happened to the victims as an event deserving of most severe criticism but commonplace nevertheless. This device takes the form of equating Auschwitz with Hiroshima or My Lai, or talking of genocide when referring to government-sponsored sterilization or birth-control programs. Equating My Lai and the death camps denies the crucial difference between isolated homicidal outbreaks in war—the consequence of anxiety, exasperation, or a temporary breakdown of controls which, inexcusable and criminal though it may be, nevertheless remains within the human dimension—and the careful planning and precise, deliberate execution of "the final solution." The essential differences are the premeditation which went into the one, compared with the breakdown of rationality and taking-over by primitive emotions characteristic of the other; and the application of all the machinery and power of the state in one case, compared to the breakdown of controls in individual persons of which the state severely disapproves in the other.

Equating what the Nazis did with the American bombing of Hiroshima seems on the surface a more appropriate comparison, since in both instances governmental preplanning was responsible for what happened. But it is actually an even more vicious distortion, because it implicitly accepts one of the biggest Nazi lies as truth— namely, that the Jews were an enemy waging aggressive war against Germany. In reality, as is well known, the Jews were Germany's most peaceful and most tragically obedient subjects. These comparisons consciously or unconsciously take the side of the Nazis against that of the Jews, and this subtle siding with the Nazis is one of the most pernicious aspects of the attitudes of all too many American intellectuals towards the extermination of European Jews. It is but the other side of the coin when the same intellectuals applaud books and films which use the death camps as background to titillate or excite, and in this way make them appear as just an ordinary part of life.

Quite opposite from that psychological defense are efforts to make the survivors appear as unusual, most superior persons because of their experiences in the extermination camps. This was attempted most effectively in Terrence Des Pres's 1976 book *The Survivor*, which has found much acclaim in intellectual circles. The book draws our attention away from the millions who were murdered, and concentrates only on the all too few who survived, and survived only because the Allied armies rescued them at the last moment. It makes heroes out of these chance survivors. By stressing how the death camps produced such superior beings as the survivors, all our interest is focused on the survival of the few, at the cost of neglecting the millions who got slaughtered.

Survivors feel exasperated and helpless when others who have not the slightest idea what their experiences were like hold forth about what these experiences were all about, and what their real meaning is. Elie Wiesel expresses well survivors' reactions to the psychological defenses presently used to avoid facing the upsetting reality of what the extermination of the Jews was all about. Speaking of those who write about the survivors, he says:

> Those who have not lived through the experience will never know; those who have will never tell; not really, not completely. The past belongs to the dead, and the survivor does not recognize himself in the images and ideas which presumably depict him. Auschwitz means death, total absolute death—of man and of all people, of language and imagination, of time and spirit. . . . The survivor knows. He and no one else. And so he is obsessed by guilt and helplessness. . . . At first the testimony of survivors inspired awe and humility. At first, the question was treated with a sort of sacred reverence. It was considered taboo, reserved exclusively for the initiated. . . .
>
> But popularization and exploitation soon followed. And then, with the passing of time, it all began to deteriorate. As the subject became popularized, so it ceased to be sacrosanct, or rather was stripped of its mystery. People lost their awe. The Holocaust became a literary "free for all," the no-man's land of modern writing. Now everyone got into the act. Novelists made free use of it in their work, scholars used it to prove their theories. In so doing they cheapened the Holocaust; they drained it of its substance.
>
> To ward off survivors' criticism, the exclusive right to that title was taken away from them. Suddenly, everyone began calling himself a survivor. Having compared Harlem to the Warsaw ghetto and Vietnam to Auschwitz, a further step has now been taken: some who had spent the war on a Kibbutz or in a fancy apartment in Manhattan, now claim that they too have survived the Holocaust, probably by proxy. One consequence is that an international symposium [on the Holocaust] was held recently in New York without the participation of any Holocaust survivors. The survivors don't count; they never did. They are best forgotten. Don't you see? They are an embarrassment. If only they weren't there, it would be so much easier.
>
> The survivors will soon be unwelcome intruders. Their assassins are now in the limelight. They are shown in films, they are scrutinized, they are humanized. They are studied at first with objectivity, then with sympathy. One movie tells of the loves of a Jewish woman and a former SS. Gone are the days when the dead had their special place, and gone the days when their lives commanded respect. People are more interested in their killers: so handsome and attractive, such pleasure to

watch. This attitude exists among Jewish and non-Jewish intellectuals alike.[4]

Confronted with the death camps, our old categories do not hold. But just because the commonly used psychological concepts do not suffice to comprehend what has happened is not sufficient reason to deny the extermination of European Jewry validity, through use of devious psychological defenses. Often I have felt like Elie Wiesel: that only withdrawal into silence will do. I think Theodor Adorno felt this way when he wrote that there can be no poetry after Auschwitz. But if we remain silent, then we perform exactly as the Nazis wanted: behave as if it never did happen. If we remain silent, we permit those who have falsified what happened to present the world with a fallacious understanding of one of the most tragic chapters of recent history. Thus thoughtful men are closed off from valid insights into what attitudes we must develop to prevent it all from ever happening again.

There are a few ways to commemorate the victims of the death camps in a dignified manner. The *Yad v'shem* in Jerusalem is the prime example.[5] But it is unique because it is in Israel, and the state of Israel itself is the most appropriate, the best, place to memorialize the victims.

I have found other places of commemoration which are also deeply moving. One is the Old-New Synagogue in Prague, the synagogue of the famous Rabbi Loew who, according to an ancient legend, created a man-like monster, the Golem. In this place where Jewish life in Prague began in 1270, there is an epitaph to the Jews of Bohemia and Moravia whose slaughter ended the long history of Central European Jewry. The memorial consists of the 77,297 names of the known victims closely engraved on the walls of the Pinkas Synagogue (which, dating from the beginning of the sixteenth century, is part of the Old-New Synagogue complex).

---

[4] Elie Wiesel, "For Some Measure of Humility," *Sh'ma, A Journal of Jewish Responsibility* 5 (October 31, 1975), pp. 314–16.

[5] *Yad v'shem* is an expression from the Bible, to be found in Isaiah 56:5. It is the promise of the Lord that He will give the righteous ones who have no children (i.e., who cannot be commemorated by them) *a memorial, an everlasting name.*

To engrave these names for eternity is a fitting monument, because as these people entered the camps they lost their names, were treated not as persons, but as things to be sorted and dispatched. The vast majority were murdered immediately; the rest were reduced to numbers tattooed on their arms, to serve as nameless, completely depersonalized slave labor until they, too, were to be exterminated.

The memorials in Amsterdam and Paris also carry legitimate meaning, marking the places where Jews, being assembled for their shipment into the camps, were still freely feeling human beings, deeply related to their families and friends. These were the places where their human autonomy ended, and here it is memorialized, because their depersonalization had only begun. The Jews brought to this place, although no longer free to act as they wished, were still at least in command of themselves even if no longer of their fate. On the transport to the death camps these people turned into shadows of their former selves, soon to be made into numbers in a hell which never recognized them as persons, but only as nameless bodies to be destroyed indiscriminately.

How can we relate today to this appalling crime? The German poet Paul Celan had been an inmate of the camps; his parents perished in the death camps. He did not try to evade this horrible experience. By confronting it within himself, he gave it poetic reality for us. Unfortunately Celan could not escape the aftereffects of his fate; in 1970 he committed suicide. But he put the whole horrendous experience into one of his untitled poems: what we must try to understand about it and have compassion with, because only in this way can we comprehend what has happened and through our feeling response transcend it. Celan wrote:

There was earth in them, and
they dug.

They dug and dug, and thus
their day wore on, and their night. And they did not praise God,
who, they heard, willed all this
who, they heard, knew all this.

They dug and heard no more:
they did not grow wise, nor contrive any song,

or any kind of language.
They dug.

There came a stillness, and there came a storm
and all the oceans came.
I dig, you dig, and the worm digs too,
and the singing there says: they dig

Oh someone, oh none, oh no one, oh you:
Where did it go, if nowhere it went.
Oh you dig and I dig, and I dig myself towards you,
and on our finger the ring awakes us.[6]

In his address of 1960 upon receiving the Büchner Prize, Celan said, "He who walks on his head sees the sky beneath him like an abyss." That is the perspective of those who have earth in them as they dig—while they are still alive, they have already returned to the earth from which they came, as they dig their own graves. Their perspective is no longer a human one, with the sky above them; all they can perceive is the terror of the abyss.

The ultimate abyss with its unimaginable murderous terror—this is what we should name that which we have come to call the holocaust, if we wish to speak correctly of this unfathomable event. The abyss of the death camps is the destructive potentialities in man enacted.

---

[6] Paul Celan, *Speech Grille and Selected Poems,* translation from the original German by Joachim Neugroschel (New York: E. P. Dutton, 1971).

The last two lines of the poem in Neugroschel's translation read:

> Oh you dig and I dig, and to you I dig in,
> and the ring awakes on our fingers.

I changed these two lines because I feel that my translation of them is truer to the original, which reads:

> O du gräbst und ich grab, und ich grab mich dir zu,
> und am Finger erwacht uns der Ring.

As I understand Celan, he did not mean to say that the other "digs in" as Neugroschel's translation suggests, since in German this would require the use of the verb *eingraben. Ich grab mich dir zu* has to be translated as "I dig myself toward you." And *am Finger erwacht uns der Ring* does not suggest that it is the ring which awakes, but rather that it is the ring—symbol of the newly established bond between the one who digs, and the other who digs toward him—which awakens them both.

.   .   .

We cannot fully grasp the nature and the implications of the death camps if we shy away from facing the destructive tendencies in man.

The aggressive part of our animal inheritance which in man has assumed its specifically human and peculiarly destructive form was called the death drive by Freud, and by Konrad Lorenz, "the so-called evil."[7] Freud believed that in man the life and the death (destructive) drives wage continuous battle, and that we can truly accept ourselves, and relate positively to the other, only when the life drives are in ascendancy—when they succeed in dominating our life as they manage to neutralize the death drive and its derivatives.

I think we cannot understand the Hitler phenomenon—and there were other monsters like him in history, although fortunately they very rarely reached similar dominance—unless we recognize by Hitler's actions and those of his henchmen that the death drive had completely overpowered the life drives. Hitler's belief that his cherished man of pure Aryan blood could flourish only when the lower races were completely exterminated created a death mania which, while it began with the Jews, did not end with them. Many others were also to be exterminated—the Gypsies, the mentally or physically deficient—while the Poles, Russians, blacks, and members of other "inferior" races were to be radically reduced in numbers under Hitler's thousand-year Reich.

Had Hitler not been so obsessed by the conviction that other races had to die for the Germans to live, he might well have won the war, and with it much of the world. Not only German Jews, but vast numbers of Polish, Ukrainian, and even Russian soldiers would have joined the German army and might have brought it victory, had Hitler's wish to exterminate some and to enslave the others not prevented him from integrating them into his army.

So it happened as it must: those beholden to the death drive destroy also themselves. In the end, Hitler wished—and even tried—to exterminate the Germans who had served him so well. His insis-

---

[7] Konrad Lorenz, *On Aggression* (New York: Harcourt, Brace & World, 1966). The English title fails to do justice to the original title Lorenz gave his book, which is *Das sogenannte Böse*.

tence that his army at Stalingrad had to let itself be killed, rather than try to save itself, is one example. Another is Hitler's carrying the war on long after it had been lost, trying to have every German fight until death rather than make peace.

However, the behavior of the Jews who, without offering resistance, permitted themselves to be walked to the gas chambers, cannot be comprehended either without reference to the death tendencies that exist in all of us. After the horrible transport into the death camps, when confronted with the gas chambers and crematoria the life drives in the Jews, who were deprived of everything that had given them security, robbed of all hope for themselves and, worst of all, deserted by the entire world, were no longer able to keep their death drive in bounds. But in their case, the death tendencies were not directed outside, against others, but turned inward, against the self.

That is why they should be memorialized at the places where they were collected for transportation—because there, although their life drives had been terribly weakened by their preceding experiences, they had not yet been extinguished. They were still wishing and trying to live, not yet entirely incapacitated by their own death drive. During the terrible transportation into the death camps, the horror of which was unimaginable, the power of their life drives must have slowly drained away. Having been on two of these transports,[8] I know that the horrors one was subjected to made one wish for death as a relief; that is, as the life drives recede, the door is opened for the death drive to overpower the individual. That is why the victims could be herded to the gas chambers without resisting: the transport had turned many of them into walking corpses. In those who were selected for slave labor, slowly the life drives returned, weak though they remained, and they tried their very best to survive.

And here, finally, I come to the American contribution to the holocaust—a sin of omission. The euthanasia program mentioned before had to be stopped, dear as it was to Hitler, because too much opposition was aroused by it. Had there been as much concern abroad about the extermination of the Jews as there had been about

---

[8] First from Vienna to Dachau, the second time from Dachau to Buchenwald. Still, these transports cannot be compared to what went on years later on the transports to the death camps.

the killing of the mentally defective and the insane, then the Nazis would probably have had to stop their extermination of the Jews also. But the world remained silent; the Pope, the world's clergy—all who had raised their voices for the mentally defective—remained silent when Jews were murdered.

This same lack of world concern, as it weakened life drives, reinforced the death tendencies in the Jews, because they felt completely abandoned, felt that nobody else cared, that nobody but they themselves thought they had a right to live. Unfortunately, one's own belief in one's right to live is not enough to keep the death tendencies within controllable boundaries. Most suicidal persons think they have a right to live; they try to commit suicide either because they are convinced that nobody else cares whether they live or die, or to find out whether this is so. They give up their suicidal ideas as soon as they come to feel that there is someone else who is deeply concerned that they live, and who is willing to go to great lengths to help them live.

The SS knew instinctively all there is to be known about the death drive; for good reason did the "death's-head units" of the SS run the camps and wear skulls on their uniforms. It was their systematic aim to destroy the strength of the life drives in prisoners.

Long before Jews permitted themselves to be transported into the death camps, long before they allowed themselves to be herded to the gas chambers, the Nazis had systematically destroyed their self-respect, robbed them of the belief that they could be masters of their fate. What happened to them impressed on them that nobody cared whether they lived or died, and that the rest of the world, including foreign countries, had no concern for their fate. One cannot meet catastrophic events and survive when deprived of the feeling that somebody cares.

The worst damage to our life drives does not come from the hateful and destructive actions of our enemies. While we may be unable to resist them physically, we can cope with them psychologically as long as our friends, those who we think ought to be our rescuers, live up to the trust we put into them.

Had the Jews felt that important voices in the rest of the world were raised in their behalf, that people in the free world cared and truly wanted them to live, they would not have needed to engage in the defense of massive denial, but could have realized what was going on, and reacted differently to it. They could then have coped better with the fact that the Nazis wanted them to perish and had planned for their destruction, although nobody can cope really well with this. But many people have enemies who wish them evil; it was the indifference of all those others who should have come to their rescue which was so finally destructive to Jewish hopes.

The Nazis murdered the Jews of Europe. That nobody but the Jews cared, that the world, the United States, did not care, was why Jewish life drives lost the battle against death tendencies.[9] This was why the camp inmates had already relinquished life as they dug their own graves, and why, as the poet put it, "there was earth in them." The most extreme agony is to feel that one has been utterly forsaken.

Murderers can only kill; they do not have the power to rob us of the wish to live nor of the ability to fight for life. Degradation, exhaustion, and utter debilitation through starvation, sickness, and mistreatment—all these seriously weaken our will to live, undermine our life drives, and with this open the way for the death drive. But when such conditions—in which the Jews found themselves because of Nazi persecution and degradation—are worsened by the feeling that the rest of the world has forsaken us, then we are totally deprived of the strength needed to fight off the murderer, to refuse to dig our own grave.

This level of despair is given words towards the end of Celan's poem by the desperate cry "Oh someone," and then there is the final giving-up, when one realizes that there is "no one." We ought to have been their someone, but we were their no one. This is our burden. Just because we cannot atone for it, it is wrong to deny or obfuscate it.

As if from beyond their grave—which was of course never allotted to these victims—the poet speaks to us with their voice: "oh you: / Where did it go, if nowhere it went." Only if we stop denying —for our comfort, and to our lasting detriment—what the holocaust

---

[9] One of the last messages received by the outside world from the Warsaw ghetto said, "The world is silent; the world *knows* (it is inconceivable that it should not) and stays silent; God's vicar in the Vatican is silent; there is silence in London and Washington; the American Jews are silent. This silence is incomprehensible and horrifying." (George Steiner, *Language and Silence* [New York: Atheneum, 1967].) But it was not only silence which met the destruction of the Jews. German newsreels show what those in the ghetto must also have observed: the frequent laughter and applause of Polish spectators as they watched houses being blown up and Jews perishing in the flames.

was all about, will it stop going nowhere; will we know where it went.

Our obligation—not to those who are dead, but to ourselves, and to those around us who are still alive—is to strengthen the life drives, so that never again—if we can help it—will these be so totally destroyed in so many, least of all by the power of a state. A true understanding of the holocaust ought to imbue us with the determination that we shall never again permit that men, overcome by their desperation and enslaved by their death drive, should walk to their death as their murderers wish.

With the poet's help, finally, I can be more specific about what is needed:

> *Oh you dig and I dig, and I dig myself towards you,*
> *and on our finger the ring awakes us.*

If, with empathy and compassion, we dig towards those who have so completely given up all hope that "there is earth in them," this will bind us together (as the ring does in a betrothal) and we both will awaken: they from their living death; we from apathy to their suffering.

That we ought to care for the other, that with our concern we ought to counteract the death-like and death-provoking desperation that there is nobody who cares for one, has been taught since the beginning of time. But in each generation, one event more than any other makes this lesson especially pertinent, giving it a character specific to that age. For this century I believe this event is the extermination of the European Jews in the gas chambers, because the way it happened was possible only in a totalitarian, technological mass society, obsessed by a pseudo-scientific delusion. (In the case of the Nazi state the particular pseudo-scientific delusion was its eugenic mission to improve the genetic inheritance of man.) Nothing will give us a more acute and pervasive understanding of the evils of such totalitarianism than when, in our minds, we dig toward the millions who have been so cruelly, so senselessly, so wantonly exterminated. It is the best we can do to forge a bond between them and us. While it will not awaken them, it may well awaken us to a more meaningful life.

"Owners of Their Faces"

They that have pow'r to hurt and will do none,
That do not do the thing they most do show,

.   .   .   .

They are the lords and owners of their faces,
Others but stewards of their excellence.

                    —SHAKESPEARE, SONNET XCIV

My reading of Paul Celan's poem was informed by what I had learned about survival in the camps from observing others and myself: even the worst mistreatment by the SS failed to extinguish the will to live—that is, as long as one could muster the wish to go on and maintain one's self-respect. Then tortures could even strengthen one's resolution not to permit the mortal enemy to break one's desire to survive, and to remain true to oneself as much as conditions permitted. Then the actions of the SS tended to make one livid with rage, and this gave one the feeling of being very much alive. It made one all the more determined to go on living, so as to be able someday to defeat the enemy.

Through their actions and the terrible conditions of life that they imposed, the SS attempted to rob the prisoners of the ability to respect themselves and care for their lives. If one thus lost all hope for the future, then one's mental state automatically precluded any possibility of believing that one could defeat the SS's purpose by surviving. Then one was deprived of the psychological relief which imagining future revenge and well-being offered, and one could no longer defend oneself against falling prey to deepest depression. When to this became added the feeling that one was abandoned by those in the outside world, then, in utter desperation, one only wished it would all be over.

Wanting to go on living even in so terrible a situation, keeping one's respect for oneself, and with it for some others, maintaining hope for one's future, and holding on to the belief—or at least the hope—that one was not abandoned were all closely related elements;

so were disgust with oneself and one's life, despair about one's future, and the conviction that one had been forsaken. If one could maintain one's self-respect and will to live despite the utter exhaustion, physical mistreatment, and extreme degradations one had to endure, then one could continue to hope that one had not been forsaken by the rest of the world, even if there was but little support for such belief. Then any scrap of evidence was sufficient to be experienced as suggesting that somebody cared.

All this worked only up to a point. If there was no or only little indication that someone, or the world at large, was deeply concerned about the fate of the prisoner, his ability to give positive meaning to signs from the outside world eventually vanished and he felt forsaken, usually with disastrous consequences for his will and with it his ability to survive. Only a very clear demonstration that one was not abandoned—and the SS saw to it that one received this only very rarely, and not at all in the extermination camps—restored, at least momentarily, hope even to those who otherwise by and large had lost it. But those who had reached the utmost state of depression and disintegration, those who had turned into walking corpses because their life drives had become inoperative—the so-called "Muslims" (*Muselmänner*)—could not believe in what others would have viewed as tokens that they had not been forgotten.

For those whose will to live and hope for the future had given way, the end was near. It came relatively rarely through outright suicide, because this meant to take some action, desperate as it was, and they no longer had the strength to act on their own. But there was also no need to deliberately do away with one's life. If one did not exercise great ingenuity and determination in the battle to stay alive, one was soon dead, given the conditions in the camps. Therefore if one gave up hope, one lost the ability to go on with the difficult and painful struggle survival required and so one died in a short time. Losing the will to live was the consequence of the waning of the life drives so that they became too weak for even the primary of their two tasks: to endow the self with the energy it needs to function and hope for the future. Forsaken already would be the closely related other task of the life drives: giving the individual the strength and desire to maintain emotional ties to others, which very much includes the ability to gain strength from their ties to him. This is why it was so vitally important for survival to believe that one had not been forsaken.

Since the "life drive," the "libido," the *élan vital*, or whatever term is preferred are but symbols for psychological processes, one may also elaborate on their meaning by saying that as a person loses interest in himself, his life, and his future, everybody and everything in the outside world of necessity loses interest for him, too. On the other hand, if everybody outside does lose, or seems to lose, interest in a person, then it requires unusually strong life tendencies, well developed self-respect, and great inner security for such an individual not to soon lose interest in himself, and become ready to give up living, particularly when the circumstances of his life are extremely disagreeable and destructive.

In the camps, because of the depth of despair which so often pervaded every moment of one's existence, I experienced more keenly than ever before, and observed in most fellow prisoners, how some small sign that others indeed cared—a message from home which gave this impression, a helping gesture from another prisoner, even an item in a newspaper which suggested that the plight of the prisoners found sympathetic attention—could instantly rekindle the will to live, if one's depression had not become so deep that nothing could relieve it. The will then once again expressed itself in both its forms: as a more determined struggle to survive because one again began to hope for one's future (the direct result of the belief that others cared), and a more positive move towards others, such as some fellow prisoner.

My quoting Celan's poem, with what it told about the utter loneliness and desperation of those who had "earth in them" and the awakening to life that could be effected when a compassionate I "digs" toward a you, was equally informed by my life's work with psychotic youngsters. Many of these—like those death camp inmates who, as the poet describes, dug their own graves—are unable to "contrive any kind of language" because none would be commensurate to their pain, despair, desolation, and living death. But also they are convinced that even if they tried to express it all, nobody would listen and have compassion, because nobody could care enough to share with them and thus relieve their horrible suffering.

Without the understanding gained from psychoanalysis I would not have been able to comprehend what the concentration camp did to people, nor why; nor the way people become psychotic, nor how to induce them to rejoin life from their psychological death. The concentration camp experience permitted me access, through empathy, to what it is like to live in psychosis; so I could later examine the issues of what causes it, and what is needed to be able to make a new beginning and escape it.

In the concentration camps, efforts to deprive the prisoners of even the smallest remnants of their autonomy were particularly vicious and all-pervasive. Nevertheless the system succeeded only to various degrees, affecting some aspects of one's life more than others. In the measure that the prisoner was deprived of autonomy it brought about a commensurately severe personality disintegration, both in his inner life and in his relations to others.

If he was not murdered, how well a person was able to survive depended on how well he managed to maintain if not some of his autonomy, at least some of his self-respect and the meaning his relations to others had for him. On the other hand, how soon and completely he lost all of his autonomy, and how far the disintegration of his personality went were mainly conditioned by two factors: the severity of the traumatization he was subjected to, as objectively evaluated; and how shattering it was experienced subjectively by him.

The latter depended to a very large degree on how securely a person's autonomy had become established in his pre-camp existence; that is, how well his personality had been integrated and his self-respect developed. Other significant factors were how intrinsically meaningful had been his life-style; how significant, satisfying, and permanent his relations with others. Most important in these respects was whether and to what degree his self-respect and security had been anchored in his innermost life—that is in who he was—or to what degree he had relied for security and self-image on the externals of existence—that is on what he only seemed to be.

Survival in the camps—this cannot be stressed enough—depended foremost on luck: to be able to survive, one had to escape being killed by the SS. While nothing one could do could assure survival, and while chances for it at best were extremely slim, one could increase them through correctly assessing one's situation and taking advantage of opportunities; in short, through acting independently and with courage, decision, and conviction, all of which depended on the measure of autonomy one had managed to retain.

Survival was, of course, greatly helped if one had entered the camps in a good state of physical health. But most of all, as I have intimated all along, autonomy, self-respect, inner integration, a rich inner life, and the ability to relate to others in meaningful ways were the psychological conditions which, more than any others, permitted one to survive in the camps as much a whole human being as overall conditions and chance would permit.

There is thus good reason to be concerned with what could be done to make it possible for all people to achieve autonomy, true self-respect, inner integration, a rich mental life, and the ability to form meaningful relations to others. It is not because they might need all of these desperately should they ever find themselves in an extreme situation, but because they need them all of their lives.

In my work with psychotic youngsters I had to cope daily with the often unbelievable ravages caused by lack of autonomy, absence of any self-respect or integration, and a complete inability to relate. I was much concerned with how all these might be restored to the children; how incredibly difficult a task this was, and how heartbreaking it would be if not achieved.

The combination of my concentration camp experience and my work with psychotic individuals motivated my involvement in two fundamental—and related—problems: what could be done, both on the larger social scale and on the narrower but much more immediately important individual level, to prevent anomie and alienation, so destructive to autonomy and security; and how to forestall personal disintegration, isolation, absence of self-respect and of respect for the other. The papers forming the rest of this book deal with those problems and also with what can be done in society, and in persons' life experience—foremost through their upbringing and education—to promote their achieving autonomy, self-respect, integration, and the ability to form meaningful and lasting relations; in short, to help them become "the lords and owners of their faces."

In the preceding remarks I drew a parallel between the personality disintegration caused by being caught in that particularly devastating maelstrom of history called the Nazi holocaust; and that which is the consequence of very unique, terrible, private experiences which lead either to a psychotic collapse of integration or an inability to establish any integration in the first place. By implication this suggests also a parallel of requisites needed to achieve recovery from such extreme traumatization—namely the regaining of autonomy, self-respect, and personal integration.

The rebuilding process is the same whether personality disintegration and destruction of autonomy are caused by real or by imagined experiences; whether these originally were mainly externally or internally caused; whether the traumatization is due to the Nazi holocaust or to having been forced to exist in a most private hell; whether one has been destroyed as a person by a government using all the machinery and power of the state for this purpose, or by the psychological abandonment and rejection of parents who, more often than not, are themselves deeply unhappy people, incapable of doing otherwise.

The recognition of this parallel served strongly to reinforce my concern with various aspects of the problem of how personal autonomy, self-respect, integration, and good relations to others could be made more available through improved conditions in both the social and the private realm. The essays which follow are in one form or another addressed to these issues. It seems therefore appropriate to introduce them with a paper which tells how this parallel came to my attention.

I have not been the only one to whom this parallel between camp experience and a child destroyed by his earliest experiences has occurred. It seems to force itself on the mind if one thinks and cares deeply for the victims of the holocaust. Another of Paul Celan's poems, "Death Fugue" ("Todesfuge"), bears this out. It was this poem which immediately established him as Germany's—and probably Europe's—most important poet of his generation. To convey the ultimate desperation reigning in the death camps, he evokes the image of a mother destroying her infant.

> *Black milk of dawn we drink it at dusk*
> *we drink it at noon and at daybreak we drink it at night*
> *we drink and we drink*

are the poem's first lines; and later on

> *Black milk of dawn we drink you at night*
> *we drink you at noon death is a master from Germany*[1]

---

[1] Paul Celan, *Speech Grille and Selected Poems*, tr. Joachim Neugroschel (New York: E. P. Dutton, 1971).

When one is forced to drink black milk from dawn to dusk, whether in the death camps of Nazi Germany, or while lying in a possibly luxurious crib, but there subjected to the unconscious death wishes of what overtly may be a conscientious mother—in either situation, a living soul has death for a master.

Schizophrenia as a Reaction to Extreme Situations

From the very inception of psychoanalysis successful efforts to help a patient achieve better integration of his personality required parallel attempts at integration on the part of the therapist. This could be easily overlooked, because in Freud's self-analysis, on which psychoanalysis is based, patient and therapist were one and the same person. Since Freud's time, unfortunately, too little attention has been paid to the fact that good psychotherapy, and particularly good psychoanalysis, requires that the therapist examine the motives for his therapeutic actions: why he decided to treat a particular patient, why it is in the patient's best interest to be treated in this therapist's manner, and what it means to the therapist to have to cope with the problems the patient brings up.

Such continuous self-examination is necessary to prevent impurities originating, for example, in the therapist's self-system and self-interests from interfering with his doing only what is best for the patient. At the same time, such self-analysis of the motives for treating a patient, and of reactions to what goes on in oneself while conducting the treatment, when honestly and conscientiously engaged in, will also further the integration of the therapist himself.

Great care to prevent the therapist's self-interests from jeopardizing those of the patient is required in all forms of psychotherapy, no matter what the nature of the disturbance from which the patient suffers. Such care is particularly necessary in the treatment of those who are least able to defend themselves and who are most vulnerable to being taken advantage of, such as psychotics and children. If the patient is both child and psychotic, precaution on the part of the therapist becomes of paramount importance. This is why in our work at the Orthogenic School in Chicago we

SCHIZOPHRENIA AS A REACTION TO EXTREME SITUATIONS: A paper with the same title was published in the *American Journal of Orthopsychiatry* 26 (1956), pp. 507–18. It is here reprinted in shortened form, with some additions and other editorial changes.

were convinced that a most significant aspect of our efforts must be the continuous self-scrutiny of every worker, and the mutual scrutiny of each other by all staff members in respect to what they did with and for the child patients, and why they did it, very much including their original and present motives for devoting themselves to the institutional treatment of psychotic children. (While such careful scrutiny had to extend to every aspect of the work, to elaborate on it here would be beside the point; elucidation of this system is detailed in my book A Home for the Heart.)

For me personally, such scrutiny of my motives soon disclosed that helping disintegrated individuals achieve their integration had a very special meaning, due to my experiences in the concentration camps. (This was in addition to the intrinsic merits of restoring persons previously unable to function to the enjoyment of life, and the many other personal satisfactions the work provided, such as those that come from growth in understanding the most complex and darkest mental phenomena, and from increasing facility in helping ever more seriously disturbed individuals to get well.) Participating in the integration of previously totally disintegrated persons, contributing actively to their integration of themselves, was in some vicarious manner a compensatory experience for having suffered disintegration while in the concentration camps, for having had to watch helplessly and passively while human beings suffered their personalities being completely disintegrated by the terrible conditions under which they were forced to live.

This relation between working for the integration of psychotic individuals and survivorship seems obvious enough. Of course, there is more than ample reason for working with psychotic children, without being motivated by being a survivor. Nearly all who devote themselves to this task have no experience with survivorship. I myself had worked and lived for many years with some autistic children before I was imprisoned in a concentration camp. And although I had at that time been vaguely familiar with what went on in the camps, it did not occur to me to see any parallel between that and the causes of the autism of the children whom I knew intimately. Without my experience of being subjected to personality-disintegrating experiences in the camps, and of observing the reactions of others to these experiences, it would never have come to my awareness that there exist parallels between these conditions and those which bring about the suffering of psychotic individuals.

Thus I knew all along that trying to help individuals who had been destroyed by the vagaries of life was one possible way to respond to the concentration camp experience and its aftermath, survivorship, as stated in

"Trauma and Reintegration." But it took many years of the most careful and prolonged observation of psychotic children before I saw how many parallels there are between the psychological conditions which had prevented these children from achieving age-appropriate integration and those conditions which had disintegrated the prisoners. These parallels were so startling and unexpected that for quite some time I hesitated to publish them. But eventually these findings became so convincing that I felt they should be made available to others.

At the time of original publication of the article it seemed best to begin with a discussion of various views on the treatment of childhood psychosis, a discussion of no interest within the framework of this book. So the beginning section of this paper has been deleted, as have some other smaller sections.

Childhood schizophrenia has been attributed either to some deviant genetic endowment, or—particularly in psychoanalytic studies of this disturbance—to parental, particularly maternal, attitudes. Hardly ever is it viewed as the child's spontaneous reaction to unique conditions of his life. While parental attitudes obviously largely shape these conditions, ascribing the child's reactions solely to them denies his autonomy in responding to what happens to him. Only if we take into consideration that the child has some freedom to respond to what happens to him does it become understandable why different children react differently to similarly destructive experiences to which their environment subjects them; some respond to them with schizophrenic reactions, others in quite other ways.

Because of the infant's complete dependency on the nurturing person and his inability to take care of himself physiologically, all too often he has been viewed as if his psychology were totally dependent on that of his mother. Actually, the infant is by no means simply a *tabula rasa*. From birth on, his psychological reactions are shaped by, but also shape, his mother's relation to him.

Strong as the impact of the mother may be, the child also responds all along in terms of his nature and his personality.

In regard to the origin of childhood schizophrenia, it can be said that the mother's pathology is often severe, and in many cases her behavior toward her child offers a fascinating example of an abnormal relation. But this proves neither that these mothers create the schizophrenic processes nor that the specifics of their pathologies explain those of the children. Therapeutic concentration on the mother, or on the mother-child relation, is the consequence of acceptance of an unrealistic ideal—that of the perfect infant-mother symbiosis, where the two together form a nearly undifferentiated psychological unit. To escape the isolation of man in modern society, to do away with the anomie from which we suffer in reality, we have created the wish-fulfilling image of the perfect twosome: mother and infant. We have thus overlooked the fact that individuation, and with it stress and pain, begins at birth.

If, on the other hand, childhood psychosis is due to spontaneous psychological developments in the child, what experiences set the psychotic process going? Observing the mortal anxiety which regularly underlies the symptomatology of these children, I was, for a time, much taken by Pious's views on the role of *mortido* in schizophrenia.[1] But his views did not fully agree with our observations at the Orthogenic School. In my ruminations, checking ideas against observations, it occurred to me that once before I had not only witnessed, but had also partly described, the whole gamut of autistic and schizophrenic reactions—observed not in children, but in adults in the German concentration camps. These reactions, in many aspects different from person to person, were all responses to one and the same psychological situation: finding oneself totally overpowered. Characterizing this situation were its shattering impact on the individual, for which he was totally unprepared; its inescapability; the expectation that the situation would last for an undetermined period, potentially a lifetime; the fact that, throughout its entirety, one's very life would be in jeopardy at every moment; and the fact that one was powerless to protect oneself.

This situation was so unique that I had coined a new term—"extreme situation"—when I had first published my description of human reactions to such an environment.[2] Since then, the discovery of the death camps has given this new concept even more sinister connotations, and it has become widely used in psychology. In this article I detailed the impact of imprisonment in concentration camps,

---

[1] William L. Pious, "The Pathogenic Process in Schizophrenia," *Bulletin of the Menninger Clinic* 13 (1949), pp. 152–59.

[2] "Individual and Mass Behavior in Extreme Situations."

particularly the far-reaching personality changes which were the consequence of having to live in this extreme situation. I had been able to observe the differences in response to extreme and to suffering experiences. The latter were dealt with by one's normal personality, but the extreme experiences led to radical changes in individual personality structures.

Though the conditions of living in a concentration camp were more or less the same for all prisoners, one could observe various types of resultant behavior which had similarities to schizophrenic symptoms—so much so that a description of prisoner behavior would be tantamount to a catalogue of schizophrenic reactions.

For example, some prisoners responded to living in the extreme situation with suicide, or suicidal tendencies, including the inability to eat. (This we may compare to anorexia or infantile marasmus.) Others developed catatonia, responding to any demand of the gestapo as if they had no will of their own, or had lost control over their bodies. Many went into melancholic depression, while others developed delusions of persecution beyond the actual persecution they experienced. Illusions, delusions, and projections were frequent. Superego and ego controls broke down, resulting in behavior which in more normal situations would be viewed as delinquent or infantile, including incontinency. Loss of memory was universal, as were shallow and inappropriate emotions. The differences in symptomatology were attributable to the prisoners' personalities, life histories, socioeconomic background, etc., but the fact that they developed schizophrenic-like reactions was the specific result of being forced to live in an extreme situation.

The difference between the plight of prisoners in a concentration camp and the conditions which lead to autism and schizophrenia in children is, of course, that the child has never had a previous chance to develop much of a personality. However, the youngster who develops childhood schizophrenia seems to feel about himself and his life exactly as the concentration camp prisoner felt about his: deprived of hope, and totally at the mercy of destructive irrational forces bent on using him for their goals, irrespective of his. Under such conditions the egos of most people are unable to give protection against the devastating impact of the external world; they are unable to exercise their normal task of assessing reality correctly or predicting the future with reasonable accuracy, thus making it impossible to take steps to influence it. Such egos appear not worthy of investment with vital energy by the total personality. Most of the very limited vital energy remaining available to a person under extremely debilitating conditions remains at the disposition of the id, and too little is available to the ego for it to exercise adequate influence and control over either the inner life or external reality.

One must not disregard the crucial differences between the life of a prisoner in a concentration camp and that of a child who becomes schizophrenic; however, their emotional responses to externally entirely different situations are strangely similar. There are important differences also in their psychological conditions, such as in intellectual and emotional maturity. To develop childhood schizophrenia, it is sufficient that the infant is convinced that his life is run by insensitive, irrational, and overwhelming powers, who have total control over his existence and do not value it. For the normal adult to develop schizophrenic-like reactions, this actually has to be true, as it was in the German concentration camps.

In our work with schizophrenic children, we found again and again that their schizophrenic symptomatology was not just a reaction to generalized parental attitudes such as rejection, neglect, or sudden changes in mood. In addition, specific events, different for each child, had convinced these children that they were threatened by total destruction all of the time, and that no personal relations offered any protection or emotional relief. Thus the psychological cause of childhood schizophrenia is the child's subjective feeling of living permanently in an extreme situation—of being totally helpless in the face of mortal threats, at the mercy of insensitive powers motivated only by their own incomprehensible whims, and of being deprived of any intimate, positive, need-satisfying personal relationship. Three examples may serve to illustrate.

One set of parents, for reasons of their own, and with no basis other than the child's reactions to the complete neglect to which they subjected him, decided that their son was feebleminded. Since he supposedly did not understand conversation, they spoke freely in front of him about how he ought to be put away, and how he should never have been born. His subsequent autistic withdrawal led to his being sent to an institution for feebleminded children, where he was also badly neglected and often deprived of meals as a punishment. This added to his conviction that his parents wished to kill him through starvation.

In another case, prolonged observation of a boy's behavior convinced us that his delusions of persecution and anaclitic depression were the consequence of a severe traumatization, possibly caused by some dark and terrible secret event which might have taken place before the child's verbal abilities had fully developed and which he therefore could not easily reproduce in any form but vague and totally destructive images. Despite the parents' cooperation with our efforts to establish a detailed early history, no information about such a secret was revealed, nor could the boy himself recollect anything but death anxiety and overwhelming rage, which he had to repress totally.

Following the lead that this child clung frantically and with great repressed hostility to his older brother, we asked him for information. In order to help our work and relieve his guilt, this brother told how, when the younger brother was not yet three years old, the older brother and some of his friends had played a hanging game, with the boy as victim. The rope had cut off the child's breathing, and he was revived only after artificial respiration had been applied. Afraid that the child might tell of this event, the older ones established a regime of terror. Repeatedly and severely they beat up this youngster, threatening even worse tortures if he should ever reveal the story. In order to make the threat more effective, they repeatedly locked him up in a dark and inaccessible excavation and kept him there for prolonged periods despite his terrified screaming.

In a third case, chance observations led an adopted boy not yet three years old to guess at his mother's adulterous relations. During the year following his discovery, which he did not at all fully understand, the mother repeatedly threatened to kill him if he should ever tell anyone about her relationship to the other man, or even mention his name. As the child grew older, he continued to be threatened daily that he would be killed if he told anyone about the mother's affair. Then, before the child was five, the mother deserted husband and son without warning.

Our observations had led us to feel that this boy stood under a dreadful fear for his life, and that he was hiding a terrifying secret, the nature of which did not seem clear to him. Finally through a former servant, who had been dismissed from the home after the affair had gone on for some time, it was possible to learn in some detail about the early and repeated traumatization of the child. Subsequently, memories of these threats were spontaneously produced by the boy in play sessions.

These examples illustrate dramatically some of the psychological factors which seem to occur characteristically in childhood schizophrenia. What about its treatment?

Kaplan, following Kanner's earlier observations on autistic children, made the important point that the schizophrenic child needs most to live with a "need-satisfying" person. He added that these children have tremendous difficulties achieving socialization because of the inability of their egos to cope with instinctual drives and reality pressures.[3]

In fact, as soon as we began our work at the Orthogenic School we concluded that to treat the schizophrenic child, he must be provided with truly need-satisfying persons not just for one hour a day, but as much as possible all the time, every day of the year. Further, such a child needs to live in an environment that imposes no demands, or only minimal ones, and which is so comprehensive and simplified that it can be mastered by even the child's weak ego; an environment which tends to reduce libidinal pressures and in which it is safe for both the child and his environment if he openly acts in line with these pressures.

Actually, these requirements are complementary. The need-satisfying person, through the physiological, psychological, interpersonal satisfactions he provides for the child, reduces the pressures of libidinal tendencies and anxieties. The absence of reality pressure in the environment in which they both live makes it possible for this person to remain need-satisfying, and permits the child eventually to recognize it. It must be an environment, for example, that accepts and respects even very annoying symptoms as legitimate expressions of

---

[3] Leo Kanner, *Child Psychiatry*, 2nd ed. (Springfield: C. C. Thomas, 1948); Samuel Kaplan, "Childhood Schizophrenia: Round Table Discussion," *American Journal of Orthopsychiatry* 24 (1954), pp. 521–23.

the child's needs or anxieties, and this again not just during the treatment hour, but all day and all night.

I cannot spell out here how this is done;[4] instead, one example may illustrate the way in which an eleven-year-old autistic boy provided himself with those experiences he needed most.

In a first reaction to the freedom to live according to his needs, this boy, whose toilet training had never broken down before, stopped defecating. He retained his stools for over two weeks, thus asserting his autonomy over his bodily functions, contrary to maternal demands. Eventually he gave up withholding his stools, but would not use a toilet. For nearly six months, he soiled himself and played with his feces. But during this time he slowly emerged from the rigid, catatonic state in which he had been for years.

After he had thus convinced himself that in the environment of the School he possessed autonomy, at least as far as elimination was concerned, in about his fourth month with us he spontaneously provided himself with the experience of being fed, first, as it were, by himself, then by a mother figure. He began habitually to put his food into his mouth, mash it and mix it well with saliva, then spit it onto his sleeve, mess it there some more, and finally eat it from his arm. Thus, in a way, he fed himself from his own body.

In a next step, he spat or put this mess of food not on his own sleeve, but on that of his counselor. Convinced of the child's deep need to do this, his counselor, to quote her, accepted this "as part of the meal, like the salt and pepper. This putting on of food is done with great deliberation. He takes the food in his mouth, chews it, puts it in his hand, presses it into my clothes, looks at it, scrapes it off the clothes, and puts it back in his mouth and eats it. I usually wear a blue denim shirt and a jacket which I put on when we go for a meal. Then when we are through I can wipe the remnants of food off these clothes and keep them to wear to the next meal. I now feel quite comfortable about his putting food on me."

Although the child repeated this ritual at least three times a day at regular meals, and often between meals, this did not yet constitute a personal relation; but it slowly grew into one. As the infant does not

---

[4] Even before this was written, attempts were made to do so in *Love Is Not Enough* and *Truants from Life*; these were continued later on in *The Empty Fortress* and *A Home for the Heart*.

at first recognize his mother as a person, but may feel that he feeds himself, so this boy first fed himself from his sleeve. As the infant later recognizes that he is feeding from the mother's body, so the boy later fed from his counselor's sleeve. Even then, he probably did not recognize her as a person, but simply felt it more pleasant to feed from her than to feed from himself. His feeling may have been something like: "There's something out there which, when it lets me eat off her, makes eating feel good."

Contrary to his past experience, when everything that came from the outside was overpowering, threatening, and unpleasant, now something coming from the outside was subject to his control; he was now the one who overpowered another person, and what came from this person was pleasant. When this eating stage was reached, day wetting, soiling, and smearing with feces disappeared with some small encouragement, to be replaced by a more active and aggressive cognizance of the environment. For example, the boy occasionally urinated deliberately on the bed of a boy whom he viewed as his main competitor for his counselor's undivided attention.

Thus, we may speculate that this boy began to unfreeze after he first learned to assert his autonomy by controlling his elimination, and then by ridding himself of his feces wherever and whenever he pleased. After such assertion of "anal" autonomy, he began to satisfy his "oral" autonomy by feeding from himself. The external world began to acquire meaning as he fed from a preferred person, and he began to master it as he asserted his urethral autonomy by urinating on undesirable objects. During this development, his incomprehensible talk couched in neologisms and echolalia changed into understandable communication, and he began participating in simple, childlike games. All this progress occurred over his first eight months with us.

It is easier to give an example of such procedures than to generalize about them, since all procedures have to be geared individually to the chronological and emotional age of the child, his personality, and the nature of his disturbance and his symptoms. But the most important fact is that these children must live in a setting that is totally therapeutic. They need an institutional treatment in which a therapist does not treat a child only for a few hours a week, but where the need-satisfying person lives with the child. True, no one person can take care of such a child all day long; others must, of necessity, share in the work. But this one, central person must live so close to the child that most of the time he can make himself immediately available day and night, when needed to help in a crisis. If this is so, the absence of the central person can be suffered for hours at a stretch without harmful consequences. That is, if the schizophrenic child has learned—and in the Orthogenic School he learns it soon— that the room where his counselor lives is just a few doors down the corridor and if he sees the counselor around many times during the day, then, as the treatment progresses, this availability eventually permits him to forgo for periods of time his or her immediate presence, which he at first requires.

Basically, what such a child needs is a mother free of the self-centered emotional demands so many mothers make, so that he can benefit from mothering without having to respond to it; so that he is free to respond in his own good time and his own schizophrenic way. Then he can begin to reestablish his autonomy.

For the child must be able to recapture autonomy not only in the treatment room, and not only in regard to his emotions. To begin life anew, the total, extreme situation which destroyed his autonomy must be replaced with a total living situation which he can master. As he was overwhelmed by his environment, now he must be able to control it within reason, and to control it successfully. This means the environment must be simple; it must not offer complex challenges, nor make complicated demands. The need of such children for consistency and their desire for simple routines must be stressed. Basically, the child has to feel as safe, protected, and in command of his environment as the happy infant may feel in his cradle.

We cannot put a schizophrenic child in a cradle, not only because he is no longer an infant, but also because it would violate whatever feeling of self-respect he might have acquired, deprive him of whatever negative autonomy he might have achieved through his symptoms, and restrict his freedom of movement and expression. Instead we must provide the child with an environment that creates only those slight challenges and stimuli which are compatible with the utter security an infant should know in the crib. We must protect the child from any hostility coming from the external world, particularly from his parents; we must provide maximum need-satisfaction; and we must demand very little socialization, so that the demands of the environment are cut down to a minimum while the pressures of his impulses become reduced. When living under such conditions, even a very weak ego can begin to function more adequately.

In practice, this certainly implies self-demand feeding of favorite foods, at any time of day or night. It means no insistence on toilet training, or other socialized behavior; such has to be the result of his desires, not of our demands. It means no restrictions on motility unless these are clearly beneficial; opportunity for total rest whenever desired, etc.

Given such indulgence, it is possible to put some limitations on the discharge of aggression as far as physical harm to others is concerned, and to limit those self-perpetuating, compulsive preoccupations, sexual or otherwise, which drain too much vital energy or build up tension rather than reduce it. We try to make it possible for the child to live according to his own autonomous desires, always with the caution that the exercise of autonomy must not lead to hardship for the child—then his ego would prove once more inadequate. For example, we must provide all the necessary material for, and encourage the construction of, safety devices, and any contraptions which the child needs to feel secure.

Living in such a benign situation, the child may become ready to start life anew. Strangely enough, we have found that it may take a schizophrenic child about as many years to do this as it takes the normal child to develop his personality. Such normal development requires two, three, or four years of living uninterruptedly in a physical and human environment that promotes autonomous personality growth. The same amount of time and conditions is required for the schizophrenic child to develop his new personality. Then these children feel reborn, and they begin a new life of their own.

Here, again, there is a striking parallel to the experience of concentration camp prisoners. A dominant topic of many prisoners' daydreams was the idea that they would start an entirely new life after their release from camp. Observation of some of these prisoners suggests that only those who really managed to begin, in a fashion, a new life after their release fully overcame the damaging influence of the camps.

Being subjected to living in an extreme situation somehow contaminates permanently the old life and the old personality. This suggests that a personality which did not protect the individual against landing in an extreme situation seems so deficient to the person that he feels in need of widespread restructuring.

Returning to childhood schizophrenia, it should be mentioned that, much to our surprise, we found quite a number of schizophrenic children who, at the crucial point in their rehabilitation when they were ready to reintegrate their personalities, also began their new life symbolically; so much so that they underwent again the experience of being born.[5] One autistic boy told his therapist about it at the moment he was symbolically giving rebirth to himself through hatching from an imaginary egg. He said, "I laid myself as an egg, hatched myself, and gave birth to me. You know, that happens to very few people."

---

[5] I detailed one such case, illustrating both the severity of the extreme situation which led to a child's schizophrenic withdrawal and the process of her symbolic rebirth, in *Truants from Life*, and another in *The Empty Fortress*.

PART TWO

Education
and the Reality Principle

The morality taught by the joint forces of home, church, and community up until roughly the middle of this century gave direct support to the school in its efforts to teach the young in traditional ways. But this is no longer generally true—on the contrary, now the morality taught to many children before they come to school, and while they attend it, is often at variance with the school's educational efforts. One result is that children nowadays are exposed to the teaching of widely divergent values, compared to an earlier era when those taught by home, church, community, and school were identical in most important respects.

For example, yesterday's conviction was that the purpose of all human activity is to gain us eternal salvation; today's popular conviction is that life is a rat race. Or compare the once-accurate belief that unless most of us work long, hard hours and are thrifty, we and our children will starve, with the present belief that economic hardships are unnecessary and that everyone is entitled to a guaranteed income. To state the problem baldly: we have an educational system resting on a morality that holds that if man is to survive in this world, it is absolutely necessary for him to acquire a specific body of attitudes, and a certain sum of knowledge and skills. But how is today's educator going to reach a youth who is convinced that society owes him a living no matter what—either because of past injustices inflicted on him or because of the expansiveness of our modern affluent society?

Let us review some of these modern views of morality which, though not always openly stated or understood as such, pervade much

EDUCATION AND THE REALITY PRINCIPLE: This paper was originally presented as one of the lectures published in *Moral Education: Five Lectures* (Cambridge, Mass.: Harvard University Press, 1970), pp. 85–107. It is here reprinted with deletions and some other changes.

of today's extracurricular life and sometimes also life in the classroom. I will cite two significant prophets of modernity: Nietzsche and Darwin.

According to Nietzsche, "fear is the mother of morality" and "morality is the rationalization of self-interest." Certainly the psychoanalyst agrees with Nietzsche that morality is nourished by fear and that, in the final analysis, the content of morality is self-interest. After all, it is self-interest that makes one wish for eternal salvation, just as it is self-interest that makes one wish to succeed in the rat race. Where these types of self-interest differ is that the first leads to entirely different behavior from the second.

But as for morality being based on fear, nowadays we want to remove fear from the life of the child. As for the content of morality, we often insist that it should not be self-interest. In short, we want the child to obey a morality whose fundamental motives we are doing our best to remove.

Darwin, the second of my prophets, stressed how relative morality is and how it arises from the particular conditions one grows up with. Thus "if men were reared under precisely the same conditions as hive-bees, there can hardly be a doubt that our unmarried females would, like the worker bees, think it a sacred duty to kill their brothers; and mothers would strive to kill their fertile daughters."

Each of the statements just quoted is an absolute, even the absolute statement about the relativity of morals. But they neglect to account for developmental psychology, especially its model of a morality that develops slowly and in stages. So long as morals were viewed as God-given, immutable, and absolute, morality was the same for young children and full-grown adults. That is, one learned well in school and lived successfully as long as one's training began with a very firm and stringent morality of absolutes, based on fear.

It was a Darwin, as well as a Nietzsche and a Freud—all raised during their formative years on a stringent and absolute morality based on fear and who continued to live the rest of their lives guided by many important elements of that same morality, although they had freed themselves of the fear—who could later afford to question morality ever more critically. They could do this in maturity without it interfering with their high ethical standards, and without going to pieces as persons or withdrawing from the world in disgust. It was precisely the absolute morality instilled in them as children which made them strong enough, later on in life, to try to reshape the world by their more mature moral concepts.

Today, however, we hope mistakenly that somehow more and more citizens will have developed a mature morality—one they have critically tested against experience—without having first been subject as children to a stringent morality based on fear and trembling.

In the recent controversy about whether our schools serve the underprivileged well, it has been pointed out again and again that current methods and procedures, including our teaching materials, are geared to the middle-class child. In fact, none of the learning our present schools expect to instill in their students can take place without what has been described as a puritanical, or a specifically middle-class, morality.

In respect to education, one of the most essential aspects of this "middle-class morality" is the conviction that postponing immediate pleasure in order to gain more lasting satisfactions in the future is the most effective way to reach one's goals—that is, accepting the reality principle over the pleasure principle. It is this morality alone that makes serious and consistent learning over long periods of time possible, whether in Communist countries or in our own.

Now, unfortunately for education, the modern views of morality cited earlier do not prepare the young to act on the basis of long-range goals. It takes mature judgment to be able to "do the right thing" when one is no longer motivated by fear, and to do it even though one knows how relative all human values are. Before the age of reason, conscience (or the superego) operates on the irrational basis on which it was originally formed; it tells the child what he must do and must not do on the basis of fear (not of reasoned judgment). Only later does the mature ego apply reason to these do's and don't's and slowly subject these earliest laws, step by step, to a critical judgment.

One primary motive for learning is the wish first to satisfy and later to modify an irrationally demanding superego to make it more reasonable—an aspect which old-fashioned education unfortunately disregarded. But if there is no excessive superego anxiety to reduce, a most important motive for learning is absent. If we do not fear God, why learn about religion? If we do not fear the forces of nature, why learn about them? The detachment that permits hard study out of sheer curiosity, out of a desire to know more, is a stance arrived at only by very few, and even by most of them only in maturity.

Thus, while conscience originates in fear, any learning that is not immediately enjoyable depends on the prior formation of a conscience. It is true that too much fear interferes with learning, but for a long time any learning that entails serious application does not proceed well unless also motivated by some manageable fear. This is true until self-interest is enlightened enough so that it alone is sufficient motive to power even hard-earned learning all by itself. Such is rarely the case before late adolescence, when personality formation is essentially completed.

This means that the small child who is taught to think (or whose life experience teaches him) that taking things without permission is all right on some occasions but not on others will have a superego full of holes—one that will not later support him toward academic achievement. Kant's categorical imperative "Act only on the basis of those principles which you can wish ought to become universal law" requires a maturity of judgment, an ability to step outside one's private world and appreciate the experience of others—neither of which is available to the young. The meager and highly subjective experience that forms the world of the child does not permit such objectivity. To the immature mind, sometimes yes and sometimes no means only I can act as I please.

A more refined morality must have as its base a once-rigid belief in right and wrong based on a fear of perdition that permits no shading or relativity. It makes no difference whether perdition for one child is tantamount to damnation in hell, and for another to the loss of parental affection. If, as modern middle-class parents are often advised, affection and approval are guaranteed to the child no matter what, there will be no fear—but neither will there be much morality.

This means that diligence, concentration, and perseverance do not come about because of self-interest alone, as we seem to want to believe, but because of an irrational superego anxiety. Only when such traits have become an inseparable part of the personality is the anxiety no longer necessary for learning. Witness the fact that many of our underprivileged children, although they know full well that in the long term it would be to their advantage to apply themselves seriously in school since they wish to find good jobs, cannot do so. In the arduous task of learning, these children's egos are not sufficiently powered by psychic energy, because they have not often enough and clearly enough experienced that the reality principle is superior to the pleasure principle.

To put it concisely: all education is based on a middle-class morality that finds its psychoanalytic equivalent in a powerfully developed reality principle, one that insists that present pleasure must be largely forgone for greater gains in the future. This morality is not learned on a rational basis, but mainly through two separate sets of experiences: anxiety instilled by the parents, and by the example of parental behavior. If parents do not live by a stringent morality, and by the reality principle, neither will their children be able to do so.

But the poor no longer fear perdition if they do not walk the narrow path of virtue, and the reality principle does not seem to work to their advantage; thus many of them—although of course not all—are not likely to present their children with an image of living on the basis of strong moral principles, or of a purposeful adherence to the reality principle. The result is that their children—and ever more also those of middle-class parents—cannot internalize a parental morality based on the reality principle as the main content of their superegos, nor later make it become part of their egos. Therefore no strong morality supporting the educational process will guide their actions.

It requires extraordinary psychic efforts to build up, all on one's own, without parental examples, a superego and an ego which embrace the reality principle and reject living by the pleasure principle. This is why most of those who grew up deprived of such parental images of a stringent morality operate for the rest of their lives largely in line with the demands of a relatively primitive ego. They seek experiences which provide immediate pleasure satisfactions and can apply themselves only to the gaining of short-range goals.

Those who live by the pleasure principle can and do make good use of educational experiences which are made truly enjoyable to them. In this manner they may acquire bits of knowledge and skills. But despite it they remain essentially uneducable and uneducated because solid knowledge requires that such isolated pieces of information become systematically woven into a consistent whole, and this demands prolonged hard work for a distant purpose. It is beyond those who cannot give up the pleasure principle for the reality principle.

Educators who try to reach their students on the basis of the pleasure principle are amazed at how fast and how much their children learn; but these children also quit as soon as learning can no longer be easily or immediately enjoyed. All other learning (which means much of it) can occur only when we have learned to function on the basis of the reality principle, because most learning gives no immediate pleasure satisfaction, only the hope of gaining greater, more valuable, and more lasting satisfaction at a much later time.

Now with modern education, this later time becomes very late indeed, perhaps some fifteen years later. The more we thus tax the reality principle by postponing the satisfactions we strive for, the more likely it is to give way. Then the pleasure principle becomes dominant again, unless the superego is much more powerful than it is now for many of our children. That explains why the longer the period of schooling, the greater the rate of dropouts—even for our nice, middle-class children, even for students at our best colleges— and the more apt they will be to seek the easy way out that drugs and alcohol seem to offer.

To be able to put off reaping rewards for fifteen years or so needs a powerful domination of the pleasure principle by the reality principle. The longer the span of time spent on education, the more dominant the reality principle must be for consistent learning to take place. This, in practical terms, is what teachers mean when they speak of the need for discipline, attention, and concentration.

Fortunately for education as it now exists, a fair number of middle-class children still enter school with a strong superego and the reality principle, if not yet dominant, at least sufficiently well established in its rudiments to permit postponing pleasure over stretches of time. Because this is so, we can still believe that our system works and that all the children fed into it do profit. Indeed it does still work, but, percentage-wise, for fewer and fewer; and their number is constantly declining. Partly this is because the time spent on education has so increased, but more important, it is because we live no longer in a scarcity economy but in theoretical affluence. The image of the affluent society plays havoc with the puritanical virtues.

How then do we learn? We learn best when our ego is well-functioning, that is, when it integrates in a constructive manner the demands of it and superego and brings them into concordance with those of reality; and when the goal of learning is in line with our ego and superego values and made further attractive because we like and admire the teacher. Whenever these conditions are not met, there is ego weakness and conflict. Such conflict, where not resolved (as by sublimation, etc.), detracts from the ability to learn or makes it frankly impossible.

Nor can the ego support learning when it is overwhelmed by other concerns. An empty stomach that clamors for food, a rotting tooth that hurts, a body abused by lack of rest, a mind that anxiously wonders what violence waits on the streets or at home, if not even in the corridors of the school—all these will distract and depress the child with their immediate pressures and prevent learning, because an ego overwhelmed by realistic worries or frustrated desires is much too weak to assert long-range goals and insist on concentration on difficult work. This means there must be not only a strong, work-oriented superego but a fairly satisfied id for the average boy or girl to enjoy the balanced state of ego (or mind) that alone permits learning in class. (The unusual ones whose academic motivation is so strong that nothing will deter them we need not worry about; they will almost always learn, no matter what.)

Now this strong superego, as suggested earlier, is unreasonably domineering at first and says "you must do as you're told" and not "it all depends." Then in the slow process of learning and maturation it more and more induces the person to say to himself, "I must do what will be best for me—and others—in the long run." I think what is wrong with the education of so many children today is that they suffer from both an ego that is weakened by the onslaught of over-aroused or unsatisfied instinctual desires, and a poorly established superego.

We no longer can or want to base academic learning on fear. We know the crippling price of inhibition and rigidity it exacts. But the child must fear something if he is to apply himself to the arduous task of learning. My contention is that for education to proceed, children must have learned to fear something before they come to school. If it is not the fear of damnation and the woodshed, then in our more enlightened days it must be at least the fear of losing parental love and respect (or later, by proxy, the teacher's) and eventually, the fear of losing self-respect.

Here again the trouble is that in order to fear the loss of self-respect, one must first have acquired it. And it is practically impossible for a youngster to develop true self-respect when he is failing in school. As the child grows older, this potential loss should be the major fear spurring all actions, including academic learning. But self-respect and its demands are merely what have taken the place of older, irrational superego strictures. If those were never established through the internalization of parental moral values, or those of religion, then nothing can replace them. Self-respect is also the heir of an earlier and even deeper respect for the parent, because he reliably protects us from pain and want and lives a life we admire. If there has been no such respect for the parent, no self-respect can take its place, with the exception of the rare individual who, all on his own, develops the inner strength to impose moral demands on himself and because he does so achieves self-respect. Those who do not, who because of their childhood experiences can neither respect an internalized parent, nor respect themselves, feel worthless, and whoever thinks himself worthless has a very hard time applying himself successfully to higher learning.

So the circle is complete: a parent who is not deeply respected will not evoke much fear about the loss of his love. Thus it might be said to the modern parent that if he no longer wants to base his child's superego on fear, he must make doubly sure that he is most highly respected. The same goes for the teacher who will later stand *in loco parentis*. Otherwise, respect for him will not lead the child to identify with him and his high standards of behavior, until they become the child's own high standards of behavior.

What *do* we do for children whose behavior in school shows they have not yet changed, or not significantly so, from the pleasure to the reality principle? Sometimes we try to start them even sooner on learning for which they have no use and which therefore falls flat; or we try to teach them on the basis of the pleasure principle—as far as such learning can go—or on what little of the reality principle they have made their own. But this type of learning never goes very far.

The fact is that so much of learning is not a pleasurable experience but hard work. There is no easy transition from pleasure to hard work, but if one has learned to find meaning in both, then one can combine them. If not, one will do only the pleasurable things and ignore the hard work. The voice of reason is very soft; it is easily drowned out by the voice of our appetites. If our teaching is based on pleasing the emotions, the noisy clamor of emotions will drown out the quiet voice of reason any day of the week.

Since many children no longer acquire an absolute sense of morality in the home and community, and do not function by the reality principle, our problem becomes how to use a child's educational experiences to reorganize his inner world and his personality, so that he may acquire the attitudes required for becoming a well-educated person through his school experiences.

Freud seemed to believe, and so do I, that this can be done only if the teacher first recognizes the necessary conditions for such learning and, second, acquires a true understanding of the slow-developing ego, including how and why morality is learned. Above all, such education, the purpose of which is to instill a more refined morality, cannot succeed unless it takes due account of a pupil's present state of ego-development, and what the teacher may infer about its history from the child's social origins. If we wish to educate the child's person, as opposed to trying to pound some information into his head—which is almost useless, since truly useful knowledge cannot thus be acquired—we must know where he comes from, who he is, and where he wishes to go; that is, we must first understand his moral existence.

The neglect of such prior knowledge is what bedevils so many of our attempts to educate the underprivileged. We resort to half-measures because we do not recognize the double character of education: that it must reach the child as the person he is at present, in order to guide him to where he should go. While most educators recognize the goal, they seem reluctant to meet the preconditions for reaching it. But without this, as Dewey and Pestalozzi before him knew, the goal will never be achieved.

So realistic teaching, including that of morality, requires us first to assess the degree to which a child coming to school has made the reality principle his own. If he has not done so sufficiently, then all educational efforts must be geared toward helping him accept it as more valid than the pleasure principle—helping him to accept and internalize it. This can be done, although it is difficult, and it becomes more difficult as the child grows older.

Our ability to postpone must be based on the repeated experience that it pays off in the future. The injunction not to grab and eat a cookie right now will be effective only if the child gets a great deal of praise and affection for the postponement, if he is not too desperately hungry at the moment, if his hunger has always been satiated pleasantly and fully in the past, and if he fears that by grabbing he will lose the source of all this very certain satisfaction. No praise will work with the hunger unstilled; no demand will be effective without the conviction that postponement will achieve greater gains but certainly no loss. No postponement is possible if all one's experience says, "What I don't grab now I'll never get."

That is why it is so often observed that the underprivileged child can learn only as long as the teacher's attention is focused on him—because then he at least gets rewarded by emotional closeness at the moment of trying to achieve. Too much of his life has consisted of the experience that if he doesn't grab it now—be it attention, praise, or other rewards—he won't get it later on. This is another reason why an education which takes so many years to produce results (jobs, money) is unable to reach children who do not believe that future rewards can result from energy spent now.

In my efforts to teach teachers this seemingly simple principle, I was nearly always up against their puritanical ethic, according to which waste is sinful and will be punished by scarcity in the future. So when the underprivileged child merely grabs as the teacher distributes clean paper or pencils or maps and, in the teacher's eyes, wastes all the supplies, these teachers react critically:

> The children who are culturally deprived in my room have a tendency to waste the paper much more than other children in the class. Some-times such a child will start to do something on a piece of paper. But if it's not up to his own standard, or what he thinks is my standard, he'll throw it away, or say "this is not good" and ball it up. Then he wants another piece of paper. He can't think of turning the paper over. He won't erase either. He has to do it completely again. He wants a perfect paper.
>
> Mostly I'm concerned because I feel we're wasting huge amounts of paper, and also it gets messy after a time. The wastebasket's always overflowing and the floor and the desks are full of it. They ball it up and into the desk it goes. After a while it gets to the point where you can't find the books, in between all the paper.

Here, the teacher's morality (based on the reality principle) re-quires an economical use of resources but clashes head-on with the children's morality (based on the pleasure principle) to the point where no learning takes place. What the teacher failed to realize is that these children, by wasting supplies and asking for more all the time, were trying to find out if the supplies *were* adequate, if there *would be* more, even if they didn't grab them now—not to speak of how exciting it is to have for once one's fill, even if only of clean paper.

Yet it is only on the basis of such pleasurable satiety, with many, many repetitions and later reflection, that we learn we can afford to postpone. Too many teachers want their students to live by the reality principle before they have had a chance to learn it and on the basis of many successful experiences make it their own. Criticism of their wastefulness only reinforces their conviction that "there isn't enough, and we'd better grab it now."

The children's closeness to the pleasure principle reveals itself not only in how they waste paper (which is easily recognized) but also in their need for perfection, in the disbelief that they can correct or erase—because to be able to correct implies the belief that things can be better in the future. It is the very belief that could enable them to move from the pleasure to the reality principle.

The fear these children reveal when through their actions they express their conviction "What I don't grab now, I'll never get" has its source in the earliest experiences, particularly those centered around feeding, whether of nutriment or love. I think it of crucial importance in our efforts to instill the morality needed for learning that we provide these children in school those basic experiences upon which rests all later adherence to the reality principle. By this I mean an abundance of the most basic supplies: food and rest, plus an emotional supply of acceptance and respect. These children must be taught it is safe to waste—not just paper, but also food—and that, contrary to past experience in the home, these will always be in ample supply.

I have said that the reality principle, and with it most learning, has a great deal to do with ego functions, and that the ego must be supported by moral conscience. But in applying this principle to education, we again seem stuck with a conception of the conscience that derives from the well-integrated middle-class family for whom it works, though no longer as well as it used to.

Piaget, who studied children at the ages when morality, or the superego, is developing, concluded that there seem to be two moralities in childhood, or at least within the culture his subjects were drawn from. Developmentally, the earlier is a morality of constraint. It is formed in the context of the one-way relations between the child as the subordinate and the adult as the dominant person. Its result is a highly personalized superego, based on having internalized the voice of very particular persons, chiefly the parents. (Later, if learning is to proceed smoothly, the teacher will have to be accepted as a suitable stand-in.) But for that, the parents have to be very important, very impressive, very dominant, and—most relevant if we want to understand the predicament of the underprivileged child—excellent providers.

Soon, however, the child develops further. He becomes more than just a member of his family; he becomes a member of his society too. Then the morality of constraint is partially replaced by a morality of cooperation, and this is tempered and refined by the spontaneous give-and-take of peer interaction. At least this is how Piaget describes the development of a conscience in Geneva, Switzerland, a rather conservative and very middle-class city where the heritage of Calvinism is still strong.

Now in Western society, particularly in America, relations between child and adult are not so unilateral as they were in Freud's Vienna or Piaget's Geneva. The parent becomes less and less domineering in the child's life, the relations between parent and child less unilateral, and the peer group more important much sooner in life— witness the earlier entrance into nursery schools, etc. If this trend continues, then the superego, even for middle-class children, may come to be based much more than it is now on a morality of cooperation with the peer group. Or to use Piaget's central concept, it will be based on having learned to obey the rules of the game.

In a consensus society, a conscience based on "obeying the rules of the game," on a "peer group morality," is remarkably unconflicted. The two separate, often conflicting, sets of mental functions known as the ego and the superego are in many ways identical where social consensus is high. In Geneva, for example, both the peer group morality and that derived from the parents match the morality of society. Ego and superego are then in harmony, and the ego (the soft voice of reason) is not only powerfully supported by the superego but is further strengthened by its success in society. The result is a strong ego. One is then well able to live by the reality principle, ready to learn to gain rewards from a society one is very much a part of, and ready to follow what the teacher requires, since she almost echoes what one's own superego demands.

This is quite different from a situation in which obeying superego demands deriving from the morality of the school and teacher put one at odds with the surrounding community. The values of the teacher are then not recognized as the embodiment of one's own superego, but as an enemy. Clearly they threaten the peer group morality, though that is one's only guide to action, if not to survival itself. In such a case the ego is split apart by trying to satisfy the two opposite demands.

In short, where consensus is low, the more a child has developed his personality on the basis of peer group morality, the less will the teacher succeed with her superego appeals. Then the child's ability to learn will hinge on whether, and how much, his particular peer group supports the demands of education.

From this analysis it becomes clear why our educational system fails the culturally deprived child. He is the child who is deprived of our middle-class culture with its roots in the stable and secure nuclear family. In his family there is little that supports the reality principle: opportunities for gratifications not enjoyed at the moment may never recur. In both girls and boys the superego is mainly derived from the relation to the father. But in many underprivileged homes no dominant, or at least reliably providing, father figure, fit to be internalized as a superego, is available to the child. Thus neither a strong reality principle nor a strong superego is ready to support education. In their stead is a morality that depends almost entirely on the peer group, but a peer group often deeply at odds with the surrounding adult world if not entirely at odds with education as represented by teacher and school.

In considering the task of the schools—to instill the morality which is needed for education to reach its goals—we must start out by realizing that the personality of the culturally deprived child is *not* identical with that of the middle-class child. What it contains, in lieu of a highly personalized morality derived from identification with the parents, particularly the father, is a morality based on the child's particular sub-culture and its norms, which as often as not are those of the slums. If we want to activate his interest in education, we must appeal to him on the basis of the demands of his own group morality, not ours.

If, therefore, we can offer tangible advantages here and now, both for him and his group and within the framework of their particular mores, we may be able to reach him. Slowly he may then want to modify his ego ideal, if not also his superego, by moving toward our standards, if only in part. All of this is supportive of my main theme: "We must start where the child is, and try to guide him to where he should be."

The catch is that this takes a lot of doing. If we pretend that teaching the three R's can come before the morality needed for education, we shall not succeed. Nor will we succeed unless we have first begun with ourselves, where *we* are. The real trick is to rid ourselves of the prejudice of our particular marketplace, because unless we begin there we shall never help the child to give up, however slowly, the prejudice of his own marketplace.

Some time ago, as a matter of fact, I tried my hand at just such a venture when I met with a self-selected group of grade-school teachers who taught mainly lower-class black children. At one meeting there had been a heated discussion in which we realized that we must encourage these children not to be quiet in class but to speak up loudly, even in disorderly fashion, because learning to speak up in class about anything they like is a key step toward learning to speak up in class about things the teacher wants them to speak up about. And speaking up on what the teacher wants discussed, even in disorderly ways, is a first step toward heeding her in other ways, such as talking in more orderly fashion. We talked, too, of how the children's peer group morality (to defy the adult middle-class world) supports their shouting all at once, and of how we, step by step, have to win over that peer group support to where it is more in accord with doing things in orderly fashion.

Soon afterward a situation confronted a teacher who had learned to apply a principle even when the situation was not identical. She told of how all year long she could not get the children to line up quietly when they went out for recess. "Every day I begged and preached to the children to be quiet and it never worked. But after our last meeting I decided to ignore the bell and pretended to be busy with something at my desk. At first they were as unruly as ever. But after a short time they began to hush each other. 'Shh! Shh!' they said, 'we want to go out.' And I've done that every day since then, all week long, and it's worked like a charm. Once in a while they don't get quiet, and I tell them, 'All right. I guess you need a little more time to be noisy.' And pretty soon they get each other quiet."

When I asked this teacher what she thought had happened, she said, "It takes the pressure off me when they put it on each other." And the children can indeed conform when the pressure is from their own peers. This they have learned to respect; it is the pressure from adults—and especially from middle-class adults—that they feel they must fight.

Once the teacher begins to think of the pressures the children are under and what she can do about them, instead of worrying about the pressure she herself feels, she will find ways, all on her own, to relieve the children's pressures on her, and everyone is better off. To understand and act on that requires no unusually inspired teachers, but only ordinary ones who have been helped to understand what is going on.

When we are no longer bound to our own morality about what the teacher's role is and what that of the child is, then we can consider instead what human beings are like and why they act as they do. We are then also free to realize that a lot of satiation has to precede any learning to live by the demands of reality, theirs and our own. But by that time their reality and ours are no longer so different.

The Decision to Fail

We have long known that a mind cannot function well if anxieties prey heavily upon it. Parents and teachers are given the sound advice to be kind and patient with the non-learning child; but too often, modern methods for dealing with children's learning difficulties depend on love alone. Benign attitudes cannot solve the problem; such attitudes may be likened to bed rest for the sick—frequently a precondition needed for therapy to succeed, but only rarely therapeutic in itself, and occasionally more debilitating than curative. To eliminate a learning block, we have to find the anxiety that lies behind it, try to comprehend the anxiety, and then work to remove it.

It is now fairly commonly accepted that troubled emotions can so distract a child that he cannot learn or pay attention in class. Systematic studies show how intimate this connection between emotions and learning ability really is. A research project run by the United States Public Health Service in the 1950s found that those adolescents who showed chronic anti-social behavior were also poor readers.[1] To study this issue, an entire school population of 45,000 children was observed over several years. In this way it was possible to spot all children who showed low reading achievement, and the group was sizable. For example, 16 percent of all fifth-graders were reading below the third-grade level. (Typically, more boys than girls were thus retarded.)

A year later, among these now sixth-grade pupils, the relative reading level of each child had stayed remarkably constant. But when the same group was restudied two years later, nearly all who had been

---

THE DECISION TO FAIL: Reprinted with minor changes and deletions from the *School Review* 69:4 (1961), pp. 377–412.
[1] A. D. Miller, "The Role of the School System in a Mental Health Program," in M. Krugman, ed., *Orthopsychiatry and the School* (New York: American Orthopsychiatric Association, 1958), pp. 135–40.

retarded readers in the fifth and sixth grades now exhibited serious social problems as well.

My experience with emotionally disturbed youngsters suggests that although reading difficulties often "show up" earlier than severe emotional disturbances, as far as causation goes it is really the other way around. Assuming normal intelligence, only the severely disturbed child will have serious trouble learning to read; this inability will stem from the same emotional problems which, in a few years, may break into grave asocial behavior.

When emotional disturbance exists in a small child but his parents are unable or unwilling to recognize it, the disturbance goes unheeded until the child reaches school. There he is singled out, not because the teacher always recognizes the presence of emotional disturbance, but because of academic malfunctioning. Just as we pay attention to a fever because it tells us infection is present, it is crucially important to note and understand the causes of emotional blocks to learning in the early stages. If the child is not helped early on, but is "carried" by the schools into later grades and into adolescence, then neglect becomes costly indeed—to the child, to his family, and to society.

It is difficult to isolate types of emotional blocks to learning, but one could divide them roughly into three groups: first, there are obstructions resulting from a way of life and methods of education shaped by our advanced technology. Second, there are learning inhibitions arising from the child's particular life history. Third, the learning experience itself may create or aggravate an existing disturbance and in this way block learning. The last two groups often overlap; to simplify this discussion, they are presented together.

Some of these learning difficulties require the services of specialists, but many others could be greatly alleviated by educators.

The many sources for difficulties having to do with modern technology have been widely discussed. Perhaps the most commonplace of these is the impact of long hours spent watching TV, and the resultant combination of overstimulation and inactivity. A less obvious block growing out of technological thinking may originate from the child observing an adult attitude regarding learning as a tool—something to be mastered and used only upon occasion.

Ordinarily, nothing is more tempting to normal children than emulating their parents, such as when they dress up in Mommy's or Daddy's old clothes and pretend to be grown up, copying parental life activities. In fact, one of the greatest supports the teacher has is the child's wish to imitate. If the child had no chance to copy the intellectual activities of his parents, he can now imitate those of the new parent-surrogate, the teacher. Good learners usually actively play at teaching and being taught, re-creating the classroom experience as they once imitated their parents.

Dressing up and playing school are merely first, external steps in the child's response to the inner and outer world of those adults who are significant to him. Recent studies have shown convincingly that the child responds to, "acts out," or reacts not only to adults' overt desires, but also to their covert ones. Regardless of what parents or teachers may try to teach the child, he will more often respond to the adult's hidden inner motivations than to the adult's overt dicta. Again and again it can be shown that a child's delinquent act—though contrary to what the parent intended to teach—was the result of what the child correctly perceived in his parent: a strong, though perhaps not consciously recognized, delinquent desire.[2]

Pupils, too, often react less to teachers' statements of fact than to the unconscious signals they send out, their tone of voice, and the things they leave unsaid. If parents or teachers stress academic achievement without concern for an ultimate goal—if we view grades or good performance in class as goals in themselves, without regard to whether the child comprehends his lessons as meaningful in a larger life design—then the child may react with apathy, since grades seem fleeting and petty purposes.

Until Sputnik and the resulting clamor about our gifted children, the question most frantically asked of our teachers was what to do about Johnny who, it seems, could not learn to read. The problems presented by the gifted reader and the poor reader are not unrelated. Behind each one lies the need for a different attitude toward scholarship.

First and primarily it must be realized that reading is not just a tool, the use of which can be learned any which way, the faster and easier the better. Any educational effort that does not emphasize the

---

[2] A. M. Johnson and S. A. Szurek, "The Genesis of Antisocial Acting Out in Children and Adults," *Psychoanalytic Quarterly* 21 (July 1952), pp. 323–43.

more significant purposes of reading is apt to be a failure. Tool thinking is concerned with tools: how best to master and perfect the use of them. The point is that one masters use of a tool for a reason—to attain some other end; mastery of the tool in itself means nothing without some application. Such tool thinking applied to learning, though it has its place in perfecting mastery of reading, will not lead to scholarship.

If we look at the reading problem and concentrate on its core—the purpose of reading—quite a bit seems to have gone wrong with the way we teach reading. It is not that children no longer learn to read; of course they do. They learn it earlier, better, and faster than ever, and many more of them learn it, in addition. If we want to be realistic in comparing reading achievement present and past, we must also ask whether, by teaching so many more faster, there is not bound to be some loss in quality. Also, it may be that for those whom we try to teach, reading no longer seems a necessary or valuable source of knowledge and stimulation. Now, besides the printed word, children can also learn from the radio, movies, and TV. Reading, which was once the unique way of acquiring knowledge, loses in attractiveness when competing with these other media. Therefore, we cannot simply compare learning in class, then and now. We must also consider reading in competition with these vastly enlarged, easily ingested other sources of information.

Another consideration is whether we teach reading as well as we could today. There, I fear, we often do a poorer job than necessary, for what we teach pupils in their primers often seems pointless, if not contrary to the purpose of teaching. This wrong direction is the result of an educational philosophy based on tool thinking rather than goal thinking. Curiously enough, this same tool thinking permeates most of the criticisms leveled at our educational system. To study more science as the way to keep up with (and, if possible, outdistance) the Soviets is simply to view learning as a tool. The same thinking underlies much of our present method of teaching reading; it is much more efficient than it used to be, but loses sight of the goal of reading—the independent acquisition of knowledge through one's own efforts, motivated by one's own curiosity. Thus our children may well learn how to read, but reading itself will have little meaning for many of them.

We seem to want scientists who spring suddenly out of the educational system like Athena, fully armed to slay the Russian Gorgon. This desire reflects a belief that there can be a sudden appearance or transmission of wisdom, without any slow process of learning and growing. But it is neither the speed with which knowledge is acquired, nor the propensity for gadgeteering in the laboratories that makes for scientific discoveries. It is curiosity, plus the interest and leisure to follow even idle curiosity, from which flows all deeper understanding.

The present attitude about education seems to be that our young people should keep their noses to the grindstone and that we, the teachers, should see that they stay there. This attitude is contrary to the way in which most advances in knowledge were gained; they began with flights of fancy. Certainly idle curiosity has its price; some of it will remain nothing but "idle," and some of the curious will be content with the mere asking of questions, without too much concern for the satisfaction of answers. But a few, spurred on by curiosity, will make the important advances—and a few is all we need.

Seen in this perspective, the problem of all teaching is essentially that of stimulating curiosity in the students, while at the same time giving them the conviction that they will be able to satisfy parts of it through reading and study. The problem of teaching to read, then, is primarily one of convincing pupils that the printed word holds the answers to important questions about which they are curious.

With this in mind, let us look at some of the primers from which children are taught to read. The first words the child learns from one widely used reader are: "Run, Ted. Run! Run! Run!" and "Jump, Ted. Jump! Jump! Jump!"

This is hardly news to the child, nor worth learning to read for, since he does this every day. Further, we know that it takes an awful lot of patience for a child of preprimer age to sit still and pay attention. To tell him in the imperative form through what he reads to run and to jump is hardly conducive to his sitting still and paying attention to his lesson. Worse, it teaches him that the written word tells him to do something that his teacher tells him not to do. Thus at the very beginning of education the precepts of the teacher, from whom he must learn, are set against the precepts of the book, from which he must learn to read.

I am told that these words are selected because children have an easy time recognizing them. So let us see what more important knowledge they lead the child to at the end of the book. The last two pages of the reader, quoted here in their entirety, convey to the child these startling pieces of new information: "Ted! Ted! Run and play. Sally! Sally! Run and play. Boots! Boots! [a dog] Run and play. Splash! Splash! Splash! Boots! Boots! Play and splash. Sally! Sally! Play and splash. Ted! Ted! Play and splash. Splash! Splash! Splash!" These are the commands given the child. These are the life activities which are impressed on him as desirable. He is asked to direct his attention to activities that will take him away from learning, and he has learned only what he has known all along without having to read about it.

Let us move on from the beginning of the reading process to some examples which may tell us whether learning to read seems worthwhile after the basic skills are acquired; that is, whether the child's reader eventually tells him that by reading he will find answers to questions of significance to him.

One of the most difficult and yet most important things that any human being has to learn is to understand himself, and how to get along with others. This means that he must learn how to form correct expectations in regard to his own behavior and that of others. The people with whom the child must first learn to get along are his mother and father. One could expect, therefore, that his readers would teach him to have realistic expectations of his parents and their interactions with him and each other.

But while parents play a large role in our readers, the stories never describe occasions on which even the slightest differences arise between parents. This tells the child that either the stories are not true, and that reading is therefore not worthwhile, or else that something is wrong with his parents, because they argue on occasion. Actually, what children need to learn is that people can have differences of opinion—even argue—and still live successfully together, and further that it is better to air these differences than to deny that any exist.

In these stories about families, the mother is always ready to go out for walks or to play; she is never preoccupied with housework. If she is a working mother, it never interferes with her ability to serve all the needs of the child and home—she seems to have unlimited time and energy. Similarly the father in the stories is never tired or in need of rest when he comes home from work. The child is thus led to draw the conclusion that his own parents are not good parents, because they do not behave like the mother and father in the stories. Instead, his parents act like human beings who are sometimes tired, preoccupied, or even irritated as they go about their chores, and this is very different from the way characters are described in the child's reader.

In many such ways, the images readers create about what are usual or desirable homes and forms of behavior completely contradict the child's everyday experiences. The result is that either these images set the child against his own life experiences or they suggest to him that little truth can be derived from reading.

With these primers, if we seriously want to promote the importance of learning to read for our children, we have to be sure that they do not take the reading matter we impose on them too seriously; otherwise they would conclude that through reading one receives only misinformation. For example, when the children in stories have accidents, as happens occasionally, they never behave as if they were hurt or scared or angry. Whatever happens to them is all great fun. Such stories do not prepare children to deal successfully with adversity, nor do they convince children that factual information can be gained from reading.

Many stories also tell how children just love to have a new baby in the family. As likely as not, the child who reads these stories is jealous of the new baby who has arrived in his own home. But because of the image created through the stories he reads, he must either not believe the story or get confused about the validity of his own emotions. In point of fact, these readers all present an adult's wishful image of how the world should be, not the way it actually is.

Learning is based on emotional security; the very insecure child, the upset child, is a poor student. If he is made to feel, through the false images of readers, that his emotions are not in accordance with what society expects of him, he will not learn well. Nearly all the emotions described in our reading books are clear-cut and positive; they are hardly ever mixed or truly negative. To insist that all children are jealous of their siblings is just as unrealistic as insisting that all children love the new baby. Most of us, as children, felt both ways: we loved the new child, but often we were angry, too, because he got in our way. If only our readers depicted attitudes toward new siblings in a realistic way, they could stimulate thinking and give a child the conviction that something of importance is to be gained from learning to read.

In older societies, with their scarcity economy, the coming of a new baby naturally led to a discussion of how this event could be managed in terms of the family's income, the additional room that was needed, and so on. These discussions were not kept from the child, and they impressed on him that, while the parents did look forward to the new arrival with love and hope, there were also serious problems to be met. The child then gained some understanding of his parents' mixed feelings which permitted him, in turn, to accept his own mixed emotions as natural.

In those times the schoolchild did not learn to read "run, run, run," when he was expected to sit still and pay attention. What he was told to learn was that *c-a-t* spells *cat* and *d-o-g* spells *dog*. While this was not very exciting or stimulating, at least it did not present contradictions. The older method of education did not prepare a child for the hardships of life or its tragedies, such as the loss of a home or a harvest, but neither did it imprint on him the notion that no financial problems existed in other homes. In still older times reading was learned from the Bible which, though filled with human tragedies, made up for them through the precept of trust in the Lord.

Today, by trying to make learning easy, pleasant, and amusing, we often end up creating vacuous images of life and people. This is further aggravated by the fact that during the child's first years in school his readers do not present him with new subject matter. The whole reading program is essentially built around things or experiences with which he is already familiar. If this then is all we learn through reading, why should we learn to read, even if the learning is made easy and pleasant?

So today, while children theoretically could learn to read better and more easily, in reality learning to read often seems pointless, because the reading matter is so empty. In the higher grades children do get to read books that are more stimulating, but by then some children have become deeply discouraged with or uninterested in education, because what it seems to offer is so dull.

These remarks are not meant to suggest that we should scrap what we have learned about the importance of making reading enjoyable, about the steps in word recognition, frequency of words, or logical sequence in the acquisition of reading skills. There can be no doubt that our present-day readers make learning easy for the child; as tools they are excellent. On the other hand, captivated as we are by our ability and success in forging these tools, we have lost sight of the fact that tools are pointless as such unless applied to a purpose. All too often in teaching, our concentration on efficiency in developing a skill at the expense of emphasis on its deeper purpose makes the skill itself seem unimportant.

In considering the second large group of causes for learning blocks, those stemming from the child's particular life history or an already existing disturbance, we must realize that a child's determination not to learn can often spring from desires as positive and at least as strong as (though different from) those that motivate the good learner. Both learner and non-learner, often with equally strong motives, seek the same goals, such as pleasing a parent, or gaining success; but what constitutes pleasing a parent or being successful in their eyes may lie at opposite ends of the continuum stretching from total failure to unusual achievement.

Sometimes this determination grows out of the parents' attitudes or social position. Typical as the source for these learning difficulties is the wish of most children to look up to their parents. The child may not wish to do better than his parents because he does not want to make them seem inferior. Out of the need to rely on them, children anxiously protect the image of their parents as the best of all parents. Because our dominant creed is that every new generation should do better than the last, adults often overlook the fact that many children have reason to wish the opposite. This emotional block to learning has a very strong, positive motivation.

It is not that these parents act as if they would resent superiority in their children. On the contrary, most of them tell the child he must acquire a better education than they themselves were able to. Nevertheless the parent who, with the very best of intentions, tries to encourage his child in this way may still make him feel guilty about his better opportunities. In order to avoid feeling guilty, the child may quit learning at exactly the same point where the education of one of his parents stopped.

But it is not only guilt which may cause a child to stop making educational progress. Many parents who sincerely wish their child to go further in his education than the level they were able to attain nevertheless consciously or unconsciously fear that if the child does, he will then have little in common with them and may stop looking up to them and seeking their company. It is an understandable anxiety, since many children in later life do discontinue contact with their parents because they have come to feel that they have little they can share with them. In such cases a child may act not in line with the parent's expressed wish that the child should achieve academically, but in accordance with the parent's unspoken anxiety. Then the child may be unable to make educational progress beyond the point where the parent fears that the child will surpass him and so break the intimate tie which up to now has bound parent and child together.

Thus, whatever the parent's openly expressed hopes for his child may be, I have known quite a few young people who either out of guilt or in response to parental anxiety dropped out, or suddenly developed severe learning blocks while continuing to go to school, at exactly the point where the education of a parent ended.

A teacher does not need to openly express critical attitudes about the child's parents or their way of life to make the child feel he must side with his parents against teacher and school. Sometimes the teacher, wishing the child to achieve middle-class standards, asks him to adopt principles of behavior that are above those of one or both of his parents. Such a child may, unbeknownst to parent and teacher, express his deep loyalty to the parent by rejecting all that school (and with it, learning) stands for, because it seems to belittle his parents or their way of life, or both.

Often severe blocks to learning are due to the child's efforts to take one parent's side against the other. This happens typically when two parents have differing levels of education and one disparages the other. But here, as when the child protects both parents against the school, the block can be readily overcome once the underlying cause is recognized. The solution is that both parents, or the parents and the school, must truly agree about what is desirable, and make this consensus clear to the child.

Two further steps are usually necessary to erase this type of learning inhibition. First, we must show our sincere appreciation of the child's wish to relieve his parent's anxiety, or to protect the pride of one or both parents by not doing better than they were able to; and, second, we must convince the child that he can do much more for his parents, and at the same time for himself, by satisfying their justified wish to be proud of his achievements.

The wish to protect a parent by not learning does not begin to cover the variety of positive reasons for unconscious, though deliberate, failures in class. Realizing that these failures are due to laudable motives is the most important step in removing them. For this reason, and also because adults do not usually see anything positive in a child's determination not to learn, I should like to add a few more illustrations.

Some children are poor learners because they do not wish to compete, feeling that competition is wrong. Such feelings in a schoolchild are easy to understand if we consider how often he has been admonished not to take advantage of a brother or sister, to let others take a turn first, to be considerate of others' feelings, and so on. Other children feel so guilty or worthless that they do not dare add to their faults by getting ahead of children they think are much worthier. In order to protect the other child (a positive desire) and not add to their own guilt, they stop learning so that others will more readily succeed. While the particular reasons may vary, a child's feeling that he has no "right" to succeed is by no means rare.

Probably the most common positive reason for not achieving academically, however, is the wish to retain closeness to the beloved mother. To learn means to grow up. Therefore many children see it as giving up mother, or certainly being mothered, and they are unwilling to do this.

Equally positive, as an underlying motive for failure, is the desire we all have to be special, different, and unique. If the need for status and self-respect is accepted as a positive motivation, then we must count the wish to be first among the lowly, rather than second among the best, with the group of learning inhibitions based on positive wishes.

The good learner who believes he can go to the top of the class is spurred by this conviction to work harder. As long as a child can believe that if he tries to do well he will succeed, he usually applies himself to gain status and self-respect. Even if his best efforts land him only in the mediocre group, he may still settle for that (as many children do), but only if he can be satisfied with being one of the gang.

If this moderate station is not enough for his self-respect and he cannot give up the need to be special, or if he is frustrated in wanting to be one of the gang because the others reject him, then the wish to be unique is reinforced powerfully. He may thus arrive at the conviction that he can gain status only by being the worst. In this way he attracts attention to himself—true, in a negative way, but attention nevertheless.

The learner who does poorly, on the other hand, often is convinced he can never make the grade. He is impelled to stop learning by his wish to maintain his self-respect. Believing that he will fail even if he makes his best efforts, he protects himself by deciding not to learn. Then he will be able to tell himself that his failure is not due to inability, but to a deliberate act of will. It is not rare for such a child to feel he can gain more status or self-respect through not learning than through diligent application.

When we wish to help such children, we must begin by realizing that almost never can a child recognize on his own that he chose failure because he was afraid he could never do best, or even average, or was unacceptable to the gang. He may be only a little readier to accept the idea that he chose to be a huge failure, rather than risk being a small failure or an insignificant success. Any such open acknowledgment would destroy the child's chance of achieving self-respect through not learning. Instead, he usually tells himself and others that he could do very well, if he wished to. Only with such claims can he get the attention accorded those who are genuinely different and still tell himself that his uniqueness is not a matter of inability, about which he thinks he can do nothing, but the result of a freely made decision. Thus he protects the image of himself as an adequate person, the image he sought by defying schoolwork in the first place.

A child's need to protect his self-respect in this way is among the most dangerous blocks to learning. Once he has fallen into such a pattern, he honestly believes that his greatest desire is not to be special but to defy school and adults by deliberately not learning.

For other reasons, too, this is an insidious process. The further the child falls behind, the more his pretense of adequacy is threatened and the more drastic are the steps he must take to protect it. That is why a fourth-grader can be satisfied that he is a big shot when he defies the teacher by not learning, while the seventh-grader must, in addition, defy police and society by delinquent acts. The fourth-grader who acts "dumb" is the easily admired clown. A few years later the same behavior makes him look stupid, and instead of being admired he is despised. By then it is usually too late to regain status by academic success, so the child tries to get it by delinquency.

When a child fails for such reasons, it is of little avail to encourage him to try harder so that he can string along within the low or middle group. His decision not to learn was made just to quiet his fear that his work would never get him higher than that low group. A much better approach is to boost the child's self-esteem, since lack of it drove him to his defiant course. This can be done, for example, by showing the child how ingenious he was in protecting himself and by giving him credit for his determination, without agreeing that its goals are desirable. Only much later, after he is convinced that we recognize his competence, can the child be helped to see that he behaved like the fox with the sour grapes. At the same time we must help him to truly achieve in academic skills. Through many such efforts on our part he may eventually recognize that defiance of learning is not the only way to gain personal distinction.

We must never forget that many learning inhibitions can come from a child's desire for inner honesty and truth, and from his effort to succeed in terms of his own life experience. In fact, given similar natural endowment, and with the whole pressure of school, parents, educational system, and society at large favoring success in learning, it often takes a great deal more determination on the part of the non-learner to fail than for the good learner to do well in school. This is so because all the breaks, all the encouragement and rewards, are in favor of the learner. If despite this powerful system of rewards a child fails, then we must assume that his motives for not learning, as likely as not, are stronger than are those of the child who is successful in class.

Different from those learning inhibitions that have positive motives are those caused by negativism. Some children may be set against the school, not because they wish to protect a parent's pride or be loyal to his way of life, but simply because they do not wish to acquire a different set of values.

Others do not learn because learning is not made attractive enough or because the teacher has hurt their feelings and they want to hurt hers in retaliation. A child may also be so tired, physically or emotionally, that intellectual exertion seems to be too much to expect of him, and he will not even do the little he could. All this is so well known that I mention it here only in passing.

Behind other learning inhibitions may lie the wish or the need to defy adults, punish a parent, or do both at the same time. A child often opposes his parents with "my teacher said so." This tempts us to overlook the fact that quite often the same child cannot accept what the freely quoted teacher says or stands for. Because he needs to defy authority and cannot do it without adult support, he claims the teacher's backing when he speaks up against his parent. The wise parent will not object to this, because to be able to use the teacher against the parent makes the teacher, school, and learning very attractive to the child. But if a child cannot so use the teacher to achieve some independence from his parents, he will have to defy the teacher instead, to gain independence from at least some adult.

Some children are quite overwhelmed at home, less frequently today by physical mistreatment than by being nagged to desperation or driven to achieve beyond their ability. Their need to defy is so great that they will defy adult authority whenever they see a chance to do so without fatal hazards. Because teachers are much more lenient than nagging or driving parents, the child who does not dare to oppose an overpowering parent defies the teacher instead, by not learning. This is usually reinforced by a secondary gain; by not learning the child can effectively punish the parents to whom he is otherwise subservient. Not learning in class has become the commonest whip that the middle-class child can hold over a parent whose pride is deeply hurt by the child's academic failure.

Similarly, intellectual superiority was, and sometimes still is, the whip that many a lower-class child, or the child of new immigrants, holds over his parents. Since this is an emotional motive for higher achievement, and often a powerful one, it does not concern us here. But as a negative motivation for academic success, it may round out our discussion of the negative motivations for academic failure.

So far we have considered those learning inhibitions that extend, more or less, over the totality of school. Equally frequent are emotional blocks to learning that spring from the avoidance of a specific learning task or a specific subject matter, for a particular reason.

Contrary to widespread belief, a child with average or better intelligence will more often have trouble because he understands some subject matter too well, rather than because he is inattentive or finds the task beyond his mental capacity. Such a child may actively reject the subject matter because it offends his moral scruples or because it scares him. Then he cannot understand because he does not wish to understand.

Usually the child has one of two reasons for this rejection: either the essential principles underlying a learning task would throw him into inner turmoil when applied to himself, or the particular content reminds him of experiences much too painful or threatening to think about. To ward off such pain, he convinces himself as well as others that he cannot understand how to apply what he dreads to apply to a personal problem; or that he cannot grasp what (if he did grasp it) would remind him of an unbearably unpleasant experience.

Children whose own history is forbidden territory, or who can make no sense or only painful sense out of their experiences, want to protect themselves from examining their personal history. One solution is to be totally uninterested in all history; or they deny that there is any sense to the historical sequence of events. To insist that such children should understand and accept as meaningful any sequence of events in the history of men or of nations means acquiring perceptions that would cause unmanageable anxiety if applied to themselves. They might have to realize, for example, that certain bad experiences of their past or present which, for emotional reasons, they wish to chalk up as due to random chance really sprang out of basic and permanent attitudes in themselves or their parents.

That one's deep suffering was and is due to chance can be accepted; one can still continue to live and to strive. Eventually the wheel of fortune turns, and what was due to bad luck may suddenly change for the better. But if we must accept our misfortunes as the result of consistent and irreversible attitudes, or the design of our parents, then we can no longer hold on to the hope that things will change for the better in the future.

Because the study of history normally means learning to make sense of a sequence of events, it is an enriching experience; merely recognizing this fact makes learning history possible and rewarding. But if the cost of this advantage is having to realize that one's own life is devoid of inner meaning, then the pain of the realization seems too high a price to pay. Thus in the case of history it is not an inability to comprehend, but rather a true understanding of its essence, that may block a student from learning.

To illustrate, though with a different subject matter, one adopted girl had severe difficulties at home although she maintained herself fairly adequately in her classes until high school, where she had to take a general science course. In this class she created continual disturbances and was in such severe conflict with her science teacher that most of the time she was sent from the room and spent her time in the office of the dean of students. The criticism at home and at school was so severe that within a few months her difficulties extended to other subjects as well. What had started as a resistance to attending only the science class became a head-on clash with all of school.

The reason this girl had to protect herself from attending the science class was that general biology and heredity were part of the subject matter. She did not want to learn about the beginning of life, since it reminded her too painfully of how badly her own had begun: her real mother had given her up, and her adoptive parents had no use for her. Up to then she had maintained herself by making believe that her adoptive parents were her true parents, despite their rejection. Now the teacher became her enemy, since she expected the child to learn and remember how life really begins, which only increased the child's violent anger against her unrewarding home. To this was added the painful reminder that the beginning of her life was so different from that of her schoolmates; and with the study of heredity came the realization that she did not even share a common heredity with her adoptive parents. Since she was too intelligent not to understand what all this meant to her personally, her only way out was to misbehave. Then she would be sent from the class and not have to hear about matters which only created a dangerous rage in her. Had all this been recognized in time, the rejection of one subject matter might not have extended to the rejection of school in general.

In this example, all of school learning became unacceptable because of a single subject matter. But it happened rather late in the girl's educational career. Things are even more serious when this occurs early and around such basic subject matter as reading or arithmetic.

For example, one boy committed a crime at an early age, probably not knowing quite what he did. His parents impressed on him how severely he would have been punished, had he not been an ignorant child. Realizing his inner destructive wishes, the only protection the child knew of consisted in not learning to read. If he could read (he thought), he could no longer claim ignorance of the law. But the pretended inability to read soon extended to all learning.

When we taught him that ignorance is no excuse before the law, he was able to recognize the protection and advantages of reading: if he could read, he could find out which actions are punishable and which are not.

It is well known that many children develop learning inhibitions because of the parental command not to know. Sometimes a child extends a parent's order not to explore his own body or what goes on in the parental bedroom to mean that all curiosity is wrong. But without curiosity one cannot learn. Teachers can get a child to repeat what he is told, but without the child's own spontaneous wish to know, it is not learning but parroting. A child can remain fixated at this level if he thinks it is bad to be curious or to wish to learn secrets.

Other children develop the notion that, while it is all right to look, they are not supposed to understand the meaning of what they see. This happens typically when a child observes his parents behaving in a way they either disapprove of (as in marital discord) or when they do not wish the child to understand their actions or motives. If such experiences are repeated, the child may get the idea that while his parents do not object to his observing details correctly, they severely disapprove of his understanding what it all means. Such children may learn to recognize letters and words but, in obedience to what they consider a parental command, remain unable to understand sentences or the meaning of paragraphs. Reading without understanding is frustrating, not rewarding; so if they are then further criticized by their teachers for not understanding sentences, such children may give up learning altogether.

It is not always parents who inhibit the child's ability to see and comprehend. The child himself may do so for what he considers valid reasons. One child claimed he could not see the words in his book clearly, and his behavior was such that there was reason to believe his vision was actually defective. Seeing the letters only vaguely, he could not read.

Eventually this boy was able to remember the first time his vision suddenly blurred; it was when he first saw his mother attending to his newborn brother. Seeing another child getting the attention he wanted was more than he could stand. So to blot out the experience, he became unable to see what went on.

The wish not to see what is painful to see is a relatively simple defense. Sometimes a more complex mechanism is at work, such as the one called *undoing*. An obvious and well-known form of undoing is technically called a *washing compulsion*. Lady Macbeth, deeply perturbed by the blood that once stained her hands, continued to clean them with such intensity that little time or energy was left for anything else in her life.

The need to undo, to reverse a too-painful situation, may also find expression in reversal. This is an exchanging of letters in reading which can so distort the meaning that no progress in learning takes place. Often the deeper purpose of such behavior can be overlooked or explained away by pointing to the similarity in the appearance of the letters. But such simple explanations may only deprive the child of the help he needs, which alone will clear up his learning problem.

Other reversals may affect not letters, but words. One child who witnessed a terrifying scene early in life was so preoccupied with what he had seen that everything else that had happened in the past re minded him only of what he once saw. Thus he read the word *was* as *saw*.

Another child wished so intensely to be a boy that for periods of time she delusionally believed she was one. She also resented her brothers' luck in belonging to the envied sex. So she went about correcting it; whenever she encountered the words *boy* or *man* in her reading, she read *girl* and *lady*; if the printed page read *girl* or *woman*, she read it *boy* or *man*. Similarly, she read all *he*'s for *she*'s and the other way around.

While some reversals can be traced back to specific events, wishes, or anxieties, sometimes any reversal will do, if the child wishes to undo or reverse not a specific event, but the totality of his life situation. The shattering event in one boy's life was his mother's sudden desertion. Without any warning she took off and was never heard from again. The wish to undo this event was so overwhelmingly important to this boy that he reversed letters in every word he tried to read.

All learning is based on the manipulation of symbols and concerns itself with abstractions. Learning is a process of intellectualization, a process in which thought is freed of its personal emotional content and achieves a higher "objective" meaning invested in symbols used in verbal or written communication. To the infant, the peculiar smell of his baby blanket, its color, texture, and the strange way it was worn down by him make it unique, entirely different from all other blankets produced in the same factory. His chair is unique to the infant, although it may be identical with all other chairs in the dining room.

As long as the child has not acquired sufficient identity in himself, he is interested only in the unique, not the general, aspects of objects. Not any blanket, but only his blanket can give him security, though all blankets may make him feel warm. As long as he cannot afford to be covered by any other than his own blanket, he is not yet able to abstract from the unique meaning objects have for him. Also he is not really ready to learn to deal with general, abstract concepts and their symbolic representations, such as words and numbers.

Some psychologists differentiate, therefore, between a perception of the world that is autocentric and one that is allocentric:

> In the autocentric mode there is little or no objectification; the emphasis is on how and what the person feels; there is a close relation, amounting to fusion, between sensory quality and pleasure or unpleasure feelings, and the perceiver reacts primarily to something impinging on him. In the allocentric mode there is objectification; the emphasis is on what the object is like; there is either no relation or a less pronounced or less direct relation between perceived sensory qualities and pleasure-unpleasure feelings.[3]

When for the child "my blanket" changes into "the blanket I used to need to be able to fall asleep," he has made (in respect to blankets) the crucial step from an autocentric to an allocentric perception of the world.

Learning to manipulate abstract symbols such as printed words or

---

[3] E. G. Schachtel, *Metamorphosis* (New York: Basic Books, 1959).

numbers presupposes at least a three-stage development. At first, the object is little else than part and parcel of the perceiving person—the baby's blanket—receiving its meaning only from the meaning it has for this person. In the second stage of development the object acquires an independent reality of its own, as the child comes to perceive it as unchanging, always one and the same. And finally, once allocentric perception is fully grasped, the object's unchanging and independent existence becomes less important, while its generic qualities acquire ever greater importance. Only then can a symbol represent different examples of the same object.

Learning in school can take place only when the mental development of the child has by and large reached this third stage of recognition. Our reading readiness tests, for example, measure this when they require the child to connect a unique object as drawn with its symbolic representation of a printed word.

Unfortunately, the child does not reach this third level all at once. For some experiences he may remain fixated on the first or second level, but for other experiences he may have reached the third level. If this is the case, serious learning difficulties may result when the child is expected to understand and manipulate the symbolic process but is still fixated on one of the two earlier levels. The learning difficulty will be most serious when he has not yet freed himself of the autocentric way of experiencing reality.

An inability to abstract and go beyond the autocentric personal and emotional meaning is behind many reading difficulties, though it need not always interfere with learning to read altogether. If everything goes well, the child who learns to read can also invest words with his own unique meaning without its interfering with his ability to read. The dog, the cat, the table, the book about which the child reads in his primer can be the unique dog, cat, table, or book to which he is closely attached. He may insist, and rightly so, that one dog is entirely different from all other dogs; and, if the teacher is wise, she permits him to learn to read and spell *dog* without having to give up the deep personal meaning his dog has for him.

The printed word is a symbol which refers to a particular object, such as a home; and, while the letters *h-o-m-e* must stand for all homes, in learning to read the child is not forced to accept this, if he does not wish to. He may think of this or that particular home. He may think that what he learns through reading about a home need not apply to *his* home. Despite the general nature of the printed word, nothing prevents the reader from giving it a meaning particular only to him in his mind.

Now it should be easy to see how to some children, one or another particular word in their readers is emotionally unacceptable. Sometimes a child will spontaneously find his own remedy to this dilemma. The pressure of his emotions will force him, in his reading aloud, to express not the thoughts presented in the book but those predominant in his mind.

Fortunately such "misreadings"—or one should say correct readings in terms of the child's interests and emotional needs, but incorrect in terms of the printed letters—are usually restricted to one word or a few emotionally loaded words. While bothersome, they need not interfere with the child's learning to read or his overall academic progress, provided the particular "loaded" words are not too crucial to an understanding of the meaning of what he reads.

But in order for this problem to remain narrowly circumscribed, it is often necessary that the understanding teacher (or, given the reality of our school situation, probably a careless one) not focus her criticism on the child's few errors. If too much is made of them, the painful emotions and then embarrassment connected with the words may force the child to protect himself further from recognizing what bothers him. He may do this by extending his misreadings to many other words, so that soon nobody, including himself, can guess what lay behind them in the first place.

The daughter of an albino developed a reading problem over a few words. The mother's pale blond hair was less of an emotional problem to her daughter than her near-blindness, which put the girl under a tremendous burden and also made her fear she might have inherited her mother's disabilities. Whenever she saw the word *blond* in her reading, she misread it *blind*. These two words meant the same thing to the girl: "my mother's disabilities." For this emotional reason they were identical to her, and she reacted to what she saw as their common essential meaning: "blindness."

In this case the teacher was aware of the mother's condition and ignored the misreading. The result was that the misreading remained restricted to these rather insignificant words, with no other effect on the girl's academic progress. Here, a deliberate and selective inattention to the reading difficulty was the best course of action (although inattentiveness is by no means suggested as the wisest procedure in all cases).

A case where such inattentiveness was similarly indicated, but was unfortunately *not* adopted, was that of a boy who had spent his first years in an institution and his life since then in many foster homes. He consistently read *house* for *home*. Never having known a home, he had at least lived in houses. When the teacher insisted that he read *home*, he changed his reading from *house* to *hole*. The teacher had shown him that she could not view a house as an acceptable substitute for a home, although he had been forced to be satisfied with it. So he retired even further, into a hole, where he buried himself emotionally. For similar reasons he was unable to read or spell *love*, for which he regularly substituted *life*. Never having known love, he tried to comfort himself with the life which still lay ahead of him.

Up to then this boy's difficulties were restricted to simple substitutions for a few offensive words; the new words were relatively appropriate, starting with the same letter, and had as many syllables as the rejected words. But his second substitution, of *life* for *love*, was again rejected by the teacher. Soon he misread all words, not just the few unacceptable ones that started with *h* (*home*), *l*(*love*), *m* (*mother*), and so on. Misreading so many words, he was constantly being corrected and criticized, until eventually he gave up reading altogether. It took years of hard work and deliberate encouragement for him to start again to just substitute words starting with the same letter for unacceptable words, and more years before the boy could again begin to learn to read, which he now learned easily and well.

Another child, a girl with a very low opinion of herself, refused to capitalize her own name or *I*. To do either would have run counter to her inner honesty, because she felt that nothing about her was, or deserved to be, big. Although she felt very competitive toward her classmates, her feelings of worthlessness kept her from openly competing. The only way she knew of not falling further behind was to keep the others from progressing. So she was most ingenious in pursuing her goal, diverting the children's attention, occupying the teacher's time. Only after she was given ample recognition for her ingenuity was she able to relent, since the recognition reduced her inferiority feelings considerably.

Although most of my examples are from the area of reading and spelling, the same psychological problems may lead to learning inhibitions in any or all subject matter. I have concentrated on reading because it is basic to all other learning experiences. Without the ability to learn arithmetic a child can still progress up to a certain level in class, while without the ability to read, he cannot. Still, it may be of interest to note briefly how arithmetic lends itself even better than reading to expressing certain crippling emotional preoccupations.

It was said that while in reading the symbol of the printed word *home* must stand for all homes, the child may have a particular home in mind and still learn to read. But not so in mathematics, where what holds true for one mathematical operation must hold equally true for all others. Arithmetic is based on the principle that units are like each other, otherwise they could not be added. Children for whom numbers have retained their autocentric meaning—so that *one* stands for the child himself, or for one of his parents, *two* for the other parent, etc.—may meet insurmountable difficulties when we ask them to add up to four or five.

One such child was adopted before the parents had a child of their own. He could readily add up to three but not beyond that, because, as he put it, to count to four was not the same as to count to three. In his life experience it was indeed not the same. The addition of a fourth to the family entailed an entirely different emotional experience than the previous condition of three. Contrary to what the teacher wanted him to learn (that four is more than three), he knew he had much more when there were only three, and that four to him was much less than three. Moreover, four, to him, was not one added to three, but rather that Three (himself) was pushed out by Four, since the arrival of the fourth member meant there was no longer any place for him in the life of his parents.

Or again, a family of five young children lost both their parents under very traumatic circumstances. The oldest boy was particularly hard-hit by the loss and the changes it entailed in his position within the family. He had a hard time with all arithmetic operations where the number *five* (the number of the children) was involved, with one exception: he had no difficulty in adding two to five, since that seemed to restore the original family constellation. But when asked to subtract two from seven, it threw him into a panic that extended for a considerable time during which he was unable to function at all.

The boy was fascinated by the number *eight* (his age when the deaths occurred) and introduced it in all kinds of anxious contexts. Whenever anything went wrong, he was convinced it was connected with eight. If somebody was late, he was eight minutes late; it would rain in eight minutes, and so on. Any arithmetical operation that involved numbers beyond eight was beyond his ken; all things had stopped for him with eight.

Other children find fractions extremely hard because in their homes it is not true that a pie is divided into six equal parts. In their emotional experience, and often in reality, the six pieces into which pies are divided in their families are never alike. Therefore they cannot accept as true and correct what the teacher tries to teach: that one sixth is exactly like any of the other five sixths.

As long as the child is not able to separate certain numbers from the emotional meaning they have for him, he cannot master mathematical processes involving them. The same is true not only for specific numbers but also for entire mathematical processes. Many children find subtraction much more difficult than addition. This is so not only because it is the reverse of the process just learned, but also because most children are emotionally in favor of adding something to their lives, but cannot afford to see anything subtracted from them. For similar reasons multiplication usually presents fewer emotional problems than division.

Conversely, there are children who have less trouble learning the more complicated processes such as division than the simpler process of multiplying. Multiplication involves a fast increase in numbers. But they may fear this more than anything else if they are afraid, for example, of the arrival of new siblings in the same sense that the Scriptures speak of multiplying. For similar reasons some children can learn to subtract but have great difficulties with addition.

There are, of course, innumerable ways in which children can express one and the same emotional problem that perturbs them. Sibling rivalry, and the wish to do away with a hated newcomer, can therefore be expressed in a variety of ways. One bright youngster could perform rather difficult mathematical problems in addition, subtraction, multiplication, and division, but only if one allowance was made: the answer was always incorrect by one. She always deducted the one who she felt was one too many in her family: her younger sister.

As if to show that this was not a case of poor learning, she occasionally found another way to do away with one. Sometimes when several rows of problems were given to her, she would solve the top row of problems perfectly well; after all, she was the first to arrive in her family, and her arrival was perfectly correct. But the second row, representing her younger sister, was full of errors; it was all wrong just as the sister's arrival in this world was "all wrong."

Thus the most common emotional difficulties that find expression in failure to learn arithmetic remain those that relate to simple numbers and their relations. Much as the most serious emotional problems originate in the very simple experiences of childhood and only much later grow more intricate, so too, contrary to what one might expect, it is not the advanced and very complex mathematical processes that often stymie the child, but the very simplest steps in addition or subtraction. Trigonometry, or complex algebraic problems or formulas, may present difficulties of an intellectual nature, but they rarely lead to learning inhibitions. The reason is that they are too far removed from the direct and tangible nature of those life experiences which arouse emotions deep enough to block the child's ability to learn.

It does not come naturally to the child to express the family constellations that upset him in such elusive formulations as algebraic equations. But simple addition or plane geometry can present insurmountable difficulties, for example, to the child who cannot understand the properties of triangles because he cannot understand the triangular relations within his family. Usually in such cases, the two parents and the child form a triangle of such complex emotional relations that the child cannot understand the first thing about its form or inherent characteristics.

Factors which may make one subject matter particularly difficult for one child may, for other reasons, make it very attractive for others. The very abstract nature of mathematics can make it also serve needs opposite to those just described. A child who feels desperately unlike the other children in his home may throw himself into arithmetic because it teaches that all numbers are basically equal in their meaning. He may make his own, as if with a vengeance, the fact that one fourth is like all other fourths, just to deny that he, one of the fourths of his family, is treated so differently from the other three fourths.

If one wants to understand what may be emotionally implied in the learning of arithmetic, one has to start with the realization that each child is unique. To some, arithmetic is very difficult because they cannot separate the abstract processes of mathematical reasoning from their emotional involvement with numbers and their manipulation. But, as just mentioned, the subject of mathematics is eminently attractive to those who can use it defensively to separate themselves from all emotions.

The story of a bright eleven-year-old boy may end this consideration of emotional blocks to learning. He was so totally unable to read that he was diagnosed as a hopeless case of *alexia* (word blindness). Just before and after he finally began to read, he had a long series of dreams. Basically these dreams consisted of one and the same central image: he was trying to go down a road but was stymied by a huge roadblock.

Before he began to read there was always just one roadblock that stopped him; convinced that he could not go on, he returned in defeat to his point of origin. As he began to make first efforts to read, the dreams changed into nightmares. Now when he came to the roadblock, he managed to bypass it by going off the road into the fields and then back onto the road again. But this did not help; on the contrary: as soon as he had bypassed the roadblock and tried to proceed, he found himself confronted with a still larger one. The two blocks between which he was caught began to close up on him and threatened to crush him. At this point he would wake up in terror.

During the months he was having these dreams the boy made no progress in reading. One day he would learn a few simple words, which the next day he could no longer recognize. But the day came when in therapy he at last comprehended what these blocks symbolized and with it what his anxiety about reading was all about. With this the dream changed. He still found roadblocks in his way, but now, after getting around one somehow, he no longer tried to proceed immediately. Instead, after getting past a roadblock, he turned to remove it before going on. This he could now do, stone by stone.

As he thus in his dreams removed block after block, he moved closer and closer to his final goal: his emotional block to learning disappeared and he made fast and steady progress in reading.

These dreams can tell us much about how to remove emotional blocks to learning: nothing could be more erroneous than to expect a child to have smooth riding after he has merely somehow gotten around his learning inhibition. On the contrary, at this point the real task of understanding its nature has barely begun. Trying to get around the block without recognizing and dismantling, i.e., mastering its cause will only lead to different, possibly larger, and more dangerous blocks on the road to academic achievement and emotional well-being.

The solution then lies in understanding first why the block was there in the first place (what the child is afraid of) and second, what purpose it served (why the child thought that not learning would protect him); then, third, after mastering the block (understanding and getting around it), it is necessary to remove it entirely before going on.

The final resolution to any deep emotional difficulty always requires the recognition that to understand what one was so afraid of, and why, is the best way to overcome the anxiety that originally blocked one.

The boy who dreamed of roadblocks was unable to learn because he felt (with some valid reason) that his parents had not wanted him to live. He feared this was true, but also doubted that it was. But he was convinced that if he learned to read, he would find written confirmation of his fear; then he could no longer doubt his parents' intention and would have to die. He removed the roadblock that prevented his learning when he was able to realize that by learning to read he could become self-supporting, could one day be independent and live on his own, irrespective of what his parents wanted.

Thus the deepest and most important motive for learning is not the approval of a vaguely conceived society, not to please one's parents or teachers, not to get ahead of the Russians. The inner conviction of the uses of learning for oneself is what overcomes educational handicaps, even the most severe blocks to learning. For education to be such an inner liberating force, it must not be degraded to the position of a tool, but made the essence of personal growth and development.

About Summerhill

Alexander Sutherland Neill's germinal book *The Problem Child* appeared in 1926; it had a deep and immediate impact on all those concerned with psychoanalytically oriented education. Much has happened since then, even in the years since his book *Summerhill* was published in this country in 1960; and so grossly have Neill and his work been misunderstood that I must strongly advise rereading him as I did recently, with today's educational problems in mind. I urge this especially for everyone concerned with the well-being of children, and for those specifically interested in what we do wrong with our methods of education.

Although Neill's work had been familiar to me since the twenties, it was only after *Summerhill* appeared that I began to have frequent occasion to be annoyed with the implications being drawn from his writings by American readers. Occasionally I was even carried away, blaming him in my own mind for how his "fans" misread him and misapplied his teaching, although I should have known better. But so persuasive were these enthusiastic followers, so insistent that their own exaggerations and distortions truly represented Neill's educational philosophy, that even I was slowly swayed.

Little by little, I began to think of Neill as somewhat foolish in his all-permissiveness—I who, of all people, should have known better. I, too, had been confronted with the same dual problem: how does one apply a psychoanalytic understanding of man to the general education of children in a residential setting; and how does one apply psychoanalytic understanding to the needs of a particular group of children? Neill dealt with a group of relatively normal or only mildly

ABOUT SUMMERHILL: This essay was printed as a chapter in *Summerhill: For and Against* (New York: Hart Publishing Co., 1970), pp. 99–118. It is here reprinted with some changes.

disturbed children; in the Orthogenic School, we dealt with most severely disturbed children.

On other grounds, I had run into similar misunderstandings of my own writings over two decades. I had always blamed myself for these, thinking I should have done a better job of explaining myself. This again made rereading *Summerhill* a salutary experience, because to think then of the distortions evoked by Neill's writing—from admirers no less than from critics—was to recognize how little he and his writings were to blame. I can now comfort myself that when my writings are misinterpreted and misunderstood, the work itself is less to blame than are those preconceived notions which the reader will find support for, no matter what the author has really said or had in mind.

Now why was it particularly easy for Neill's work to be so grossly distorted? I believe it is because Neill the person and the educator was so much greater a man, so much more deeply human, so much more outstanding a molder of youth, than he was a philosopher, a student of psychoanalysis, or a theoretical psychologist. He was deeply attuned to the psyches of children, and this comes through most clearly in his actions, in the many concrete examples he offers of how he operates; his book is essentially a set of such examples, which are rich in psychological wisdom. When, however, it came to trying to explain his philosophy, he was often woefully inadequate and naive. At such times he was not above dodging an issue with a sleight-of-hand—as when asked, for example, why he played down the teaching of Latin or mathematics. He replied, "If the experts in mathematics and Latin have great minds, I have never been aware of it." Neill was actually well aware that among mathematicians, as among Latinists, great minds are as frequent—that is, as rare—as they are among persons of any other calling. Neill would know better than anyone how to deal with a child who wanted to concentrate on those subjects, or how to accept with deep empathy the child who wanted nothing to do with those subjects. But when the subject was posed as a theoretical question, the great clinician of education was at a loss for words and he took too simple a way out.

In a more serious vein: when asked how he justified prohibiting intercourse among his preadolescent students, he replied that his school would otherwise be closed. This is probably true, but it hardly clarifies the deeper issue: if he believed—as he indicated in his writings—that sexual activity should not be inhibited, how does one deal with the way such sexual activity may affect the psychology of a prepubertal girl, with what it could do to her view of herself, later on, if she had intercourse, even if at a specific moment she was attracted to it? What would happen to a thirteen-year-old if she got pregnant? How would that affect her development, in our society, if she was either forced to give up her child, or compelled to become a mother long before she wanted to?

Having said this, I must add that I have no doubt that had one of the Summerhill children become pregnant, Neill would have helped her to deal with her predicament with utmost sensitivity and understanding. But a terrible predicament it would nevertheless be, in today's world. Thus his answer hardly meets the problem of whether or not to bless preadolescent sexual intercourse in our society, nor does his philosophy suggest how to prevent such activity if we do not approve of it.

If his girls did not get pregnant, even with the very great freedom he believed so salutary for them, it is because most of the children who came to him were raised in a Victorian atmosphere of severest repression. Many came from British public schools with their repressive practices, and from homes where spanking brought obedience and sexual taboos were rigorously imprinted. Even after Neill had lifted innumerable prohibitions, these children were left with enough of a superego-anxiety to prevent excess. More important, the man who tried to free them of their crippling anxiety became so beloved to them that soon they could not help but identify with him and with his school, and then they were unwilling to do anything that might endanger its operation.

This would never work with children who had too little superego to begin with, as is true of so many of our difficult children, whether raised in slums or in over-indulgent homes. What Neill failed to see is the extent to which his system worked because it was the very antidote for the particular disease his children suffered from: over-repression. That is why he could generalize that what is good medicine for those suffering crippling inhibitions is also the best for all—which it is not.

In his philosophizing, Neill was thus charmingly naive. One can and does love him for his naiveté; it is so much a part of what is very good in him. But if one tries to apply his philosophy as he stated it, rather than flexibly applying what the man really stood for, then one does indeed end up making a fool of the man and his teaching.

Neill's basic philosophy is naively Rousseauian, with the human infant born inherently good: if only evil society, especially his bad parents, were to let the child grow up naturally without anxieties and inhibitions, he would mature all on his own into the most glorious human being. As for psychoanalysis, Neill has taken from it only that repression is bad, and that neuroses are brought on by sexual inhibitions.

True, Neill wrote before ego psychology became the cornerstone of psychoanalytic theory and practice. But he remained unaware that while anxiety causes neurosis, anxiety is also what keeps society going. Anxiety is one of the mainsprings of creativeness, invention, and progress, particularly in its sublimated form. Yes, anxiety about loss of self-respect is even the wellspring of Neill's own success, which can only be described in terms of another pair of old-fashioned virtues: personal honesty and common decency. He was utterly honest in all his human interactions, and his highest value was common decency, which he expected the children to make their own guiding principle.

He failed, however, to take account of the existential anxiety which, according to some psychoanalysts, originates in separation anxiety. Nor did he talk about our deep inner conflicts or our psychosocial crises: he took no note of the continuous battle between id and superego, of eros against the instinct of aggression, to mention only two of these conflicts. His naive optimism stands here in stark contrast to Freud's pessimism about human nature.

Neill's simple views of man, and why things go wrong with man, contradict those of Freud, who recognized that the inner complexities which man is heir to cause his eternal inner struggles. Neill came to psychoanalysis by way of the Wilhelm Reich of *The Function of the Orgasm*—he who held that the source of man's conflicts is society, not the nature of man. Eventually, Reich's failure to integrate psychoanalysis and Communism forced him into cosmic speculations, and to putting man in an orgone box. Neill's greater closeness to life and to children kept him from ever putting children into boxes.

But lacking psychological sophistication—sophisticates never understand children, who are so obvious if we can accept their obviousness—Neill remained unaware of the reasons why the things he did worked. He believed they worked because he was on the side of the children, which indeed he was. Since he believed children are born without sin, and that their difficulties come not from within themselves but from a bad society, his solution was to protect children from society, to take their side against it. Would that things were that simple!

Since Neill did not worry about psychology, about exactly how the changes in his students came about, he did not realize the fact that all was due to how they identified with him. He did not realize that Summerhill worked not because it was just the right setting in which to raise children, but because it was nothing but an extension of his personality.

Everything about Summerhill expressed Neill. From the moment they came there, children were enveloped by Neill—by what he stood for and lived for. Everywhere there was the powerful impact of his person, most of all his common decency. And sooner or later, most children would come to identify with him, however reluctantly. When, for example, a child would call him a fool, Neill believed this was a salutary effect of having given the child the freedom to oppose him. But the child did not oppose him; he loved him. Neill had indeed given the child freedom—so much so that trust was born; trust enough for the child to declare his love and admiration, albeit in somewhat abusive form—as is natural with preadolescents, who have a tendency to hide their deepest loves because they fear revealing them would make them too vulnerable.

Since the changes Neill produced in his children were based on identification, he succeeded only with those who could identify with him. And many could, because he was simply one of the grandest men around. But let a smaller person try to apply Neill's naive philosophy, and chaos would follow. Neill's view of man is incorrect, though his view did inspire him to feats of true greatness. Most of all, Neill was all of a piece, with hardly a flaw in his personality—excepting always his naiveté. In a great man, this is rather an asset. But what a liability it becomes in smaller men!

Having been head of a boarding school for over a quarter of a century, I cannot help comparing Neill's experiences with ours at the Orthogenic School. My reevaluation of Neill's book will thus be flavored by my own convictions and experiences, and I must in fairness warn the reader of this.

What far outweighs Neill's lack of psychoanalytic depth is his deep respect for the child as a unique human being. Implied in all that he says—though he is explicit enough when talking about parents—is the belief that one cannot truly respect another person unless one respects oneself highly.

Among other things, one's self-respect requires that one does not make a fool of oneself. Certainly, respect for a child entails our not letting the child make a fool of himself. But this is exactly where so many followers of Neill go astray: they pervert his teaching of true freedom to imply that one should permit a child to make a fool of himself, the adult, or both—all equally destructive. In short, they somehow infer that one should give a child enough rope to hang himself. Essential to everything Neill says is the principle that we must teach a child to understand what a rope is all about, so that he will never use it to hang himself or another.

When Neill wrote *The Problem Child* in 1926 and *The Problem Teacher* in 1944, these books were addressed to the readers and problems of that time. Since most children who came to him then were suffering from a too-rigid, too-punitive type of rearing, he was mostly concerned with showing the evils that this led to. Nowadays, many children suffer far more from a reverse kind of rearing, namely having things too loose, too much their own way. Those who believe that this is what Neill recommends should carefully read his assertion: "To let a child have his own way, or do what he wants to *at another's expense*, is bad for the child. It creates a spoiled child, and the spoiled child is a bad citizen."

Neill was very aware that we cannot permit immature minds to impose their will on us; this may be illustrated by his story of a boy who was trying to terrorize others: " 'Cut it out, my boy,' I said sharply, 'we aren't afraid of you.' He dropped the hammer and rushed at me. He bit and kicked me. 'Every time you hit or bite me,' I said quietly, 'I'll hit you back.' And I did. Very soon he gave up the contest and rushed from the room."

Here is a lesson for some of our permissive parents and schools. What Neill knew, and what everyone not shackled by preconceived notions soon learns, is that to submit to coercion leaves both child and adult with nothing but hatred or contempt for each other. If we permit someone to coerce or intimidate us, we stop being of much use to that person. We cannot help him because he does not respect us;

and furthermore, we cannot help him because we dislike him, whether or not we admit that to ourselves.

Every one of Neill's specific reactions—as opposed to his stated philosophy—remains valid even for situations he could not possibly have considered, because those situations did not exist at the time *Summerhill* was published. Neill's criteria apply because they stem from his deep respect for the person. On the very first page of *Freedom—Not License*, his sequel to *Summerhill*, he says: "I define license as interfering with another's freedom. For example, in my school a child is free to go to lessons or stay away from lessons because that is his own affair, but he is not free to play a trumpet when others want to study or sleep." Maybe the passage hit me because student activists—against the expressed desire of the students taking it—had just interrupted one of my classes, believing, like many of Neill's American followers, that they were fighting for their freedom, while in fact they were undermining all freedom by practicing license.

Would that our militant students, concerned as they are with their individual freedom, with being authentic and creating a better society, had learned what Neill, that great educator, considered the basic requirement for any better society: namely, respect for the individual. One must be convinced that one has no right to interrupt what others are doing, although one has every right to abstain from what is being done if that is one's wish.[1]

---

[1] In defense of many militant students, I should add that they do respond to what might be called "Summerhill" methods of education, which are simply good educational methods, period. The group who tried to break up my class did so because they were annoyed with a statement I had made. Since in my classes I discuss only what the students want to talk about, I told them I was quite ready to discuss it. I invited them to say what they had on their minds, which they did for a while. Then the rest of the class, on their own, voted by overwhelming majority that the group should desist, and that I should continue from where we had left off.

Before doing so, I encouraged those who preferred to hear more of what the militants had to say to meet separately with them, because I did not believe they would profit from my teaching when they thought there was something else more important to listen to. Since I really meant what I said, the militants left—angry with me, but in peace. It was a large class, and I do not know how many left with them, but the majority did not.

Because I respected the militants and their concerns, they were able in re-

On the basis of my own experience, I can only underscore what Neill says about the freedom of the child: "It all sounds easy and natural and fine, yet it is astounding how many parents, keen on the idea, manage to misunderstand it." He cites the example of parents who let their four-year-old son bang on a neighbor's piano with a wooden mallet, while they looked on with a triumphant smile, meaning, "Isn't self-regulation wonderful?" Unfortunately, these are parents who do give their child enough rope to hang himself by. They are the same "young enthusiasts for self-regulation" Neill speaks of "who come to my school as visitors, and exclaim at a lack of freedom in locking poison in a closet, or our prohibition about playing on the fire escape. The whole freedom movement is marred and despised because so many advocates of freedom have not got their feet on the ground. . . . One such protested to me recently because I shouted sternly to a problem boy of seven who was kicking my office door."

One more delightful story to show Neill's common sense—that characteristic most needed in all our dealing with children—and how sorely lacking it is in those who understand neither the value of freedom nor the viciousness of license:

A woman brought her girl of seven to see me. "Mr. Neill," she said, "I have read every line that you have written; and even before Daphne was born, I decided to bring her up exactly along your lines." I glanced at Daphne, who was standing on my grand piano with her heavy shoes on. She made a leap for the sofa and nearly went through the springs. "You see how natural she is," said the mother. "The Neillian child!" I fear that I blushed.

Having so often had the identical experience with parents who had read every line I had written without understanding my meaning at all, my heart went out to Neill. "It is this distinction between freedom and license that many parents never grasp." But then he goes on to explain that "the proper home is one in which children and adults have equal rights." And here, as in many other places, while in total agreement with Neill's meaning, I think it better to talk of appropriate rights rather than equal rights. The right to play with toy

turn to respect mine. This, however, does not work as a trick. Emotionally wrought-up persons, more than others, can "smell" if one really cares about their needs. They can respect the other person's needs only if they feel that their needs have been respected first.

guns means very little to adults, while the right to read in peace means very little to the young child. So it is an appropriate right for the child to play with guns, as it is the appropriate right of adults to read in peace.

Perhaps I am in a better position than most to judge what is involved in operating a Summerhill. For example, in my own work, as at Summerhill, boys and girls come to us as young as age five, others as late as fifteen or older, and these children will remain with us for many years.

What most readers of *Summerhill* do not understand is that while such an educational setting imposes few specific demands, and never trivial ones, it is really among the most demanding of educational institutions. Such a setting demands of the child that he develop a very high degree of self-respect; and with it, true respect for others. This is much harder to learn than how to automatically get to class at nine o'clock, and to pay attention when there. It is even harder than Latin or trigonometry.

Applying this to the particular situation of the Orthogenic School, I am always impressed with how, on casual acquaintance with our institution, visitors are astonished by our so-called undemandingness about etiquette, manners, and behavior. At the Orthogenic School, our inner attitude toward children is much like Neill's, although with different children and a different philosophy, our practices are quite distinct. What visitors overlook is that the absence of minor demands is for a purpose, and that purpose is to free the child's energy for the enormous task of rebuilding his misdeveloped personality.

While concentrating on so major a task, the child should be encouraged to do it in ways that are age-correct for him. This means our respect for the child's freedom demands we accept his doing things in ways that many peace-loving, middle-class parents in America cannot accept. It means that if children want to play with guns and act out battles, we must respect such desires. We must not be so distrustful of them as to assume that if they play war as children, they will therefore grow up to be war-loving, murderous adults.

By playing at war, children can realize in their own ways what is wrong with war. If we do not push them into some particular mold concerning war and peace, they can later, as grownups, be free of the military spirit. Instead, the modern peace-loving parent often mistakenly forbids all war games. All these parents should read what

Neill says of children at Summerhill, who when they want to make things "always [make] a toy revolver or boat or kite." He understands how little difference there is to the child between a revolver or a gun, and a boat or a kite. The difference between them exists only in the mind of the adult, not in the mind of the child. And the adult who imposes this difference on the child destroys the child's freedom.

In another context Neill tells us: "A parent's fear of the [child's] future affords a poor prognosis for the health of the child. This fear, oddly enough, shows itself in the desire that his children should learn more than he [the parent] has learned." It is the parent who has never really learned to control his own aggressive impulses who also feels the greatest need to keep his child from playing war games. But by forcing such limitations on the child's play, the parent convinces the child of how deeply he distrusts him as a person, because the parent seems convinced that as the child grows older, he will not be able, on his own, to decide that peaceful cooperation is better than violence.

At the same time, if we let children make and use swords, then it is our obligation to see that they do not get hurt. "I'm always anxious when a craze for wooden swords begins. I insist that the points be covered with rubber or cloth," says Neill. How much easier it is to simply prohibit children from playing with swords.

If Neill were to work in an American setting today, his actions would be very different from those described in *Summerhill*, where the problems he dealt with are so largely those of children brought up in Victorian ways. Things have not changed as to what constitutes the right way to educate children, but specifics have changed. For example, Neill tells us in *Summerhill* that "parents are spoiling their children's lives by forcing on them outdated beliefs; they are sacrificing their child to the past."

This statement is dated, although the warning implication it carries is still valid: parents should not sacrifice their children to their own neurotic anxieties. Today in the United States, I think the danger to middle-class children is that they are sacrificed by their parents not to the past, but to the future. Few middle-class American children suffer because the authoritarian religion against which Neill rages is imposed on them. Instead, children are sacrificed by parents who burden them with the future by telling them from early childhood on of their obligation to correct the evils of the world. Other parents sacrifice their children to the future by insisting that if success later in life is to be won, the child must devote his present existence to preparation, and don the straitjacket of competitive education.

In one sense, quite a few very liberal, well-educated, middle-class families—those most apt to believe they are raising their children in the philosophy of Summerhill—do sacrifice their children to the past: not, as Neill suggests, by asking them to relive it, but by imposing on them the obligation to correct the errors of the past. Whether the child is burdened with reliving the past as it was, or burdened with reshaping the future, he is being sacrificed to parental concerns. Too many parents deceive themselves by assuming they believe in Neill's freedom, while not granting their own children what Neill calls a child's most important privilege: the right to play in the present; that is, to play with guns at age ten. Instead, such parents ask their child at this age to join in their worries about the politics of the nation, and do the work of the future.

Neill believed that to rear children well requires that "parents come to some sort of compromise agreement; unhealthy parents either become violent [i.e., forcefully suppressive] or they spoil their children by allowing them to have all the social rights." In the term "forcefully suppressive," he included the imposing of social or political convictions. Neill says, "A child cannot have real freedom when he hears his father's thunder against some political group." He recognizes that to give a child freedom is not easy, because "it means that we must refrain from teaching him religion, or politics, or class consciousness. . . . I would never consciously influence children to become pacifists, or reformers, or anything else. . . . Every opinion forced on a child is a sin against that child. A child is not a little adult, and a child cannot possibly see the adult's point of view."

This is as true today as it was when Neill wrote it, and I wish that all liberal parents concerned with freedom would recognize how they deprive their children of freedom when they "thunder against" various inequities, justified as this may seem to the parents. They thus deprive their child of the most important thing of all: the right to form his own inner opinions, influenced not by their authoritative preachments, but only by his own direct experience with life.

Neill does not "preach to children that slums are an abomination unto the world. I used to—before I realized what a humbug I was about it." His reason for refraining is not that slums are not an abomination—they definitely are—but that if we have failed to erase them, we have no business bothering our children with a problem that is still ours, not theirs.

The same goes for atomic war: "Today, even small children cannot help hearing about coming wars with the terrible atom bombs. . . . Healthy, free children do not fear the future. They anticipate it gladly." It is only when we impose our anxieties about the future (as of wars) on our children that they come to fear the future and with it, all of life. In this way, as Neill points out, we make them unhealthy because we force on them what he calls "the sick fear of tomorrow."

I do not share Neill's conviction that if only we could avoid all sexual repression and encourage free sex play, particularly masturbation, in children, all the evils of the world would dissolve. No doubt, we could and should be much more accepting of children's sexuality. But like his views about man, Neill's views about sex derive directly from Reichean thought in the early days of psychoanalysis. Neill fails to consider the tendencies toward aggression which, according to students of animal behavior, are probably inborn in man, or certainly are a significant part of his makeup.

Believing with some of our present social critics in man's innate goodness, Neill concludes, as they do, that our sex-repressive (exploitative) society accounts for all the conflicts and contradictions we encounter in life. He ignores Freud's recognition that the greatest danger to human society does not come from repression, but from the instinct of aggression, from man's tendency towards destruction and self-destruction. In advocating complete sexual freedom, Neill does not concern himself with the fact that among preliterate tribes where sex repression is very minor, man's anxiety is more pervasive, if anything; and that in those societies, man must strive even harder to limit his anxieties through taboos and through what are often crippling rituals.

Neill also fails to consider that in such societies there is very little freedom in arranging one's life. Instead, all energy must go into securing sheer survival, since without repression and sublimation no higher forms of social organization are achieved, nor is that technology developed which alone protects us against sickness and famine.

I do not believe that man can live free of anxiety.. For while it is true that anxiety brings about neurotic behavior, anxiety also brings about our highest achievements. All depends on how well we are able to sublimate these anxieties, and set them to constructive use.

While Neill is excellent at reducing neurotic anxiety, he neglects existential anxiety and what I consider the prime task of psychoanalytic education: transforming this force of anxiety from one that shrivels us into a force that expands us and our lives.

In the same context, I think Neill errs when he thinks that if a seven-year-old looks frightened at the sight of a cow and says, "No, no, moo cow eats you," it is because the child was brought up all wrong. Young children believe in the *lex talionis* wherever they are raised. Since they know we eat the cow's flesh, they believe the cow wants to eat ours, too. The source of such a belief is an inner anxiety, independent of sex repression, in which some of our own destructive tendencies find expression.

Thus, while I do not doubt that children would be much better off if they enjoyed greater sexual freedom than most of them do, I question if the gain would be all Neill believes it would be, if only we allowed our children total freedom in sex play. Certainly he is right when he says: "There would be infinitely less sex crime in the world if sex play (or sex in general, I might add) were accepted as normal." But this, too, has to be qualified in terms of what is age-correct; freedoms in this area, too, must be in line with man's normal growth and development.

As a little boy (and a girl as well) should be free within himself, and free in terms of parental influence, to play with guns, and because of such freedom feel no need to concentrate his interest on guns as an adult, so as a child he should be free to be interested in sexual activity appropriate to his age. He should be able to engage in masturbation without undue fear, but he should not need to do so provocatively, destructively, or excessively. He certainly should not concentrate on that at the expense of his interest and energy in social play, nor at the expense of his relating to others. He certainly should not, as a child, engage in sexual intercourse. He should not need to use heterosexual relations as a substitute for masturbation or aggression.

But compared with Neill's overall grasp of what children need for growing up well, as every page of his book testifies, these are small qualifications. For when it comes to the practical problems of how to deal with children and sexual issues, Neill is eminently sound. I could not agree more that it is "far better and safer to postpone an answer than to tell a child far too much" about sex, or at too early an age. Also that much of so-called sex instruction will not do because, as he says, "It's just a form of awkward lessons in anatomy and physiology."

Neill is also completely right when he says that what stops us from giving a child all the knowledge about sex he asks for is the problem of how to make things clear. Neill might be writing of today when he says: "The modern parent may have no temptation to follow that kind of [sex-repressive] teaching, yet may succumb to something similar: the worship of the sexual function as a new-found god." Despite his theoretical overvaluation of sex freedom, in practice Neill realizes that to make too much of sex itself is also confusing to the child: "We all have been so conditioned about sex that it is almost impossible for us to see the middle, natural way; we are either too pro-sex or too anti-sex."

But it is not only in matters of sex that we push the children in terms of our anxieties, instead of understanding and accepting what is age-correct for them. Certainly it is destructive to the child to be induced to be competitive about his own education. Having just been criticized severely because I suggested that not everyone need go to college, and that many youngsters would be much better off if, after high school, or perhaps even earlier, they were to receive a high level of preprofessional training or training in social services, I was delighted to read: "Over the years, we have found that Summerhill boys who are going in for engineering do not bother to take the matriculation exams. They go straight to practical training centers."

Here is a prescription that applies to all children, but especially, at this moment in time, to many of our underprivileged youth who could well use the chance to do what so many Summerhill boys do who "have a tendency to see the world as a ship's steward."

Neill finds it as destructive to the child to be induced to cooperate at too early an age as to be forced to compete. "There is no case whatever for the moral instruction of children. It is psychologically wrong. To ask a child to be unselfish is wrong. Every child is an egoist and the world belongs to him. When he has an apple, his one wish is to eat that apple. The chief result of mother's encouraging him to share it with his little brother is to make him hate the little brother. Altruism comes later—comes naturally—*if the child is not taught to be unselfish*. It probably never comes at all if the child has been forced to be unselfish." But again, it is not quite as simple as Neill believes when he says that "there is no need whatsoever to teach children how to behave. A child will learn what is right and what is wrong in good time—provided he is not pressured."

The child will learn to behave only if he is surrounded by right human examples which are so attractive to him that he will want to copy them, to shape his personality and values in the image of those he admires and with whom he identifies. But he will identify out of anxiety, out of fear of losing the good will, or the presence, or the respect of the loved person. There is no socialization nor any learning without fear. Under primitive conditions or in a scarcity economy, the fear is that we will starve if we do not learn how to gain our livelihood. In middle-class society, the fear, at first, is separation anxiety; then the fear of loss of respect of a person we love; and finally, the fear of loss of self-respect. The values of what is right and what is wrong are not God-given, nor are they born in us, needing only unfolding.

On the other hand, children do have sufficient good sense to realize what is good for them and what is not, provided their own needs have been sufficiently satisfied so that they know what those needs are. "The truth seems to be that children take a much longer time to grow up than we have been accustomed to think. By growing up, I mean becoming a social being." And they become social human beings through experiences with other persons—not through teaching of theories, nor through experiences which do not involve anyone else.

It was these socializing experiences that Neill provided for the Summerhill children in all of life, by day and by night. His giving was what socialized the children—not their inborn nature, which is at best a potential to be realized through a great deal of living and learning. The socializing process takes time, much longer than we assume. That is why our push for early academic education often produces very bright but totally unsocialized persons—people who know a lot, but who do not know how to live in a community of others.

But if the human example can do all that, children must not be overwhelmed, not by our presence—which should be there to take or leave, but available when a child needs it—nor by our presents, of which "children today get far too much, so much that they cease having appreciation for a gift." Children who have been given too much—be it toys, or academics, or stimulation, or the license to act without regard for others—are all spoiled children, unable to appreciate freedom, either their own or that of others. "Later in life, as the spoiled brat gets older, he has even a worse time of it than one subjected to too much discipline. The spoiled child is terribly self-centered." This is a caveat to remember: that too little discipline may in the long run be more damaging than too much. If this is what experience has taught Neill, of all people, we ought to heed his warning.

But the best discipline of all for the child is the self-discipline of the parent and the educator. This is the kind of self-discipline that prevents us from acting out on others our own anxieties and needs, certainly not on our children. This discipline permits us to be on their side instead of forcing them to be on ours. For things to work out to our liking, one's personal life should be such that one would wish his child to emulate this life and take it as a model.

Neill's life and work are, indeed, such a model, even if we cannot agree with his theoretical formulations. Let us hope his followers will realize the facts and try not to set his philosophy into deadly practice, but rather to live as honestly and with as much respect for self and for others as Neill did in his long and enormously fruitful and satisfying life.

Violence:
A Neglected Mode of Behavior

These violent delights have violent ends.
—*Romeo and Juliet*

Man and society were born of both violence and gentle cooperation; to neglect either in our efforts to better human relations would be fruitless. Aggression and violence are concepts so closely related as to be interchangeable, and if we are serious about understanding aggression and its role in society, we have to start with an examination of the desire to do violence. Shakespeare's good friar of Verona knew that violent delights have violent ends. But if these delights were not enticing, would we not shun them, since we all know they lead to disaster?

Some years ago Robert Warshaw wrote a defense of the classic Western movie, arguing that the gunfighter is a moral hero.[1] This assertion is startling, since few of us would define the movie cowboy as our moral hero, or gunfighting as an ideal way to solve moral problems. But let us remember that sword-bearing Achilles is regarded as the moral hero at the beginning of Western civilization. Because of distance in time, the vast difference in settings, and our veneration of the *Iliad*, it is often difficult to recognize what Simone Weil pointed out—that the *Iliad* is, in fact, a poem of violence.[2] The very first lines of the *Iliad* tell that it is the anger of Achilles that causes utter devastation and hurls untold heroes to their death, their corpses becoming a feast for the dogs.

VIOLENCE: A NEGLECTED MODE OF BEHAVIOR: Reprinted with changes and additions from the *Annals of the American Academy of Political and Social Science* 364 (1966), pp. 50–59.

[1] Robert Warshaw, *The Immediate Experience* (Garden City, N.Y.: Doubleday, 1962).

[2] Simone Weil, "The *Iliad*, or the Poem of Force," *Politics*, 2, 11 (November 1945), pp. 321–31.

Violence existed long before Homer. But with him appeared the new humanizing Greek spirit, which informs his poem. Although he did not offer a solution, Homer represented violence as the central problem that must be dealt with by a world striving to become civilized. Several centuries later in his *Oresteia*, Aeschylus, the first great tragic poet, attempted a solution by depicting the origin of Athenian civilization as lying in the termination of a murderous vendetta, accomplished thanks to a careful weighing of all the issues involved in a spirit of justice and humanity. The concept that henceforth and for all times to come rampant violence such as blood feuds would be outlawed and replaced by communal justice was, according to the poet, the foundation for all great achievements of Athenian culture.

Long before Aeschylus, the *Iliad* had demonstrated that nothing good can ever come from having recourse to violent means. Paris, who broke the peace of Menelaus' home, had to perish. So did the greatest hero, Achilles, who had joined the avenging party; and to be killed was the fate of Agamemnon who had led it.

The human race in the *Iliad* is not divided into victorious heroes and victims. If there were conquering heroes, violence might seem justified, at least to the victors. But in the course of the *Iliad*, if the Greeks win one day, the Trojans do the next; in the end, both Hector and Achilles perish. In this poem there is not a single man who does not, at one time or another, have to bow to force. The concept that the use of violence leads to retribution with almost geometrical rigor was a main subject of Greek thought; it is the soul of the *Iliad*. Therefore, our first great epic impresses on us that we should think seriously of what our inner and outer attitudes to violence ought to be.

This may lead to the explanation of why the gunfighter of the Western film has taken such hold of our mass imagination. The Western, Warshaw thinks, "offers a serious orientation to the problem of violence such as can be found almost nowhere else in our culture. One of the well-known peculiarities of modern civilized opinion is its refusal to acknowledge the value of violence. . . . We train ourselves to be shocked or bored by cultural images of violence, and our very concept of heroism tends to be a passive one: we are less drawn to the brave young men who kill large numbers of our enemies than to the heroic prisoners who endure torture without capitulating."

What we seek in the Western is "the image of a single man who wears a gun on his thigh. The gun tells us that he lives in a world of violence, and even that he 'believes in violence.' But the drama is one of self-restraint: the moment of violence must come in its own time and according to its special laws, or else it is valueless. . . . Really, it is not violence at all which is the 'point' of the [classic] western movie, but a certain image of man, a style, which expresses itself most clearly in violence."

The Western hero suggests that "even in killing or being killed we are not freed from the necessity of establishing satisfactory modes of behavior." This has become our problem: establishing "satisfactory modes of behavior" although we live in a society where violence is rampant. The gunfighter in the Western has found his solution to the problem. Obviously, it cannot be our solution, but Warshaw suggests that at least he has taken the problem seriously. We ought to do the same.

Nowadays, parents are encouraged a great deal to accept their children's primitive desires so far as intake and elimination are concerned. We even tend to be more understanding about sexual behavior and more accepting in our emotional attitudes. But what measures are we taking to help our children do a better job of mastering the disturbances which come from our innate tendency to act aggressively? We try to satisfy other instinctual drives within acceptable limits or, if this doesn't seem feasible, to channel them into safe directions, so that they do not generate so much pressure as to cause explosive outbreaks or a crippling of the total personality. In regard to violence there seem to be no such reasonable efforts, but a covert denial of its existence as a drive.

We disapprove when our children play at war, or cowboys and Indians, as if the play were for real. But if parents who object to this kind of play were consistent, they would have to outlaw even chess, because it is definitely a war game, the goal of which is to destroy the opponent's king. But they do not, because parents enjoy their adult forms of war and other extremely competitive games. Yet they somehow think that their children should not engage in their childish forms of such play; war games are only for adults!

In respect to gun play, we react as if the play were reality, which it definitely is not. Children's play is closely related to daydreams and dream fantasy. By inhibiting their aggressive fantasy play, we behave as if even thinking and dreaming about violence were evil. This attitude prevents children from forming a clear understanding about the world of difference that separates violent fantasy from acting violently in reality. If the child is not permitted to learn early what this difference consists of in respect to violence (to use Warshaw's terms, if he has not been given a chance to establish satisfactory modes of behavior in respect to violence) then, later on, he may not be able to draw a clear line between violent fantasies and violent actions.

By outlawing the child's violent fantasy we totally neglect what even Plato recognized: that the difference between the good and the bad man is that the first only dreams of evil deeds, while the latter engages in them. The ancient Greeks knew that the crucial difference between good and evil does not reside in a difference of fantasy content—and children's play is nothing but the child's giving form and expression to his childish fantasies—but whether or not fantasy remains just that, or is acted out in reality with real consequences.

Children are told not to hit or swear at their playmates. They are supposed to refrain from destroying their toys or other property—so far, so good. But then what outlets for violence are provided for them? It is so unreasonable, but let a parent meet with violence acted out by his youngster, and likely as not the parent will slap the child or thunder at him, thus demonstrating that violence is all right if one is older and stronger, and makes use of it under the guise of suppressing it. So we end by using violence to suppress violence, and in so doing teach our children that, in our opinion, there is no reasonable or intelligent way of dealing with it. Yet the same parents, at another moment, would agree that suppression is the worst way to deal with the instincts.

Unlike Wertham, who—as do many others—pleads for the protection of the innocent so that they won't be seduced by, for instance, the comics,[3] I am convinced that neither comics nor even television seduces innocent people. It is high time that both the myth of original sin and its opposite—the myth of original innocence—were dispatched to the land of the unicorns. Innocence is neither an inborn characteristic nor a useful protection or defense; most of the time it is

---

[3] F. Wertham, *Seduction of the Innocent* (New York: Rinehart, 1953).

little more than ignorance, too often clung to for (false) security. Comic books are apt to reinforce delinquent tendencies and teach new, asocial ways of acting only to those in whom delinquency is already a part of their make-up.

The prevalence of images of violence in films and on the TV screen encourages the random discharge of violence, while at the same time increasing the fear of violence without in any degree promoting an understanding of the nature of violence. We need to be schooled in how we may go about developing measures to contain, control, and channel the energy that is discharged in violence into more constructive directions. As mentioned before, what is absent in our education and in the mass media is the teaching and promotion of "satisfactory modes of behavior" in respect to violence.

But the basic issue is the delinquent and violent tendencies inherent in us, not their expression in comics, films, and TV, or even whether these feed such tendencies or make their control more difficult. The behavior of children and adolescents in regard to violence merely reflects the pattern among adults. If adults did not like to see violence depicted in the mass media, the media would not show it in such wide variety and with such prominence, and then children and youth would have much less chance to watch and be influenced by it.

Particularly in matters of violence, there is no protection in ignorance. Elsewhere I have tried to point out that ignorance of the nature of violence, as during the Nazi regime, did not lead to bliss but to death. Those under Hitler's power who despite Nazi persecution wished to believe that all men were good, and that violence existed only in a few perverted men, failed to protect themselves effectively and all too many of them soon perished. Violence exists, surely, and each of us is born with his potential for it. But we are also born with opposite tendencies, and these must be carefully nurtured if they are to counterbalance those which push us to act violently. To nurture such countervailing forces, however, one must know the nature of the enemy, and this is not achieved by denying its existence.

By asserting that there is, or ought to be, no place for violence in our emotional make-up, we evade the issue of how to educate for the control of our violent tendencies. In this way we try to force each individual to suppress his violent tendencies, since we have not taught him how to control or neutralize them, nor have we provided outlets by proxy for them in society. This is why so many people are eager to find at least imaginary satisfaction of their violent tendencies in the fantasy images of violence provided by the mass media.

If these violent images have become ever more prevalent, even in supposedly objective reporting of the news, it is one indication of how widespread is the fascination with violence, and the felt need for violent discharge in imagination. What is very wrong, however, is that the news shows that give such prominent footage to violence fail to counteract this with some equally or more prominent depiction of peaceful and cooperative achievements—and these occur at least as often and are considerably more important for society's well-being than the incidences of violence. The resulting impression from this one-sided reportage is that only violence is exciting, and non-violent achievements are not.

In many programs full of violent action, there is hardly any difference between the violence engaged in by criminals and that carried out by the law-enforcing and law-abiding elements of society. This suggests that there is simply no way of controlling violence in satisfactory ways. The combination of the parental demand for suppression of violence, and the fear created by violence, which is depicted as being both omnipresent and controllable only through counter-violence, plus the media's stimulation to act violently, leads to a building-up of violent tendencies in some people, to a pitch where they can no longer deny or control them. This may then lead to sudden eruptions in isolated acts of explosive violence.

These outbursts are conspicuous: by their spectacular nature, they even give the impression that ours is an age of violence. So we clamor for still greater suppression of even small eruptions of violence that could act as safety valves, draining off small amounts and leaving a balance that the individual could assimilate. Even among psychoanalysts, Freud's death or destructive instinct is not quite respectable, because we decree that what is not supposed to exist cannot and does not exist; all evidence to the contrary is simply disregarded, or explained away, for example, by the theory that violence is caused only by frustration.[4]

---

[4] It is of course true that when we cannot have our way, this is frustrating and may make us angry; we then may try to get our way, no matter what, by violence. But frustration of desires results, more often than not, in a passive giving

What we need is an intelligent recognition of "the nature of the beast." We shall not be able to deal capably with violence until we are ready to see it as part of human nature. When we have gotten well acquainted with this idea, and have learned to live with the need to domesticate our violent tendencies, then through a slow and tenuous process we may tame them successfully, first in ourselves, and on such basis also in society. But we shall never succeed in taming our violent tendencies as long as we proceed on the assumption that because violence *should* not exist, we might as well act as if it did not.

Violent action is, of course, a short-cut toward gaining an objective. It is so primitive in nature that it is generically unsuitable to gain for us those more subtle satisfactions we seek. That is why violence stands at the very beginning of man's development into a socialized human being. The heroic sagas marking man's entry into a more civilized and humane world are dominated by themes of violence; and it is also characteristic of our own entrance to life. Often violent temper tantrums, so typical of the child about to become a complex human being, show both: how violent and destructive outbursts preceded our developing ability to master inner drives and deal constructively with the problems presented by the fact that the external world is often frustrating; and the need to achieve such mastery if we are to cope well.

Although we do not wish to acknowledge how universal this really is, a birthday party of happy, normal children could instruct us. The birthday child, in his natural eagerness to get at the enticing present, will tear the wrappings off the package to get at the toy. If the box he is ripping should be part of the game, so much the worse for the box. Thus desire begets violence, and violence may destroy the object desired. In this sense, as in many others, violence is both natural and ineffective. It rarely reaches its goal or else, in getting at it, destroys it. True, discharge itself is a goal—but then once we have discharged our anger, we no longer question what caused it, nor do we seek

---

in. It all depends on a person's propensity to have recourse to violent means to gain his ends, or to give up in resignation. Also some of the most deeply felt frustrations are not caused by others, or by external circumstances; they are the consequences of inner dissatisfactions with ourselves for not being able to be the person we want to be. Only somebody lacking in self-control and with a strong tendency to project inner difficulties onto outside figures will discharge disappointments with himself in violent outbursts against others.

better ways to deal with the causes. Then nothing prevents what enraged us from happening again, leading once more to an outburst of violence.

To recount the evils of violence here is unnecessary. What is to be considered is whether our attitudes toward violence are reasonable given our goal to contain it, and what ways might better serve our ends.

The obvious is often neglected when we think about violence: whether or not it will be used or avoided depends entirely on what alternative solutions are known to a person facing a problem. Aeschylus understood this, and thus I evoked his *Oresteia*. In it Athena offers a substitution for ancient revenge for murder which is better than another murder. Violence is the behavior of someone who cannot visualize any other solution to a problem that besets him; this shows up most clearly in gang warfare.

Today we are constantly bombarded by images of the "good life" of ownership and consumption, but for a great number of people the means to consumership are slim. This is particularly true of many young people before they find a secure place both in our economic and our social systems, and even more so if they are from marginal or sub-marginal backgrounds. They often feel helpless to provide themselves with what they feel is even a minimal satisfaction of the demands we create in them. So they see no alternative for reaching their goals except through violence, and the pressures of frustration—and the very real chance that they might get away with using violence—only tempt them more to use it. Nothing in their education has equipped them to contain their violence, because during their whole educational life, its existence has been denied.

Yablonsky, in an analysis of what makes for the violent gang,[5] remarks with irony that the views and outlook of gang members, as in a nightmarish mirror, merely reflect the official ethos. The purpose of violence for the gang members is to achieve precisely the same major values as in respectable society: success and prestige in the eyes of one's peers. One homicidal youngster was quoted in explanation of his actions as follows: "I'm not going to let anybody be better than me and steal my 'rep' [reputation]. . . . When I go to a gangfight I punch, stomp and stab harder than anyone."

---

[5] L. Yablonsky, "The Violent Gang," *Commentary* 30 (August 1960).

Yablonsky says the very fact that senseless, unpremeditated violence is most respected by the gang shows the function that violence serves for them. Despairing of alternative solutions, or, perhaps more correctly, convinced that for them no alternatives exist, these youths seek a quick, almost magical way to power and prestige. With a single act of unpremeditated intensity, which has no ulterior purpose besides proving to oneself and others one's ability to act outrageously, gang members try to establish a sense of their own existence, and through it forcefully convince others of their potency.

Unfortunately, youth gangs are merely one extreme result of a situation that breeds violence also among normal, decent human beings. While similar situations exist all over the United States, a typical account is in Lewis's *Children of Sánchez*,[6] the scene of which is laid in highly urban Mexico City. Jesus Sánchez tells the story of his life, that of a man who is tied deep within himself to the old communal ways of his village, but who wishes desperately to make a go of life in a twentieth-century big industrial city. We watch how he is defeated again and again in his aspirations. Yet he is kept going, driving himself beyond endurance, by the desire to see at least his children succeed in this world which is so alluring but frustrating at every turn. Finally, bewildering frustration and the fact that Sánchez can see no other way out lead both him and his children to acts of violence, simply because they know of no other solution.

It is not only the lower-class world of the gang, or the children of Sánchez, who share the feeling that no alternatives exist and that there is no way out. The whole of our society seems caught in a spirit of believing that we lack alternatives. "Red or dead" used to be one slogan implying that we should either prepare for ultimate violence by creating weapons which are ever more destructive, or be ready to surrender without resistance to Communism if it should knock at our door. This anxiety about alternatives trickles down to attitudes about college boards and grades and so on through the fabric of our lives.

Ours is by no means an age of greater violence than others—on the contrary. Witness the near-abolishment of capital punishment, and the fact that public executions are no longer widely attended spectacles. As a matter of fact, the chances for discharging violent tendencies in socially approved ways at least vicariously are now so

---

[6] Oscar Lewis, *The Children of Sánchez* (New York: Random House, 1961).

severely curtailed that their regular and safe discharge is no longer possible.

The essential questions are: How can violence be husbanded? How can it be discharged in ways which are, if not socially useful, at least relatively harmless? Rural life used to offer the child at least a chance for some vicarious discharge of violence: in my native Austria, slaughtering the pig was a distinct highlight in the lives of peasant children. Chopping wood and similar forms of aggressive manipulation of nature provided other socially useful outlets and contributed to the well-being of the family. Such discharges were safe; they aroused no counter-aggression in the target.

Competitive or spectator sports are no real substitute because in the first place, they raise aggressive feelings of competition to the boiling point. And secondly, each time one wins, another must lose; and every lost game builds up more aggression than the player may have discharged in playing.

Maybe if our educational system were to acknowledge aggression, our children would not be glued to the television screen to see a bit of violence. According to our experience at the Orthogenic School, children seem to want to learn about aggression, not just discharge it— although they want that too. Right now, for example, the stories read in schoolrooms do not contain any incidents of aggression; no child in them ever hits, becomes angry, or destroys things in an outburst. The worst they ever do is to tease or pout. All of them live on Pleasant Street, in Friendly Town.

Perhaps there was some psychological wisdom to those old-fashioned readers where the child was told over and over what cruel fate befalls the evil-doer. While these stories scared children, they at least allowed for some vicarious discharge of hostility. Being relieved somewhat from hostility, the children's positive tendencies could be freed for the learning process. We could do even better: we could tell children through stories that people sometimes do get angry at each other and quarrel, but that they can make up, and if they do they will have a better life together.

It is peculiar to our culture that, in encouraging an extremely competitive spirit, we stress those aggressive emotions that power competition although aggression itself is tabooed. And although children have many experiences which arouse their violent anger, they are not supposed to express it.

One boy from birth on grew up in a variety of foster homes where he was treated badly. He was unable to learn and so repeated first grade three times. Finally he landed at the Orthogenic School, but there, too, he could not learn to read simple words like "come be with me," because no one had ever wanted to be with him, or had invitingly called out to him. But when we acknowledged the validity of his anger and of his violent feelings, given his life experience, he found it easy to learn to read and print words as complicated as *fighting, soldier, submarine, fireman*—all terms that were in line with his dominant feelings. The first two of these words had to do with his wish to do battle against a world that had mistreated him, and with the profession especially equipped to engage in warfare. The third word reflected his desire to remain hidden—and thus safe—while attacking those who had an easy life on the surface in contrast to his own life, which, he felt, had had to proceed underground. The fourth word suggests that after he had thus discharged violent anger in fantasy he had become ready to consider that the fire of his fury might be extinguished by a person who knows how to do so.

If we do offer children a chance to learn about what is foremost in their minds, or, actually, what is most deeply buried there, then they learn fast and furiously,[7] like the Maori children described in Ashton-Warner's *Spinster*.[8] The heroine of this novel, a teacher, realizes that her young Maori students can write exciting stories of their own; only the titles of their stories are less apt to be "Fun with Dick and Jane" than "I Am Aggressed Against." One of them named Tame writes:

> I ran away from my
> mother and I hid
> away from my mother
> I hid in the Shed and
> I went home and
> got a hiding.

---

[7] This familiar construction, "learning fast and furiously," tells how well known (though neglected) is the fact that we learn fast and well if, through the act of learning, we can also discharge fury, or "attack the problem," as we say.

[8] Sylvia Ashton-Warner, *Spinster* (New York: Simon and Schuster, 1958).

Having just read this, the teacher goes to the standard primer and turns curiously to the page from which this child is supposed to learn to read. There she finds the following story:

> Mother went to a shop.
> I want a cap, she said.
> I want a cap for John.
> She saw a brown cap.
> She saw a blue cap.
> I like the blue cap, she said.

Irini, a six-year-old, asks the teacher to spell several words, and then writes with concentration. Finally she brings the teacher what she has written:

> Mummie said to Daddy
> give me that money else
> I will give you a hiding.
> Daddy swear to Mummie
> Daddy gave the money
> to Mummie. We had
> a party. My father
> drank all the beer by
> hisself. He was drunk.

The teacher turns again to the primer and finds a story about parents:

> Look at the green house.
> Father is in it.
> It is father's home too.
>
> There is Mother.
> She is in the green house.
> She can see us.
> Let us run to mother.

It is easy to see significance in the contrasts between the Maori tales and those in the British primers. Ashton-Warner describes how she had to find what she calls "key words" in order to get her Maori children interested in reading and writing.

Long before she published her story, the children of the Orthogenic School had forced us to similar conclusions. If we wanted these children to learn, we had to convince them that reading, writing, and spelling would help them with what concerned them most deeply.

Once we did that, children who for years had resisted learning even the simplest words—who had been unable to learn to read from primers that pictured life as all sweetness and light, when their world was full of anger and violence—were suddenly eager to read. Some who for years had not learned to read a single word then learned to recognize, read, and spell a hundred words or more in a couple of weeks' time.

When we thought they were ready for it—that is, when we felt that these children's built-up resentment of learning had waned—speaking briefly to them in terms they could understand we introduced them, for example, to the idea that it sometimes feels good to write about one's angry thoughts, and it doesn't hurt anybody. On these occasions we told them that the hardest thing to do, and therefore the biggest problem in learning and living, but also the most important one, is mastering one's own scary ideas. But learning words that help us separate the fearsome event from what we only think about this event is greatly helpful. This is because while scary events that really happen are overpowering, our process of merely thinking about them, or talking and reading about them, need not be. In these ways, we explained, we can come to understand and learn to deal with things we fear.

After such explanations, three children picked *scary, fire,* and *hit* as the first words they wanted to learn. To me it seems that in those three words the children, without knowing it, outlined a course on how to deal with destructive tendencies, at least in the classroom-learning situation. One word, *hit*, refers to violence; the second word, *fire*, to a form of inanimate destruction; and the third word, *scary*, to the outcome of aggression and destruction.

If we permit children to speak openly about their aggressive tendencies, they can also come to recognize the scary character of these tendencies. Only this kind of recognition can lead to something better than, on the one hand, denial and suppression, and, on the other, explosion into violent acts. Thus education can bring about the conviction that in self-protection, and to avoid scary experiences, one must deal in constructive ways with tendencies to violence, both one's own and those of others.

A small sample of the emotionally charged words the Orthogenic School children usually learned to read after seeing them once, and to spell and write after only a few repetitions, is: *fire, knife, cut, crash, shoot, kill, hit, bite, teeth, cry, fight, jail, scream, yell.* Consider how much aggression these words reveal, and the children's desire to learn about them.

It is just as enlightening to see how closely the words selected by emotionally disturbed children in the U.S. compare with what Ashton-Warner's normal Maori children learned to read: "Rangi, who lives on love and kisses and thrashings and fights and fear of the police and who took four months to learn: come, look, and and, takes four minutes to learn: butcher-knife; gaol; police; sing; cry; kiss; Daddy; Mummie; Rangi; fight."

Each of the Orthogenic School's children selected different words to learn, because what was emotionally significant to one was not so much so to others. But the interesting thing is that all the children learned all the emotionally charged words, even ones not too meaningful to them, once they saw that these were important words to another child. They thus shared not only learning, but each other's emotions.

As we developed our teaching method, we realized that angry or scary words sometimes aroused too much emotion. We then devised many categories of words so that the child could choose which he preferred to learn, categories such as: angry words, scary words, not-nice words, nice words, warm words, and cold words.

Some of the nice words the children selected included *orange juice, milk, play*, and *hot dog*. These tell us something about the satisfying experiences that children need to counterbalance violence. In view of the fact that most primers concentrate on what we would call nice words, it is of interest that the children learn not-nice and scary words much faster and more permanently than even the nice words they themselves selected to learn. These not-so-nice words are what they wish to read and write when given a chance because in doing so they can express important feelings which adults wish them not to have—that is, feelings they wish the child to deny and repress. This can also be seen from what youngsters write on their own surreptitiously, on the walls of public and semi-public places such as toilets. They put these words on walls not just because they are not permitted to read and write them in more respectable places; they do so also to assert their interests, but mostly to defy adults and affirm their wish to act independently, even contrary to what adults demand of them. It is this desire which may later explode into violent action.

To make a comparison between self-motivated and adult-imposed "normal" learning: although the children with whom we worked did not, like Rangi in *Spinster*, learn ten words in four minutes, one of our boys who had barely managed to learn four nice words in one day learned ten self-chosen angry words on the same day, including such difficult ones as *witch*, *tornado*, and *fighting*. This shows that the wish to express and master what is important to us is a powerful motivating force for learning to read and understand a word and thus the phenomenon to which it refers, pleasant or not. Learning about the world's and our own biggest and most pressing problems and how to cope with them very much includes learning about our emotions, including violence: what it is really like, what causes it, what are its (deplorable) consequences, and how these may be avoided. Denial and repression will do no good; mastery through understanding is still the best way to equip our children for dealing with their own difficult and disruptive emotions, among which their violent tendencies are those creating the most severe problems for themselves and society. But so far we have failed to tame violence successfully.

A British physicist who has speculated about the next development in man came to the conclusion that only when we fail to succeed in our actions do we take recourse to finding solutions in thought.[9] He writes: "Thought is born of failure. Only when action fails to satisfy human need is there ground for thought. To devote attention to any problem is to confess a lack of adjustment which we must stop to consider. And the greater the failure the more searching is the kind of thought which is necessary."

Freud spoke of thought as the uniquely human ability to engage in actions with the least expenditure of energy, and with the smallest risk possible.

Instead of simply condemning violence we should think very seriously about it from an early age on and all through life: about what causes violence in ourselves and in others; what could be done to prevent these causes from occurring, or from resulting in violent actions; how the energy aroused by stimuli which evoke violent feelings could be channeled into constructive behavior; and if none of this should be possible, how violence could be controlled in ways which

---

[9] L. L. Whyte, *The Next Development in Man* (New York: New American Library, 1950).

do not bring about a renewed desire to commit violence. This would require our truly accepting that the propensity to act violently is part of our nature. But since it is the part which can and still does cause untold troubles, we ought to devote most careful thought and planning to educate and refine, in short, to sublimate, those emotional energies which otherwise may explode into violence. Obviously such life-long education and sublimation is the opposite from simply insisting that violent tendencies should not be permitted to exist, or that the propensity to act violently is not universal; and from suppressing violent thoughts or fantasies out of the fear that these might break out in violent actions. If we relinquish the easy but ineffective solutions of denying or suppressing our violent tendencies, we may then learn to deal with them at all times rationally. If we do, then our failure in dealing with violence would be less, and we might learn to cope with violence in thought only; that is, with the smallest danger to ourselves and others.

Mental Health
and Urban Design

When considering problems of urban design as these relate to the mental health of inner-city dwellers in the U.S.A., many of whom are black, it may be permissible to begin with a Negro proverb out of West Africa which says, "There is no home that isn't twice as beautiful as the most beautiful city." To this I would like to add: provided that this home offers satisfaction in the present and the promise of an even better future to come.

Why talk of homes, when the problems posed here are the spatial arrangements prevailing in the inner city; how these affect the mental health of those living there, and how they could be improved to better the mental health of children growing up there? Because particularly in the case of children, mental health is created or destroyed in the home. The child's outlook on life is shaped by how he experiences his home, and what goes on in it. One might call this the human dimension in the design of the home. In the inner city, as everywhere else, it is the key element shaping our lives, and the measure of this critical dimension is not space but time—namely the future. The home environment must generate hope for the future, if the child is to grow up to be a mentally healthy adult.

To what extent does physical design affect the psychology of hope?

Much has been made of the fascinating findings on overcrowding and its consequences, as tested by the behavior of rats. These findings have been widely accepted as indicative of what overcrowding may be

MENTAL HEALTH AND URBAN DESIGN: This essay was written as a contribution to a symposium on "The Social Impact of Urban Design" which was published under the same title (Chicago: The University of Chicago Center for Policy Study, 1971). It appeared there as a chapter called "Mental Health in the Slums" (pp. 31–47). It is here reprinted with some additions and eliminations.

doing to men—that is, if they live like rats.[1] But while drawing parallels between animal behavior and human behavior is fascinating, it is also questionable; to arrive at conclusions about humans from such parallels is extremely dangerous.

Some biologists, foremost among them Huxley, have made the important point that while man is an exceedingly young species, and very much in evolution, he is no longer evolving in the zoological sense. No longer do our instincts or bodily organs evolve. Instead, unlike other animals, we perfect our tools, our machines, our thoughts, and our social organizations. Huxley is convinced, and so am I, that our next steps in evolution must be of a psycho-social nature, and part of what evolves must be our habitats. Rats create their habitats on the basis of instinctive behavior, not thought and planning. This is even more reason why city planners shouldn't look to rats to teach them lessons; and why any conclusions about man that are drawn, say, from rat behavior and how rats are affected by overcrowding are erroneous. While animals can react only by instinct, man, through organization and his social institutions, through planning and design, can do a great deal to counteract the devastating effects of overcrowding.

It is interesting to speculate about which animals man selects to study and learn from. One day dog eats dog; the next day he is man's best friend and epitomizes unselfish devotion. One day the wolf is the dangerous animal to be kept from our door; the next day it is a she-wolf who will nurse abandoned children.[2] One day monkeys do better with terry-covered wire mesh than with a mother; the next they cannot live without a real monkey for a companion.[3] One day too many animals in the pen kill each other off; the next it's their mutual cooperation in close living that assures their survival.

When I was young, entirely different animals were being studied

---

[1] John B. Calhoun, "A 'Behavioral Sink,'" in Eugene L. Bliss (ed.), *Roots of Behavior* (New York: Harper and Brothers, 1962), pp. 295–315, and "Population Density and Social Pathology," *Scientific American* 206 (February 1962), pp. 139–46.

[2] See "Persistence of a Myth," in *The Empty Fortress*.

[3] H. F. Harlow, "The Nature of Love," *American Psychologist* 12 (1958), pp. 673–85; H. F. Harlow and M. K. Harlow, "Social Deprivation in Monkeys," *Scientific American* 207, No. 5 (1962), pp. 136–46.

intensively; and the lessons their way of living seemed to teach humans about their own aroused just as much excitement then as is now stirred up by the study of overcrowding in rats, or among the Sika deer, or the sticklebacks.[4] At that time, what gave us pause were studies of the complex animal societies formed by ants, bees, or termites. We were very much taken with the marvelous communities these animals organized for themselves; how peacefully and well they lived with each other compared to man; how suitable for survival was the hierarchical order of the society in which they lived; how excellent was their social cooperation. In short, what we learned from these animals was how an appropriate social organization can assure the outstanding success of even the densest kind of crowded mass living.

Today we seem interested only in those animals, and those experimental conditions, which suggest that mass living, in and of itself, is insufferable. What impresses us is not what can be learned from animals that live peacefully together although crowded into the narrowest spaces, but the lessons to be learned from animals of the same species that fight viciously for territory when their living space becomes restricted—how they then engage in aggression against each other, neglect their young, or stop reproducing.

All this leaves one with the uneasy feeling that this or that animal is selected for study when the behavior of its particular species seems to support preconceived notions about human beings, while those animals whose behavior contradicts the same notions are paid no attention.

Hall, for example, in *The Hidden Dimension*, devotes about thirty pages to discussing what can be learned from animal behavior about crowding. He is aware that there are as many animals which cannot bear crowding as there are animals craving close mutual contact. But Hall dismisses the latter, which would seem pertinent if we want to know how animals can fare well despite terrible crowding, in less than a page. And he does this even though he recognizes that it is "possible to observe a basic dichotomy in the animal world. Some species hud-

---

[4] John J. Christian, with Vagn Flyger and David E. Davis, "Phenomena Associated with Population Density," *Proceedings, National Academy of Science* 47 (1961), pp. 428–49; K. Lorenz, *On Aggression* (New York: Harcourt, Brace and World, 1966); Niko Tinbergen, "The Curious Behavior of the Stickleback," *Scientific American* 187, No. 6 (December 1952), pp. 22–26.

dle together and require physical contact with each other [not just for their well-being, but for their survival]. Others completely avoid touching. No apparent logic governs the category in which a species falls. . . . Curiously enough closely related animals may belong to different categories. The Great Emperor penguin is a contact species. . . . The smaller Adelaide penguin is a non-contact species . . . it is somewhat less adaptable . . . than the Emperor, and its range is apparently more limited."[5]

So while Hall states that the non-contact animal is less adaptable —and man is certainly the most adaptable of all—he says nothing further about the adaptable Emperor penguin in his treatise, but goes on to discuss the behavior of the less adaptable non-contact species.

I find more apt for illustrating the human dilemma an animal metaphor in Schopenhauer, who once compared human beings, and the human condition, to two hedgehogs (but our porcupines will do as well) who are trying to survive a very cold winter. To avoid freezing to death they hole up in a cave. But since it's very cold, even in their cave, they seek warmth and comfort from each other by drawing close together. Unhappily, the closer they get to each other, the more they prick each other with their quills. So in disgust they draw far apart, to avoid pricking each other. But in doing so, they lose all the comfort and warmth they could give each other from their body heat, and again they risk dying from the cold. So they draw closer together again, until through this continual back-and-forth movement they eventually learn how to live with each other in optimal comfort and warmth.

The affluent society has changed all this. In the cave of the "porcupines" there is now central heating. The middle classes, remembering too well how they suffered from pinpricks when they tried to avoid freezing to death, have drawn far away from each other in their now well-appointed and well-heated caves. Each person has fled to his very own room, preferably with his own private bath.

Unfortunately our slum dwellers, at the opposite end of the scale, are still very crowded together and so they prick each other badly all the time. This is even less bearable for them today than it used to be,

[5] Edward T. Hall, *The Hidden Dimension* (New York: Doubleday and Company, Inc., 1966).

because they are all now aware that in our affluent society, over-crowding is no longer necessary or even common.

Before they moved to the big cities, many slum dwellers lived in small shacks. And as recently as colonial days, even the wealthy lived in confining quarters. But this was more bearable because the church, town meetings, and the pub all served as extensions of the social living which went on indoors, and the entire village was an extension of it outdoors.

As for the shack out in the country, the living sphere there was even larger and less limited; the entire landscape surrounding it was, in one's experience, part of where one lived. It invited physical and mental roaming. This outdoor space, which could be taken in by the person sitting on the doorstep or on the porch, seemed to center around the inhabitant.

In fact, so far we are not at all certain whether man is a contact or non-contact species. The hedgehog simile suggests that he holds an intermediate position, where too much or too little contact space is equally damaging. Too little, as in the slums, leads to defensive social isolation, anonymity, feelings of incompetence, anomie, even violence. Too much, as in some suburban homes, leads to physical isolation and provokes a different type of anomie, such as that of "hippies" who crowd together ten or more to a small room, trying to combat what they know is their desperate physical and emotional isolation.

I came to use the simile of the hedgehogs in my thinking, because it was confirmed by my experience with the kind of human and spatial arrangements which seem best for rehabilitating psychotic youngsters suffering from extremes of isolation. Contrary to what was widely advocated, we found that accommodations for six, seven, or eight such children, living and sleeping together in one sufficiently large room, worked much better than the customary one or two to a private room typical of private mental sanatoria. This is not comparable, however, to the hideous crowding of many into a single ward which is typical of our public mental institutions.[6]

Here, in my special field, we see duplicated the same errors that characterize both our private and public housing. In private housing

---

[6] Since this and the following remarks referring to the experience with spatial arrangements at the Orthogenic School were written, this topic has been dealt with much more extensively in *A Home for the Heart*.

there is often far too much living space for optimal contact; in public, far too little. Long before Chombart de Lauwe published his findings,[7] we had found that both too little and too much living space (*Lebensraum*) is equally destructive to human well-being. De Lauwe found that when the available space was below eight to ten square meters per person, it doubled the social and physical pathologies. But both types of pathology also increased (though less sharply) when the space available rose above fourteen square meters per person.

These data were derived from French living conditions, which are typically more crowded than American. At the Orthogenic School, we found that our youngsters need more living space than the French, and that about sixteen square meters per person is the ideal for them. But this is so only if, in addition to a "private" sphere, enough allowance is made for public meeting rooms (dining room, play and recreation room, gymnasium, outdoor play areas, etc.).

One institution decided to model itself on the image we had created, but tried to do better by allowing each patient about twice the living space. The result was that far from being drawn out of social isolation, each patient tended to seclude himself more within his spacious living area. Far too little interaction occurred, as each patient tended to "get lost" within his wide private circumference. Whether for this or other reasons, the institution decided a few years later to withdraw from long-term residential treatment and to concentrate on short-term and outpatient therapy instead.

Of course, floor space alone does not begin to tell the story. All depends on how the living spheres are spatially organized; whether or not they are so arranged as to invite use without any one activity crowding any other or becoming too isolated.

One thing we know about slum children is the great difficulties many of them encounter in school and later in life because their verbal capacities have not been properly developed. Their vocabularies are inadequate to meet easily and successfully the requirements of modern living. We also know they have not learned to converse and communicate freely and with pleasure on a wide variety of topics

---

[7] Paul Chombart de Lauwe, *Famille et habitation* (Paris: Editions du Centre national de la recherche scientifique, 1959), and "Le Milieu social et l'étude sociologique des cas individuels," *Informations Sociales* 2 (Paris, 1959), pp. 41–54.

because at home they were not talked to enough, or else they were merely screamed at or shut off. To think the thoughts we want such children to think and make their own requires bigger spaces for inter-action than are presently available to them and their parents. "Indi-viduals must have . . . considerable neutral ground between them. . . . In my house we were so near that we could not begin to hear."[8]

I don't know how large, exactly, the kitchen-living-dining room in public housing projects ought to be, but I do know that it will have to be much larger than that presently provided. This is even more true regarding the play space for children. It is in play, as Piaget has shown us, that one learns to obey in good spirit the rules of the game: that is, how to get along with others even if one has disagreements; to wait one's turn without getting restless; to accept temporary defeat because one knows that one will get another chance to succeed.

It is enjoyable play experiences that prepare one to later enjoy the give-and-take of social behavior and to conform to the rules govern-ing life in society. Thus it is another great deficiency in the rearing of many slum children that they have not learned how to play well. But children cannot learn to play in cramped quarters, particularly at a young age when they have to develop their locomotor skills. They must have sufficient unencumbered space to crawl, walk, and play.

In this respect, the often considerable spaces between the high-rises of our public and private housing projects are wasteful as far as living space for the inhabitants is concerned. These spaces do provide light and air for the living cubicles, but they are not extensions of indoor living spaces. The height of the buildings themselves, the dis-tance of these grassy plots from above, the insignificance of a person seen when looking down—these do little to invite the dweller above to amble out of his indoor confinement. Even if he does, he gets none of the feeling of being in the out-of-doors part of what still belongs to his personal world. These plazas or lawns are not experienced as belonging to oneself or one's community. They are at best con-veniences, at worst reminders of one's smallness; in neither case do they enrich one's experience of oneself. They completely fail to pro-vide a feeling of security and expansiveness; and this they could sup-ply, were the buildings and the spaces between them designed differently.

---

[8] H. D. Thoreau, *Walden.*

Occasionally I have seen, in these interstitial areas, what seemed like very attractive equipment: play sculptures, or benches and tables for adults who wished to have a bite outdoors, play cards or chess, or simply relax alone, or with family or friends. Walking about, I found them inviting, and wondered why they were so little used.

Then I observed some children's play there, and saw the same problem of proportion mentioned above. A child would climb up on one of these concrete animals, or up on the jungle gym, hoping, as children do, that from up there he could look down and survey the world, feeling elated to be so big and tall. But as his gaze met the high-rise and went upwards, he felt dwarfed on his perch. The very height of the building destroyed what the child strove for in his fantasy play. If even the tall trees are dwarfed by this building—his home—how much more is he, just a small boy. And soon the child would climb down, often leaving the playground itself. The area cheated him out of the heightened feeling of self he had been after, as it does the adults, for different reasons.

Even sand play seemed less attractive than usual in these places, for much the same reason. The young child gets tremendous satisfaction out of building castles in the sand which will tower over all his surroundings. But in these playgrounds, even the biggest sand tower is ridiculously small; it serves only to impress one even more with how hopeless it is to try to assert one's existence through one's personal achievements, vis-à-vis the buildings.

There are other important reasons why these outdoor spaces, which should be friendly expansions of the indoor living areas, are experienced as inimical territories. The child who plays in front of his home experiments with how safe it is to venture out into the world, while at the same time he continues to be protected by the security of the home. For this to occur, his mother should be easily able to survey what goes on where the child plays; his shout should bring her to his rescue in no time at all. A mother should be able to let her child venture out without anxiety because a simple call to him will return him to the safety and comfort of her closeness. That is how it ought to be, but things are exactly the opposite in these housing projects.

A mother looking out from the eighth- or tenth-floor window can barely make out what goes on down there; she certainly cannot hear it, what with the noise of the city. So she cannot feel secure about letting her child play outdoors. The child does not feel protected by the nearness of his parent, or by the feeling that his cry for help will be heard or answered. So what should be the experience of a safe and enjoyable venture into the outside world becomes an experience which only demonstrates the dangers and unfriendliness of the wider world, and how unprotected one is, exposed to all its vagaries. Thus playing outside his home, which should offer the child the experience that the world outside is a friendly one, permitting him to look forward with confidence to his future life in a widening world, does exactly the opposite: it impresses the child with the inimical nature of a world which begins at his doorstep.

A man's home is supposed to give him the feeling that there inside it, at least, he is the master. The high-rise, by its overpowering size, makes us feel puny and cheats us of the feeling of mastery a home should provide. It makes us want to assert our mastery in some other way.

So psychologically there are reasons why anger is vented against a building that so dwarfs man's existence. Young males particularly, unsure of their virility, express this anger, and they start by getting even with the building. By defiling it they try to imprint it with their superiority, but often things don't stop there. They are goaded to assert their virility by overpowering human beings too, to begin ridding themselves of all the feelings of smallness accumulated in the years spent growing up there. The vastness of the building also creates anonymity within it, and this is another reason to make oneself known in and out of the building by cowing others with violence.

The home, the community, and the school are the three centers of any child's life. School is the child's first experience with an institution created by society just to serve him so that he, in turn, will make his contribution to society. More than anything else, the school will shape the child's view of society and his behavior within it. If he remains anonymous there, in his first encounter with the wider world, the child will come to expect that this is how his life in society will unfold for him. But if in school he finds understanding, stability, security, and personal attention to his individuality, he will believe these will also be available to him in society, and he will strive for them.

All this is well known, but important to remember because spatial arrangements are part of how society speaks to the individual. To him, they represent society's view of him and all those who are expected to use them. Society supposedly creates its structures according to what it thinks will best serve their occupants.

But no more dismal view of man can be imagined than the one that seems to inspire our public school buildings. Unlike our public housing, public schools usually have well-designed entrance halls, but these, and possibly the auditoriums and libraries, are the limits of good architectural planning and design. These as showplaces in the building get all the architect's attention, but the place of learning— the classroom—gets none. Good design just seems to be absent when it comes to beauty, comfort, and the sense of purpose in the places where children are to learn, walk, and eat. In fact, the design of these public buildings seems to do more justice to traffic flow than to the needs and comfort of living human beings.

Consider the corridors in most of our schools. The first thing that strikes one is their appalling length. Our big schools, by their very size, rule out any chance for intimacy and defy the human dimension. No school should serve more than three to five hundred youngsters. Only an educational factory serves several thousand. And if anyone thinks that the largeness of our schools is justified by our having to educate so many children in ways that are economical, let me point out that it doesn't cost much more to build several schools of human dimensions than it does to build a few large factories of learning.

Cost differences would certainly be reduced by eliminating the salaries of many persons now needed to organize, run, and police our unwieldy schools. Communication between teachers is barely possible in these super-schools, so that large amounts of time and money have to be spent on writing, reproducing, and reading memoranda. Teacher turnover, the biggest single problem in education, would certainly be alleviated if teachers could once again consider themselves teachers instead of keepers of a welter of report sheets. No doubt the quality of teaching would also be vastly improved.

Schools should be designed so that all the classes a given child will attend—except for gym and a few labs—are located close together. If a corridor is needed, it should be used by two or three classes of roughly the same age level. Then the corridor could be their territory, part of their own familiar living space at school, decorated and arranged in ways appropriate to them, and partly *by* them. This common anteroom could then become a space for informality, for making friends.

Instead, modern high schools are planned so that, at set intervals several times a day, a few thousand pupils rush in every direction for five minutes. Instead of relaxing and socializing between classes for ten or fifteen minutes in *their* corridor, youngsters in the high schools merely jostle a horde of other youngsters, most of them essentially strangers to each other. They run like mad and arrive at their next class out of breath and out of sorts with each other and the school.

I do not wish to dwell on the vast and unnecessary expense involved in building and maintaining these corridors. After all, that's only money. But I am concerned because it is generally impossible to distinguish them from corridors in an office, a factory, or a jail. Certainly these corridors are long—generally much too long—and usually clean, and hopefully wide and light enough, but there it ends.

Yet corridors could educate and give the feeling that they were built as something for the children to enjoy, not to be funneled through. But these corridors are so structured as to compel us to hurry through them. We cannot tarry to enjoy momentary leisure, to let our thoughts wander as we stroll, to develop personal relations. This is what slum children need most to learn to do, and there is no place to do it in our schools.

To make matters worse, most school corridors double as locker rooms. Unfortunately, as far as design is concerned, no thought is given to these lockers, although they figure importantly in the lives of the students. This increases the impression that the architect-as-artist withdraws from the scene whenever direct basic human use is concerned. And the modern architect may have to do just this because success doesn't really seem to crown those who design for what feels good, but the opposite: those who design for show and looks alone.

We all know what we mean when we speak of a locker-room spirit. Now, it may not be a completely desirable spirit, but it does work—it makes for friendships. Yet in our schools we don't even give our students the locker rooms that might make for this spirit. As a result, the corridor is neither a place for informal encounters, which it could be, nor does it invite companionable walking, which it could do. In most schools it is a causeway where our future citizens learn that life in our society is, if not a rat race, at least a corridor race.

I single out corridors and locker space because they, much more than the classroom or the library, tell the child in silent language about the spirit and intention of the school, and thus those of the society that built it for him. After all, the classroom and the library were built for what the school wants of the child: that he should learn. Therefore these speak most of what we want of the child and much less of what we want *for* him. The other places—the corridors, the locker space, the lunchroom—are not for learning, but belong to the social life of the child. Yet if the good life does not begin at school, few children will believe that school is meant to help them reach the good life.

The slum child especially has little hope for the future. The promises we make about what the future will hold for him if he does well in school are revealed as empty promises by the school building itself, if not as out-and-out lies by which we try to seduce him to do right now what we want him to do. Only what makes life good for him right now will make the school acceptable—even desirable, if we do the job well.

If it were not bad enough to herd children through the school corridors, we do the same in the lunchroom. Eating together is the greatest socializing experience in life, beginning with the infant's earliest relations when he is fed by his mother. Family members who have been dispersed throughout the day return at sundown to eat and visit together. When youngsters congregate to have a good time, they eat and drink as they talk a mile a minute. As adults, if we want to honor someone or to get to know him more than casually, we invite him to dinner. Serving our friends good food and drink makes for good spirit; those we break bread with are never quite strangers again. We also know that too much confusion or clatter interferes with the sociability and friendship that might otherwise develop during eating experiences. We expect to enjoy ourselves when we eat, and we get angry when our meal is too much disturbed.

The cafeteria is the place where children could and should socialize; this, if anywhere, is where they could come to feel attachment for their school and their friends. But compare this potential with the actual situation: typically, the cafeteria is much too large a room, seating far too many youngsters at one time. If our public housing units are poorly designed machines for living and our schools are factories for learning, these cafeterias are but feeding machines of the worst type. Scant architectural attention has been paid to the possibility of breaking the one huge room into many small ones, each with its own individual stamp. Not only are these rooms huge, but virtually no effort has been made to decorate them or otherwise lend appeal.

The long counters, the dismally arranged tables, the prison-like seating arrangements—all testify to a total lack of ingenuity in planning. The chaos and noise are unbearable unless rigid discipline is clamped down. Here, where children should be freest to interact, they are most severely regimented. Instead of enjoying their meal they have to gulp it down; instead of enjoying each other they spend their time fighting against noise, haste, and crowded seating arrangements.

No wonder, as all school administrators know, one of the biggest school problems is keeping order in the cafeteria. What makes it all the more offensive is that the middle-class teacher eats not with the inner-city child, but with other teachers in their own lunchroom. This proves again to the inner-city child that the school and the teacher are not there for him, but that he is there for them, to be manipulated as they see fit. He is again part of the masses, badly crowded together, while spacious arrangements and unhurried eating are only for his betters.

Therein lies the essence of my complaint. All of this reinforces an outlook on life that the slum child acquires long before he enters school: that life in our society for him is nothing but a long series of miseries, of dog-eat-dog, of nobody caring about anybody else.

There are many other things wrong with our school buildings. The toilets are degrading, for example, and they induce sexual acting-out or the taking of drugs. But there are a few more things to be noted about the most critical of buildings, the child's home.

We all know that the basic personality is formed in infancy and childhood. But in our huge public housing projects today, as in our slum buildings, even the best parent cannot shelter his preschool child against the traumatization coming from his surroundings, short of locking him into the apartment. The traumas children are exposed to in these huge housing projects or in slums are so severe that one can only wonder that the children do not later, as adolescents and grown-ups, suffer even severer pathology than they actually do.

The parents of children living in the slums or public housing are not only poor, but most of them—partly through a process of self-selection and partly through rejection by society—are the lame ducks, the left-behinds, the emotionally sick and disturbed. The reason is that all those with a healthy ego strength have more vitality and manage to move out, since they do not want to live in such conditions. For the most part, only the weakest and most disturbed members of the group remain living there for any length of time.

The result is that the child, from an early age on, even if he or his own family is sound, is nevertheless a witness at close quarters to events traumatic in terms of his personality development: desertions; fights within families; physical assaults—even mutilations; criminality; gang warfare; all types of sexual perversion; and dope addiction and its consequences. All this and more goes on daily in slums and most public housing projects.

Since this child has nowhere else to go, he has to watch in terror when the ambulance carries out the slashed and the dead; and when the policeman comes, handcuffs the man next door, and drags him out. These are his introductions to society, made before he comes to school—though one's first experience with what society can offer should make one feel protected. Unfortunately, the small child in this situation does not usually get correct information, so that not even the ambulance symbolizes help. On the contrary, it is just something from the frightening outside world that takes people away. But if this outside is an enemy, neither is there any safety inside, with its shootings and switchblades, with the drunks and the dope pushers and the addicts.

Even the inanimate offers little enough comfort on the inside. The cinder-block walls in the apartments of public housing projects, while sturdy, prevent any decent display of things on the walls to individualize living, nor do they permit any hanging of shelves where floor space is already at a premium. The absence of lockable closets and cabinets means it is not possible to place poisonous substances or dangerous implements out of children's reach. All this makes for more screaming at children, for further danger, aggravation, and grief.

The overcrowding in the slum, the arrangement of many apartments along a narrow corridor in much of public housing, the thin walls—all these prevent even the best of parents from really sheltering their children. There are so many children on one corridor of one building that it automatically leads to a jungle-like organization of the children among themselves, where the bigger ones terrorize the little ones. There is so much chaos, so much frightening noise, bad smell, and filth—in short so many overwhelming and chaotic experiences—

that all the growing child's energy goes into just warding these off, into an anxious watching and fighting for sheer survival. Hardly any energy is left him for building his personality along more constructive lines. Even watching the deterioration of the building—at least the public housing was clean and good-smelling when he moved in—and seeing it getting worse step by step gives the child the feeling that life, as it moves on, just gets worse.

Here, the slum school is no help. On the contrary, it reinforces the conviction of a slow deterioration everywhere. Often when the school year begins, both the school building and the classrooms are well organized, good-smelling; everything is in good order, and clean. The children, too, begin the academic year accordingly: clean and nicely dressed. But as the school year wears on, the building, the classrooms, and particularly the toilets are more and more neglected. So often is the physical appearance of many children. Thus, the school, which more than any institution tells the child what society is all about, reinforces the slow erosion of any hopeful anticipation of a better future. Most of the children simply go on learning how to survive in the slum, rather than enjoying exposure to a different way of life that would get them out of it.

If the school is part of the housing project itself, this is more of a hindrance than a help. While it is good to have the school within walking distance, even this normally good spatial relation turns sour for the slum child. When the school is located within the project, it means that the child never escapes the devastating and depressing atmosphere of his particular sub-community or society. With slum life so marked by the bullying and extortion of younger children by older ones, school also means that the child never escapes the bullies who threaten him if he doesn't comply, whether it is money that is demanded, or joining the delinquent gang, or sexual submission.

Once school is over, the younger children don't dare use the playground or its equipment, because they would only be pushed away or beaten up by older children. Typically, playground equipment is destroyed for want of supervision by experienced group workers, who are badly needed. It is incredible how terrified the little children are of the older ones because of their continuous experience of being bullied, pushed around, and having their toys taken away from the earliest age on. The only thing such children can look forward to is getting older, so that they can then bully or extort in turn from the younger ones. In class they cannot pay attention to the teaching or learning because for their survival they must pay attention to their gang leader's plans, and what the rival gang is up to.

Yet nothing I have described up to now can begin to compare with the heritage of despair that surrounds these children. The dwellings are such an accumulation of poor, disturbed, utterly desperate people that the general attitude gives the children an indelible image of utter hopelessness. Except for the most fortunate and sturdy, defeat is assumed from the start.

It is not the crowding per se, but the inner climate in the slums and housing projects that makes them human sinks inviting comparison to rats' nests under forced, overcrowded conditions. It is not even the way these people are crowded together (bad as it is) that contributes most towards hopelessness, anomie, violence, and crime. Most important is the absence of the inner feeling that one is working toward a goal. One of the worst features of the resulting defeatism is the widespread attitude that there is nothing the slum inhabitant can do. It is a fatalistic attitude according to which even self-generated events are ascribed to chance. For example, if someone gets burned, it is not regarded as a matter of carelessness that could be prevented next time, but as just a piece of bad luck, chalked up to fate. So also with the shootings, the arrests, the desertions, and all other happenings of life. But good things, too, are regarded thus. Success is not ascribed to effort or determination; it is again luck, this time good luck. This attitude shows up most clearly in the inability of project inhabitants to organize themselves for improving the building or the spaces around it.

It takes quite a bit of hard work, for example, for the inhabitants of one corridor to consistently keep it in order. It is as if they planned to agree with the animal experimenters who show that overcrowded rats cannot keep their nests clean. However, rats cannot get together, talk things over, and plan for the improvement of conditions they suffer in common.

The reason behind project dwellers' failure to act is the feeling that the project is not a home, but a trap. Contrary to the spirit of the saying that any home is more beautiful than the most beautiful of cities, beautifying a trap just emphasizes that that's what it is. Or, as one author put it, "Harlem is ugly, rotten, decaying, just because it wants to be ugly, rotten. . . . To paint the store fronts, to wash the windows, to plant flowers, to sweep the sidewalks, to wash the stoops would mean an acceptance of Harlem as home. The Negroes I knew in Harlem didn't think of Harlem as home but as a trap."[9]

And so the slum or public housing unit, as it now exists, cannot be a home for children to grow up and out of, but a trap they and their parents want to tear down and destroy. What they cannot accept or realize is that it is their thinking of the building as a trap that makes it one.

People have lived in ghettos much worse and much more crowded than most of our slums. Certainly the Jewish quarters of Europe, such as, for example, the one in Venice from which all got their name, were much more crowded, poorer in living space and facilities, and more inescapable than even our worst slums of today. To use some random examples: the Jewish ghetto in Cologne was the narrowest street in town; it was even called the "Narrow Street." In the Frankfort ghetto 4,000 persons lived in one short gloomy street, twelve feet wide, where the roofs of the small houses met at the top, making for gloomy darkness all day. In some cities the brothels were placed in the one small street in which Jews were permitted to live, to add to their ill repute. In the infamous Roman ghetto, at times as many as 10,000 inhabitants were herded into a space smaller than one square kilometer. In nearly all ghettos several families often had to occupy the same room.

Nevertheless, all this had no serious moral consequences. The purity of family life was a successful antidote to what otherwise would have been poisonous conditions. The method used by the leaders of the community to prevent demoralization was to impose ever more stringent laws governing ever more aspects of life in ever greater detail. This forestalled the ill effects that the worsening of external conditions might otherwise have had on the life which went on in the ghettos. It is a prime example of how through better organization human beings can prevent the external conditions of their lives from causing them to deteriorate as persons.

Although the living conditions were nearly always desperate in these ghettos, they were never devoid of hope or pride. An incredible amount of effort went into the most careful organization and regula-

---

[9] Julius Horwitz, *The Inhabitants* (New York: The New American Library, 1960).

tion of all aspects of ghetto life, to prevent the inhabitants from deteriorating into the hopeless despair that makes for a slum existence. It required particular skills in living, special family conditions, but most of all a tight communal organization.[10]

I believe our slums could be rehabilitated. But it would take infinitely greater efforts, a much longer time, and might even be more expensive than simply providing our slum dwellers with the type of spatial arrangements that would greatly facilitate their escape from their present psychology of despair.

In our worst slums, there are those who have not given up hope, either for themselves or their children. There are those who wash their windows, no matter what they see through them; who do not accept their dwelling unit as a trap, but try to make it a home; who still hope that if they themselves cannot escape, their children will.

It takes the death of hope to imbue children with the feeling of "What's the use?" And hopelessness on the part of the parent makes for pathology in the slums, just as it can in the suburbs. Conversely, wherever a group living on one corridor does get together to clean and maintain it for a while, it is a great reassurance to them and their children that not everything "just happens," that it is not beyond their own power to improve their own lot.

I do not minimize the extent to which the deterioration of buildings results from lack of proper upkeep by absentee landlords, from inadequate garbage collection, and so forth. But I think that unless the inhabitants themselves also work to improve their own living conditions, no amount of maintenance is going to change their children's outlook on life. As long as the children are young this miasma of despair is inescapable. By the time children are old enough to ride away from their project alone on a bus it is too late. By then, the basic conviction that everything is fate and that fate is against them is so ingrained that for most, it is too late to reverse this attitude toward life.

The spatial needs of the child of the ghetto are what all children need: space where he can roam and play safely and a home that can truly protect him from the dangers surrounding his personal world. If

---

[10] For the conditions in the Jewish ghettos, and the organized counter-measures of the communities, see, for example, Israel Abrahams, *Jewish Life in the Middle Ages* (New York: Meridian Books, 1958).

we want to open the ghetto child to all the hopes of a middle-class existence, we must give him from the start the place where the middle-class existence begins: a home that's his own.

In Chicago there is a rather old housing project which avoided practically all the pitfalls referred to above. Apparently it gave dwellers exactly what they wanted most: something like a house of their own. It is called the Altgelt Gardens, and each dwelling—the larger ones in the form of duplexes—has a direct entrance from and exit to the outside. Each family can mingle with or insulate itself from its neighbors as it wishes. It is therefore a housing project in which true family life can and does develop; so much so that by now some of the children who grew up there have chosen to live there as married people.

This project is very successful by comparison to many others, because at least it gives the ghetto dweller something like a place of his own. But it does not, in fact, belong to the dweller, and therefore only partially succeeds. It looks like a home of one's own, but one does not in fact own it. To that degree it does not nourish the sense of hope which can best erase the fatalism of despair.

Given these considerations, I cannot fathom why there is such concern about how cheaply per square foot our public housing can be erected. I find it impossible to convince architects, much less boards of directors, that to make economy the central issue in such buildings is the silliest consideration of all. I always tell them that if they want to save money, they should not erect such buildings at all. To build them cheaply just means that they will never achieve their purpose, and if that is so, why build them at all? But they *are* built, and then prove unworkable. They change nothing in the mental condition of our inner-city dwellers. The building is soon abused and the children are no different than before. All this makes me sometimes feel that our public housing for the inner city is built to make sure we perpetuate the inner city by perpetuating the conditions that made for inner-city problems.

To review intelligently the economics of public housing, I would have to discuss the psychology surrounding public housing, and this is a subject all by itself. So let me use a suggestive example. During the last few years we have heard a lot about the long hot summers, what they do to slum dwellers, and what they are apt to do, because of the heat, to communities. But still, we do not air-condition our public housing, though we do that in all newly built private apartment buildings, including much student housing. A careful cost analysis might prove that given expenses for police, riot damage, and the cost of arrest and trial, it wouldn't be more expensive to air-condition these buildings. Then, on a hot summer night, everyone would be cool, comfortable, and fairly contented at home. What I am sure of is that if we could assign a negative dollar value to human misery and a positive one to human comfort and a satisfying life, then not to air-condition these buildings would be penny-foolish.

Psychoanalysis has taught us that our first enclosure, the home, is experienced as a symbolic mother. Like the real one, it can be good or overpowering; one that envelops us with comfort and security, or rejects us with neglect and indifference. The weaker we feel as individual persons in society at large, the more profoundly we must know we are welcome and safe in our home.

As long as the child can run home to mother, slam the door shut on this fearful outer world, and be safely at home, he will know he has a place in this world. While the safely middle-class family can manage successfully in an apartment, because of its built-in sense of hope for the future, the ghetto dweller, more than anyone, needs a place of his very own to have and to hold, so that he finally comes into his own.

Private houses require a down payment and monthly installments, so that they are so far open only to former ghetto dwellers of the lower middle class. But we must make them available to the poorest segments of our population. If we do, if we give them the right surroundings and public facilities, we shall indeed have given the children of ghetto dwellers the right spatial distance from horror and the right spatial closeness to hope.

Growing Up Female

In the sixteen years since this essay was first published—it was written a few years earlier—the problems it deals with have become, if anything, more acute. Greater numbers of women are now working. They have made significant strides toward achieving social, economic, and occupational equality with males, and women now more frequently hold positions of considerable importance and prestige. With all this, women have gained much more independence—but they have had to pay a price for it.

An increasing number of marriages now end in divorce, and many more women are having to raise their children without the help of a husband—in general, the number of single parents has jumped significantly in the last decade or so. While women have made great progress towards sexual equality and have achieved considerably greater sexual freedom, this has not necessarily made for greater enjoyment of sex; sexual freedom does not seem to offer deeper and more lasting emotional satisfactions than a good marriage.

The achievements of the women's movement have led to severe identity confusion among many women. The change in social roles women fulfill in society and the home, and changes in their views of themselves and of their relations to males, have led to parallel and equally widespread identity confusion among males regarding their relations to females and their sexual role. All this has made social and sexual relations more problematic for both females and males.

While a traditionally ordered society tightly shackled both females and males to narrowly defined social and sexual roles, society thus provided people with certainty regarding their identities. A few always revolted against being forced to live a life contrary to their desires and suffered, or were made to suffer, for it. But the vast majority had neither the strength

GROWING UP FEMALE: This essay, which appeared originally in *Harper's* 225 (October 1962), pp. 120–28, is here reprinted with some editorial changes.

nor the opportunity to revolt, and so they more or less accepted and settled into the roles which society decreed. Where there is no doubt, there is also little insecurity. While such tightly regulated social and sexual roles did not permit much freedom or individuality, there was also little need for developing a strong personal identity; identity was settled at the moment of birth.

The historical role for each sex allowed only restricted satisfactions. But as long as nothing better was thought possible, and religion sanctioned these roles, it was easier to make one's peace with the considerable deprivations they imposed, even when there was little satisfaction in sex or the relations to one's partner.

With the breaking down of ancient customs and traditional sex-related traits, and the new freedom to be oneself in whatever way one wishes, comes the difficult task of achieving personal identity, and the related task of gaining autonomy. This is what a technologically advanced society requires of one, if we are not to risk eventually being forced back into rigid patterns of living by a totalitarian system.

The externals of women's lives have changed since this article was written, and so have the externals of male attitudes towards females. Therefore some of what is said here about external arrangements in women's lives no longer applies to the same degree. But the internal difficulties of achieving a secure personal and sexual identity have, if anything, become even more of a problem. Persons who have not achieved a secure identity for themselves cannot provide each other with those complementary experiences that make for a happy marital relationship. Although in many more cases both partners in a marriage now have an independent life in society, this has not necessarily made it easier for them to be happier with each other.

The greatest happiness in marriage can come about only when true independence as socially equal human beings is enriched and made continually fascinating and satisfying for both partners by their being sexually completely secure with each other. This security is based on a complementary attraction, enriched by the specific differences in personality and sexual experiences that come from one partner being female, and the other male.

In the last analysis, it is very difficult to attain one's full identity as a person all by oneself, as in a vacuum—one must relate to others. I believe that the essence of a healthy heterosexual identity requires that it be proven again and again by the depth of satisfaction that a relation which is close emotionally and completely gratifying sexually provides when the particular *female qualities bring out the best in the male; and simultaneously the particular male qualities bring out the best in the female.*

By what models is a modern girl to measure herself in her growth? Many a psychologist or educator today will find few questions more recurrent or troubling than this one. On every side one encounters growing girls and educated women who seem to have followed out the respected modern formulas: they have "done well" at school, at finding jobs, at finding husbands, at running homes, at planning activities of all sorts. And yet they remain, as Veblen put it, "touched with a sense of grievance too vivid to put them at rest." They are frequently baffled by this and so, unhappily, are some of the psychologists they consult. In trying to help women—to "accept the womanly role," for example—counselors often seem to aggravate the grievance, rather than cure it.

What I shall try to show in this article is that the grievance is very real and justified, although it is barely understood. The ways in which we bring up girls in America, and the goals we set for them, are so strangely—and often painfully—contradictory that it is only too predictable that their expectations of love and work and marriage should frequently be confused, and that deep satisfactions should elude them. Very few human problems have been so transformed by the convulsive growth and evolution of modern society as those of women; but the parents and psychologists and educators who guide young women today have scarcely begun to inquire into what a modern and satisfying female life might really be.

Many of women's special difficulties spring from the distorted images of females that preoccupy so many men. Freud was probably right in thinking that the male infant's overattachment to his mother projects him into a continuing emotional predicament that is peculiarly difficult for most men to solve, and often warps the demands they make on women. Bound emotionally to the infantile image of his mother as unassailably pure, a man may seek out a superior woman he can worship. Or, trying to break the infantile bond, he may choose a woman who appears inferior to himself. The different kinds of emotional balm men seek from women are as various as their frustrations when they do not find it. But the female who needs and wants a man—and all normal women do—is often placed in a sadly absurd position: she must shape herself to please a complex male image of what she should be like—but alas, it is often an image having little to do with her own real desires or potentialities; these may well be increasingly stunted or concealed as she grows into womanhood.

Such irrational demands on women are nothing new, as we can learn from the Bible. In the purely psychological sphere, relations between the sexes have always been difficult. But we often forget that until the modern industrial era, the great majority of people had little time or energy to devote to purely emotional "satisfactions" and "relationships." Life was still taken up with the basic necessities of food, clothing, and shelter. To secure them, most men and women and their children worked extremely hard—and often worked together—in their homes and shops and fields. If the family was to survive and prosper, the women and girls simply had to do their heavy share, and this earned them a certain respect. It would seem from the available evidence that enough good feeling existed between the sexes to make their emotional difficulties manageable—especially if sex as such was satisfying. What we call "psychological satisfactions" today was frosting on the cake—the cake of economic survival and simple sex.

Now the technological revolution has brought us to precisely the opposite situation. Many women no longer need be bound to men by economic necessity; they rarely share any work with their husbands, and their time is often their own. Women are at last reaching that stage where they can shape their personal relations the way they choose. What choices are they making, and how successful are they?

Most women claim to base their personal relations on what they conceive to be "love"—on "emotional satisfaction." In this, they are clearly the children of modern technology and the easy life it brings. So too is psychoanalysis itself, which aims to make emotional satisfaction more possible. But now a savage paradox is slowly—all too slowly—dawning on the psychoanalysts and many of their female patients: it appears that relations entered into chiefly to gain psychological satisfaction more often than not end in psychological despair. "Love," as Saint-Exupéry put it, "does not consist in gazing at each other, but in looking outward in the same direction." For what kind of love, and what kind of life, are we preparing our girls today?

Paul Goodman has suggested that boys today are growing up in ways that he calls "absurd." But how much more absurd are the ways in which we raise our daughters! We tell them early that they are very different from little boys and give them dolls to play with rather than baseballs. But we also provide them, from kindergarten on through college, with exactly the same education given to boys—an education clearly designed to prepare boys for a life of competition and independent responsibility.

Consider the contradictions that are thrust upon the growing girl. For fifteen years or more she is officially encouraged to compete with boys in the schoolroom, to develop her mind and her initiative, to be second to none. She may study the same physics and history as her boy-friends, work part-time at jobs not too different from theirs, share many of the same political and social interests. And then our curious system insists she "fall in love" with a potential husband: she is, in fact, expected to enjoy giving up what she may have loved until then, and suddenly find deep fulfillment in taking care of a child, a home, a mate. Her life is to be filled with what are, to her husband, after-hours occupations, and the training of her youth is seemingly intended to fall away like an afterbirth. After years of apparent equality, it is made clear that males are more equal, and most females resent this, as they should. Our educational system has ostensibly prepared them for a kind of liberated marital and occupational life that in fact rarely exists in our society; at the same time it celebrates the values of an antiquated form of marriage inherited from a time when women were prepared for little else.

If many girls seem to accept these hypocrisies calmly, perhaps it is because they have been made aware, quite early in the game, that their role in society will in fact be very different from that of the boys sitting next to them in the classroom. The boys have no doubt that their schooling is intended to help them succeed in their mature life, to enable them to accomplish something in the outside world. But the girl is made to feel that she must undergo precisely the same training only because she may need it if she is a failure—an unfortunate who somehow cannot gain admission to the haven of marriage and motherhood where she properly belongs.

Actually, the gravest damage is done long before this. The little girl's first storybooks and primers, for example, hardly ever show a woman as working or active outside the home. It makes no difference that many millions of American children under twelve have full-time working mothers. A little girl is expected to shape herself in the image of the maternal housekeeper of these ridiculous primer stories, and never mind what certain unfortunate mothers may be obliged to do. As if to emphasize society's ambivalence, this image of the stay-at-home is usually presented by a female teacher, who may well be a working mother, a contradiction that is not lost on the little girl and tends to teach her that she will have to live a life of contradictions. In these early years, it is rare indeed for girls to hear the slightest suggestion that they might one day do the interesting work of this world quite as well as many men, or even better.

It is little wonder then that as adolescence approaches, many girls are already convinced that what really counts is not any commitment to their studies—although they may be conscientious about them—but their ability to carry on social, emotional, and sexual relations that will make them popular and ultimately attract the right boys. Here matters are made more difficult by the fact that young girls tend to mature faster physically and emotionally than boys, although the boys may do better academically.

The girls soon perceive that they are ahead of the boys in the maturity and sophistication of their desires. The boys seem more childish, less grown up, less certain about their ability to cope with the other sex. What is more, the boys often come from homes where Mother knows best, and they find themselves ruled by female teachers who day after day impress upon them their authority and competence. In this situation it is not easy for a boy to gain confidence in his maleness, to say the least. (Later on, of course, both sexes are exposed to male teachers in high school and college, but by then it is often too late to undo the damage.)[1]

The high school and college girl must face a frequently awful predicament. She—and usually her mother also—feels she must be popular with boys. To get the dates she wants, the girl must try to reassure the boys that they are really superior to her; but deep down

---

[1] Many boys drop out of school before they meet with many male teachers; in order to protect their own male image, they reject this continuing domination by females. Similarly, the aggressive delinquency which gets boys into trouble is often no more than a desperate attempt to assert their maleness. Since the girls in school are often more mature socially and sexually, the boys find that they can clearly assert male superiority in school only through aggressive and competitive sports. Having learned this, they choose aggressive ways to prove themselves male when outside the school.

she cannot believe in this pretense, and she may well resent the necessity for it. Once she has gained the ultimate objective and is safely married, she will, as likely as not, drop the mask and begin to assert in her home what she is convinced is a superior maturity. By then, however, it may no longer exist, for boys typically catch up with girls in this respect during their mid-twenties. And in the meantime the boys are generally given a good deal more freedom to experiment—to "sow their wild oats."

A good many young men, for example, may skirt marriage until they are into their thirties; they are allowed to go their own way, suffering no more than a mild nagging and some teasing from their friends. It is tacitly acknowledged that they need more time to find themselves in their work before they settle down, and they remain popular in both married and unmarried circles. Such men are considered failures only when they cannot support themselves, or make headway in their careers. By contrast, the situation of an unmarried young woman is altogether different, often cruelly so. No matter how gifted she may be in her work—or how brilliantly she has put her education to use—a woman bears a suspicion of failure if she does not marry young.

Indeed, the pressures upon the young girl to marry safely and quickly may seem inexorable just when she is trying to embark on her own path; and these pressures are exerted in ways unfamiliar to boys. During his first years at college, for example, a boy is likely to undergo a "crisis of identity," exposed as he is to conflicting new ideas and ways of acting, and given chances to experiment. As a junior or senior, however, he may start to find himself through serious academic work. A girl may undergo a parallel experience, only to discover that her new dedication to scholarship may rule her out of the marriage market. Fearing that her single-minded absorption will allow her chances to slip by, she stops dead in her tracks; or worse, she cannot make up her mind about what she wants, and she may suffer a college-girl "breakdown."

Nor does this happen only in college. Many a girl emerges from high school with a vague feeling that she can, she should make something of herself. But everyone around her insists that she will find fulfillment through marriage—and her friends are getting married. So she buckles down to a brief course in beauty culture or secretarial work. Later, as the wife of a clerk or skilled worker, she is as restless and bewildered as the college girl who gave up an interest that was becoming "too absorbing," so that she could marry off into the suburbs. Neither girl can quite understand what has gone wrong—she is, after all, an undoubted success in the eyes of others.

And what in fact has gone wrong? What happens when the young bride at last enters the home she has been taught to think of as her true domain? In truth, she may find that the much-touted labors and pleasures of the hearth are among the sad delusions of our times. For if it is hard for male youth nowadays to find meaningful work, as Paul Goodman has argued, the fate of the homebound wife is surely harder.

Of course, modern labor-saving devices have abolished most of the backbreaking housework of the past—and good riddance; but at the same time they are doing away with the real satisfactions this work once yielded. Using her husband's money to buy machine-made clothes for her family involves no unique or essential labors on a woman's part. Much the same can be said about cooking with prepackaged ingredients. What remain, apart from child-rearing, are the most stultifying mechanical tasks—dusting, making beds, washing, and picking up. And beyond these lie chiefly the petty refinements of "homemaking"—what Veblen described as the occupation of ceremonial futility.

The very people who sell women products for the home are shrewdly aware of this futility. A study by the sociologist Florence Kluckhohn has shown that advertising aimed at the housewife often subtly describes the home as a kind of penal colony from which she should escape as quickly and for as long as possible. Typically, an ad for an automatic stove shows a woman putting on her hat, leaving, and coming back hours later to find the dinner all cooked. The advertiser, as Mrs. Kluckhohn points out, does not say where the woman has been; just to get away, it is implied, is a blessing.

Since work around the house is often less than interesting, children are the natural target for the young wife's energies. Here, at least, she feels considerably more sophisticated than her mother. After all, she has had extensive schooling, and has perhaps worked briefly at a demanding job, and motherhood has been depicted to her as another tremendous and enlarging experience—the climax, somehow, to all that has gone before. Yet, in fact, the care of an infant forces a woman to give up most of her old interests, and unless she is fascinated by the minute developments of the baby, she seldom finds that any new and different enrichment has entered her life to replace her relinquished satisfactions.

This impoverishment is particularly acute when a woman has her first child. Later on, the concerns of her older children may enliven her days while she cares for a newcomer. Then, as the time for nurturing babies and taking care of small children passes, many middle-class mothers come to find existence empty without small children to care for. Reluctant to return to the outer world—or lacking confidence in her ability to do so—the housewife must find something to occupy her which seems vital and demanding of her concentration, so she continues to devote herself to her children.

Things change when children become of school age—and change once again when they are in their teens. Schoolchildren certainly need a mother, but they actually need far less of her than she may devote to them. Chauffeuring children around the suburbs, for example, takes time and requires someone who drives a car, but this person need not be a mother. The children themselves would prefer to be free of arranged rides and the tight scheduling this imposes. The same goes for arranging children's social life, which again they would much prefer to do themselves.

Of course the professed concern of many mothers is to watch over their children's educational life, and help them with their problems in growing up. But in these things, too, the children would often rather be on their own, except for those occasional crises when the parents are needed for support. And sadly enough, the modern mother is often in a poor position to give support when her child is doing badly in school or is not very popular or feels defeated. Having invested so much emotionally in her child's achievement, a mother's pride suffers at his failure and as likely as not, she administers a bawling-out when understanding and compassion are needed. Thus she may fail as a mother because her inner needs make her work at it too hard. The children of women who do interesting work of their own during the day often find more sensible and sympathetic mothers to help them with their studies and problems in the evening. On the other hand, the mother who urges her girl on toward intellectual achievement while staying at home herself poses a contradiction that is probably not lost on the girl.

When motherhood does not bring satisfaction, the woman turns to her husband with the demand, spoken or unspoken, that he somehow make up to her for what she is missing in life. She waits for him to come home with word of the outside world and its events. At the same time, she may work hard at being a wife, trying to advance her husband's career, plotting to get him ahead socially. But even if this sort of thing works, he may resent it—it will not be his success, but hers.

Sometimes a wife will spend her husband's money heedlessly and push him to achieve higher earnings and status, blindly demanding things to make up for her empty feelings about her life. Other wives simply nag, or they repress their resentment altogether and accept the prospect of a stultifying life. The husband begins in turn to resent his nagging wife and even his family life; or he may resent his wife for her passive dreariness. In either case both suffer, often without in the least knowing why. Living with such parents, a growing girl may well absorb and keep for life a distorted view of what a man is for, and how he can be used.

No doubt it will be argued that there is more to a modern woman's life than this—that labor-saving devices have so freed housewives from their chores that they can undertake useful and interesting activities of all sorts without actually taking jobs. Such claims seem questionable. Undeniably, a good many housewives do find time for activities outside the home, but all too often the activities themselves are really frivolous or makework, creating futile and unrewarding experiences. Such activities often include gardening—which has replaced the conspicuous embroidery of an earlier age—or the ubiquitous bridge circle and country-club life. There are also activities like the PTA, the League of Women Voters, and charity work which pass as "constructive" and "valuable." Close examination, however, reveals that these pursuits are often used to cover up a lack of really serious and interesting involvement. And according to a recent study, "Volunteer workers are increasingly being assigned to fund-raising or low level routine, from which little achievement satisfaction is possible."

To quote Veblen again, "Woman is endowed with her share—which there is reason to believe is more than an even share—of the instinct of workmanship, to which futility of life or of expenditure is obnoxious." When this impulse is denied expression, a woman feels that sense of grievance which runs like a vivid current through the lives of so many women today.

If the instincts for workmanship are widely frustrated in many modern women, this is even more true in regard to their sexual instincts. Of course, sexual difficulties are neither a recent curse of the young, nor limited to girls. But the way we prepare our children for sexual life has burdened girls far more than boys.

In Latin countries, as in many other lands, girls are prepared from early childhood to accept a yielding and passive role, not only in sexual relations, but in the life of the family, where the man traditionally dominates. But the American girl is raised in contradiction. On the one hand, she is told that to be feminine means to be yielding and courted, and that she must respect this norm. She certainly cannot, for example, ask a boy she likes for a date, nor can she pay the expenses when she goes out with him (although she may sometimes "go dutch"). She may feel most reluctant simply to call up a boy to talk with him, or to ask him to take a walk with her.

Yet at the same time today's young girl has been taught from childhood to think and act for herself; to strive for success, and compete equally with boys at school. What she has *not* been taught is that men and women are neither wholly similar, nor wholly opposite, but complementary. She has never been encouraged to quietly consider the ways in which she and the boys she knows are alike—the talents and aspirations they could build up together and the emotional needs they share—and the ways in which they are not alike, as in their sexual functions. As a result, the girl does not know where and when to be "feminine" and where and when to be "equal."

The adult world has led her to think that the "active woman" is somehow an unfeminine and sexually inadequate woman—something patently untrue. Women who strive to "wear the pants" do so for defensive and neurotic reasons, just as the very need to be dominant, whether in man or woman, is due to feelings of inferiority or to thwarted desires. But it is quite a different thing for a girl to do purposeful work, not because of some twisted drive, but because she wants to realize her own potentials. Unless we distinguish clearly between the two kinds of striving we stifle the healthy growth of girls by labeling natural ambition as unfeminine.

At the same time, girls are led into an equally dangerous misunderstanding about the sexual act itself. While men and women need not be so different in their personal aspirations as our society now pretends, they are different in the way they experience sex. Here much confusion was created by Wilhelm Reich and his rather too facile following among the intelligentsia; he led both partners to expect that they could and should have a parallel orgastic experience. Too often, a parallel experience is mistakenly thought to mean a similar if not identical experience; the emphasis upon the desirability of orgasm may lead to frustration in both man and woman.

This problem is very different in some societies, where modern technology has not affected the lives of women and their expectations. There it is still sufficient for a woman if her lover or husband enjoys sex with her. Since his enjoyment proves her a good woman, she too can enjoy herself; she does not worry whether she is frigid or torrid, and as likely as not she achieves total release. Since her lover is not obliged by any conscious code to provide her with an orgasm, he can enjoy himself, experience orgasm, and thus help her to feel fully satisfied herself.

In our own society, boys need as much as ever to have their virility attested to by their sexual partners; and girls have a parallel need. But today the boy wants his girl to prove him a man by her so-called orgastic experience, and the girl is even worse off. She not only has to prove him a man by making him experience orgasm; she must also prove her femininity by orgastic release or else fear she is frigid.

She is quite used to performing with males on equal grounds, but she has too little sense of how to complement them. She cannot suddenly learn this in bed. Trying to make sure that the man has an orgastic experience, and also wondering if they can have one themselves, many women become so worried that they truly experience little satisfaction, and end up pretending. Sexual intercourse cannot often bear the burden of *proving* so many things in addition to being enjoyable. It becomes another competition between man and woman: who can make whom have an orgastic experience. And the lovers cannot even enjoy their mutual desire or the forgetting of self in the act.

With both sex and household work often less than satisfying, it is not surprising that so many modern marriages turn sour, and that the phenomenon of homosexuality looms as importantly as it does today.

Many young wives soon realize that their husbands are neither willing nor able to complement them in their motherly tasks in any satisfying way. Resentful, in many cases, of her husband's fuller life, a young wife may nevertheless try to force him to share motherhood with her. But irrespective of whether or not he attempts to do so, and however hard she may try, a woman cannot find compensation in marriage itself for her own thwarted aspirations.

The results are often men who want women, but don't know what to do with them when they get them; and women who get men, but who are disappointed in them and in themselves when they live together. Mutually disappointed, it is natural that each sex should seek out its own as company; for only then can they really be themselves on a truly equal basis, freed of anxiety, disappointment, or inferiority-feeling. Who has not observed the tendency of the sexes to segregate themselves in certain married circles? However, when relations between the sexes are so plagued, then a kind of homosexuality may also become rampant. And indeed, psychiatrists have recently been noting an alarming rise in both female and male homosexuality.

Higher statistics concerning "female homosexuality" may reflect an increasing number of women who are unwilling to pretend they enjoy having a role forced on them that frustrates their aspirations; and so they seek the company of a partner who can share them. Sometimes two such women find it convenient to live together, whether sex is involved or not, and slowly, as in a good marriage, the partners blend their lives.

In some cases—but much less often than is sometimes assumed—this leads to a desire for sexual relations. But unlike most male homosexuals, such women can often switch their sexual attention to the other sex if they can find a male who really wants and needs to "look outward with them" (and I would add inward) in the same direction. (This, of course, does not hold true for a hard core of female homosexuals.)

The upbringing of most girls today also fosters something resembling female homosexuality. This is because the old intimacy between mothers and daughters who actually worked together for the survival of the family has now practically vanished. As discussed, many women now feel compelled to prove themselves good mothers by making sure their daughters are "successes" in life, and so it is difficult for warm confidence to grow between them. The daughter of such a woman naturally longs for real affection, for the sharing closeness to another woman, for the tender loving care that she wanted from her mother, and never got. When they meet with a rewarding response to this need on the part of a mature woman—which need not, and preferably should not, be of a gross sexual nature—some young women are enriched by it, and are then better able to move on to a successful heterosexual relation.

At this point the prospects for the young female hoping for a satisfying marriage may seem fairly bleak. Whether marriage as we know it is obsolete, I do not know, but frankly I doubt it. Despite its shortcomings, marriage is still the best institution we have developed to combat loneliness and to provide a structure within which two adults can find intimate satisfaction and continue to grow; not to mention the child's need for two parents.

But no institution can provide intimacy or anything else; it can at best provide a framework. This framework itself cannot ensure that youthful love will be transmitted into two fulfilled lives, since our children need to be prepared for marriage by a kind of upbringing very different from the ones they are getting. People must learn to expect far less of the institution itself and much more of themselves in the way of hard work to help each other live interesting and satisfying lives. They must not marry so early that they peg each other to permanent immaturity, out of anxiety, emptiness, or because they feel unable to make a go of life all by themselves. And they must recognize that a woman's place cannot automatically be confined to the home.

Fortunately, there are more than a few mature marriages to be found. In these, the partners have come to see that the feelings of love—and the affection for idiosyncrasies of personality—which lie between them can count for very little by themselves in making their relations work. In the long run, the crucial questions for a married couple concern the kinds of worlds in which they can actively interest themselves as man and woman, and as parents—very much including their connections to their work as well as to each other. If these connections act to bring the members of the family together, then the marriage has a strong chance of survival.

But, of course, this is not so easy. Often the husband's work may split him off from his wife instead of bringing them together. A rather extreme form of this dilemma was presented in a novel called *Command the Morning* by Pearl Buck. She wrote about the wives of scientists working on the secret atomic project at Los Alamos during the war, all of whom were tiresomely caught up in the usual antiquated variety of American marriage. These women had to live lonely lives with secretive husbands who could not share with them the excitement of their work. The only other alternative was to look for some secret excitement of their own, in promiscuous adventure. Only the heroine, a female physicist, is shown to have a complete life, for she shares the creative suspense of the scientists. As she and one of the scientists become involved in work together, they inevitably fall in love. Unfortunately Miss Buck was unable to conceive of any outcome for this affair except a conventional homebound marriage, or no marriage at all. It was apparently beyond her to imagine a marriage where both partners could still love each other and remain part of the same working world. And so, of course, she had the female physicist reject her lover and the prospect of imprisonment in domesticity, so that she didn't have to give up her science.

Obviously I do not think these are the only choices to be made. But I have no doubt that Miss Buck speaks for a great many people who do think so. When such choices do arise, how do we advise young girls to deal with them?

Recently I discussed this problem with some psychoanalytic friends. The majority of these analysts still embraced a nineteenth-century solution to the problem similar to Miss Buck's: a woman belongs in the home, at least for the sake of her children while she is raising them. Her life can be made more bearable if she is helped to gain some meaning from her after-hours community activities, from aesthetic pursuits, and from her sexual life with her husband—or, if need be, from some extramarital sexual adventures.

Such analysts advise a woman to seek meaningful work until the time she gets married or pregnant. Then, she should make an about-face in her way of life, if not also in her emotions. She should then accept the so-called womanly role, stay at home, and raise her children for a decade or longer, during the very years when she is in the prime of life. During this period she must be helped to be not too frustrated a wife, so that when the children are at last in grade or high school, she can make another about-face, recognize the limitations of the PTA life, and return to the more satisfying occupation she pursued before her marriage and children.

What such advice disregards is that having a mother at home who is dissatisfied with her life is no help to the child, even if she does not take it out on the child that his presence prevents her from having a more interesting life. A mother unhappy about the limitations imposed on her life will not be able to make her child happy in his.

Nevertheless the route of working before childbirth, and again after the children have become adolescents, is actually the one that many mothers—voluntarily or involuntarily—have chosen to follow. But one result of such switching back and forth in their major commitments is that many women resentfully feel that they lived a meaningful life only before they got married—a feeling that can have disastrous effects on them, their marriages, and their children. This "switching" solution, in short, leaves the conflict between self-realization and child care unexamined.

I am convinced that modern women will have to confront this conflict, and solve it. It might mean adopting the system found in some other societies where women work—i.e., entrusting part of the infant care to the older children, or sharing it with relatives. It might well mean more arrangements whereby young children are entrusted to the care of well-qualified professional people, at least for part of the time.

Some kind of change along these lines is badly needed, but it will not be an easy reform to make, given the resistance which may be expected. In trying to bring such a change about, women unfortunately will not be able to count on much support from their therapists. For, as we have seen, the preconceptions of many a psychologist about the proper feminine role prevent him from really helping a girl to grow up successfully female—that is, generically female in her sexual and emotional relations and in child-rearing, and yet able to develop as fully as a male can in all other respects.

Psychoanalysts' inability to do full justice to this female situation stems from the very nature of psychoanalysis as a method essentially concerned with the exploration of the unconscious recesses of the mind and of infantile fixations. Psychoanalytic therapy is little concerned with how society ought to be organized or even how the patient ought to organize his life in society—its proper task is to help the individual solve some problem which prevents him from being what he wants to be. How the patient arranges his life after this has been achieved is entirely up to him, for enabling the patient to live an independent life is the goal of therapy.

This is why psychoanalysis may help a girl greatly in dealing with problems of sexual repression or preoedipal and oedipal fixations, just as it may help a young student overcome his inability to study—these are problems of personal self-realization. But it cannot help a girl decide what kind of woman she wants to be or what role she wants to play in the community, any more than it can help a student decide what subject to study or what career to choose. These are problems of social self-realization, and to deal with them as personal psychoanalytic problems may muddle and aggravate them.

Since each different female must find her unique solution to the problem of whether or not to combine marriage and motherhood with work, we cannot look to psychoanalysis as such for leadership in solving this issue. But paradoxically enough, hope for a more rational approach to the problems of women can be found in the discoveries of Freud himself.

Freud felt rather uneasy in discussing the psychology of women. Basically he remained caught up in his own nineteenth-century middle-class background, with his typical overesteem for his mother and his compensatory feeling that he should dominate his wife. He accepted this view as part of the "natural order of things," and, as we have seen, its shadow still hovers over today's psychoanalysts, and our society generally.

But it is worth noting that Freud himself, while always the courteous gentleman when with his wife, often turned for companionship to intellectually active women who, according to his own view, had chosen the unfeminine role in life. He lived domestically as superior male, but in his work sought the company of women he treated as equals.

Freud thus stood at the threshold of a new era in the relations of man and woman, and was not able to cross it. But he did forge the tools that now might enable us to take the steps impossible for him. He was able to demonstrate that the repressive sex taboos of his time were in fact a counterpart of the Victorian overvaluation of the forbidden woman. By showing us how to uncover these repressions, he opened a way for healthier and more satisfying sexual relations to develop between men and women in the years that followed.

Like most great reforms in man's thinking, this one grew from the most honest and most searching examination possible of the contradictions between what people glibly profess, anxiously evade, and blindly do. We should by now be capable of extending a similar self-examination to the contradictions in our attitudes toward women.

If we do this, I suggest we shall find that although women have been accorded votes and education and jobs over the years, our view of them and their potentials is still far from psychologically mature. Indeed, it is in many ways still biased in the unhappy limitations it imposes on the possibilities for women to make the most of their capacities. A rational and psychologically balanced view would appreciate and enjoy the ways that women are truly different from men, but it would recognize that in most respects women have far more in common with men than our society is now willing to grant.

Above all, such a reform in attitudes must take place among those who have anything whatever to do with bringing up the young. For until parents, teachers, and psychologists honestly perceive the prejudice in their assumptions about the proper roles for women, equal education of the sexes will continue to be a mockery, and we must expect the continuing disintegration of young marriages as emotional distance grows between immature couples. Only a thorough effort by their elders to grow up in their thinking will enable our boys to become adults so secure in their masculinity that they can be truly male in their relations to their female partners, very much including in the sexual relation; and this without any need to assert what used to be viewed as the traditional male role in home or society—because maleness and femaleness reside in how one feels about oneself and the partner, in short in who one is, and not in what one happens to do in the home or society. Only efforts to raise boys and girls to this realization will enable our girls to accept marriage and motherhood as an important part of their future, but a part that will not waste—in desperation, resignation, or boredom—the best of their lives and possibilities.

PART THREE

Unconscious Contributions to One's Undoing

The inner life and the outer are not just inextricably interwoven, they are but two different expressions—or if we look at them, offer two separate perspectives—of one and the same phenomenon. If an experience has made a deep impact on us, its integration will affect and be reflected in both our inner and outer lives, albeit in different manners and degrees. Such integration may require alterations in our attitudes and feelings about ourselves and our lives, and what we do about this makes up our external behavior. In fact, integration of a truly important experience requires both that we deal constructively *with what it did to us* as an inner experience, and also that *we do something about it* in our actions relating to it.

For example, when helping a child to cope with the destructive consequences of being abused by a parent, it is hardly ever sufficient to simply stop the occurrence of mistreatment. It is also necessary to help the child overcome the damage to his emotional well-being and personality which results from having been abused. The child must be helped to master, and with this integrate, the psychological damage he has suffered.

The abuse must also be permanently halted, whatever steps this may require, such as removing the child from domination by the abusive parent, or helping the parent to overcome the difficulties which caused his abuse of the child. In order for the child to integrate this damaging experience—which, when not integrated, continues its destructive impact—things must happen both in the child's inner and in his outer life. Although the measures which need to be taken may differ greatly in form and degree, these steps ought best to proceed parallel to each other.

Our efforts at helping the child overcome the experience of abuse by a parent will not be successful unless he himself works at it. For example, the child will have to free himself of the feelings of incompetence and worthlessness which he may have developed in consequence of being so painfully rejected by the person who ought to be his protector. But he must also take measures to forestall further abuse as much as he can, given his age and his limited power to influence his fate.

The need for parallel alterations in one's inner state of mind and in one's actions out in the world seems obvious when what needs to be integrated is the consequences of insults both physical and psychological, as is true for the abused child, and also for the Nazi concentration camp survivor. However, matters are not much different when the abuse is not physical but solely psychological, and even when it is not obviously wreaked by others, but mainly self-inflicted, such as when a person is beset by irrealistic fear of a parent or ridden by guilt. For example, if a person is debilitated by the consequences of an economic, social, and psychological dependency on his overindulgent and/or overcontrolling parents, his course of treatment must help him overcome the painful psychological consequences of his dependency, and also help him develop the strength to gain his economic and social independence in all those respects realistically possible.

The foregoing may shed some additional light on the concentration camp survivors' wondering whether they have some special responsibility because they were saved, and their guilt feelings. The survivors feel that their camp experiences traumatized them, although many know consciously only that they have suffered greatly and had terrifying experiences which shook them to the very roots of their existence.

If after liberation a survivor shoulders responsibilities he had not made his own before, this may suggest to him that such a change in his external behavior is a sign that he has integrated the effects of his traumatization. But this is not always so. Because while significant inner changes bring about parallel changes in outward behavior, the opposite is not necessarily true. Alterations in external behavior often occur simultaneously with inner changes to which they are related, but by no means always.

By writing and publishing the essay "Individual and Mass Behavior in Extreme Situations" I tried to increase awareness not so much of the abominable mistreatment of inmates in the German concentration camps, but rather of why they were treated in such a manner. At that time the gestapo was still using the camps to create anxiety in the rest of the population, to dominate them more effectively. In line with what has just been said, writing this essay was an attempt to do something *about* my experience, directly by making others aware of the camps, and indirectly by spreading the idea that the spirit which created these camps must be eradicated permanently.

Writing about it was also unconsciously an attempt to lay my experience to rest by distancing myself from it and gaining intellectual mastery over it. But the latter required more than a mere retelling of my experiences. To achieve some understanding of what had happened to me and to many, many others, and to arouse my readers to action toward preventing the continuance of the concentration camp system, required a full integrative effort.

Trying to understand why something of far-reaching importance happened to one is often a significant development in attempts at integrating the experience and its consequences. For example, in psychoanalytic treatment patients often find it quite easy to remember what happened to them, and even how they reacted to it. It is usually much more difficult for them to fathom why it happened to them. Doing this is usually a necessary step toward comprehending what is much more difficult and painful to recover—namely, why deep down they responded in particular ways to their experience. And all these insights need to be gained in ever more complete form, although their working-through—that integration into the personality which alone constitutes cure—does not necessarily take place in the neat sequence which has been suggested.

Returning to the example of the abused child, given the appropriate age and intelligence, the child is usually soon able to describe fairly accurately what happened to him and how he reacted to it— such as with anxiety, pain, hate. But quite often before the child can comprehend what all this has done to his internal life, for example, his view of himself, his expectations for the future, his attitudes to others besides the abusing parent, and much more, he must try to unravel why the parent mistreats him. Difficult as it is to understand others, when they have great importance for us and our lives, such understanding is often a necessary step toward understanding ourselves better.

An adolescent girl was quite conscious of her reactions to the frequent and severe beatings which her father inflicted on her. She "knew" what they did to her. It took considerable work until she realized that despite the father's mistreatment, it was not her relation to him which was behind her suicidal depression—although all along she had known that her miserable home life contributed to it—but rather her relation to her mother who, in her overt behavior, was quite nice to the girl. Over time she began to understand that she was used by her mother as a lightning rod to deflect the father's violence away from the mother, and that the father's brutality gave the mother the much-enjoyed opportunity to feel morally superior to her husband.

Then the girl began to understand that her suicidal reactions were due to her hopelessness about receiving the love she so desperately craved from her mother, and that her father's beatings by comparison made little lasting impression on her. Finally she came to understand that she had chosen to offer herself as a target for the father's violence by deliberately provoking him and by creating situations which she knew led to a breakdown of his controls in order to give her mother what the mother desired most: not to have to suffer from her husband's violence, while still being able to enjoy her superiority over him. The girl had done this in the vain unconscious hope that the mother, moved by the daughter's mistreatment, would make up for it by loving her.

Thus, however innocent and hapless a victim of violence or any other traumatizing experience may be, integrating the trauma requires dealing with the problem of whether or not one has made any contribution, however small and insignificant, to being victimized, and in case one did, realizing how and why. In my initial essay on the concentration camps, I tried to describe what happened to the prisoners in the camps, how they reacted to it, including how they tried to defend themselves against it, and why it happened, namely what were the gestapo's purposes. Then a next step in understanding seemed needed. It required many more years of work for me to approach the painful problem of whether and why in addition to being forced by circumstances beyond their control to let things happen to them against their will, the Reich's victims may in some way and to some small degree have also permitted some of it to happen to them, from conscious or, more likely, from unconscious causes.

If this was the case, if something within the victims contributed to their not protecting themselves more effectively against their being destroyed, then this, too, had to be understood. Not because this could lead to a complete understanding of what had happened, and why—the events were so enormous and cataclysmic that it will never be possible to understand them completely—but because it might contribute to preparing oneself better in the future for defending oneself against possible destruction.

In this sense, an examination of whether it might not have been possible to respond more effectively, to protect oneself better, against the danger of one's destruction thus might be regarded as a doing something both *with* and *about* the events whose aftereffects need to be integrated by the survivor. This is so because a true reintegration ought to protect one better than the old one it replaces. The old integration could not draw on past experiences to devise means to protect the individual better against traumatization; but to be successful the new integration must.

One of the ways this new integration can be promoted is to gain awareness of that in oneself which, unbeknownst to one and against one's conscious will, has cooperated to some small degree with the destroyer. Understanding why and how this may have happened is one way to forestall it happening again. This is part, then, of doing something *with* the experience.

But at the same time, understanding the possibility of such unconscious contributions to one's undoing also opens the way for doing something *about* the experience—namely, preparing oneself better to fight in the external world against conditions which might induce one unconsciously to facilitate the work of the destroyer. In one way or another the essays which follow are addressed to these problems.

The Ignored Lesson of Anne Frank

When the world first learned about the Nazi concentration and death camps, most civilized people felt the horrors committed in them to be so uncanny as to be unbelievable. It came as a severe shock that supposedly civilized nations could stoop to such inhuman acts. The implication that modern man has such inadequate control over his cruel and destructive proclivities was felt as a threat to our views of ourselves and our humanity. Three different psychological mechanisms were most frequently used for dealing with the appalling revelation of what had gone on in the camps:

(1) its applicability to man in general was denied by asserting—contrary to evidence—that the acts of torture and mass murder were committed by a small group of insane or perverted persons;

(2) the truth of the reports was denied by declaring them vastly exaggerated and ascribing them to propaganda (this originated with the German government, which called all reports on terror in the camps "horror propaganda"—*Greuelpropaganda*);

(3) the reports were believed, but the knowledge of the horror repressed as soon as possible.

All three mechanisms could be seen at work after liberation of those prisoners remaining. At first, after the discovery of the camps and their death-dealing, a wave of extreme outrage swept the Allied nations. It was soon followed by a general repression of the discovery in people's minds. Possibly this reaction was due to something more than the blow dealt to modern man's narcissism by the realization that cruelty is still rampant among men. Also present may have been the

THE IGNORED LESSON OF ANNE FRANK: This article appeared originally in *Harper's* magazine, November 1960, pp. 45–50. Although it is here reprinted with some additions, deletions, and textual alterations, its essential content remains unchanged.

dim but extremely threatening realization that the modern state now has available the means for changing personality, and for destroying millions it deems undesirable. The ideas that in our day a people's personalities might be changed against their will by the state, and that other populations might be wholly or partially exterminated, are so fearful that one tries to free oneself of them and their impact by defensive denial, or by repression.

The extraordinary world-wide success of the book, play, and movie *The Diary of Anne Frank* suggests the power of the desire to counteract the realization of the personality-destroying and murderous nature of the camps by concentrating all attention on what is experienced as a demonstration that private and intimate life can continue to flourish even under the direct persecution by the most ruthless totalitarian system. And this although Anne Frank's fate demonstrates how efforts at disregarding in private life what goes on around one in society can hasten one's own destruction.

What concerns me here is not what actually happened to the Frank family, how they tried—and failed—to survive their terrible ordeal. It would be very wrong to take apart so humane and moving a story, which aroused so much well-merited compassion for gentle Anne Frank and her tragic fate. What is at issue is the universal and uncritical response to her diary and to the play and movie based on it, and what this reaction tells about our attempts to cope with the feelings her fate—used by us to serve as a symbol of a most human reaction to Nazi terror—arouses in us. I believe that the world-wide acclaim given her story cannot be explained unless we recognize in it our wish to forget the gas chambers, and our effort to do so by glorifying the ability to retreat into an extremely private, gentle, sensitive world, and there to cling as much as possible to what have been one's usual daily attitudes and activities, although surrounded by a maelstrom apt to engulf one at any moment.

The Frank family's attitude that life could be carried on as before may well have been what led to their destruction. By eulogizing how they lived in their hiding place while neglecting to examine first whether it was a reasonable or an effective choice, we are able to ignore the crucial lesson of their story—that such an attitude can be fatal in extreme circumstances.

While the Franks were making their preparations for going passively into hiding, thousands of other Jews in Holland (as elsewhere in Europe) were trying to escape to the free world, in order to survive and/or fight. Others who could not escape went underground —into hiding—each family member with, for example, a different gentile family. We gather from the diary, however, that the chief desire of the Frank family was to continue living as nearly as possible in the same fashion to which they had been accustomed in happier times.

Little Anne, too, wanted only to go on with life as usual, and what else could she have done but fall in with the pattern her parents created for her existence? But hers was not a necessary fate, much less a heroic one; it was a terrible but also a senseless fate. Anne had a good chance to survive, as did many Jewish children in Holland. But she would have had to leave her parents and go to live with a gentile Dutch family, posing as their own child, something her parents would have had to arrange for her.

Everyone who recognized the obvious knew that the hardest way to go underground was to do it as a family; to hide out together made detection by the SS most likely; and when detected, everybody was doomed. By hiding singly, even when one got caught, the others had a chance to survive. The Franks, with their excellent connections among gentile Dutch families, might well have been able to hide out singly, each with a different family. But instead, the main principle of their planning was continuing their beloved family life—an understandable desire, but highly unrealistic in those times. Choosing any other course would have meant not merely giving up living together, but also realizing the full measure of the danger to their lives.

The Franks were unable to accept that going on living as a family as they had done before the Nazi invasion of Holland was no longer a desirable way of life, much as they loved each other; in fact, for them and others like them, it was most dangerous behavior. But even given their wish not to separate, they failed to make appropriate preparations for what was likely to happen.

There is little doubt that the Franks, who were able to provide themselves with so much while arranging for going into hiding, and even while hiding, could have provided themselves with some weapons had they wished. Had they had a gun, Mr. Frank could have shot down at least one or two of the "green police" who came for them. There was no surplus of such police, and the loss of an SS with every Jew arrested would have noticeably hindered the functioning of the police state. Even a butcher knife, which they certainly could have taken with them into hiding, could have been used by them in self-defense. The fate of the Franks wouldn't have been very different, because they all died anyway except for Anne's father. But they could have sold their lives for a high price, instead of walking to their death. Still, although one must assume that Mr. Frank would have fought courageously, as we know he did when a soldier in the first World War, it is not everybody who can plan to kill those who are bent on killing him, although many who would not be ready to contemplate doing so would be willing to kill those who are bent on murdering not only them but also their wives and little daughters.

An entirely different matter would have been planning for escape in case of discovery. The Franks' hiding place had only one entrance; it did not have any other exit. Despite this fact, during their many months of hiding, they did not try to devise one. Nor did they make other plans for escape, such as that one of the family members—as likely as not Mr. Frank—would try to detain the police in the narrow entrance way—maybe even fight them, as suggested above—thus giving other members of the family a chance to escape, either by reaching the roofs of adjacent houses, or down a ladder into the alley behind the house in which they were living.

Any of this would have required recognizing and accepting the desperate straits in which they found themselves, and concentrating on how best to cope with them. This was quite possible to do, even under the terrible conditions in which the Jews found themselves after the Nazi occupation of Holland. It can be seen from many other accounts, for example from the story of Marga Minco, a girl of about Anne Frank's age who lived to tell about it. Her parents had planned that when the police should come for them, the father would try to detain them by arguing and fighting with them, to give the wife and daughter a chance to escape through a rear door. Unfortunately it did not quite work out this way, and both parents got killed. But their short-lived resistance permitted their daughter to make her escape as planned and to reach a Dutch family who saved her.[1]

This is not mentioned as a criticism that the Frank family did not plan or behave along similar lines. A family has every right to arrange their life as they wish or think best, and to take the risks they want to

---

[1] Marga Minco, *Bitter Herbs* (New York: Oxford University Press), 1960.

take. My point is not to criticize what the Franks did, but only the universal admiration of their way of coping, or rather of not coping. The story of little Marga who survived, every bit as touching, remains totally neglected by comparison.

Many Jews—unlike the Franks, who through listening to British radio news were better informed than most—had no detailed knowledge of the extermination camps. Thus it was easier for them to make themselves believe that complete compliance with even the most outrageously debilitating and degrading Nazi orders might offer a chance for survival. But neither tremendous anxiety that inhibits clear thinking and with it well-planned and determined action, nor ignorance about what happened to those who responded with passive waiting for being rounded up for their extermination, can explain the reaction of audiences to the play and movie retelling Anne's story, which are all about such waiting that results finally in destruction.

I think it is the fictitious ending that explains the enormous success of this play and movie. At the conclusion we hear Anne's voice from the beyond, saying, "In spite of everything, I still believe that people are really good at heart." This improbable sentiment is supposedly from a girl who had been starved to death, had watched her sister meet the same fate before she did, knew that her mother had been murdered, and had watched untold thousands of adults and children being killed. This statement is not justified by anything Anne actually told her diary.

Going on with intimate family living, no matter how dangerous it might be to survival, was fatal to all too many during the Nazi regime. And if all men are good, then indeed we can all go on with living our lives as we have been accustomed to in times of undisturbed safety and can afford to forget about Auschwitz. But Anne, her sister, her mother, may well have died because her parents could not get themselves to believe in Auschwitz.

While play and movie are ostensibly about Nazi persecution and destruction, in actuality what we watch is the way that, despite this terror, lovable people manage to continue living their satisfying intimate lives with each other. The heroine grows from a child into a young adult as normally as any other girl would, despite the most abnormal conditions of all other aspects of her existence, and that of her family. Thus the play reassures us that despite the destructiveness of Nazi racism and tyranny in general, it is possible to disregard it in one's private life much of the time, even if one is Jewish.

True, the ending happens just as the Franks and their friends had feared all along: their hiding place is discovered, and they are carried away to their doom. But the fictitious declaration of faith in the goodness of all men which concludes the play falsely reassures us since it impresses on us that in the combat between Nazi terror and continuance of intimate family living the latter wins out, since Anne has the last word. This is simply contrary to fact, because it was she who got killed. Her seeming survival through her moving statement about the goodness of men releases us effectively of the need to cope with the problems Auschwitz presents. That is why we are so relieved by her statement. It explains why millions loved play and movie, because while it confronts us with the fact that Auschwitz existed it encourages us at the same time to ignore any of its implications. If all men are good at heart, there never really was an Auschwitz; nor is there any possibility that it may recur.

The desire of Anne Frank's parents not to interrupt their intimate family living, and their inability to plan more effectively for their survival, reflect the failure of all too many others faced with the threat of Nazi terror. It is a failure that deserves close examination because of the inherent warnings it contains for us, the living.

Submission to the threatening power of the Nazi state often led both to the disintegration of what had once seemed well-integrated personalities and to a return to an immature disregard for the dangers of reality. Those Jews who submitted passively to Nazi persecution came to depend on primitive and infantile thought processes: wishful thinking and disregard for the possibility of death. Many persuaded themselves that they, out of all the others, would be spared. Many more simply disbelieved in the possibility of their own death. Not believing in it, they did not take what seemed to them desperate precautions, such as giving up everything to hide out singly; or trying to escape even if it meant risking their lives in doing so; or preparing to fight for their lives when no escape was possible and death had become an immediate possibility. It is true that defending their lives in active combat before they were rounded up to be transported into the camps might have hastened their deaths, and so, up to a point, they were protecting themselves by "rolling with the punches" of the enemy.

But the longer one rolls with the punches dealt not by the normal vagaries of life, but by one's eventual executioner, the more likely it becomes that one will no longer have the strength to resist when death becomes imminent. This is particularly true if yielding to the enemy is accompanied not by a commensurate strengthening of the personality, but by an inner disintegration. We can observe such a process among the Franks, who bickered with each other over trifles, instead of supporting each other's ability to resist the demoralizing impact of their living conditions.

Those who faced up to the announced intentions of the Nazis prepared for the worst as a real and imminent possibility. It meant risking one's life for a self-chosen purpose, but in doing so, creating at least a small chance for saving one's own life or those of others, or both. When Jews in Germany were restricted to their homes, those who did not succumb to inertia took the new restrictions as a warning that it was high time to go underground, join the resistance movement, provide themselves with forged papers, and so on, if they had not done so long ago. Many of them survived.

Some distant relatives of mine may furnish an example. Early in the war, a young man living in a small Hungarian town banded together with a number of other Jews to prepare against a German invasion. As soon as the Nazis imposed curfews on the Jews, his group left for Budapest—because the bigger capital city with its greater anonymity offered chances for escaping detection. Similar groups from other towns converged in Budapest and joined forces. From among themselves they selected typically "Aryan" looking men who equipped themselves with false papers and immediately joined the Hungarian SS. These spies were then able to warn of impending persecution and raids.

Many of these groups survived intact. Furthermore, they had also equipped themselves with small arms, so that if they were detected, they could put up enough of a fight for the majority to escape while a few would die fighting to make the escape possible. A few of the Jews who had joined the SS were discovered and immediately shot, probably a death preferable to one in the gas chambers. But most of even these Jews survived, hiding within the SS until liberation.

Compare these arrangements not just to the Franks' selection of a hiding place that was basically a trap without an outlet but with Mr. Frank's teaching typically academic high-school subjects to his children rather than how to make a getaway: a token of his inability to face the seriousness of the threat of death. Teaching high-school subjects had, of course, its constructive aspects. It relieved the ever-present anxiety about their fate to some degree by concentrating on different matters, and by implication it encouraged hope for a future in which such knowledge would be useful. In this sense such teaching was purposeful, but it was erroneous in that it took the place of much more pertinent teaching and planning: how best to try to escape when detected.

Unfortunately the Franks were by no means the only ones who, out of anxiety, became unable to contemplate their true situation and with it to plan accordingly. Anxiety, and the wish to counteract it by clinging to each other, and to reduce its sting by continuing as much as possible with their usual way of life incapacitated many, particularly when survival plans required changing radically old ways of living that they cherished, and which had become their only source of satisfaction.

My young relative, for example, was unable to persuade other members of his family to go with him when he left the small town where he had lived with them. Three times, at tremendous risk to himself, he returned to plead with his relatives, pointing out first the growing persecution of the Jews, and later the fact that transport to the gas chambers had already begun. He could not convince these Jews to leave their homes and break up their families to go singly into hiding.

As their desperation mounted, they clung more determinedly to their old living arrangements and to each other, became less able to consider giving up the possessions they had accumulated through hard work over a lifetime. The more severely their freedom to act was reduced, and what little they were still permitted to do restricted by insensible and degrading regulations imposed by the Nazis, the more did they become unable to contemplate independent action. Their life energies drained out of them, sapped by their ever-greater anxiety. The less they found strength in themselves, the more they held on to the little that was left of what had given them security in the past— their old surroundings, their customary way of life, their possessions —all these seemed to give their lives some permanency, offer some symbols of security. Only what had once been symbols of security now endangered life, since they were excuses for avoiding change. On

each successive visit the young man found his relatives more incapacitated, less willing or able to take his advice, more frozen into
inactivity, and with it further along the way to the crematoria where,
in fact, they all died.

Levin renders a detailed account of the desperate but fruitless
efforts made by small Jewish groups determined to survive to try to
save the rest. She tells how messengers were "sent into the provinces
to warn Jews that deportation meant death, but their warnings were
ignored because most Jews refused to contemplate their own annihila-
tion."[2] I believe the reason for such refusal has to be found in their
inability to take action. If we are certain that we are helpless to
protect ourselves against the danger of destruction, we cannot contemplate it. We can consider the danger only as long as we believe
there are ways to protect ourselves, to fight back, to escape. If we are
convinced none of this is possible for us, then there is no point in
thinking about the danger; on the contrary, it is best to refuse to do
so.

As a prisoner in Buchenwald, I talked to hundreds of German
Jewish prisoners who were brought there as part of the huge pogrom
in the wake of the murder of vom Rath in the fall of 1938. I asked
them why they had not left Germany, given the utterly degrading
conditions they had been subjected to. Their answer was: How could
we leave? It would have meant giving up our homes, our work, our
sources of income. Having been deprived by Nazi persecution and
degradation of much of their self-respect, they had become unable to
give up what still gave them a semblance of it: their earthly belongings. But instead of using possessions, they became captivated by
them, and this possession by earthly goods became the fatal mask for
their possession by anxiety, fear, and denial.

How the investment of personal property with one's life energy
could make people die bit by bit was illustrated throughout the Nazi
persecution of the Jews. At the time of the first boycott of Jewish
stores, the chief external goal of the Nazis was to acquire the possessions of the Jews. They even let Jews take some things out of the
country at that time if they would leave the bulk of their property
behind. For a long time the intention of the Nazis, and the goal of

---

[2] Nora Levin, *The Holocaust* (New York: Thomas Y. Crowell, 1968).

their first discriminatory laws, was to force undesirable minorities, including Jews, into emigration.

Although the extermination policy was in line with the inner logic of Nazi racial ideology, one may wonder whether the idea that millions of Jews (and other foreign nationals) could be submitted to extermination did not partially result from seeing the degree of degradation Jews accepted without fighting back. When no violent resistance occurred, persecution of the Jews worsened, slow step by slow step.

Many Jews who on the invasion of Poland were able to survey their situation and draw the right conclusions survived the Second World War. As the Germans approached, they left everything behind and fled to Russia, much as they distrusted and disliked the Soviet system. But there, while badly treated, they could at least survive. Those who stayed on in Poland believing they could go on with life-as-before sealed their fate. Thus in the deepest sense the walk to the gas chamber was only the last consequence of these Jews' inability to comprehend what was in store; it was the final step of surrender to the death instinct, which might also be called the principle of inertia. The first step was taken long before arrival at the death camp.

We can find a dramatic demonstration of how far the surrender to inertia can be carried, and the wish not to know because knowing would create unbearable anxiety, in an experience of Olga Lengyel.[3] She reports that although she and her fellow prisoners lived just a few hundred yards from the crematoria and the gas chambers and knew what they were for, most prisoners denied knowledge of them for months. If they had grasped their true situation, it might have helped them save either the lives they themselves were fated to lose, or the lives of others.

When Mrs. Lengyel's fellow prisoners were selected to be sent to the gas chambers, they did not try to break away from the group, as she successfully did. Worse, the first time she tried to escape the gas chambers, some of the other selected prisoners told the supervisors that she was trying to get away. Mrs. Lengyel desperately asks the question: How was it possible that people denied the existence of the

---

[3] Olga Lengyel, *Five Chimneys: The Story of Auschwitz* (Chicago: Ziff-Davis, 1947).

gas chambers when all day long they saw the crematoria burning and smelled the odor of burning flesh? Why did they prefer ignoring the exterminations to fighting for their very own lives? She can offer no explanation, only the observation that they resented anyone who tried to save himself from the common fate, because they lacked enough courage to risk action themselves. I believe they did it because they had given up their will to live and permitted their death tendencies to engulf them. As a result, such prisoners were in the thrall of the murdering SS not only physically but also psychologically, while this was not true for those prisoners who still had a grip on life.

Some prisoners even began to serve their executioners, to help speed the death of their own kind. Then things had progressed beyond simple inertia to the death instinct running rampant. Those who tried to serve their executioners in what were once their civilian capacities were merely continuing life as usual and thereby opening the door to their death.

For example, Mrs. Lengyel speaks of Dr. Mengele, SS physician at Auschwitz, as a typical example of the "business as usual" attitude that enabled some prisoners, and certainly the SS, to retain whatever balance they could despite what they were doing. She describes how Dr. Mengele took all correct medical precautions during childbirth, rigorously observing all aseptic principles, cutting the umbilical cord with greatest care, etc. But only half an hour later he sent mother and infant to be burned in the crematorium.

Having made his choice, Dr. Mengele and others like him had to delude themselves to be able to live with themselves and their experience. Only one personal document on the subject has come to my attention, that of Dr. Nyiszli, a prisoner serving as "research physician" at Auschwitz.[4] How Dr. Nyiszli deluded himself can be seen, for example, in the way he repeatedly refers to himself as working in Auschwitz as a physician, although he worked as the assistant of a criminal murderer. He speaks of the Institute for Race, Biological, and Anthropological Investigation as "one of the most qualified medical centers of the Third Reich," although it was devoted to proving falsehoods. That Nyiszli was a doctor didn't alter the fact that he—like any of the prisoner foremen who served the SS better than some

---

[4] Miklos Nyiszli, *Auschwitz: A Doctor's Eyewitness Account* (New York: Frederick Fell, 1960).

SS were willing to serve it—was a participant in the crimes of the SS. How could he do it and live with himself?

The answer is: by taking pride in his professional skills, irrespective of the purpose they served. Dr. Nyiszli and Dr. Mengele were only two among hundreds of other—and far more prominent— physicians who participated in the Nazis' murderous pseudo-scientific human experiments. It was the peculiar pride of these men in their professional skill and knowledge, without regard for moral implications, that made them so dangerous. Although the concentration camps and crematoria are no longer here, this kind of pride still remains with us; it is characteristic of a modern society in which fascination with technical competence has dulled concern for human feelings. Auschwitz is gone, but so long as this attitude persists, we shall not be safe from cruel indifference to life at the core.

I have met many Jews as well as gentile anti-Nazis, similar to the activist group in Hungary described earlier, who survived in Nazi Germany and in the occupied countries. These people realized that when a world goes to pieces and inhumanity reigns supreme, man cannot go on living his private life as he was wont to do, and would like to do; he cannot, as the loving head of a family, keep the family living together peacefully, undisturbed by the surrounding world; nor can he continue to take pride in his profession or possessions, when either will deprive him of his humanity, if not also of his life. In such times, one must radically reevaluate all of what one has done, believed in, and stood for in order to know how to act. In short, one has to take a stand on the new reality—a firm stand, not one of retirement into an even more private world.

If today, Negroes in Africa march against the guns of a police that defends *apartheid*—even if hundreds of dissenters are shot down and tens of thousands rounded up in camps—their fight will sooner or later assure them of a chance for liberty and equality. Millions of the Jews of Europe who did not or could not escape in time or go underground as many thousands did, could at least have died fighting as some did in the Warsaw ghetto at the end, instead of passively waiting to be rounded up for their own extermination.

Eichmann:
The System, The Victims

The task Hannah Arendt sets for herself in *Eichmann in Jerusalem* far transcends discussion of the crimes of one man, since the book deals with the greatest problem of our time—not only genocide, one of its ugliest expressions. Totalitarianism in one form or another is the most important issue of our day. Had the Eichmann trial concentrated primarily on this issue, then it would truly have been the trial of the century, for totalitarianism did not end with Hitler. The majority of mankind is ruled by totalitarian governments, and even nations that are at present democratically governed are not entirely free of totalitarian tendencies. The reason is that modern technology-oriented mass societies have a tendency to transcend the human dimension—to manipulate the individual for the purposes of the state, rather than have the state serve the individual.

This is the virtue of Arendt's book—that it views Eichmann and his trial as posing the problem of the human being within a modern totalitarian system. But in a way this is also its shortcoming: the issues are so vast that we do not seem able yet to cope with them intellectually, although her book is certainly a most serious and in part successful effort to do so.

In order to deal with totalitarianism on a human scale, Arendt had somehow to reduce it to its human basis. She does this by pursuing three basic threads of the theme: the man Eichmann; the impossibility of judging totalitarianism by means of our traditional system of thought, including our legal system; and the hapless victims. But so interwoven are these three issues because of the nature of the subject and the way Eichmann's trial was conducted, that neither Arendt nor I can deal with them separately.

EICHMANN: THE SYSTEM, THE VICTIMS: This review-essay of Hannah Arendt's book *Eichmann in Jerusalem: A Report on the Banality of Evil* (New York: The Viking Press, 1963) appeared in the *New Republic*, June 15, 1963, pp. 23–33. It is reprinted here in shortened form, and with some other changes.

Hannah Arendt's previous works, *The Human Condition* and *The Origins of Totalitarianism*, show her to be singularly well equipped to understand how Eichmann's deed, his trial, and his victims are all part of the same problem. So while her book is nominally about Eichmann in Jerusalem and though the trial is discussed in a very personal, erudite, and critical way, in a deeper sense it is more than an essay on the banality of evil; essentially, this is a book about the incongruity of it all.

For example, by all "scientific" standards Eichmann was a "normal" person. "Half a dozen psychiatrists had certified him as 'normal' —'More normal, at any rate, than I am after having examined him,' one of them was said to have exclaimed, while another found that his whole psychological outlook, his attitude toward his wife and children, mother and father, brothers, sisters, and friends, was 'not only normal but most desirable'—and finally the minister who paid regular visits to him in prison . . . reassured everybody by declaring Eichmann to be 'a man with very positive ideas.' " Obviously our standards of normality do not apply to behavior in totalitarian societies.

This book is about the incongruity of the murder of millions, and of one man being accused of it all. It is so obvious that no one man alone can exterminate millions. The incongruity is between all the horrors recounted, and this man in the dock, when essentially all he did was talk to people, write memoranda, receive and give orders from behind a desk. It is essentially the incongruity between our conception of life and the bureaucracy of the total state. Our imagination, our frame of reference, even our feelings, are simply not up to grasping it.

We can witness our inability to grasp tragedy every day. If one individual suffers, or a few—as in an airplane crash, a mine explosion, or typically as when a neighbor's child has a serious accident— immediately our sympathy is roused to the quick. We feel for the victims, and their relatives. We anxiously wait for further news. We all hope and some pray. We feel compelled to do something to help.

But let thirty thousand be killed by a volcano erupting, where we are not on the scene to see it—then we are not deeply moved. We may collect money, we may talk and read about it, but we still are not really shaken up inside. Our emotions are still the emotions of the small clan or village. We react with deep feeling to what we see and can feel in ourselves, to what is immediately before our eyes, or what we can understand from personal experience. We have not yet learned to deal with the experience of the total mass state. We simply cannot think in terms of millions—or, at least, most of us cannot— but only in terms of the individual. A few screams evoke in us deep anxiety and a desire to help. Hours of screaming without end lead us only to wish that the screamer would shut up.

This, then, is a book about our inability to comprehend fully how modern technology and social organization, when made use of by totalitarianism, can empower a normal, rather mediocre person such as Eichmann to play so crucial a role in the extermination of millions. By the same incongruity, it becomes theoretically possible for a minor civil servant—say a lieutenant colonel, to keep the parallel to Eichmann—to start the extermination of most of us by pressing a button. It is an incongruity between the image of man we still carry— rooted though it is in the humanism of the Renaissance and in the liberal doctrines of the eighteenth century—and the realities of human existence in the middle of our current technological revolution. Had this revolution not permitted us to view the individual as a mere cog in the complex machinery—dispensable, a mere instrument —and the state to use him as such, Eichmann would never have been possible. But neither would the slaughter at Stalingrad, Russia's slave labor camps, the bombing of Hiroshima, or the current planning for nuclear war. It is the contradiction between the incredible power technology has put at our disposal, and the insignificance of the individual compared to it.

It is the incongruity between the banality of an Eichmann, and the fact that only such a banal person could effect the destruction of millions. Had he been more of a man, his humanity would have kept him from his evil work; had he been less of a man, he would not have been effective at his job. His is exactly the banality of a man who would push the button when told, concerned only with pushing it well, and without any regard for who was pushed by it to his death, or where.

Even our language has become incongruous; it fails us because our words are symbols for events occurring in an entirely different context; they refer only to matters of a different magnitude. To "kill" applies to the murder of an enemy in war, or for personal gain, or out of personal hate. It implies something akin to a face-to-face encounter. Dillinger was a killer, Eichmann was an instrument in the destruction of millions; yet anything that he did not consider strictly legal revolted him. As he truthfully stated, he never killed a man. Legalized mass murder, by order of the state—this he did not mind; on the contrary, he could enjoy the efficiency, the "scientific" attitude, with which he executed his duty.

Eichmann's "expert" knowledge of the Jewish problem was in all respects woefully inadequate, as Arendt shows in detail; it mainly consisted of his having read two books. But to him this seemed a scientific approach to the problem of first the forced emigration, and later the extermination, of all European Jews. This again is of crucial importance, because without such legalistic or scientific detachment, the inhumanity of totalitarianism cannot be understood. It was not simply one person's pseudo-scientism leading him astray. This is amply documented by the "scientific" experiments on human beings who were all killed by the experiments, a result foreseen by the experimenters who, in terms of their training and position, were well-qualified scientists. They were—in many cases—prominent physicians, distinguished university professors and what not, all trained in pre-Nazi times, all sworn to the Hippocratic oath. Some of the greatest physicians of Germany knew and officially approved of what their colleagues were doing. They too did what they did only because it all seemed perfectly legal; all was in order within the frame of reference of the totalitarian state. The old-fashioned term "murderer" cannot apply to them, or to Eichmann, because it is a term remaining within a human orientation.

Arendt believes, and so do I, that some of the characteristics of the Third Reich are inherent in modern totalitarianism, while others more peculiar to it can fortunately remain so. Today as then, for example, we still respond to devices used by the modern mass state for exerting control through the impersonal bureaucracy, impersonal tastemakers, and impersonal sources of information; all hide individual responsibility behind a screen of objectivity and service to the community. This is why Arendt is not satisfied with studying the personality of an Eichmann as a unique phenomenon, but devotes equal attention to the system and what it did to its victims.

Those who wish to learn from these events for the future must accept not only the possibility, but the probability, that most people are neither heroes nor martyrs—that under great stress and misery a few become heroes, but most people deteriorate rather rapidly, and that inhumanity could be found among both Nazis and their victims. Students of society or of man have learned to take for granted that nobody, including the students themselves, is ever free of human failings. Just because we know that none of us is entirely free from guilt for what has happened, we can afford to investigate even the guilt of the victims. This Hannah Arendt tries to do around the specific event of the Eichmann trial.

Those who will view this book only as an account of the trial—critical, highly personal, perhaps even biased in part—will be dismayed by it because they will miss what her book has to teach. Yet to write the history of just another prominent Nazi was hardly worth Arendt's effort, nor was describing a trial that served propaganda as much as justice. If only one more miserable political criminal was being tried, then it would have seemed petty to take the court to task for the way it conducted the trial, because the accused's guilt was clear to begin with, and he admitted to it. Or why would Arendt drag into her account of the trial the fact that Jews, and even Jewish leaders, lent an unwilling heavy hand in the extermination of Jews? This had nothing whatever to do with the accused. His guilt was not an iota less because they did so.

Many will harp on all this because they fail to grasp the real issue. Judge Musmanno, who reviewed her book in the *New York Times Book Review*, could see it only as a most unfair account of a trial, as if the trial itself had been her topic. He failed to understand that the issue was not Eichmann, but totalitarianism. He writes, for example, that "Miss Arendt devotes considerable space to Eichmann's conscience and informs us that one of Eichmann's points in his own defense was 'that there were no voices from the outside to arouse his conscience.'" Musmanno righteously adds, "How abysmally asleep is a conscience when it must be aroused to be told there is something morally wrong about pressing candy upon a little boy to induce him to enter a gas chamber of death?" Asking such a rhetorical question is playing up to the gallery, or the emotions of the audience, as did Attorney General Hausner (according to Arendt), because it was never proved that Eichmann did such a thing, or knew about it. Of course, he knew about the killings; he never denied it. But what Arendt is talking about is the dreadful situation that in a totalitarian state there are no voices from the outside to arouse one's conscience. This is the important issue she deals with, as Musmanno's emotionally loaded question tries to make us forget. For us who were not Nazis, the issue is the absence of these voices, our voices. This is what makes living in a totalitarian society so desperate, because there is nobody to turn to for guidance, and there are no voices from the outside.

How silent one's voice becomes under totalitarianism is well known by those who were inside concentration camps. They did not raise their voices to tell about it as long as they remained within range of the system. Maybe my own conscience was "abysmally asleep," but when I was released from the camp, I did not tell about it, not so long as I or my mother was still on German soil. All I did tell others was to get out of Germany in a hurry, or they would perish. That is how little my conscience spoke as long as I had to fear being returned to the camp.

To prove that Eichmann could have heard the voice of conscience, Judge Musmanno quotes the story of Pastor Grueber, whom the court lauded as "one of the just men of the world." Undoubtedly he is a wonderful man, and like everyone else, I admire his courage and moral convictions. But Arendt's account shows how softly even this man's voice spoke. On one occasion he asked Eichmann to let unleavened bread be sent to the Jews in Hungary for Passover. And he intervened on behalf of those Jews who had been wounded in World War I, those who had received high war decorations, and the widows of men killed in that war. But when asked by the court directly if he had tried to influence Eichmann, when asked, "Did you, as a clergyman, try to appeal to his feelings, preach to him and tell him that his conduct was contrary to morality?" he had to answer that he had not, because "words would have been useless."

And so indeed they might have been. If conscience spoke so little and so softly out of the mouth of one of the most courageous of men, how can one doubt that Eichmann felt that no voices spoke up to reproach him? That they did not is no excuse for Eichmann. Those who think that Arendt quotes all this to exculpate him will miss her point. Her point is that even a saintly man like Probst Grueber spoke so softly that his voice remained inaudible, and that this is the tragedy of the honest man in a totalitarian society. This is why a Pasternak remained quiet under Stalin, while the Ehrenburgs praised him.

This is also why Arendt goes to some length to discuss a different attitude toward the handing over of Jews and how it affected Nazi functionaries in countries like Denmark or Bulgaria, where there was strong resistance to it not only among the population but also among high government and church officials. She speaks of the slow erosion of doctrinaire Nazi attitudes in these Germans because they were exposed to voices that objected to Nazi morality—voices that were loud and clear and numerous enough to make themselves heard.

Since Arendt sees the trial's importance in its revealing of the nature and the still very present dangers of totalitarianism, she is critical of the legal basis of this trial. She does not accuse the judges or Attorney General Hausner of having failed to mete out justice, or having failed to conduct a trial that was as fair as one could expect it to be under the circumstances. She is critical because the court vacillated between trying a man and trying history, and to this she objects.

To try Eichmann for the deeds of the state which he served—this the legal system by which he was tried did not permit. Had that been attempted, then hundreds of thousands of others would have had to be tried too: all the Germans, and many Jews too, who in some fashion helped in the killing of Jews. As those who arranged for the Nuremberg trials recognized, it was impossible to bring to justice all who participated in the crimes against humanity. For when such crimes are committed, where is one to draw the line? A lieutenant colonel, such as Eichmann, stands neither very high nor very low in the hierarchy. Since he in particular was on trial, was the line to be drawn at the level of captain? And if so, why this arbitrary cut-off point?

To avoid all these and many other difficulties, Eichmann had to be tried as a person. But to do so required that he be viewed as a man of extraordinary qualities; that is, as a monster. This Eichmann certainly was, but as part of a monstrous system; as a man, he was blatantly not. That is why both Arendt and the court were unable to restrict themselves to the trial of one man, but resorted to "painting the broader picture." To the court, this larger picture was that of anti-Semitism, and Arendt is critical of the court on this score (or so it seems to me), because such an approach obfuscates the fact that only one individual was on trial for his life; to mix up his trial with that of a system such as totalitarianism, or of an idea such as anti-Semitism, is questionable if one wishes to uphold the concept of individual responsibility.

That is, both the prosecuting attorney and the judges wanted to see Eichmann's deed as horrendous—which it was—but not as something radically different from other persecutions of the Jews. That is why, as far as the prosecution was concerned, "it is not an individual that is in the dock at this historic trial, and not the Nazi regime alone, but anti-Semitism throughout history." And this is why Israel's Attorney General Hausner began his opening address with Pharaoh in Egypt, and with Haman's edict, "To destroy, to slay, and to cause them to perish."

Not by the furthest stretch of the imagination could Eichmann be justly put to death for Pharaoh's deeds. Nor can any court within our legal system try an idea, such as anti-Semitism, nor can events in the history of man, such as the history of anti-Semitism, be tried. If we begin to try ideas, we end up with witch-hunts; or condemnations without due process, such as characterized the McCarthy era in America.

Why, then, were all these images evoked? The court did so because it viewed Hitlerism as a chapter, though the most lurid chapter, in the history of anti-Semitism. But in Arendt's opinion, which I share, this was not the latest chapter in anti-Semitism but rather one among the first chapters in modern totalitarianism. For this reason it is unfortunate, as Arendt stresses, that Eichmann was not tried by an international tribunal. To ensure against further chapters, as much as a writer can, Arendt tries to show the full horrors of totalitarianism, which go very far beyond those of anti-Semitism. A more complete understanding of totalitarianism requires that we see Eichmann as basically a mediocrity whose dreadful importance is derived only from his more-or-less chance position within the system.

To believe otherwise, to believe that there exists true freedom of action for the average individual within such a system, is so contrary to fact that neither prosecuting attorney nor judges attempted to show that Eichmann enjoyed such a freedom. Only the extraordinary person, at great risk to himself, retains limited freedom in such a state.

It is in this sense that totalitarianism exists wherever the state abrogates the rights of the individual and makes reason of state the highest principle, overruling all others. That principle in Hitler's state was to make the German people supreme, and to eliminate all racial impurity from the soil of the greater German Reich. Toward this end he exterminated not only millions of Jews but also many other people considered inferior. Individuals counted for nothing, and if they stood in the way of reaching this ultimate goal they were exterminated—not to serve individual hatred or personal advantage, but to obey the supreme law. Hence Eichmann's revulsion at those who enriched themselves, and his outrage at what he considered the barbarity of the Rumanian pogroms. Hence also, as Rousset[1] has pointed out, the requirement of the state that wherever possible, the victims should acquiesce in their destruction so that they, too, like victims in some barbarous rite, should be part of the universal effort to do what was best for the state.

If one regards the Nazi extermination of the Jews as a chapter in the history of anti-Semitism, then Eichmann and his kind are indeed the greatest anti-Semitic monsters of all—and this the court tried to establish. If, on the other hand, the "final solution of the Jewish question" was merely one part of the master plan to create the thousand-year totalitarian Reich, then Eichmann becomes a cog, sometimes an important one, sometimes less so, depending on his position in the overall machinery. In this case the cog was of such personal mediocrity that he really could not quite comprehend his role. Arendt shows again and again how he was beholden to clichés, was in many ways unable to form opinions or think on his own, was carried away by his own phraseology.

At least one of these clichés is deeply significant here. Again and again Eichmann spoke of *Kadavergehorsam*: freely translated, "the obedience of a corpse." This was by no means a term born under Hitler—it was taken over from the Prussian Army tradition. This corpselike obedience was expected of every good German soldier, and was considered one of his greatest virtues. If this was so in the German army of pre-Hitler days, when at least some shreds of democratic thinking were afloat, and when autocracy was tempered by some nodding acquaintance with humanistic ideals, how much more powerful did it become under Hitler, that throwback to the creed of the god-emperor who brooked rival deities even less than his imperial Roman antecedents.

And it is true: whoever embraces such *Kadavergehorsam* in re-

---

[1] David Rousset, *The Other Kingdom* (New York: Reynal & Hitchcock, 1947).

gard to anything his supervisors may require is no longer a man but a living corpse. Here the obedient servant of Hitler and the prisoner who walked to the gas chamber became alike as true symbols of the total state. The rewarded servant and the prisoner to be murdered, each had lost his free will, his ability to act out of personal conviction. The difference is that the Eichmanns were delighted with such conditions and felt it their duty to impose them on others, while the prisoners were herded into them by police and fellow prisoners. But in the end result, the corpselike existence, the difference between them is much smaller. That Eichmann not only chose such flagrant denial of any-thing that we consider human—worse, that he imposed it on others—this is reason enough to judge him. But let us also remember how in a large part of this country a short century ago such *Kadavergehorsam* was imposed on many and considered their most desirable attitude—those whom arbitrary fate had condemned to the role of slave.

One could wish that the court had this issue in mind when it went way beyond the trying of Eichmann to discuss Jewish failure to resist. To decide whether or not Eichmann was guilty of the crime he was accused of was supposedly the purpose of the trial. Eichmann admit-ted his guilt, which was also well established through corroborating evidence. Then why call all these witnesses for the prosecution? For the trial it was immaterial to discuss why Jews did not fight back. Yet the court asked witness after witness: "Why did you not protest?" "Why did you board the train?" "Fifteen thousand people were stand-ing there and only a hundred or so guards facing you. Why didn't you revolt and charge and attack?"

Arendt is probably correct about the motives of the court. She believes that these questions were asked to convince all Jews that there can be no strength in Jewry unless it is supported by the state of Israel. She feels that by bringing out the lack of Jewish resistance, the Israeli authorities were trying to show that no such resistance was possible because no Jewish state existed to give it strength.

If this was the reason of the court, perhaps it was also why the same court neglected to shed light on the unfortunate and desperate cooperation of Jewish leadership with the SS. Because it was the misfortune of the Jews of Europe that they too saw Hitlerism as only the worst wave of anti-Semitism. They therefore responded to it with methods that in the past had permitted them to survive. That is why they got involved with executing the orders of the state; that is why the Jewish leaders and elders, with heavy hearts, cooperated in arranging things for the Nazi masters. Arendt claims, and her thesis will long be fought over, that without this collaboration Hitler could never have succeeded in killing so many Jews.

This is the part of her book that will be most widely objected to. I do not claim to know whether she is right or wrong in her argument: that if the Jewish organizations had not existed, the extermination of the Jews could never have attained such tremendous proportions. But she certainly makes her point effectively.

Because of her concentration on the injustice bred by totalitarianism, Arendt at times creates an ambiguity in her evaluation of guilt. Thus on cursory reading she seems to plead that Eichmann was a victim and that Jewish leaders were heavy with guilt. In fact, Arendt saw rightly that Eichmann was not the greatest villain of all. But to say so leaves her open to the misunderstanding that she did not think him much of a villain, when she certainly did think him so.

I believe that Arendt's purpose was to paint the broader context of the trial as she saw it, which went far beyond anti-Semitism. This was of greatest interest to me, because it has to do with the much more important issue: how and where can an individual resist, or fight back, in a totalitarian society? Jewish witnesses who testified seemed to think that nobody could, certainly not the persecuted Jews.

Arendt's point—and it is well taken—is that any organization within a totalitarian society that compromised with the system became immediately ineffectual in opposing it and ended up helping it. "The gravest omission from the 'general picture' [that the court tried to paint of the extermination of the Jews] was that of a witness to testify to the cooperation between Nazi rulers and the Jewish authority." Eichmann himself asserted that without such cooperation the extermination would have run into serious difficulties. He said, "The formation of the Jewish Council and the distribution of business was left to the discretion of the Council. . . . These functionaries with whom we were in constant contact—well, they had to be treated with kid gloves. They were not ordered around, for the simple reason that . . . that would not have helped matters any. If the person in question does not like what he is doing, the whole works will suffer." In cross-examination, Judge Halevi found out from Eichmann that the Nazis had regarded this cooperation as "the very cornerstone" of their Jewish policy.

That the SS state could not have functioned without the cooperation of the victims, I can testify to from my own camp experience. The SS would have been unable to run the concentration camps without the cooperation of many of the prisoners—usually willing, in some cases reluctant, but all too often eager cooperation.

This cooperation the court deliberately refrained from bringing to light, although it freely brought out the absence of resistance. According to Arendt, the court did not raise the question "Why did you cooperate in the destruction of your own people?" but this question was shouted out by spectators who were only too familiar with the contribution of prominent Jews to the Jewish fate. When Baron Philip von Freudiger, formerly of Budapest, gave testimony, this question was screamed at him, so that the court had to interrupt the session. Arendt reports: "Freudiger, an orthodox Jew of considerable dignity, was shaken: 'There are people here who say they were not told to escape. But fifty percent of the people who escaped were captured and killed'—as compared with ninety-nine percent, for those who did not escape." A fateful comment on the consequences of Jews being kept in the dark by Jewish leaders.

From this and much more Arendt concludes that "If the Jewish people had really been unorganized and leaderless, there would have been chaos and plenty of misery but the total number of victims would hardly have been between four-and-a-half and six million people."

Thus only fighting partisans or those who went underground had a chance to survive—those who made no effort to compromise or meet the oppressor halfway, and who shunned principles such as that by sacrificing thousands one might save tens of thousands. Because accepting such principles implied some cooperation with the enemy in the sacrifice of the thousands.

In retrospect, it is quite clear that only utter non-cooperation on the part of the Jews could have offered a small chance of forcing a different solution on Hitler. This conclusion is not an indictment of Jews living or dead, but an empirical finding of history. To deny or ignore it may open the door to the genocide of other races or minority groups. Active resistance arouses admiration; watching violent subjugation of the victim evokes revulsion; while passive compliance permits most of us to put it all out of our minds fairly soon.

Perhaps an example from the American scene may illustrate.

Many of us were impressed by the way Negroes in Birmingham marched, singing and upright, to jail. But much deeper feelings were aroused in us when we saw pictures of a solitary Negro being dragged down by policemen because he refused to march to jail on his own. The response of the German people to the crimes committed against the Jews might have been very different if each Jew who was taken had to be dragged down the street, or shot down on the spot. However, this experience did not often confront the German people. When ordinary German citizens witnessed utter brutality against Jews, some applauded, but among others there was at least some adverse reaction; and the Nazis were extremely sensitive to it.

Arendt also tells of how two small actions against Jews were used for testing out what the popular reaction might be. Perhaps if these Jews had not, on their own, packed their things and marched themselves to the train that took them away, if they had had to be openly shot, or dragged down the streets, the Nazis might have learned that such methods aroused too much resistance. There is little doubt that they were astonished at the lack of popular opposition to the extermination program. But there was also little reaction because the Jews cooperated so smoothly, following the advice of their own leaders.

When, then, or at which point, is an individual still able to save his soul and perhaps also his life, although enveloped by a totalitarian society? Interestingly enough, this very point could be identified clearly in the Eichmann trial. Arendt pays great attention to it. One can only regret that the court did not.

This moment of choice came when Eichmann for the very first time visited the extermination camps and saw what happened to the Jews. He nearly fainted. But instead of heeding his emotional reaction, he pushed it down to go on with the task that he had been assigned and that he embraced as his own obligation. This was Eichmann's point of no return. Then and there he abdicated from reacting as a human being and made himself a mere tool of the state. Such, I believe, are the moments when the vital decision has to be made, because these are situations where one is confronted in a personal, immediate way, not an abstract one, with the issue of the human being versus the totalitarian state.

For all too few Germans this moment came as Hitler gained power; for others it happened with the euthanasia program. For more Germans it came with Stalingrad. Such a moment of truth came certainly to every prisoner in the concentration camps, when he was confronted with the problem of whether or not to cooperate with the SS and help in the running of the camp. It came to many Germans, and it must have come to many Jews, particularly to Jewish leaders. My thesis is that if one does not stand up to one's experience in accordance with one's values, if one takes the first step in cooperating with the totalitarian system at the expense of one's convictions and sentiments, one is caught in a web that tightens with each step of cooperation until it becomes impossible to break free.

I have spoken about the incongruity of it all. There was no less incongruity in the trial itself. Here was a lieutenant-colonel who admitted his guilt, but also stated that he had done nothing but his duty. And here was all the machinery of a state, trying to convict him of a crime he had already admitted to committing.

Initially I said this was not the trial of the century, though it dealt with the crime of the century. At one time the crime of Leopold and Loeb was rightly called the "crime of the century," but since then it has been superseded by crimes such as Eichmann's. These two boys committed a most inhumane act, not for gain or out of hatred, but to assert principles. It was a crime committed because of the most inhumane principles and to assert their superiority. To their crime, too, the old legal maxim *"Cui bono?"* did not apply. Neither Leopold nor Loeb profited from their crime, nor did Eichmann in any appreciable way from his. He recognized that his advancement probably would have been quicker at the front or through other services, although he was certainly serving the principles of his masters, and in part to get his promotions.

Leopold and Loeb's trial was the trial of the century because, thanks to Darrow, the incredible inhumanity of their deed was put within the broad context of human nature. The result was that despite our revulsion at their crime, enough empathy was aroused with these errant human beings so that the trial left us not only shaken with helpless indignation but also aroused in us the determination to create a better society, one that could not and would not produce another Leopold and Loeb.

Eichmann's trial was not the trial of the century, because as a trial it had altogether too many shortcomings. It was a trial where the witnesses for the prosecution had their day in court, but not those for the defense. It was a trial where there was no balance between the machinery available to the prosecuting attorney as compared to that of the defense. It was a trial where important witnesses for the defense were prevented from appearing in court because they were given no assurance of immunity. (Obviously only those who had intimate knowledge of Eichmann's work could have borne witness on his behalf as to whether or not he personally was eager to see all Jews exterminated, or was only following orders. But the only ones who could answer such questions were those who had seen him at his gruesome work, because they had been his collaborators. Hence they risked prosecution under the same Nazi Collaborator Law that Eichmann was tried under. They could have come to Israel and appeared as witnesses only if immunity had been granted them. This Israel refused to do—had to refuse, because their victims might have prevented their leaving Israel alive—but it deprived Eichmann of his chance to produce witnesses on his behalf.) It was a trial where most of the time was spent on issues that had no direct bearing on the guilt of the accused.

It was a trial where the state spoke with rightful moral indignation about crimes against humanity, to an accused it had kidnapped in violation of international law. The legal background of this trial also illustrates the inappropriateness of our legal concepts for dealing with twentieth-century totalitarianism. And here again I speak not as an expert or as a lawyer, but rather as a citizen concerned with what our laws can and cannot do for us all.

The basic principle underlying the law under which Eichmann was tried is derived from the charter of the Nuremberg trials. They served as precedent, for example, for convicting a man without his having been found guilty by a jury of his peers. According to this charter the greatest crime of all was the crime against peace, which was called "the supreme international crime . . . in that it contains within itself the accumulated evil of the whole: war crimes, and crimes against humanity." Of those who sat in judgment at Nuremberg, at least one nation had engaged in unprovoked aggressive war against Finland, while two had committed crimes against humanity according to this charter; one by using slave labor. Another nation had clearly acted against the Hague convention by dropping atomic bombs, indiscriminately killing civilians. Still, these things happened before the Nuremberg trials.

Since then, many wars have been waged, but no court has tried anybody. Crimes against humanity are unfortunately still not tried, or only by the victors, with only the vanquished as the accused.

Such are the realities of political life in our twentieth century. I regret them but I do not object to them, because I know that these same realities induced me (in my more optimistic moments I like to think, forced me) to do things in the concentration camp (and probably outside as well) that would not stand up too well under closest scrutiny.

Unlike Arendt—and despite her cogent argument for an international court—I do not object to Israel's trying Eichmann, or to its trying him the way it did, because I believe we must deal in some fashion with the Eichmanns of this world. I am convinced that the fact that our legal procedures are not adequate for doing so must not permit the Eichmanns to remain unpunished. But the trial does demonstrate that our existing laws are as inadequate for dealing with totalitarianism as we are unprepared as individuals to meet its challenge.

Arendt seems to object to the trial as propaganda. This to me is its main justification, given the irregularities of the trial and Eichmann's having been kidnapped. Personally I would have preferred the solution Arendt suggests, that Eichmann should have been killed by a Jew, as the Armenian Tindelian killed Talaat Bey (the great killer in the Armenian pogroms of 1915) and the Jew Schwartzbard killed Simon Petlyura (who was responsible for the pogroms during the Russian civil war). If such an executioner of Eichmann had then been tried, through that trial all the crimes of Eichmann could have been forced on the conscience of the world without extraneous questions such as the kidnapping and the legality of the trial interfering with the clear message of the murderous nature of totalitarianism.

However, if Eichmann's trial did not serve justice entirely well, it did something much more important, and this for the living rather than for the dead: it brought the world face to face with those dangers of totalitarianism that it seems all too willing to avoid examining.

Surviving

It was not the film Seven Beauties as such that induced me to discuss it at length. It was the near-universal acclaim with which it was received in this country and what this suggests about our reactions to survivorship today that I believe merit serious attention. Similarly it seemed important some eighteen years ago to discuss The Diary of Anne Frank because of what its reception revealed then about the public reactions to the extermination of European Jewry.

"Survive! No matter how. Survival alone counts!" or "There is no meaning to survival!" Which is the vital urging, which the nihilistic warning, of Lina Wertmüller's film *Seven Beauties*? Or are both messages given equal importance in this film? If the latter is true, the film would make its urging and its warning a mocking of us—the observers who are pulled first one way, then in the opposite direction, as the ludicrous turns into horror, and the dreadful becomes farce.

Watching this contradictory, grotesquely violent, deeply disturbing film, one is captivated by its terrifying and its morbidly funny scenes, and most by those which are both at the same time. The film keeps one spellbound; not least because it is a story about survival. And while the survivors of the German concentration and death camps are dying out, we all live under the specter of Auschwitz and Hiroshima, atomic bombs and genocide, the concentration camp in its German and its Russian varieties.

Pasqualino, a petty crook, is the film's anti-hero. He is so devoid of any consciousness of himself and his time that he as little understands how he first comes to murder out of the most ridiculous private

---

SURVIVING: This essay appeared under the same title in *The New Yorker*, August 2, 1976, pp. 31–52. It is reprinted here with some minor changes.

reasons, as he later lacks all comprehension of why he becomes for political reasons the hapless victim of murderers. He fools himself into believing that he knows why he kills: to protect his honor and that of his family; although he does not really care, and they would be quite happy—as a matter of fact, happier—without this "honor." Pasqualino is a vain, bumbling, but ruthless show-off when he thinks he has the upper hand, and a groveling liar when he is down. He murders to maintain the low respect he credits himself with as a petty Mafioso; but in murdering he violates even the most minimal gesture of Mafia honor, which requires giving the other fellow a token chance to defend himself before one shoots him down. He brutally rapes an utterly helpless woman when he believes he can get away with it, and invites his own rape when he thinks it may help him survive. This is the person who is made to stand for the archetypical survivor, the image of us all.

What meaning can we find in this film and the critical response to it? Each generation must cope with its own history. The most difficult part of this is coming to terms with the traumatic events; for the present generation, these events are the Vietnam war, and all that followed. But in some fashion the members of each generation must also master the crucial problems in the lives of their parents; and for the older generation the traumatic events were the second World War and the universe of the concentration camps. (Not that the latter is not still present in important parts of the world.) Although the attempt never works, the easiest way to try to cope with the world of one's parents is to practice indifference to it—to adopt the attitude that one must live one's own life and cannot be bothered by what revolutionized the lives of one's parents. Thus, Israeli youth do not want to hear about the holocaust; they feel that they cannot bear the burdens of their parents in addition to their own.

Thirty years makes a difference, but does that mean that the unimaginable abomination—the unspeakable horror of yesteryear—has today become a topic suitable to be turned into a farce? And, if so, what does this tell us, the observers and one-time participants, who accept it? Not to want to know about the concentration camps is one thing, but to turn one into the setting for "death-house comedy" (*Time*'s apposite description) is something different. Just because the comedy in *Seven Beauties* is macabre, grotesque black comedy, it succeeds in neutralizing the horror that, although clearly shown, becomes through this juxtaposition the *frisson* that makes the comedy more effective.

A survivor of the camps is hardly the right person to appreciate the "raucous humor" (as one reviewer described the mood of the film) of seeing prisoners who have been hanged or have hanged themselves in desperation, who suffocate in the mire of feces in an open latrine, who are slaughtered in other ways; or the "winning . . . shabby, transparent charm" (same reviewer) of the rapist whose pretended love for the murderous camp commander, a woman, is rewarded by promotion to *Kapo*, or prison foreman, and who, with only the slightest hesitation, selects six prisoners at random to be killed to fulfill the terms of the deal he has made with her. Old men should not invoke their by now ancient concerns and try to impose them on the different perspectives of those in a new generation, who feel they must interpret the past not in its own terms but in theirs. Why spoil the enjoyment of those for whom the gas chambers are a hoary tale, vaguely remembered, best forgotten? Out of such considerations, I would have kept silent but for my conviction that this film and, more important, most of the public reaction to it interpret survivorship falsely, in terms both of the past and of the present.

In its own way, *Seven Beauties* is a work of art, and an artist has every right—in fact, it is his artistic obligation—to give body to his vision of the world in which we live. This permits us to react—positively or negatively—to his vision and in this way to enrich our understanding of and refine our sensitivity to the human condition, which is, of course, our own. If the artist uses irony to achieve his goal, he presents his vision as if seen in a mirror that distorts, to make us aware of what would otherwise escape us, to force us to respond to that which we would rather avoid. Is *Seven Beauties*, then, a film using mocking irony to enrich us? Or is it entertainment using horrible props to take us more effectively on a ride so engrossing and emotionally exhausting that we are fooled into believing, because of the strength of our feelings, that we have gained in consciousness?

If the film is to be taken for mere entertainment, I must state my disgust that the abomination of genocide and the tortures and degradations of the concentration camp are used as a special, uniquely macabre titillation to enhance its effectiveness. But I believe that Lina Wertmüller, the director, had more in mind, even though at certain moments the opportunities her story offered for sophisticated death-house comedy may have carried her away. On the basis of this film as well as her others, I believe she is serious about her art and about her views of life, politics, human beings, and the relation between sex and politics.

I also believe that *Seven Beauties* is a somewhat uneasy, indirect, camouflaged—and therefore more dangerous, because more easily accepted and hence more effective—justification for accepting the world that produced concentration camps; it is a self-justification for those who more or less readily accepted a concentration camp world and profited from it. But it is also a self-justification for those who today do not wish to consider the problems that that world posed, and instead settle for the easy solution of a completely empty survivorship; it is a self-justification for those who try to evade the predicaments of the world of the present, of which concentration camps in their Russian form are still very much a part, and who do not wish to struggle with the difficult issue of finding alternatives to such a world.

Strong objections were raised to *Seven Beauties* by Pauline Kael, in *The New Yorker*, and also by Russell Baker, in *The New York Times*. Baker correctly said that "it has been ecstatically reviewed by New York movie critics" (including Vincent Canby, of the *Times*). John Simon called it "a masterpiece" in a long evaluation in *New York*, and it received rave reviews in *Time* and *Newsweek*. This was not the reaction of reviewers only; in my experience, the vast majority of those who saw the film were deeply impressed by it. More important, it seemed to shape their views about matters they had been little familiar with before, including the all-important issue of survivorship.

This is sufficient reason to take the film seriously, whatever Wertmüller's motives in making it may have been—offering questionable entertainment, justifying the acceptance of Fascism, or rousing us to deeper consideration of the world we live in. The generally positive response to *Seven Beauties* suggests to me that one generation after the Nuremberg trials, any manner of accepting Fascism and of surviving under it seems to have become acceptable, and not just in Italy—where the reasons for such acceptance can be easily understood—but also in the United States. However, I am discouraged equally by the overwhelmingly uncritical acceptance of this film and the much rarer rejection of it by those who, in my opinion, did not take it and the reaction to it seriously enough. In a review of Wertmüller's recent films titled "All Mixed Up," in the *New York*

Review of Books, Michael Wood refers to her as having "a stunning visual intelligence accompanied by a great confusion of mind." And *Seven Beauties* is confused—or, at least, confusing. How, then, is one to explain the critical acclaim it received, and the audience reaction to it? Should one assume that those who respond positively to it suffer from a parallel confusion? This may very well be the case.

It is risky to assess the director's state of mind from her film and that of its viewers from their reaction to it. But my impression is that the confusion might well be the consequence of Wertmüller's consciously holding and wishing to express certain values, ideas, and attitudes while simultaneously giving expression to opposite ones—owing to overriding unconscious desires. For example, I believe that consciously Wertmüller rejects Fascism, machismo, and the world of the concentration camps but that unconsciously she is fascinated by their power, brutality, amorality—their rape of man. In *Seven Beauties*, the horror of the concentration camp—and all it stands for—is very much a part of this fascination. Consciously Wertmüller wishes to believe in the goodness of man, symbolized in the anarchist Pedro, the unpolitical Francesco, and the Socialist whom we encounter on his way to spend twenty-eight years in prison for believing in the freedom and dignity of man, but unconsciously she ridicules all three for their inefficiency. Goodness is weak, and fails; only evil triumphs.

Wertmüller's fascination with the rape of man is most clearly shown in the two scenes that are essentially rape scenes—her protagonist, Pasqualino, in an asylum with a bound patient, and the loathsome female commander demanding that Pasqualino perform sexually or die. Nobody who is not fascinated by rape would dwell on these scenes, much less make one of them the centerpiece of the film. Both Pasqualino's act of rape and his being raped impress on us that this is what makes for survival. If survival justifies rape in both its active and its passive forms, then it justifies practically any other evil.

It is not the film's unconscious fascination with the concentration camp world that mainly concerns me, but the fact that the film fascinates many members of the American cultural élite. This fascination also has its expression in the fact that accounts of Naziism written by one of the Nuremberg criminals—Albert Speer—are best-sellers not only in Germany but in the United States; and so are sympathetic biographies of Hitler. Nothing could be more dangerous than if disappointment with the obvious shortcomings of the free world and life in it should lead to an unconscious fascination with the world of totalitarianism—a fascination that could easily change into a conscious acceptance.

Thinking about *Seven Beauties* brought back memories of audience reactions to Rolf Hochhuth's play *The Deputy*, which deals seriously with the world of the concentration camps and the moral problems it poses—problems that *Seven Beauties* mocks. I saw *The Deputy* both in the United States and in Germany. In the United States, the audience was deeply moved, and left the theater with the conviction that the only moral position possible was that of the hero —to take a firm stand against evil, even if it meant risking one's life—although, out of anxiety, most people, including oneself, might not act in accordance with such a demanding moral obligation. Americans were profoundly disgusted or depressed and disheartened by a Pope's shirking his responsibility to speak out against genocide. In Germany, I met with an entirely different reaction to this play: the theatergoers were pleased with it and relieved by what they experienced as its message. They felt fully justified by the play. It showed that those who tried to fight evil perished, and that even the Pope acquiesced, and this proved to the members of the audience that they had been right not to pay any attention to the concentration camps that existed in their midst. The reaction of the German theatergoers was easy to determine, because their interpretation of the play was important to them, and so they loudly reassured one another. The gist of what they said was, "The play proves that it would have been pointless to worry about the camps, because worrying would not have helped; even the Pope could do nothing. One would only have risked one's life stupidly." This was their reaction despite the fact that the play's message was that the Pope—and others—should have and could have done something to stop the evil. It concerns me deeply to note that *Seven Beauties* left American audiences with a reaction all too similar to the Germans' reaction to *The Deputy*. These audiences seem to accept the completely erroneous implication that to survive in the camps one had to act as if one were vermin, as Pasqualino does in the film, but in fact the exact opposite was true: while moral convictions and acting on them did not guarantee survival—nothing did, and most prisoners perished—these things were nevertheless important ingredients of survival.

Thus, what is crucial about this film is not Wertmüller's intentions in making it—not even the welcome demonstration to her fellow Italians that to oppose Fascism, while virtuous, would have been pointless, because it would have been completely ineffective—but that it justifies evil by implanting a smug conviction that nothing could have made any difference and, by implication, that nothing would make any difference today. Most disturbing are the reactions of the audiences—how the film shapes their views of the world of the concentration camps, of Fascism, of the survivors of the holocaust. Having been an inmate of German concentration camps and one of the all too few fortunate survivors, I cannot claim disinterested objectivity in the questions that the film poses. Having wrestled with the problems of survivorship, I cannot remain indifferent to the views that this film presents, particularly since it presents them so effectively.

Whatever Wertmüller's intentions, her film deals with the most important problems of our time, of all times: survival; good and evil; and man's attitudes toward a life in which good and evil coexist side by side, when religion no longer offers guidance for dealing with this duality. The late Hannah Arendt, in her book on the Eichmann trial and, with it, the concentration camps, stressed the utter banality of evil. I agree with her thesis. But what must concern us primarily is that evil is evil; we must not permit its banality to detract from this fact, as *Seven Beauties* does, for the film's central figure is banality personified.

Not that in this film evil as such is denied; far from it. It could not be denied in concentration camp scenes. If it were, we would be revolted, and the film would lose its effectiveness. But in this film the senseless banality of evil is so forcibly impressed on us, and is so inextricably interwoven with the comic, that evil loses nearly all its impact. While the horrors of war, Fascism, and the concentration camp are clearly and overtly presented, covertly they are much more effectively denied, because what we watch is a farce played in a charnel house, and, furthermore, because survival despite evil and survival through doing evil seem to be in the end all-important, regardless of the form that either the evil or the survival takes.

All those in *Seven Beauties* who are good, who have human dignity, perish. This in itself would not invalidate the picture of the world that the film presents. We know that in real life those who prevail, like Pasqualino, often do not hesitate to take ruthless advantage of others—that they care only about their petty selfish concerns, and not at all about good and evil. And we are well aware that the good often fail, are taken advantage of, perish. But in this film we are made to feel that human dignity is a sham, because when we encounter its assertion in the concentration camp we are first much taken by it, but then are given to understand that it is senseless. This is not because those who act with dignity are destroyed or destroy themselves but because their destruction happens in a ridiculous way.

From its start, the film presents good and evil to us, but makes it as nearly impossible for us to truly embrace goodness as to fully reject evil. Before the film's story begins, we are shown a series of newsreels of Fascism: demonstrations, marches, Mussolini exhorting the masses, Mussolini shaking Hitler's hand; war, the bombing and destruction of cities, the killing and maiming of people. Though all this is presented as horrible, we are entertained by an amusing mocking cabaret song accompanying the newsreel scenes. And Mussolini and Hitler are also presented partly as comic figures—an approach that is supported by the song, in which all the contradictions of life are accepted at the same time. The song says "Oh yeah" equally to "the ones who have never had a fatal accident" and to "the ones who have had one." And though most of the lyrics and the singing bitingly reject the world of Fascism we see on the screen, they are also funny, and this quality simultaneously adds to the rejection and takes the sting of true seriousness out of it.

We see Mussolini in all his bombast and Hitler with his funny mustache as we hear the words of the song: "The ones who should have been shot in the cradle, pow! Oh yeah." Then, "The ones who say follow me to success, but kill me if I fail, so to speak, oh yeah. . . . The ones who say we Italians are the greatest he-men on earth, oh yeah." The song is mockingly comic rather than tragic, and so robs the scenes of war and destruction of much of their impact. And Mussolini and Hitler are so pompous that we cannot take them seriously.

Hitler is shown here as the man with the funny mustache, as he was in Chaplin's film *The Great Dictator*. But that film antedated Auschwitz and Treblinka. Chaplin made us laugh at what we should have taken dead seriously. To laugh at Hitler was one way to live with him, but the most dangerous, the most destructive way. Because so many people thought they did not have to take seriously the ideas Hitler presented in his grandiose speeches, he was able to make our world a shambles. Because they laughed at this silly man with his funny mustache, they were caught utterly unprepared for their fate; if they had taken him seriously they might have saved themselves. Laughter can be freeing, but it can also induce a false sense of security when one is in greatest danger. The newsreels and the song accompanying them in *Seven Beauties* take us back to the period when we thought that we did not need to take Hitler and Mussolini seriously. But the war scenes show us at the same time what happened because we didn't take these men seriously. This is a contradiction that runs all through the film. Has the time really come when we should feel that the men responsible for the murder of millions are figures to be laughed at?

The film's irony, its farcical scenes, its contradictions prevent us from taking seriously the concentration camp world it so gruesomely presents. *Time* says that the film is "liberating." By making us laugh at Fascism, the concentration camp, the holocaust, it does show us one way to become liberated from this burden—something that many people desire, particularly those who lived contentedly under Fascism and those others who do not wish to be haunted by its memories. But is this a liberation that enhances our life or one that debases it? Wertmüller's film suggests the latter, just as at its end her hero, *the* survivor, remains an empty shell. Pasqualino is not a person whose experiences have added to his depth; understanding, compassion, the ability to feel guilty, all of which were lacking in him before, continue to be lacking in him, despite world-shaking experiences that one feels should have changed him completely. It is this depiction of the survivor that robs survivorship of all meaning. It makes seeing the film an experience that degrades.

As the story begins, we see two Italian soldiers, Pasqualino and Francesco, who have deserted from the Italian army. They meet by chance in a German forest. Pasqualino, concerned only with his personal advantage, has robbed a dead soldier of his bandages and put them on himself, enabling him to pretend that he is seriously wounded and thus to make his escape. Francesco, having previously saved his men from being sent to Stalingrad by getting them trucks to escape in, is now himself fleeing from being court-martialed. From a distance, the two watch a group of Jews being lined up and shot by German soldiers. This sight makes Francesco speak of feeling guilt over having played along with Fascism when he should have fought it. Pasqualino's response is that to have fought it would have been pointless suicide. Francesco denies this, asserting that it would not have been useless—that he should have taken the risks involved. He accuses himself of having killed, without reason, innocent people he did not even know during the war. Pasqualino replies that he himself has killed for a reason.

With this remark, the scene shifts to prewar Naples, and we see the killing. We watch Concettina, Pasqualino's ridiculously fat sister, make a fool of herself as the cheapest type of vaudeville singer—as he will soon make a fool of himself, first in bungling the murder of Totonno, the pimp who made Concettina into a whore and promised to marry her (or so she claims, to pacify her vociferously outraged brother), and then in disposing of the corpse. In reality, Concettina was eager to exchange her life of squalor in a mattress factory for the life of a whore. Pasqualino browbeats his sister, then shoots Totonno while the pimp is half asleep. He commits the murder supposedly to save his honor and that of his family but actually to gain the respect of Don Raffaele, his gangster boss—who, however, knows how useless Pasqualino is. He orders Pasqualino to dispose of the body, and Pasqualino does so most clumsily. All this Pasqualino undertakes in order to be able to continue his easy life under the protection of the Mafioso boss—a life based on the exploitation of his hardworking mother, who adores him, her only son, and of his seven fat, ugly sisters, the film's "seven beauties."

In Francesco and Pasqualino, not only good and evil are contrasted but also guilt resulting from indecision and absence of guilt even in the face of brutal murder. Francesco's guilt over having acquiesced in Fascism stands in stark contrast to Pasqualino's acceptance of it. By grandiloquently asserting—like Mussolini—that it is right to kill to gain respect, Pasqualino denies that he has any cause to feel guilty. Yet to be able to choose good over evil and to feel guilty if one has failed to do so is decisive both for preserving our humanity and for giving meaning to survival, and in the movie these problems of

guilt and choice are presented repeatedly, mainly in the contrast between Francesco and Pasqualino. In the crucial last scene between
them, in the concentration camp, Francesco objects to Pasqualino's
sending others to their death to save himself, but Pasqualino nevertheless does so. Francesco revolts, although he knows that in doing so he
risks his life. Then Pasqualino, to save himself, fatally shoots Francesco. Francesco demonstrates the crucial problem of the survivor:
guilt, which arises from the ability to know that one must not
acquiesce in the evils of a concentration camp world, must not buy
one's own life at the expense of the lives of others—even though fear
may force one to act against this knowledge. Pasqualino does not
suffer guilt, although he kills to gain prestige, sends others to their
death, and acquiesces in his own rape to save his skin. At least, we are
led to believe that this is how he manages to survive.

The dangerous seductiveness of *Seven Beauties* lies in its presenting this problem of the survivor clearly but denying its validity. By
means of the movie's clever artistry, the problem is made to seem
immaterial, because survival alone counts—nothing else. It is not just
that *Seven Beauties* denies the crucial importance of coping with
one's guilt in achieving survival but that it falsely asserts the overween-
ing importance of survival as such, no matter what—as if the problem
and survival were not inextricably connected.

At the same time that *Seven Beauties* opened in New York and
was widely acclaimed, long excerpts from *The Survivor*—a new book
on the concentration camps by Terrence Des Pres, a professor of
English at Colgate University—were published in such different
magazines as *Harper's*, *Dissent*, and *Moment*. This is another indication that a new generation is trying to come to terms in its own way
with what used to be called the concentration camp world. For many
people, the millions who were murdered no longer arouse much interest; they seem to have been forgotten; they no longer count. Maybe
this attitude is inevitable; our business is with the living, not the dead.
But I believe that it is another matter when the horrors of the camps
are used and their history is misconstrued to propagate a questionable
message: survival is all, it does not matter how, why, what for. This
questionable approach also implies that it is both wrong and silly to
feel guilty about anything one may have done to survive such an

experience. By quite different routes, Professor Des Pres, in his book, and Wertmüller, in *Seven Beauties*, arrive at parallel conclusions about what is required for survival in a world dominated by the concentration camp or standing under its specter. According to them, the main lesson of survivorship is: all that matters, the only thing that is really important, is life in its crudest, merely biological form.

Presenting a small segment of truth and claiming that it is the entire spectrum can be a much greater distortion than an outright lie. A lie is much easier to recognize as a distortion, since our critical abilities have not been put to sleep by having been fed some small segment of truth. The filmmaker and the writer, to make palatable their wrongful distortions of what is entailed in survivorship, weave misleading myths around the truism that one must remain alive. Saying what everybody knows and nobody has ever doubted hardly justifies a film or a book about survival in the concentration camp world. If a presentation of what is involved in survival is to have any meaning, it cannot restrict itself to stating simply that unless one remains alive one does not survive. It must tell what else is needed: what one must be, do, feel; what attitudes, what conditions are required for achieving survival under concentration camp conditions.

The kernel of significant truth in the truism that survival is based on staying alive is that in the concentration camp staying alive required a powerful determination. Once one lost it—gave in to the omnipresent despair and let it dominate the wish to live—one was doomed. But Professor Des Pres and Lina Wertmüller go way beyond this. Des Pres states that the lesson to be learned from survivorship is that man's true obligation is "to embrace life without reserve," which must, by definition, entail doing so in all ways, even those which until now have been unacceptable.

Des Pres leads up to this dictum by saying that we must "live beyond the compulsions of culture" and "by the body's crude claims." Wertmüller's film gives these principles visible form and symbolic expression. Pasqualino embraces life without reserve as he accepts without compunction Fascism, murder, rape. He lives beyond the compulsions of culture as he rapes a mental patient who is helplessly tied down, and as he hands over other prisoners to be deprived of their lives to secure his. By voluntarily managing an erection in intercourse with a ruthless killer, he survives by the body's crudest claims. All this is made more obvious because we watch it in direct connection with seeing Pedro and Francesco perish just because they transcend the body's crude claims to keep on living, at no matter what price; just because they adhere to basic moral principles—which can be viewed as mere "compulsions of culture" if one wishes to deny the importance of morality.

The facts of the concentration camp are exactly the opposite of what Professor Des Pres says and what *Seven Beauties* depicts. Those who had the best chance for survival in the concentration camps— minimal as it was—were like Pedro and Francesco: they tried as much as was feasible to continue to live by what Professor Des Pres calls the compulsions of culture, and, despite the omnipresent crude claims of the body in a situation of utter physical exhaustion and starvation, nevertheless tried to exercise some small moral restraint over the body's cruder demands. Those who, like Pasqualino, made common cause with the enemy, the camp commander, thus sacrificing the lives of others to gain advantages for themselves, were not likely to remain alive.

The prisoners, to survive, had to help one another. While this is not shown in the film, it was so obviously the reality of the camps that Professor Des Pres cites many examples of prisoners' helping others, in line with what they viewed as their moral obligation—sharing some morsel of food, performing some extra hard labor that others were incapable of, protecting others at the risk of their own lives. But Des Pres then misrepresents the motives of this behavior. It is true that some prisoners lived by the principles he formulates, and to which *Seven Beauties* gives visual expression. That is why, in reference to them, there was a camp saying—"The prisoners are the prisoner's worst enemy." Not because such prisoners were more cruel and vicious than the SS—although a very few were, to gain favor with the SS— but because if one received help from other prisoners one had a chance to survive, while without it one did not. Therefore, fellow prisoners or prison foremen who did not give help where this was possible seemed to be the worst enemies, because something could rightly be expected of them.

Thus, while it does not accord with the reality of what was likely to happen in the camps, there is some psychological validity to Pedro's act of suicide in direct consequence of Pasqualino's betrayal of his fellow prisoners. Francesco is reacting to the same betrayal when he provokes the SS by calling to the prisoners to revolt. Emotionally, disappointment in fellow prisoners was extremely hard to bear, because one expected more and better of them than of the guards, whose vileness one learned to take for granted, much as one hated them for it. In reality, nearly all prisoners made common cause against the SS most of the time. Many times, prisoners supported one another in small ways that, given the desperate conditions under which they lived, took on large dimensions. In supporting one another, the prisoners did not live "by the body's crude claims," nor did they "live beyond the compulsions of culture," nor did they "embrace life without reserve." On the contrary, such behavior, far from facilitating survival, actually endangered it.

The principles that Wertmüller and Des Pres present to us as guidelines for survival were in fact those by which the Nazis, and particularly the SS, lived, or at least tried to live. They subscribed to the philosophy that one must "live beyond the compulsions of culture"— witness the infamous statement "When I hear the word 'culture,' I draw my gun," made first by, of all people, the president of the German academy of poets, Hanns Johst, and later approvingly repeated by such Nazi leaders as Goebbels. With their racist doctrines, such as the overriding importance of "pure Aryan blood," and in many other ways, they glorified living "by the body's crude claims."

In theory, it might just be possible to assert that the validity of Nazi doctrine is what survivorship proves—so many Nazis and Fascists did manage to survive the war rather well. But I am convinced that survivorship, if it proves anything at all, proves nothing like the validity of Fascism. When a large and significant segment of those who speak for the American intellectual establishment seems ready to accept the most basic principles of Nazi doctrine and to believe the suggestion—presented in carefully camouflaged but convincing forms in *Seven Beauties* and Des Pres's critically celebrated book—that survivorship supports the validity of those principles, then a survivor must speak up to say that this is an outrageous distortion.

The harsh and unpleasant fact of the concentration camp is that survival has little to do with what the prisoner does or does not do. For the overwhelming majority of victims, survival depends on being set free either by the powers who rule the camps or—what is much more reliable and desirable—by outside forces that destroy the con-

centration camp world by defeating those who rule it. Even Solzhenit-
syn, who demonstrated the greatest moral courage, the most
remarkable ability to survive under unspeakably horrible conditions
—to the extent that he has rightly come to stand for all survivors—
would not have survived if he had not been set free by those who rule
the Gulag Archipelago. He could not have spoken up if there had not
been an outside world, independent of the world of the concentration
camps, that exerted the powerful pressure that permitted him to do
so.

The completely misleading distortion in *Seven Beauties* and the
articles excerpted from Des Pres's book is the pretense that what the
survivors *did* made their survival possible. For the fictional Pasqualino as much as for the real prisoners Professor Des Pres discusses
in his writings, it was the Allied victory (or, in some instances, its
imminence) that permitted survival. Until the Nazi governmental and
war machinery was thrown into nearly complete disarray by Allied
bombings and by defeat in the field (notably after Stalingrad), not
more than a dozen or so of the many millions of concentration camp
prisoners managed to survive by their own efforts—that is, to escape
from the camps and get away with it before the Allied forces tri-
umphed. All others, including me, survived because the gestapo chose
to set them free, and for no other reason.

If one wishes to speak in a sensible way about survival, one has to
divide it into two aspects that have little to do with each other. The
first aspect is liberation, and this depends not at all on the prisoner
but on the arbitrary decisions of the jailers, or on what seems politically expedient to them, or on their being defeated by outside forces.
The second is what the prisoner can do to remain alive until the
moment when, by chance or luck, he is liberated. But whatever he
does is of no avail if he is not set free.

Important and fascinating as the problem is of what the prisoner
can do even under the unbelievably oppressive conditions of the
concentration camp, much as it can teach us about the human condition, it has little relevance to the question of survivorship unless we
always keep in mind that survival demands first and foremost the
destruction of the concentration camp world and the arrangement of
things so that no new concentration camp world can come into being.
Any discussion of survivorship is dangerously misleading if it gives
the impression that the main question is what the prisoner can do, for

this is insignificant compared to the need to defeat politically or militarily those who maintain the camps—something that the prisoners, of course, cannot do.

This unpleasant truth about the prisoners' helplessness to survive unless they are liberated is ignored by the film and the articles, which try to replace it with the comfortable belief that the prisoners managed to survive on their own. It is what people seem to wish to believe thirty years later about the German camps, if one can trust the response to the film and the articles. Moreover, it can permit us to forget about Russian and other concentration camps of today—and the wish to do this may have fathered the film and the articles, and may explain their ready acceptance.

Seven Beauties does permit the thoughtful viewer at least a tiny glimpse of this truth, for Pasqualino reappears in freedom only after Naples has been occupied by Allied soldiers. But the film denies the truth about the causes of Pasqualino's liberation by impressing on us that it was his managing an erection and his killing other prisoners—including his friend Francesco—that secured his survival. The film further denies reality by indicating that there is no worthwhile difference between the world of the concentration camp and that which Pasqualino enters after leaving the camp. Survival in the camp, we are shown, depended on whoring, and liberated Naples is shown in the film to be nothing but a huge whorehouse, with the Allied soldiers as the whoremasters.

That this is the impression Wertmüller's film gives is attested to by what John Simon writes about it. Pasqualino pleads insanity to escape death for the murder of Totonno and is placed in an insane asylum, where he commits the rape. Speaking about Pasqualino's having got his release from the madhouse by volunteering to join the Italian army, Simon writes that from this "madhouse full of tragicomic adventures"—referring to rape as a tragicomic adventure—"one can be rescued only by transfer into a worse madhouse: the army."

The army as madhouse seems to have become a fashionable cliché. In a film about life under Fascism, about the concentration camp, about survival, one might rightly ask: which army? The all-too-efficient Nazi army, which we have seen killing prisoners, exterminating Jews, and which as long as it existed maintained a world of concentration camps? Or the army whose victory the prisoners prayed for and dreamed about, since they knew that it was their only hope for survival? This army without whose victory Hitler and Mussolini and their successors would now rule most of the world, making the German concentration camps part of the present—is this army a worse madhouse?

But in terms of *Seven Beauties* what Simon writes is not far off the mark. In this film, we are given to understand that under Mussolini only a few Neapolitans were whores—hence Pasqualino's outrage when his sister Concettina became one. We are shown that all Pasqualino's sisters have become whores because of the Allied army. So Fascism is evil, but in this film the Allied victory has not liberated the camps that play such a central role in it; instead, it has turned the whole world into a bordello. One can understand why the many millions of Italians who were quite satisfied with Fascism would like to view the Second World War this way, since it would justify their acceptance of Fascism and its evils. But one cannot help wondering for what strange reasons American intellectuals have embraced this view of things.

Professor Des Pres, as an American speaking to Americans, uses other methods to obfuscate the fact that only the Allied victory liberated the concentration camp prisoners and hence permitted the survival of quite a few—all too few, unfortunately. He does so, first, by not mentioning this basic fact of survival, and, second, by giving the impression that the prisoners, entirely on their own, were able to defeat those who kept them imprisoned. Political reality seems to count for little in a supposedly scholarly discussion of what is involved in survival. Professor Des Pres also uses other props to buttress his theories. Among them are a claim that those driven to their death are accused of having gone "to their death like sheep," and that those who survived are accused of being "tainted with something called 'survival guilt.'" Yet he fails to present evidence that these claims were ever made in a critical manner. I believe that Des Pres erects straw men in order to knock them down, and in this way to convince us of the validity of his spurious conclusions. To say that the victims of the gas chambers "went to their death like sheep" is a scandalous use of a cliché, not only incredibly callous but utterly false. Nobody who knew the camps and thought about them could possibly give credence to it. As early as 1943—long before the liberation of the camps, long before their existence was officially acknowledged in this country or was at all widely known—I wrote about the temporary personality changes that occurred in the prisoners and the far-reaching adjustments they made. Sheep cannot produce personality changes in themselves; these can be effected only by thinking and feeling human beings, and adjustments can be so far-reaching only because the people involved feel so deeply.

It is also untrue that the SS drove the prisoners as if they were sheep to their death—or, if they let them live for a time, to their barracks, to work, or, as we see in the film, to the deadly roll calls. The analogy is false, because prisoners were of no value to the SS, while sheep are of considerable economic value to those who herd them. Sheep do not know that they are being driven to the slaughter. The prisoners, after their transport, after parents had been separated from children, husbands from wives, knew how desperate their fate was, although many who were taken directly to the gas chambers did not know exactly what was in store, for the SS wished to keep them in the dark, and they were given to understand that the gas chambers were shower rooms. But the vast majority of prisoners nevertheless walked passively as they were directed, knowing more or less what was going on—and this raises more serious problems about man's behavior when his will to resist has been completely broken. This is a problem that Professor Des Pres does not discuss. He can afford to neglect it by paying attention only to the survivors. But I believe that the survivors' problems and the problems of those who did not survive are most intricately interwoven. So is the problem of the prisoners who knew that these newcomers were being driven to their death and did not shout out to them not to permit it—to resist. However, those who would have given the warning and those who would have heeded it would all have been immediately killed.

We see Pedro and Francesco call out such warnings in *Seven Beauties*, and also see them die because of it. It is one of the innumerable contradictions of *Seven Beauties* that it shows the prisoners as utterly passive, permitting themselves to be herded to the roll call—an impression that is reinforced by the guards' using dogs to help herd them—yet shows Pedro and Francesco heroically resisting such degradation and trying to rouse all the other prisoners to do the same. The picture that the film renders of the prisoners is wrong, because it shows only heroic resistance that fails to benefit anybody; helpless passivity; and, in Pasqualino, the saving of oneself by siding with the enemy.

The reality of the camps was entirely different. To stay alive, prisoners had to try at all times to be active in their own behalf, and this is something that Professor Des Pres rightly stresses; as a matter of fact, it is what his whole argument is about. In *Seven Beauties* we see prisoners, whether in the barracks or during the roll call, helplessly and passively awaiting their fate. Yet in reality, even while seemingly standing passively at attention, prisoners, to survive, had to engage in protective behavior. Those endless roll calls were physically and morally so destructive that one could survive them only by responding with determination to their destructive impact, through action when this was possible and, when it was not, then at least in one's mind—and this was true for practically everything else that made up the prisoners' lives. Like the many thousands of others who experienced it and survived, I remember vividly a bitter-cold winter night at Buchenwald when the prisoners were threatened with having to stand at attention at roll call for the entire night as punishment because some prisoners had tried to escape.[1] Roll call was taken with the prisoners standing ten rows deep. Those in the front row were doubly exposed—to the ice-cold wind and to the mistreatment of the guards—while those in the other rows were somewhat protected from both. Soon the prisoners, with the connivance of indifferent prisoner foremen, or under the direction of responsible foremen, took turns standing in the front row, so that this extra hardship was shared by all but the extremely weak and old, who were exempted.

The SS soon observed what went on, but most—though not all, some SS men being more vicious than the average—pretended not to see, as long as the prisoners changed places only when the SS men did not seem to be looking in their direction. The reason was that among the values of the SS was an appreciation not of mutual help but of an *esprit de corps*, at least up to the time Germany's defeat became clear to them. While they tried overtly to break such a spirit in the prisoners, covertly they had some grudging admiration for it, and utterly despised the prisoners who did not act in accordance with it. Thus, the total passivity of the prisoners in *Seven Beauties* is one of the

---

[1] They succeeded only for a short time; see footnote 12, pp. 64–5. From the beginning of the German concentration camps, in 1933, until the forties, only three prisoners managed to escape and survive, and this only because they were helped by SS friends.

many devices that the film uses to indicate that in order to survive one had to play entirely along with the oppressors, when actually the opposite was true.

To survive, one had to want to survive for a purpose. One of the simplest ideas that prisoners hung on to—for life, because the thought gave them the strength to endure—was revenge. This is an idea not available to Pasqualino, because a little murderer like him can hardly believe that one day he will take revenge on the big murderers. An idea that sustained many, even in the worst moments, was that of bearing witness—telling the world of the abomination, so that it could be prevented from ever happening again. Some wanted to stay alive for those whom they loved. Some were sustained by thoughts of the better world they would create, their eyes having been opened to what was really important by the infernal experiences they had lived through. Only active thought could prevent a prisoner from becoming one of the walking dead (*Muselmänner*) whom he saw all around him—one of those who were doomed because they had given up thought and hope. By showing the prisoner who has thoughts of a better world committing suicide, like Pedro, and having Pasqualino, who has no thought whatever of creating a better world, survive, *Seven Beauties* reverses what survival was all about.

In order to further convince the reader of what the prisoners could accomplish in defeating the rulers of the camp, Des Pres refers to the prisoners' having been likened not only to sheep but to monsters—a simile entirely of his invention. In the vast literature on the camps, nobody else has referred to the prisoners as monsters. Des Pres writes, "But they were neither sheep nor monsters who burned down Treblinka and Sobibor, who blew up the crematorium at Auschwitz, who succeeded in taking command of Buchenwald during the war's last days." Here the impression is created that the prisoners, all by themselves, were able to assure their survival, and this is completely untrue. Of the commando of 853 prisoners who conspired to blow up one of the four crematoria in Auschwitz not a single one survived. Some died in the blast; all others were immediately shot down. Whatever little open resistance there was in any camp, it led to survival only when the Allied armies had already reached the immediate vicinity; otherwise, the result was always death. The few instances of active fighting back—incredibly few, given the millions of prisoners involved—are therefore immaterial to the question of survivorship; witness the absence of active fighting back among the millions who went through the Russian camps and those who died there.

The statement about the "taking command of Buchenwald" by prisoners "during the war's last days" is partly correct, because the event referred to did occur—on April 11, 1945, which was indeed one of the last days of the war in Germany. But as far as the prisoners' taking command is concerned, it was a non-event that Des Pres has made to appear an event of the greatest import. What actually happened has often been described accurately, but it has more often been turned into a myth, given permanent form by the Buchenwald monument, which through fictional stories glorifies Ernst Thälmann, the leader of the German Communists, as having provided the impetus for resistance—with which he had nothing whatever to do. What happened was that when two American tank columns had reached the immediate vicinity of Buchenwald, the camp commander, to save his life, turned the camp over to the SS-appointed top prisoner of the camp and ran away with the rest of the SS. Only then did the prisoners "take command." Within three hours of the commander's departure, the first American motorized vehicles entered the camp.

Christopher Burney has given a completely trustworthy account in *The Dungeon Democracy*.[2] It is a report with which Professor Des Pres should be familiar, because we are told, in an introductory note to the *Harper's* article, that he "studied the entire record compiled by those people who survived the camps"—a formidable achievement, because the literature is vast and exists in many languages, most of it not translated and much of it not yet printed but available only in manuscript or on microfilm. In any event, *The Dungeon Democracy* was written in English and printed in 1945, almost immediately after the liberation. Burney, who was an English prisoner at Buchenwald, writes,

> April 11th. Pister [the camp commander] called the *Lagerälteste* I [the chief prison trusty, appointed to this post by the SS] and Fritz Edelmann and said: "I am leaving now. You will be Commandants of this camp and will hand it over to the Americans for me." . . . Throughout the morning there was machine-gun and artillery fire quite close, and

---

[2] Christopher Burney, *The Dungeon Democracy* (London: W. Heinemann, 1945).

we saw groups of German artillery and infantry withdrawing along the plain. At about midday the SS sentries left their posts and disappeared. Two hours later, when the coast was well clear, daring prisoners hoisted the white flag . . . and [we] . . . saw them taking the hidden weapons from the "secret" dump. They were very childish, forming bands of different nationalities and marching about looking as if they had defeated the entire Wehrmacht.

This, years later, has been turned into the myth that the prisoners took command of the camp by defeating the SS.

C. J. Odic, as prisoner-physician, was in an excellent position to observe all that went on. His truthful account[3] deflates the myths of Buchenwald's liberation. After stressing the fact that plans and some serious preparations by the prisoners for action were made only after the SS operating the camp had been thrown into nearly complete disarray by the devastating Allied air raid on August 24, 1944, he says that these plans were never executed. The camp was liberated by two tank columns, he writes, and continues:

This was all. The Battle of Buchenwald had been won. We were free. Soldiers had crossed the Atlantic to achieve it. All that remained was to create the myth. The camp suddenly crawled with ancient heroes. . . . They demonstrated that they had not lost their keen sense of opportunity: it was they who had conquered Buchenwald. The newspapers believed this story. . . . Our fate deserves to be treated more seriously.

There is the myth of the eight hundred guns; there is the myth of a camp that liberated itself, and did it before the arrival of American columns. In front of them marched a hero. . . . In Paris he is French, in Warsaw he is Polish, in Germany a member of the future Reichstag. . . .

What gives the claims [that the prisoners liberated the camp] the lie is that there were neither killed nor wounded prisoners. [Dr. Odic knew, because on liberation he was immediately made physician in charge of the hospital services.] The mass that rushed to the tower [from which the SS had controlled the camp] ahead of the Americans did not have to fight; the tower was deserted, and so were the other positions of the SS. The SS suffered no attack, whether from the rear or the flanks. . . . Is it necessary to ascribe to us a role that we have not played?

---

[3] C. J. Odic, *Demain à Buchenwald* (Paris: Buchet Castel, 1972). The quotes are translated by me.

Was our elation at being liberated not sufficient? . . . The American Army conducts a raid across Thuringia. It advances. It occupies Buchenwald. It restores to the thousands of prisoners whom it delivers the right to be human.

The issue of guilt is closely connected with that of morality. In a world that has no place for morality, no guilt can exist. According to Professor Des Pres, "the survivor's special importance" is that "he is the first of civilized men to live beyond the compulsions of culture," and thus "is evidence that men and women are now strong enough, mature enough, awake enough, to face death without mediation, and therefore to embrace life without reserve." It is hard to know exactly what is meant by the phrases "face death without mediation" and "embrace life without reserve." But it is a well-known fact of the concentration camps that those who had strong religious and moral convictions managed life there much better than the rest. Their beliefs, including belief in an afterlife, gave them a strength to endure which was far above that of most others. Deeply religious persons often helped others, and some voluntarily sacrificed themselves— many more of them than of the average prisoners. For example, the Franciscan priest Maximilian Kolbe, the original of the hero of *The Deputy*, asked for and took the place of a prisoner who was to be killed. Father Kolbe was killed. The prisoner survived.

It will be startling news to most survivors that they are "strong enough, mature enough, awake enough . . . to embrace life without reserve," since only a pitifully small number of those who entered the German camps survived. What about the many millions who perished? Were they "awake enough . . . to embrace life without reserve" as they were driven into the gas chambers? Would they not have much preferred some mediation if it could have stood between them and death, or could even have taken some of the horror out of their dying? What about the many survivors who were completely broken by their experience, so that years of the best psychiatric care could not help them cope with their memories, which continue to haunt them in their deep and often suicidal depression? Do they "embrace life without reserve"? Do the psychotic breakdowns and severe neuroses of many survivors deserve no attention? What of the horrible nightmares about the camps which every so often awaken me today, thirty-five years later, despite a most rewarding life, and which every survivor I have asked has also experienced?

Langbein, whose account of Auschwitz is so far the most complete one that has been published, sums it up by saying, "Even if the life of many former Auschwitz prisoners proceeds normally during the day, theirs is different from that of all others: there remains the night, the dreams."[4] Langbein presents example after example of survivors who continue to be deeply disturbed. One can only wonder at the audacity of Professor Des Pres in speaking about survivors embracing life without reserve when one recalls the many who, because of what happened to them or their parents or children in the camps, have never been able to live anything like a normal life. And what of those survivors who were maimed, castrated, sterilized? Those who immediately begin to cry helplessly when they are reminded of the camps? The children who, having spent time in the camps, needed psychiatric treatment for years before at least some of them were ready to try to cope with life?

Des Pres's conclusions about survivors embracing life without reserve, and their having learned to live by the body's crude claims, are particularly startling because he writes at length about prisoners who helped others—that is, who acted morally, although in doing so they risked their lives. Despite his insistence on the unselfish behavior of many survivors, he objects to the idea of guilt, the pangs of which are a most powerful motivation for moral behavior—much stronger than any fear of disapproval by others. Des Pres writes that the average survivor should not and does not feel guilty, since guilt is one of the most significant "compulsions of culture," of which Professor Des Pres claims that the survivor has freed himself. By asserting that the average survivor is not guilty—and nobody in his senses has ever claimed he *was* guilty—Des Pres obfuscates the real issue, which is that the survivor as a thinking being knows very well that he is not guilty, as I, for one, know about myself, but that this does not change the fact that the humanity of such a person, as a feeling being, requires that he *feel* guilty, and he does. This is a most significant aspect of survivorship.

One cannot survive the concentration camp without feeling guilty that one was so incredibly lucky when millions perished, many of them in front of one's eyes. Lifton has demonstrated that the same phenomenon exists for the survivors of Hiroshima, and there the

---

[4] Hermann Langbein, *Menschen in Auschwitz* (Vienna: Europaverlag, 1972).

catastrophe was short-lived—although its consequences will last a lifetime.[5] But in the camps one was forced, day after day, for years, to watch the destruction of others, feeling—against one's better judgment—that one should have intervened, feeling guilty for not having done so, and, most of all, feeling guilty for having often felt glad that it was not oneself who perished, since one knew that one had no right to expect that one would be the person spared. Langbein presents abundant evidence for the guilt-feelings of survivors, as can every psychiatrist who has worked with them. Elie Wiesel, whom Professor Des Pres quotes with approval in other contexts, wrote, "I live and therefore I am guilty. I am still here, because a friend, a comrade, an unknown died in my place." Wertmüller, by showing Pasqualino—who had no guilt-feelings even before his concentration-camp experience—as being completely free of them after his liberation, deprives his experience and his survivorship of all meaning. At the same time, this makes her image of the survivor untrue.

Professor Des Pres states explicitly that survivorship teaches us to live by the body's crude claims, beyond the compulsions of culture. *Seven Beauties,* through the events we watch, implicitly tries to convince us of the validity of this statement. Just after the first encounter between Pasqualino and Francesco, they see Jews being murdered, which leads to their conversation about guilt or its absence, and the flashbacks showing Pasqualino's murder of Totonno. From this, we turn to Pasqualino in Germany, where neither the Jews' murder nor the memory of Totonno's spoils his appetite or his good humor. In a hilarious scene, he enters an isolated German house in the forest and steals food as he banters with a speechless old woman. He is hungry, and he does not allow his memories to diminish his enjoyment—not just of the food but of how he again has managed to put something over on someone else for his own benefit.

When he brings some of the stolen food to Francesco, they are caught by a German patrol. Next, we see images of the horrors of the concentration camp: prisoners hanged, stacks of corpses, prisoners

---

[5] Robert Jay Lifton, *Death in Life: Survivors of Hiroshima* (New York: Random House, 1967).

dragged away to the gas chambers, the vicious guards directed by the even more vicious female camp commander. Pasqualino and Francesco are befriended by Pedro, the anarchist, who has failed in attempts to kill Mussolini, Hitler, and Salazar because he made dud bombs; one guesses that this, in turn, was because a man who loves men is not good at killing them, for even in the camp Pedro believes in man—in the new man, who will discover harmony within himself. When Pasqualino sees all around him prisoners mistreated and murdered, he decides to seduce the camp commander to save himself—obviously a ridiculous idea.

Another flashback now occurs—from the horrors of the concentration camp to Naples again, when the Mafia boss Don Raffaele tells Pasqualino he must get rid of the body of Totonno. In a macabre but comic scene, Pasqualino cuts the body into pieces and, in a whole series of funny scenes, disposes of the three suitcases into which he has packed parts of it. Thereafter, comic and macabre scenes follow each other in quick succession, including a hilarious trial, in which Pasqualino gets let off the murder charge and is sent to the insane asylum. There he rapes the woman who is tied down, possibly for or after shock treatment. He is discovered, himself put in restraints, and given shock treatment, and then is offered the chance to volunteer for the army. He gladly accepts. The scene moves back to the concentration camp and to the central event of the film, to which everything else has led up: the sexual encounter between Pasqualino and the camp commander—a convincing demonstration of how far he is ready to go to survive. The suicide of Pedro and Pasqualino's shooting of Francesco are the direct consequences of what happens between the commander and Pasqualino.

The movie is full of vague references that tease us by arousing our curiosity about their meaning: allusion to real and fictional characters and situations which hold out the promise of helping us understand better, so as to give greater depth to what we see on the screen, and which arouse deep feelings in us—but we never find out what these really mean. For example, the camp commander seems modeled on Ilse Koch, the infamous wife of the equally infamous commander of Buchenwald—a couple whose nefarious deeds were too much even for the Nazis, who brought them to trial. Of course, there could really never be a female camp commander, given the Nazi view of the male and female roles in society. Ilse Koch's power to destroy was based entirely on her husband's unlimited power as commander of the camp.

Unlike Ilse Koch, the commander in *Seven Beauties* is apparently a very unhappy woman of considerable depth, who is a connoisseur of the finer things of life: several times we see a famous picture in a prominent place in her room. Is the purpose of presenting her this way to make us realize that even so vile a Nazi could be, under all the incredible brutality, a good person, with fine aesthetic appreciation, just doing with disgust her hated duties when she would much rather attend to better things—as Rudolf Franz Hoess, the commander of Auschwitz, wished us to believe? Is the purpose of repeatedly showing this painting to demonstrate that the Fascists had as much in their favor as we are shown was to be held against them? Or is it to demonstrate that in them, as in the rest of us, good and bad were equally mixed, and that we have no cause to see them as more vile than those they murdered? Or is the purpose to remind us that the Nazis raped art as they did people, despoiling the great museums of the world? But if that is it, then the choice of the painting—Bronzino's *Venus, Cupid, Folly, and Time*—is wrong, since that painting remained in the possession of the National Gallery in London throughout the war. The painting has rightly been called a haunting work of art and a picture of singular beauty. It shows Venus seducing her son Cupid, so that out of love for her he will destroy Psyche, the soul—as the commander destroys Pasqualino's soul by forcing him to kill at her bidding. Is the picture given such prominence, then, to remind us that the pleasures of love are futile while the evil of it is real? In one of the figures of the painting, we see what the art historian Panofsky called "the most sophisticated symbol of perverted duplicity ever devised by an artist."[6] In many ways, the Bronzino work is a picture of treacherous duplicity, as is what we watch happening between Pasqualino and the commander. Is that its meaning? There is no doubt in our mind that Pasqualino, as much as the commander, acts with duplicity; we do not need the painting to tell us this. Is its purpose, then, simply to underline the idea that survival requires not only raping, whoring, and killing but also extreme duplicity?

We detect another allusion in the movie when the camp com-

---

[6] Erwin Panofsky, *Studies in Iconology* (New York: Harper & Row, 1962).

mander strikes a pose well known as one of Marlene Dietrich's in *The Blue Angel*. That German film, released in 1930, was, in a way, a forecast of Germany's disintegration. Is that what the commander's pose should make us think of? Or is it that in *The Blue Angel*, too, a woman utterly destroys a man who supposedly believes in "honor" and in being "respected" but who is no good?

A female camp commander was needed in the film—and so, contrary to the facts, one was used—to make its essential point about survival. True, there can be no survival of the species without sex. But if sex is engaged in with a partner one loathes and for no other reason than survival, if it is also the worst possible degradation of oneself and the worst possible exploitation of the sexual partner, then such survival is not worth having. We have been well prepared for a view of sex as exploitation in *Seven Beauties*, because earlier in the film we have been shown sex only in this and in no other form. Pasqualino's sister was sexually exploited by the pimp Totonno. Not interested at all in his sister but only in his "honor," Pasqualino exploits his sister's sexual misadventure to establish his reputation. His sister exploits sex to earn money to pay Pasqualino's lawyer. Pasqualino sexually exploits a mental patient while she is in restraints. Little wonder that in the camp he decides, in line with his past life, that his only chance for survival is to exploit sex. He pretends to love the camp commander he fears and hates.

The commander, for her part, realizes that by sexually exploiting a man whom she utterly loathes she can destroy him much more effectively as man and human being than she could by merely killing him. The men of the SS, though vile, were not stupid. They knew that the prisoners hated them and would have liked nothing better than to kill them. Not for a moment did an officer—to say nothing of a camp commander—believe that a prisoner could love him. The female commander says to Pasqualino, "Your thirst for life disgusts me. Your love is disgusting to me. In Paris, a Greek made love to a goose; he did this to eat, to live." And, moments later, "You found strength for an erection. That's why you'll survive, and win in the end." This erection, brought about solely by the wish to survive, becomes not only the means of survival in *Seven Beauties* but also the symbol of what survival is all about.

Living in accordance with the body's crude claims is what makes life worth living, or, at least, what makes survival possible—this is the lesson that Pasqualino's story teaches. He survives because he manages intercourse, and because he kills—both indirectly, by handing over six randomly chosen prisoners to be killed when he is ordered to do so, and directly, by shooting Francesco. He does survive by committing these acts, yet it is not the concentration camp conditions that basically impel him to commit them: he has been living the same way all along—he killed Totonno without a thought in order to continue in Don Raffaele's good graces, and with relish raped a mental patient who resisted as strongly as she could. Thus, it was not just fear for his life that led him to do those evil deeds that the film suggests were necessary for survival; to satisfy the body's crude claims, at greatest expense to others—this principle has guided his actions all along.

Here, however, the film is true to the realities of the concentration camp in a certain way: prisoners did not suddenly begin to behave in the camps altogether differently from the way they had behaved in freedom. The extreme conditions of the camps brought out in often-exaggerated form the values by which the prisoners had lived, but rarely changed them. One was forced to do things one would not normally have done, but internally there were always limitations derived from previous behavior patterns. The amoral persons in most cases acted as amorally as before, or worse. Decent ones tried to remain decent—at least, as much as possible. That is why Pedro is shown continuing to fight for human dignity and freedom, even if it costs him his life, and why Francesco continues to say no, as he asserted before he came to the concentration camp that it is necessary for man to do, and so is killed by Pasqualino, who never says no, regardless of the consequences.

Pasqualino's experiences seem to teach that one lives only by or for sex. But this sex for which he lives all through the film is shown as utterly ugly—as giving, at best, the crudest bodily satisfaction. There is never any love, respect, tenderness for the partner. On the contrary, Concettina, who becomes a whore, is repellent in her ugliness; there is nothing appealing in her love for Totonno. We see Pasqualino twice using a woman for sex with total disregard for her feelings, and we see the camp commander showing utter contempt for his.

This film, by truthfully suggesting that people remain more or less the same even under concentration camp conditions, but also by showing the camp in all its gruesomeness, in all its brutality and horror, and then showing life outside the camp as being equally gruesome, brutal, and horrible, posits the argument that there is not much reason to get excited about the concentration camp world or the Nazis and Fascists; after all, there is little difference between genocide and everyday life. Murder and rape are shown as omnipresent; even if somebody is tried for murder, the trial is nothing but a farce, for this is how Pasqualino's trial is depicted. By condemning the concentration camp but also condemning life outside it, the film implies that there is no cause to condemn the world of concentration camp totalitarianism: it appears as little (or as much) justified as life in general.

This disturbing debasement of life, inside and outside the concentration camp, is achieved in *Seven Beauties* through extremely clever and effective psychological play on our emotions. From the film's beginning, with the newsreels of Fascism and war, and the song accompanying them, scenes follow in rapid succession, without any transition that would permit us to readjust emotionally. The most horrible aspects of reality are grippingly presented, to be followed immediately by an entirely different scene that, without at all denying what we have just gone through, loosens the grip in which the preceding scene has held us, and turns our emotional reaction into an opposite one. The series of flashbacks and returns to the present permits these many fluctuations. We experience horror, then something grotesquely comic or funny, then scenes of brutality, then farcical humor again. With this technique, the horror becomes background for the comic scene, and the comic scene wipes out not the fact of the horror but its emotional impact, with the result that the horror adds, by contrast, to the effectiveness of the comic experience. Such quick manipulation of our emotions makes it impossible for us to go on taking seriously our emotional reaction to what we see on the screen, even though we do go on responding to it; it all changes too often, too radically, too rapidly. The film induces us to commit ourselves to not taking any event or situation seriously—not even one that would ordinarily upset us greatly or move us deeply.

For example, Pasqualino is confronted with the problem of how to dispose of the corpse of the man he has killed. Don Raffaele gives him hints. Grandiloquently, he tells Pasqualino that Naples is the land of imagination—echoing Mussolini's statements about Italians. To emphasize the similarity to Mussolini, the film shows Don Raffaele against the background of an emptily heroic piece of sculpture. With exaggerated Mafioso pride, he tells Pasqualino that the Neapolitans invented cement shoes, and that those of Chicago and New York are but cheap imitations—that the Neapolitans invented the oversized coffin, so that at a funeral nobody knows how many corpses are being buried. Then we see in a comic scene a corpse put into a coffin that is already occupied. Don Raffaele tells Pasqualino that there used to be five hundred skeletons in an old bone house, and now there are more than five thousand—and we watch as new skeletons are added to old ones. All this is macabre and very funny, because of the comic-strip manner in which these grotesque ideas are presented.

The comic scene between Don Raffaele and Pasqualino dilutes the reaction we have when we watch a scene in the concentration camp where naked corpses of prisoners are stacked, and new ones added, like the skeletons in the bone house. And, having accepted the idea that this is farce, we cannot quite free ourselves of the merriment we experienced in watching the bone-house scene when, moments later, we see killings in the camps. We recognize that we have been induced to see one as leading to the other, but, having formulated a gallows-humor attitude toward stacked skeletons, we cannot easily switch to the utter revulsion that, without comic preparation, the concentration camp corpses would normally evoke. If we do experience revulsion at this scene, we come to mistrust our emotions, as we now realize that our previous attitude of amusement was terribly wrong. But if so, how can we trust our present feeling of revulsion? Might it not turn out to be equally in error?

This technique of confusion would not work so well if it happened only once, but it happens many times in this film—probably more often than I can recall after having seen the movie only twice. The technique is used in all the crucial events of the film—in another instance, the killing of Totonno by Pasqualino. We have no sympathy for Totonno, who promised to make Concettina into an artist and to marry her but instead turned her into an occupant of his whorehouse. His overbearing, arrogant manner has also turned us against him. His being murdered, therefore, leaves us indifferent, and the chopping up of his corpse and its disposal in three suitcases, their being sniffed and barked at by a blind man's dog, and their being taken to the railway station and dispatched as a "shipment of provolone" are all comic scenes. Thus, we have formed an attitude toward murder which we recognize as all wrong when we see murder in the concentration camp. But how can we change our feelings about murder so fast, and, if we can, which is the valid feeling?

What is true for the most impressive events of the film also holds for its most important figures. Although we know better, we cannot help having some liking for Pasqualino, because he is so well portrayed by Giancarlo Giannini as the prototypical "little man," who will be a Fascist under Fascism, a Communist under Communism, and a democrat in a democracy. But this portrait of the little man, which the film makes us believe in, is a lie. The typical little man does not rape a mental patient or kill his best friend—not under Fascism or Communism nor in a democracy. The average little man does not think of or manage an erection and intercourse with an absolutely abhorrent woman, even if his life is at stake; that is, unless in addition to being banal he is also a consummate scoundrel, as is Pasqualino. While typically little men are banal, only very few are also evil. Contrary to some popular notions, evil is neither romantic nor tragic; more often than not, it is banal. But just because evil is usually banal and so is the little man, the little man's banality as such does not make him evil, as the film wishes us to believe. This film views the average man with the arrogance of intellectual superiority.

Shorn of the persuasiveness of Giannini's acting and the skillful *mise-en-scène*, Pasqualino is a very bad person, and his villainy is by no means mitigated by his banality and pettiness. His dullness is just barely hidden behind a suave verbosity; he is a smooth Neapolitan who speaks only in platitudes. He has no idea in his head beyond how to exploit others and how to take advantage of the moment; the ultimate consequences of his actions for others, or even for himself, do not concern him. He is unable to love anybody but himself and does not love even himself very well. When he is confronted with evil of real magnitude, he lacks all comprehension of it; hence he views the camp commander as an ordinary petty villain like himself, whom his most elementary tricks will seduce. We are made to like this man at one moment and despise him the next; the result is that we again feel we cannot trust our reactions, and we therefore permit ourselves to be carried away by what the film wishes us to believe.

On first seeing Pasqualino on the screen, we rather like him, discovering only later what an obnoxious scoundrel he really is. We are immediately revolted by the commander, a ruthless and sadistic killer, apt boss of a pack of murderous guards and their man-eating dogs.

The more we see of Pasqualino, the emptier he becomes as a person, while the opposite is true for the commander. And the closer she gets to being a woman, the more grotesque this mass of flesh becomes, but also the more human, and the greater depth she reveals, not least because of the way she is acted by Shirley Stoler. She is shown not only imprisoned in her body but feeling it and suffering from it. Her disgust with Pasqualino and with his lie of loving her—which she, knowing how repulsive she is, does not believe for a moment—is but a small reflection of her disgust with herself. If she were a real person, one might think that her keeping constantly within view Bronzino's painting, in which Venus is beauty incarnate, is to remind herself at all times of how ugly she is. We see her drinking champagne, and we feel that she drinks not to make herself forget what she does to the prisoners but, rather, to induce a stupor so that she will not feel her utter failure as a woman. When she compares Pasqualino to a man who, to earn money, had sex with a goose, she is comparing herself to this stupid animal. When she says that Pasqualino, because he managed an erection, will survive and win in the end, while she is doomed, her dreams unattainable, she implies that, unlike Pasqualino, she is unable to have sex without the appropriate feelings, and that since she knows that no man can have these in relation to her, she feels doubly doomed.

The result of all this is that, while the commander remains loathsome, there are moments when we cannot help feeling sympathy—if not for her, then for her misery—so imprisoned is she in her hated self, as she seems imprisoned in her uniform and her role of killer. We have come to sense that her being dead to the feelings of the prisoners is but a reflection of her being dead as a human being. She has made herself dead to all feelings to keep from being destroyed by the realization of how ugly and unlovable she is.

But this portrayal of a concentration camp commander is no less a lie than the portrayal of Pasqualino as a sometimes charming but always utterly unimportant little man. If any one thing characterized the rulers of the concentration camps, it was their inability to reflect on themselves, to see themselves for what they were. Had they been able to recognize themselves as they really were—which the camp commander in this film is shown as being able to do—they could not have carried on for a moment. In reality, the concentration camp commanders had strong convictions about the importance of the work they were doing—incredible though this may seem, given what the work consisted of. Least of all did they feel doomed—that is, not until Allied troops actually reached the camps. As a matter of fact, far from feeling doomed, they showed much greater determination to survive and ingenuity in doing so than Pasqualino does. How else could so many of them have managed to escape being caught and to establish themselves contentedly in some faraway Latin American country, or even at home, in Germany or Austria? When it comes to staying alive no matter what, it is not the Pasqualinos of this world but the former SS members who win the prize.

Even if we knew nothing about the concentration camps except what *Seven Beauties* shows us, we would be sure to sense that the portrayal of the commander, convincing though it might seem, could not be true. Somebody with so much insight into herself could not behave toward the prisoners as we see her do. So in regard to her, too, our feelings become confused by the film. Overall, unless one comes to distrust the film's story completely—and, if one can believe the reviewers, few do—then one distrusts one's feelings and is swept into the film's version of truth.

On thinking about this film after having seen it, we may well have strong reservations about how our emotions have been manipulated. But we cannot help admiring the consummate artistry with which we have been made to ride with furious speed the roller coaster of our ambivalent emotions as our feelings for the main characters change, and as comic humor is extracted from abomination. Pasqualino's psychological rape by the camp commander, for example, parallels his earlier physical rape of the patient, who, in her bonds, was as helpless in relation to him as he is in relation to the camp commander. Both scenes are horrid, but both have their definitely comic aspects, and these are so marked in the first rape scene that when we are watching the second scene we still feel the aftereffects of our reactions to the first. These two scenes of forced intercourse, outside and within the camp, are part of Wertmüller's statement about the close parallels between the normal world and what goes on in the camps—a parallelism that seduces us into thinking that the camps were not extraordinary. If they were not, we could have lived then with the concept of them, and could live comfortably with the memory of them now—

and that would mean that we did not need to correct radically our view of ourselves and our world because the concentration camps existed and exist.

In the film, one rape scene negates the other, even as Wertmüller stresses their inherent identity. For example, before Pasqualino rapes the mental patient, he lifts her nightgown and looks at her genitals with sexual excitement, and these moments of the scene, though both horrible and comic, give us a sense of his vitality, of the strength of his sexual desires. Before the camp commander has intercourse with Pasqualino—an act that, given their difference in size and power, is like linking a huge, impassive female animal to a tiny male who is destroyed by her—she lifts Pasqualino's jacket and looks at her victim's genitals, as he did with his victim. But she does so with disgust, with feelings of doom—exactly the opposite of vitality and sexual desire. This detail of lifting up the clothes and looking at the partner's genitals binds the two scenes together and at the same time makes them opposites. Thus, the scenes reinforce each other and also cancel each other out. What we experienced as comic before we now experience as depressing. Once more, we cannot trust our feelings; they have led us astray.

Even the deaths of Pedro and Francesco have their comic moments. Pedro, unable any longer to stand the degradation of the camp and the betrayal of his fellow men (by Pasqualino's choosing which ones are to be killed), jumps into the open cesspool of the latrine while other prisoners are defecating into it. But his death, because of the way it is acted, has a liberating, almost a joyous feeling. And asserting one's human dignity by shouting, "Brothers, I go to jump into the shit!" and suffocating oneself in feces has a comic quality that is nearly as strong as its morbidity. This comic quality, however, does not exist for those who—like me—witnessed in the camps prisoners dying in this way not by committing suicide but by being pushed by the SS into the latrines, where they suffocated. One can only be revolted to see, thirty-odd years later, the most horrid and degrading murder made to look as if it were a liberating act—the vilest death made to look comic. Suicides in the camps were easy and frequent. All one had to do to die was to give up trying hard to remain alive. Or one could run into the electrically charged fence; nearly always it killed immediately, and if it didn't the guards in the towers that overlooked the camp shot any prisoner who looked as if he were trying to escape.

Francesco, revolted by Pasqualino's sacrifice of the other prisoners to buy his survival and secure his promotion to prison foreman, or *Kapo*, and challenged by Pedro's assertion of his human dignity, also rebels. Pasqualino is handed a gun and is ordered to shoot Francesco. At first, he hesitates, but finally he does shoot when Francesco asks him to, saying that fear will make him defecate in his pants. Asking to be killed to prevent one from soiling one's pants, while it has some psychologically valid undertones, is nevertheless comic. The most tragic assertions of human dignity, even at the price of death, are thus reduced to jumping into feces and a comic avoidance of a pants accident.

This scene, like nearly everything else in the film, is completely untrue to the reality of the camps. No SS man would be so stupid as to hand a prisoner a loaded gun and order him to shoot another prisoner. The SS man would know that in doing so he was signing his own death warrant and probably that of a few other SS men. A prisoner who took a gun from the hands of the SS to kill a friend and did so would have known that he could not survive, and since he was sure to be killed, would have concluded he could at least take some SS men with him, and would have done so.

But this distortion of the reality of the camps is small compared to that which shows that Pasqualino is helped to survive by sacrificing other prisoners wantonly, and killing even his best friend. A Pasqualino would not have survived on the strength of managing an erection or being in cahoots with the commander. Such things would have done him no good—would, at best, have bought him a short reprieve, as they did for the many *Sonderkommandos*, or Special Detachments, of prisoners who did the bidding of the SS by working in the gas chambers and crematoriums and were all killed by the SS after about four months.

Pasqualino as we see him in the film after his encounter with the commander and his "promotion" would have survived but a few days at most in a real camp. If the SS had not seen to it, the prisoners would have: a *Kapo* who had no moral, human, or political convictions, who did not hesitate to hand over prisoners to be exterminated, and who killed one himself was far too dangerous to the rest of the prisoners to be permitted to live. To quote only one witness (Langbein): "When a prisoner became a collaborator of the SS he had to expect to be subjected to the merciless revenge of his fellow-prisoners." Nothing in the film gives the impression that this commander would have made special efforts to protect Pasqualino, whom she considered a "worm," against the rage and retribution of his fellow prisoners. While it was practically impossible for prisoners to make sure that another prisoner would survive, it was incredibly easy to kill one. There were innumerable ways to get rid of him, of which denunciation to the SS was the simplest. Even a *Kapo* could not survive without breaking rules, and if he was denounced for this he was likely to be killed. Also, there was always jealousy within the SS. If a prisoner was a favorite of one SS man, this fact did not endear him to the other SS men. So if a favored prisoner was denounced to an SS man who disliked the man who favored him, the prisoner would be, in the camp jargon, "finished off." There were also many other ways to do away with a prisoner who had betrayed his fellows. He could be killed during the night, when there were hundreds against one. Even if he had been a favorite of the SS men, they ignored the killing. One prisoner less did not matter.

I mentioned before that the SS men had a certain *esprit de corps*, deviant and even perverted as it often was, and that they admired *esprit de corps*. When they ordered one prisoner to kill another—for example, by burying him alive—they always threatened to kill him if he disobeyed the order, but they did not necessarily carry out this threat. There were instances in which a prisoner refused to kill another and both were let go for the time being. And there were instances in which a prisoner began to obey such an order and then the SS ordered the two to change places: the one who was originally to be killed became the murderer of the one who was to be the executioner. If a prisoner killed another as he had been ordered, the SS despised him for being a traitor to his comrade and usually finished him off soon. If Pasqualino had indeed survived, it would have been only because the camp was liberated within a short time after his encounter with the camp commander.

In one of the film's sudden changes of scene from the most awesome to the most grotesque, we are transported from the concentration camp and Pasqualino's killing of Francesco to liberated Naples —destroyed by war but teeming with life like one huge bordello. Not just Concettina but all her sisters, and all the women of Naples, have now become whores, and all American soldiers are but whoremasters. The whoring seven sisters now live in sleazy affluence, where before they had lived in "honest" poverty.

Then we hear the shout "Pasqualino's back!" A sweet little street singer whom he befriended before he murdered Totonno and who has been in love with Pasqualino all along comes to meet him. If this were a medieval morality play, she might save his soul because befriending her was his only decent, unselfish act. But *Seven Beauties* is not a morality play, and has nothing to do with man's possible salvation. So Pasqualino, without any special feeling, sees that she, too, has become a whore. The implied moral is that those who overcome Fascism—in this case, the Americans—degrade even good human beings like this girl as effectively as the SS degraded prisoners in the camps.

I asked a relatively small but random sample of intelligent viewers of the film—all of them under forty—who were deeply impressed by it how they thought Pasqualino had survived. They all said he survived because of his will to live—his vitality—which is what the film wishes us to believe. Not one of these highly intelligent, college-educated, otherwise well-informed people spontaneously said that Pasqualino survived because the camps were liberated by the Allied armies. And it is difficult for someone seeing this film to realize that these "whoring soldiers" risked their lives and liberated Europe. Thus, the film, made by an Italian woman who says she is a Socialist, conveys the message that those Americans who fought Fascism were as bad as what they defeated. It also conveys the message of a Fascist machismo: managing an erection assures survival, even in the concentration camp.

Shall we then conclude that Fascism was not really bad, because under it—as we have seen earlier in the film—only a very few women were whores, whereas afterward all were? Before, Naples was an intact city; now we see it in ruins, like its women. Would it, then, not have been better if all these whoremongering soldiers had not come to Europe—and had not done away with the concentration camps, the horrors of which we have just been shown? Or does Wertmüller mean to say that nothing makes any difference—Hitler or the end of Hitler, concentration camps or the liberation of concentration camps? Did she shock us with the horrors of the camps only to tell us that nothing makes any difference? Or was it all done to entertain us? Then how disgusting it is to use genocide to amuse.

Maybe we can find an answer in the film's ending. Pasqualino asks the girl who loves him, "Did you make money?" She nods, and he says, "Good, now quit and we'll get married. No time to lose. I want kids, lots, twenty-five, thirty. We've got to defend ourselves. See all those people? Soon we'll be killing each other for an apple. There's got to be lots of us to defend ourselves. Do you understand?" To which she can only answer helplessly, "I've always loved you." Pasqualino, the survivor, is his old selfish, stupid self, untouched by his concentration camp experience, ready to fight others for his advantage, intent on what he wants, with no thought for what she who has waited so patiently for him might want for herself or for the two of them. His plans for their future are the film's final, coarse irony, because he asks her, "Understand?" when he understands nothing.

I have questioned whether this film urges us to embrace life or tells us that life is meaningless. Pasqualino's nihilistic vision of a battle of all against all for the survival of the strongest is a Fascist vision, a complete perversion of Pedro's deeply significant admonition to Pasqualino in the concentration camp. In that scene, Pasqualino speaks about wanting to live and have children. Pedro objects, warning him of the dangers of overpopulation, saying that soon the world will be as crowded as the prisoners are in the barracks, and that people will kill for a slice of bread. Maybe not to the uninformed viewer but to anybody who knew the camps, to the survivor, Pedro's warning is movingly significant and hopeful, as he makes clear when he adds that "a new man . . . must be born. A civilized man. A new man who can rediscover harmony within himself." A man who can live in harmony with others must come into being to restore rightness to the world.

The prisoner, cramped into an unimaginably small space, could not so much as lie down without taking away some of the space of the prisoners who lay next to him; still, they managed. Although they were starving, they did not fight each other for the slice of bread they so desperately needed to stay alive; some even shared it. (The greatest crime in the camps was stealing another prisoner's piece of bread; for this the other prisoners exacted the most severe punishment, as they had to if they wanted to live. But it hardly ever happened.) Thus, Pedro's message contains the true lesson of the concentration camp: from having not enough space to lie down at night, from living in starvation, the survivor ought to have learned that even under such conditions, or particularly under such conditions, one can discover a life of harmony which permits one to make do, to get along with others, and to live in harmony also with oneself.

The last exchange in the film is between Pasqualino and his mother, who, happy that he is back, tells him not to think about what has happened to him: what's past is past; all that counts is that he is alive. His reply, at the very end of the film, is his nonchalant "Yes. I'm alive." Pedro's warning about a world where man eats man and only the strongest and most aggressive survive—as Fascism has taught—is taken for a prediction; his hopes for a better future of true humanity, for which he lived and died, are forgotten. Pasqualino survives, but without feeling, and without any purpose other than propagating himself. He does not feel guilty for Pedro's death, which he brought about; or for having said yes to Fascism; or for having killed Francesco and butchered Totonno. What more impressive demonstration could there be that only the ability to feel guilty makes us human, particularly if, objectively seen, one is not guilty? It is the true survivor's feeling of guilt that separates him from those who applaud the film. Those who see survival as a mere staying alive wash their hands of the true survivor.

From the beginning of time, those who have borne witness have been an embarrassment. To those who have been carried away by Wertmüller's film, or by Des Pres's writings, what I have written here has perhaps caused embarrassment. Survivors won't be around much longer, but while they are, they cannot help objecting—not to their being forgotten, not to the world's going on as usual, but to their being used to bear witness to the opposite of the truth.

Our experience did not teach us that life is meaningless, that the world of the living is but a whorehouse, that one ought to live by the body's crude claims, disregarding the compulsions of culture. It taught us that, miserable though the world in which we live may be, the difference between it and the world of the concentration camps is as great as that between night and day, hell and salvation, death and life. It taught us that there is meaning to life, difficult though that meaning may be to fathom—a much deeper meaning than we had thought possible before we became survivors. And our feeling of guilt for having been so lucky as to survive the hell of the concentration camp is a most significant part of this meaning—testimony to a humanity that not even the abomination of the concentration camp can destroy.

PART FOUR

Remarks on the Psychological Appeal of Totalitarianism

For Americans, it is hard to understand how people who have known freedom could succumb to the spell of totalitarianism. In fact, such regimes are adept in the use of powerful psychological motives that can induce even former opponents of a totalitarian regime to voluntarily accept it after it has become securely established, and they then make its values their own.

To comprehend the nature and psychological appeal of modern totalitarianism, it is useful to consider how it differs from other types of despotism recorded in history. Like the modern totalitarianism of Stalin, Mussolini, Hitler, and Franco, despotic systems of the past permitted no opposition; those who fought the regime were crushed. But in past times, either the despot did not demand voluntary agreement from his subjects, that is, an inner acceptance of his creed and methods, or else he could not enforce this demand. Everybody was supposed to obey the tyrant; but if they did, he usually cared little what they thought about him as long as they kept these thoughts to themselves, if for no other reason than that he had no way to find out what they thought. Whatever system of spying the medieval despot employed was of very limited effectiveness, compared to electronic listening devices, for example. In modern totalitarian states, the mass media provide nearly unlimited opportunities to influence everybody's thoughts. In addition, modern technology facilitates surveillance of even the most private activities. This and much more permit a totalitarian dictatorship to insist that its subjects are to think on their own—possibly because the complexity of modern technology and mass society requires this in many areas of human endeavor—

REMARKS ON THE PSYCHOLOGICAL APPEAL OF TOTALITARIANISM: Reprinted with considerable changes and additions from the *American Journal of Economics and Sociology* 12 (October 1952), pp. 89–96. Included are segments of an afterword to Charlotte Beradt's *The Third Reich of Dreams* (Chicago: Quadrangle Books, 1968), pp. 149–70.

but nevertheless arrive at exactly those convictions which the state wishes them to hold.

Thus while in past dictatorships an opponent could survive within the system and still maintain considerable independence in thought and often, to some degree, in action, and with it retain his self-respect, in the modern totalitarian state it is not possible to retain that self-respect and live in inner opposition to the system.[1] Every such modern non-conformist is confronted with a dilemma. He can expose himself as an enemy of the government and thus invite persecution and, more often than not, destruction. Or he can overtly profess to believe in something that covertly he deeply rejects and despises.

The consequence of this is that the unwilling subject of a totalitarian society comes to trick himself, to look for excuses and subterfuges. In doing so, he loses exactly that self-respect which he is trying to maintain, a self-respect he needs desperately in order to retain his feeling of autonomy. An example of the way this works may be seen in the Hitler salute. This salute was deliberately introduced so that wherever people encountered each other—at public and private meeting places such as in restaurants, railroad cars, offices, or factories, and on the street—it would be easy to recognize anyone who hung on to the old "democratic" forms of greeting his friends. To Hitler's followers, giving the salute many times each day was an expression of self-assertion, of power. Each time a loyal subject performed it, his ego was boosted.

For an opponent of the regime it worked exactly the opposite way. Every time he had to greet somebody in public he had an experience that shook his ego and weakened his integration. Had it been only his superego that objected to the salute, it would have been easier; but the salute demand split the opponent's ego right down the middle.

According to psychoanalytic theory, the task of the ego is to protect the inner and outer well-being and, most of all, the survival of the individual by mediating between the external and internal worlds and bringing them into concordance.

---

[1] This difference has been discussed, for one example, by Robert Waelder, "Authoritarianism and Totalitarianism," in Wilbur and Muensterberg (eds.), *Psychoanalysis and Culture* (New York: International Universities Press, 1951), pp. 185–95.

The ego of the German anti-Nazi supported his desire to enjoy the fruits of freedom—thus it was against everything Hitler stood for, and it sided with the superego in the conviction that totalitarianism was a vile system one ought to resist. But this was only part of the ego's function. Many times a day it had to oppose both these stands in order to fulfill its main task—protection of the individual from destruction (by the gestapo)—for example, by giving the Hitler salute.

Thus the opponent of the totalitarian regime, who needed a strong ego to be able to survive in an inimical society, and to hold on to his convictions when relentlessly bombarded by the mass media with messages which tried to invalidate all he believed, found himself in situations which disintegrated his ego because it was forced to do battle on two opposite fronts: to assert the wish for freedom, and to protect him against being destroyed by the state because he resisted its demands.

The Hitler salute is a small example to illustrate how difficult it is to retain one's ideal of personal freedom and inner integrity, including the power to remain in opposition, when one lives in a totalitarian society. If the situation forced an opponent of the system to give the Hitler salute—that is, to raise his right arm and say out loud "Heil Hitler," thus asserting his loyalty to and admiration of the Führer, a person he hated—he immediately felt a traitor to his most cherished ideas. The only way out was to pretend to himself that the salute did not count, that given the reality in which one found oneself it was all right to render the salute, because it was the only way not to be arrested by the gestapo. Still, one's integration depends on acting in accordance with one's beliefs. So one could retain one's integration while saluting only by changing one's belief that saluting was bad.

Doing this was further forced on the individual because this salute was to be given so many times each day, not just to all officials such as teachers, policemen, mailmen, etc., but even on meeting one's closest friends. Notwithstanding that one thought a friend felt the same way one did oneself—of which one could rarely be quite sure—others who saw that one did not give the Hitler salute might report this, and often enough did. It is possible once in a while to act openly against one's convictions, when forced to do so by necessity, and still maintain some semblance of integration through mental reservations about doing it. But this deception becomes extremely difficult when it has to be repeated all the time. In addition, most of us would hesitate to make a big fuss—which refusing to give the Hitler salute created—in often-repeated everyday situations; we do not wish to embarrass through our deviant behavior some person we meet by chance. Refusing to salute was made more troublesome because one not only placed one's own life in danger, but also that of the other person, since he was required to report any failure to give the salute to the authorities. Thus many times a day the anti-Nazi either had to become a martyr and simultaneously test the courage and convictions of the other person, or lose his self-respect.

A young German psychologist recalled how this had worked in her life. She had been a child during the early years of Hitler's regime. Her father, whom she loved and whose values she shared, was a strong opponent of the Nazi movement. But she had to go to school, and there she had to swear allegiance to the Führer and give the Hitler salute many times each day—on meeting her classmates, at the beginning of each class in greeting the teachers. For some time she mentally tried to cross her fingers. She maintained to herself that the oath and salute did not count because she did not mean them. But as she did what her safety required, she loathed herself, and it became ever more difficult to maintain her self-respect and still keep up the pretense. Finally, rather than act a lie any longer, she gave up her mental reservation and swore allegiance and saluted like anybody else.

Some older observers at that time were keenly aware that the system created unmanageable conflicts within their psyche, and that in the battle between moral conviction and self-preservation the side of them that wanted to live would eventually win out over principles and, for safety's sake, side with the system. For example, before he left Germany in 1933, the theologian Paul Tillich thought in his conscious mind that he would never make his peace with Hitlerism but, as he reported many years later, "My unconscious knew better," and that is why he left Germany in good time to prevent his unconscious from eventually overpowering his conscious convictions.[2]

When our conscious mind is in conflict with our unconscious, nothing reflects this better than the content of our dreams. A typical example is one man's dream during the early days of Naziism, in which he decided to protest openly against the actions of the Nazi

---

[2] *New York Times*, December 23, 1965.

regime. Obeying what his conscious mind viewed as his moral obligation, in the dream the man carefully went about writing a letter with his protests. But when it came to mailing the letter, he dreamed that he put a perfectly blank piece of paper in the envelope, which he then sealed carefully. Not only did this man dream that he made a typical "Freudian" slip, as his justified anxiety made him act contrary to his conscious intentions, but his dream also revealed that in the end his anxiety—or self-preservation—would win out over his convictions, exactly as Tillich had known it would in his case. This dreamer realized even in his sleep how destructive such inner conflicts and the way reality forces one to resolve them are to one's self-respect. He had first felt very proud in his dream that he dared to lodge the complaint, and later deeply ashamed that he did not. In the end, the dream left him feeling defeated and discouraged with himself.

Inner conflict about giving the Hitler salute was experienced by many Germans, and this conflict found unconscious expression in many of their dreams, one of which may serve to illustrate. Shortly after Hitler came to power, a man who owned a factory dreamed that Goebbels was paying a visit there. "Standing in front of all the workers, I had to raise my arm in the Nazi salute. It took me half an hour to get my arm up, inch by inch. . . . There I stood in my own factory, arm raised, pilloried right in the midst of my own workers. And so I stood until I woke up."[3]

In his dream this man, deeply opposed to Naziism, was dealing with a problem that also occupied his conscious mind: should he, or would he, compromise his convictions in order to retain his factory? (At that very early time in the Hitler regime refusing to give the salute did not yet endanger a person's life, only his livelihood.) The dream foreshadowed what his decision would be, although it was made only with the greatest reluctance. The man's inner mental struggle about what to do was given visual and temporal expression by the long and difficult physical struggle to raise his arm. He could do this in his dream only very slowly, and it took him half an hour to complete the gesture. But once the fateful decision was made, he could no longer undo it; this was why he stood in his dream with his arm raised until he awoke.

---

[3] These two dreams and many similar ones, including those discussed at the end of this essay, are reported in Beradt, *op. cit.*

The dream was even more explicit about what went on as far as this man's moral existence was concerned. The man said that in his dream the struggle to lift his arm "broke my backbone" (*brach mir das Rückgrat*). In German as in English, to have a strong backbone is a symbolic expression for having convictions, and acting in line with them. Thus the dream revealed that the dreamer knew that only he himself could break his own moral backbone, and that no regime could do that to him. It was not Goebbels who forced him to salute, but he who forced himself to salute in order not to give open expression to his conflict with the regime. The fact that the regime was able to force people to do this to themselves shows how devastatingly effective the system was.

Since our dreams give form to what goes on in our minds, one might speculate what his dream might have been like had this dreamer deep down not known that the unconscious desire to play it safe would force him to act against his convictions. Had he believed that he would live up to his conscious convictions, he might have dreamed that he, with the help of his devoted workers, threw Goebbels out of the factory. Or he might have dreamed that he refused to give the salute, and proudly walked out, to the admiration of his workers.

The dreams of those who actively fought the system and who were not beset by inner conflicts about doing so were very different. They were not free of anxiety, since some dreamed about being caught and tortured by the gestapo, a realistic fear which had entered their dreams. In other dreams, however, they were successful in defeating the Nazis. None dreamed that they forced themselves to obey the enemy by suppressing their own convictions.

What was true for the Hitler salute was of course true for all other features of the Nazi regime. The inescapable power of the modern totalitarian system rests exactly on its ability to reach into even the most minute and private life activities of the individual, by means of the mass media and other aspects of modern technological society. Another example comes from the experience of the young schoolgirl mentioned before: one day the girls in her class were asked to take a census of the population. To exclude herself would again have meant to risk the well-being of herself and her family, and the request seemed innocuous enough. But while taking the census, the girl suddenly found herself confronted with the task of asking for the details in the life of a Jewish family. She realized that these Jews hated her as a representative of the regime, and she resented this, and them. Then she realized that this resentment of the Jews was what the regime wanted her to feel, and thus she also realized the power the regime had over her to make her feel what she did not want to feel. This realization made her despise herself. The girl also hated herself for aiding in the program against the Jews through the census. Certainly, she hated the regime that forced her into this predicament—but she ended up hating herself even more. And while her hatred of the regime was impotent, thus adding to her feeling that she was impotent —a feeling destructive to one's integration—her hatred of herself for what she was doing was potent, and additionally destructive to her self-respect.

Thus the totalitarian regime finds almost daily tasks which each subject must perform or risk his own destruction. Most opponents of the system, when fulfilling these requirements, start out hating it and themselves. They soon find themselves in severe inner conflicts about whether to act in line with their convictions and run the risks involved, or play it safe and feel like a coward and betrayer of most cherished values. While the regime can easily flourish despite their hatred of it, they suffer seriously from this conflict between their overt behavior and their secret values; thus the regime is destructive to their inner integration and—since they act against their convictions—their self-respect. Self-respect and being well integrated, it must be stressed, are the only psychological buttresses which can prop us up, and give us the strength to keep going in a world which threatens us at all times with destruction.

In most instances, the opponent of the system could not find respite even within the womb of his own family. Only very rarely did an entire family consist of non-Nazis. Children in particular were susceptible to the indoctrination in school, the Hitler youth organizations, etc. And they were coaxed to spy upon their parents, and report them to the authorities. Not many children did. But those children whose parents were anti-Nazi were projected into a difficult conflict about whether to be true to their parents, or to their obligation to the state, which had indoctrinated them with the idea that it was their duty to denounce disloyal people. Such conflicts of loyalties tear a child apart, and he hates those who project him into such a psychological impasse.

In most cases the child ended up hating the political views of the parent—if not the parent himself—since these created such problems for him. The parent, on the other hand, knowing the pressures exerted on his child, had to try to hide his true opinions from him, not just in order not to be betrayed, but in order to keep life from becoming exorbitantly difficult for the child. Thus even home and family offered no relief from dissimulation; one had to continue it even within one's four walls, even in one's most intimate family living.

The difficulties an opponent of the regime found himself in with his children extended to his relations with his marital partner, and those with all other relatives and friends. Even when husband and wife were both in opposition to the Nazi state, given their different life experiences and situation in society, each objected most to some particular feature of the system, while having made his or her peace with many others. Thus they would disagree with each other on what to oppose, and how; what to accept, and what risks it was reasonable to take. This robbed them of much of the support they could have given each other, had they been able to agree.

The convinced Nazis were in accord on all issues; this was a strong additional bond which tied the families of followers of the system more securely together. Opponents, to the contrary, were not only battling the system, but also more often than not were in disagreement with each other—if not in principle, then on how to proceed. There was always the vexing problem of how one could resist without endangering not only oneself but also the rest of the family, and the deeply perturbing question of whether one had the right to put the freedom, the livelihood, the very existence of one's marital partner and one's children in jeopardy because of one's political and moral convictions.

Such interfamilial political opposition lent itself well to the externalization and rationalization of all interfamiliar conflicts which originally had nothing to do with politics, such as those between marital partners, but also those between parents and children, and siblings. For example, the wife of a high government official was strongly anti-Nazi. Her husband, a very decent man, did not like many things his position in the regime forced him to do. But he had to do them, to keep his position. His wife could and did stay home most of the time and could, for example, in this way avoid giving the obnoxious Hitler salute or participating in any of the innumerable official and party functions—the two having become identical—which her husband had to attend, and where he had to pretend adherence to the system.

None of the family really wanted the husband to relinquish his position and let the family sink into utter poverty. Then there was the real possibility that if he made his reservations known—such as ·by resigning his position—the entire family would be ostracized, and some members might suffer persecution. So while enjoying, or at least making use of, the comforts of living which her husband's overt compliance with the Nazis secured for her and the rest of the family—including not having to go out and give the salute, which enabled her to continue acting in line with her values—the wife was still very critical of her husband for not living up to his convictions. Old marital disagreements fed into the conflict and acerbated it, until husband and wife avoided each other studiously.

Resentment at being criticized and shunned by his wife set this man against her anti-Nazi position. Fear that her position might become known and endanger them all provided additional reason for objecting to her attitude and behavior, which isolated the family, making the man's official life with his colleagues very difficult. Looked down on at home for a mere going along with official policy in order to survive in his position, while receiving considerable approval out in the world for whatever pretended acceptance of the system he managed, this man slowly but surely gave up many of his inner reservations about the system, since these created such hardships at home and at work. By finally making his peace with the regime, uneasy as it remained, he at last could be as loyal to his values as his wife was to hers, something she had urged him to be all along. He then could stop feeling inferior to his wife who acted in accordance with her values; he could even feel morally superior to her—as she had acted so long to him—because although she rejected his political views, she nevertheless profited from what he did.

The children took sides with one or the other parent. The sons had long been convinced Nazis, so after his conversion the father, who had been rejected by wife and daughter, began to enjoy the full support of his sons; then he was no longer isolated in his family. The sons did not like their mother's attitude but had come to pay no attention to her, whom they viewed as odd, uninformed, and old-fashioned. As a child, the daughter had strongly sided with her mother—as she later thought, not so much in opposition to her father, but very much out of a competition with her brothers; and also because her mother's values made a strong appeal, and her consistency a deep impression on the daughter.

As she grew into puberty, the daughter began to realize that the political conflicts between her parents had their source to a large degree in marital discord of long standing. This conflict between her parents was very painful to her, and she wished for a harmonious home. It soured her on all politics, since holding political views seemed to her to be nothing but a pretense for fighting one another, and because politics had robbed her of the kind of family life she so much desired. But with this she lost her anti-Nazi convictions, or her pro-democratic ones, since all politics appeared to her as equally bad.

All the daughter desired was that the family should become reunited, and that her parents should live peacefully with each other. As she entered adolescence, the girl realized that the family could not be united on the basis of the mother's convictions, because then her father would lose his job, and then neither she nor her brothers would be able to go to the university, etc. At that time she still admired her mother for acting on her convictions, but she also hated her for breaking up family cohesion. This projected her into a deep inner conflict, created by that existing between her parents.

As the girl grew older and better able to assess situations realistically, she saw that her mother had broken all contacts with the outside world, becoming completely isolated even within the home, in order to retain her convictions. The girl herself found it ever more difficult not to go along with her peers, and so she finally turned Nazi. Rejecting all her mother had stood for freed the daughter of the inner conflict between her admiration for her mother's courage—considerably weakened since she no longer shared the mother's political opinions—and her resentment that the mother had caused such a severe break in family relations. At the same time this switch freed her of the conflict between her values and those of society. Rejecting her mother's politics because of the pain it had caused her and the rest of the family added fervor to her acceptance of Hitlerism. For the first time the girl experienced a feeling of inner well-being, the result of having freed herself of her inner conflicts. She did not ascribe this new ability to enjoy life to the resolution of an old inner conflict, however, but saw it as the consequence of the positive outlook on life which embracing Naziism had brought her, and this recommended it additionally.[4]

On the crudest external level, then, the appeal of totalitarianism is that in accepting it, one can attain conformity with one's peers and the rest of one's world, and stop being an outcast. On an inner, higher level the appeal is that of reestablishing one's inner integrity, which is endangered if one must act differently from the way one feels. In some people the pressure to solve these conflicts became so great under the Nazis that they committed suicide. Others gave themselves away to the gestapo through chance careless behavior, unconsciously motivated by the wish to end it all even if it meant going to the concentration camp, because they could no longer bear their inner conflicts.

The vast majority of former anti-Nazis gave up the fight and made their peace with the system. Without joining the party, without accepting all of its values, they came to see much good in it, although they remained critical of a few aspects of the system. But they became convinced that they had to live with and in it. In order not to feel cowardly, not to feel that they had betrayed their values, and to be able to live in peace with their families and neighbors, and—very important, although they might not always admit it to themselves—in order not to feel threatened by the secret police but to be able to take advantage of what the system offered to its followers, most people accepted most of the system.

The Hitler salute, such a relatively insignificant feature of the system but one which nevertheless could exercise such powerful influence, was a very external thing; so was the Hitler picture on the wall,

---

[4] As one would expect, the resolution on such a superficial level of so deep an inner conflict as is brought about by conflicting loyalties to the contradictory values of one's parents can be but a temporary one. It could be maintained only as long as great external pressures and inducements for it continued. At the end of the Nazi period when it became obvious how vicious the regime had been, the girl, now a young adult, reverted to her original values and experienced severe guilt for having relinquished them. She devoted much of her later life to compensating for her participation in the evils of the Nazi state, insignificant though it had been. It was her guilt which motivated her to tell me her story, in the unspoken and probably unconscious hope that due to my experience I might be able to help her with it. Thinking that she was much too critical of herself, to the best of my ability I tried to make her see this and to be less hard on herself.

and so, for that matter, was the Stalin picture. These became tremendously important only because they reminded the non-conformist every minute of his conscious life that he could not afford to live in accordance with his inner convictions. While these mechanisms were rather crude psychologically, this should not blind us to the fact that they were extremely effective.

There are also more subtle appeals. I discussed and gave examples of how a freedom-loving person who lives in a totalitarian state feels daily, hourly, a conflict between his values and what he must do in order to survive. To this I would like to add that the power which can create such a deep inner conflict in him, that can force him to act against his convictions and his desires, much as he hates it, exercises a tremendous hold over him. Being subject to such a strong external controlling force reactivates childish attitudes and feelings. Only in infancy do other persons—the parents—have such power to throw us into desperate inner conflicts if our desires are contrary to theirs.

It is not so much the actual power of the parent that makes him appear omnipotent to the child. In the beginning the infant feels quite free to take candy out of the candy jar or money out of mother's pocketbook, or to embark on sex activities. The parent may inhibit all this, but the child will still do it surreptitiously. But one day, the child will suddenly realize that the parent, without being present, has created through his past interdictions a nearly unbearable conflict in the child's mind: a conflict between his own desires and the parent's prohibition. At this point, the parent begins to appear all-powerful, godlike, to be feared as potentially destroying. The child has become disciplined.

Similarly, the power of the totalitarian system can create unmanageable conflicts in the minds of the persons living in it. The child, like the non-conformist, originally resisted the power that thus controls him. But the power is so strong that it also exercises enormous appeal—after all, nothing succeeds like success—and successful power over the child has such a great appeal that it becomes internalized as a superego.

It may be argued that this is valid only for the child, as a result of his biological helplessness. Once the child is grown up with his superego well established and his ego functioning, no external power can ever again exercise such fascination over him.

But this argument overlooks the very essence of totalitarianism, which is that it sets out to destroy the independent ego, as well as the independent superego. The parent seems omnipotent because he has the power to withhold the substance of life—food. The totalitarian system has exactly the same power; when living in such a society, an opponent fears not only that he may be deprived of the substance of life, but of life itself. As the child's freedom of movement can be inhibited by the parent, the totalitarian society can similarly inhibit its recalcitrant citizens.

One important difference between the two circumstances is that certain mental abilities are needed for making decisions when working, for instance, in a factory. Workers therefore cannot be as much controlled externally as the child. But workers who still had an independent ego or superego were sent to perform strictly menial labor in the camps. They returned to factory work only after they had internalized the totalitarian superego.

If we think now for a moment about the pre-Hitler German system of child-rearing, where the child was supposed to be seen but not heard, we can understand the special appeal the totalitarian regime had for German youth. In almost all societies, children suffer from the restrictive influence of adults. The totalitarian system turns these youngsters loose, asks them to speak up, to check on their parents and report them if they do not obey the laws of the system. As the examples have shown, this develops another intense conflict in the child who comes from a home that is not in agreement with the state, or for the child who on his own has developed critical attitudes. Now two different superego systems of value seem to clash with one another. Which shall the child obey: the superego system derived from the parents or that derived from the state?

We must not forget that totalitarian systems have so far arisen in societies characterized by a strongly hierarchical organization. If they were not outright feudal, they were paternalistic. The ruler of the country, the executive powers such as the police, the military, the teacher, etc., were powerful paternal, or perhaps we should say superego, surrogates. Superego surrogates or substitutes are persons in authority who are psychologically identified with parents and whose commands are therefore accepted like the internalized commands of the parents (or of the superego).

Frequently, even in the concentration camps, belief in the power and justice of the police was so strong that prisoners were not willing to believe that they had been unjustly persecuted. Rather, they searched their minds to find some guilt in themselves. The inner desire to be loved by the superego is extremely strong, and the weaker the ego becomes, the stronger is this desire. Since in the totalitarian system the most powerful superego surrogates are the rulers and their representatives—in short, the system itself—one can gain approval of the superego surrogates only by going along with the system.

A superego that requires personal responsibility and free choice can become very discomforting, even threatening, because one can never be quite sure that one is doing the right thing. Therefore the desire to be told what to do arises. Obeying orders allows one to avoid inner indecision that might create conflict and then either internal guilt, or, in a totalitarian state, the real danger of being destroyed. If we have only to follow demands that are imposed on us, we can feel free from guilt ourselves, and safe.

It is very painful to harbor within oneself and live permanently with a personal superego that remains critical of the actions of the society in which one must live. In general, it is possible only if alternate superego images are available. This is sometimes difficult for Americans to understand, since they have been brought up in a free society, surrounded by various sets of superego images from which to choose. There are, for example, the contradictory superego images of the puritan and the libertarian, of the man in the gray suit and the cowboy, and so on, in the American society. But in Hitler Germany all superego images were geared to one another, so it became extremely difficult to develop or to maintain a highly personal superego at variance with existing society.

It was stated earlier that the modern totalitarian society, in contrast to the tyrannies of earlier days, demands spontaneous assent and total conformity in all life activities, even the most private. It is relatively simple to keep one's mouth shut. But it is much more difficult, when one is in opposition to the society in which one lives, to go through the motions of living as though one were in accord with it.

Reflecting back for a moment to the dreams of Nazi opponents mentioned earlier, to dream that one is breaking one's own backbone and forcing oneself to do something for which one hates oneself— such as standing at attention giving the Hitler salute—is one of the most painful dreams imaginable. Dreaming such dreams is not only terribly disturbing, it is also a most convincing demonstration that the regime has the power to invade and dominate even one's most intimate life, of which dreams are a significant part.

Thus the opponent of the system, even in the earliest days of Naziism, could not find respite even in his sleep from the ever-present danger that the regime might destroy him; nor from the conflicts within himself over whether to act in accordance with his convictions, or to play it safe. This conflict pursued him into the safety of his home, tore him apart in his bed at night. His unconscious, working on him in his dreams, convinced him that true safety could be found only by doing what the regime demanded.

Some dreamed that one must not think forbidden thoughts, as did the man who dreamed he wrote a letter of protest but mailed a blank piece of paper. Other dreams went even further by telling the dreamer he must not even dare to dream what he was forbidden to think. This may be illustrated by two other dreams, again from the early Hitler days. In one a lady was watching *The Magic Flute*. Since she knew a figure taken for the devil appears in this opera, in her dream she had the thought that Hitler was just like this devil. For thinking this just to herself, she dreamed she was immediately arrested.

In another man's dream, an atlas was seized and confiscated by the police, because while looking at it in his dream, the man had thought of emigrating to a free country. Such dreams illustrate the conflict which rends the inner life of the opponent of the system: his rational mind, supported by his superego, told him that Hitler is like a devil, that one should plan for escape into the free world; his unconscious told him: you must not even think—or dream—such thoughts, because to do so leads to your destruction. Even in dreams the ego was torn apart between its desire to obey the superego by doing the right thing—that is, oppose the system—and the opposite wish to obey the regime even in one's most private thoughts, so as not to endanger one's life.

As these dreams show, in totalitarian societies opponents live in the continuous anxiety that they may make a slip, that they may reveal their inner feelings and risk total destruction, of themselves and maybe their families. Therefore, opponents have to become perfect actors. But in order to be a perfect actor one not only has to act, but to feel, to live the role.

Only by becoming the obedient subject of the totalitarian state can one feel sure that one will be observed obeying all its orders.

Thus we can finally see that the attraction of accepting totalitarianism is the prospect of gaining the inner peace that comes with having resolved severe inner conflicts, and the outer peace of feeling secure. Unfortunately, for the person who was originally opposed to the system this peace is achieved at the price of losing autonomy, self-respect, and human dignity. There is much truth in the remark that the peace which reigns in a totalitarian society is bought at the price of the death of the soul.

Alienation and Autonomy

Autonomy is a Greek word, implying freedom, independence, and self-direction. The word *alienation* is from the Latin, and denotes "the condition of being an outsider or in a state of estrangement." When the words are defined so, who would not want to be autonomous and who would not want to avoid alienation? But things are not quite so simple—these two terms also underlie two more modern concepts: the state of being inner-directed versus that of being other-directed.

These two human conditions were created not by God or the devil, but by ourselves. In theory their goals are as distant from each other as antipodes. And in practice, man wants both to be enriched by the most sublime individual achievements of culture, and to enjoy all the advantages gained through an impersonal technological mass civilization; to be both self-directed and also beholden to the other. What is posed in those two words as a dichotomy is really a question of finding the right mixture. It's the age-old problem of what and how much to render unto Caesar.

Europeans used to compare their ancient culture to a supposedly barren American technical civilization with a feeling of superiority. But for the old European countries, there is no longer an easy way of denying their own longing for all the comfort and ease of living which modern mass production can provide. As some countries become more affluent and therefore more acquainted with anomy, they begin to realize that it seems impossible, as yet, to enjoy the advantages of one without suffering the other. A recent experience brought that into sharp focus for me.

ALIENATION AND AUTONOMY: This paper was originally presented as the sixth of the 1966–67 Monday Lectures at the University of Chicago. It was subsequently printed in a collection of these lectures titled *Changing Perspectives on Man*, Ben Rothblatt (ed.) (Chicago: University of Chicago Press, 1968), pp. 149–71. It is reprinted here with some changes.

I happened to be in Europe during the time of the 1965 riots in the Watts district of Los Angeles. As I read the European papers anxiously to learn what had occurred, I was startled by the sober, sympathetic attitude toward our difficulties taken by the European press. On previous occasions I had found that internal American problems had evoked European condescension; it had been a favorite pastime, particularly in liberal circles, to bait Americans about the mistreatment of our Negro population. This time the European attitude seemed strangely different. Essentially they seemed to be saying, "What do the Americans expect? If their government goes out of its way to make the alienated groups aware of their alienation from society, if it raises hopes in them it cannot possibly fulfill at present, then insurrection must follow by necessity."

This change in attitude may very well reflect the difficulties then besetting Europe's large urban centers. At the very time of the Los Angeles riots there was rioting in Stockholm six days in succession, and for two days it even spread to Oslo. It started when the police tried to separate two fighting gangs in Stockholm, who then made common cause against the police and proceeded to riot in the streets. So in Europe, too, large groups have become alienated and are reacting explosively to their predicament.

There seems a way out, but it is hardly ever spelled out or accepted in principle—certainly not in the United States. Essentially, it is based on the idea that autonomy is only for the few—the select—and the best that can be done for the masses is to protect them from the experience of alienation, and society from its consequences. This can be done, so it is thought, by arranging things so that "the lower orders" know and keep their places, both in the family and in society; socially, politically, and economically. Their children should learn from the beginning to obey and to accept the leadership of their betters.

Once more it is suggested that the philosophers ought to be kings. This means that "the higher orders," but only they, must be so brought up that they do not fall into the dangers of the alienated existence. It means their being educated not only for autonomy, but even more for responsibility, for consciousness of the self, and for the refinement of the sensibilities. This, as a matter of fact, was the rather simple fashion in which the European more or less class-oriented educational system used to deal with the problem of the alienation of the masses. But as can be seen from the riots in Stockholm, which were certainly not started by what we call college-bound youths, the system no longer works very well.

The idea seems widespread that in other times man enjoyed great autonomy; that he used to be inner-directed, and has only recently begun to suffer from alienation. In the face of this fallacy, it may be useful to review some well-known historical facts: first, riots have occurred all through history. Second, when they failed to occur, it was not because the potential rioters were autonomous or inner-directed, but because they were forcibly restrained and so beaten down by toil and deprivation that they could not muster the strength either to riot, or to conceive that they, too, deserved a place in the sun, or to act on this conviction when they did feel deprived. As long as man was chiefly part of his family or a kinship group, when his entire life was confined to his village, his church, his farm, or the guild, tradition decreed what he could do with his life, his priest thought for him, and the lord of the manor imposed his will on him. Firmly rooted in his immediate surroundings, man was not alienated in this situation, but he certainly wasn't autonomous either. Contemplating what life was like then for the vast majority, one might conclude that where there is no autonomy there is also no alienation. But are we willing to pay the price?

With this question in mind, let us look for a moment at some of the conditions of life in these earlier days. Historians explain to us that in the villages of France, where the vast majority of the population lived in the eighteenth century—when France was the most advanced country of the Western world—the median age of marriage was higher than the median age of death. The average life-span was perhaps a third of ours, and appreciably less for women, because of so many deaths in childbirth. In some years, the greater part of entire communities died of starvation, and this appears to have been a common occurrence; only a small richer stratum survived.

In Sweden, a country where currently the entire population seems to enjoy if not autonomy at least a reasonable degree of security, recent research shows that in earlier centuries one year of starvation was often followed by a year of epidemics which finished off the young, the old, and the debilitated. Tawney wrote about nineteenth-century England: "It isn't that one class is rich, and the other is poor. It is that one class lives and the other dies."

The story these historical records tell still represents current conditions in most of Africa, Asia, and Latin America. The uncomfortable truth is that the vast majority of the human race still lives on a meager level of existence. These people enjoy neither privacy nor culture nor autonomy. Alienation would seem to them a very small price indeed to pay for gaining access to some of the socio-economic advantages and socio-human experiences—including the alienating ones—many of us enjoy today.

Do I suggest then that alienation is the necessary price if larger numbers of men are to enjoy some autonomy? Possibly so, but we are still posing the question far too radically as either-or. Unfortunately, this is how it is posed by many who realize that the advantages of industrialization are unavoidably tied to alienation, and who therefore try to beat their relative alienation by escaping into the extremes of solipsistic isolation. Reactions of this kind are reflected in those who think that since modern man seems to have to live in a state of relative alienation, it is better to start him out in total isolation in a Skinner box, or to educate him through teaching machines instead of through human contact and experience.

At the other extreme are those who engage in extremes of deviate sex, violence, or drug-induced madness. They fool themselves into thinking that because they do these things on their very own, the act has gained them autonomy. Neither course is the answer—not a self-chosen machine-dominated existence nor a self-chosen escape into a paroxysm of the senses that ends only by dulling them.

It is a mistake to try to make a good thing of alienation by mechanizing all aspects of human existence beyond reason, in order to enjoy greater material advantages. It is also a mistake to embrace alienation by denying the world altogether because it is difficult to abide in it and still remain self-determined. The real issue is: how to achieve a vital and optimal balance between relative alienation and relative autonomy—between self-direction and beholdenness to the other? The riots of Watts, Berkeley, and Stockholm included discontented groups from both the highest and the lowest levels of education, if not also social status. But these groups are alike in their suffering from alienation and their striving for autonomy.

That is why my thesis is that, contrary to widespread opinion, these two, alienation and autonomy, while antithetical as concepts, are in fact correlated; the more there is of one, the more there can be of the other, while the less there is of autonomy, for example, the less there is also usually of alienation. Our present dilemma is that until this connection between them is recognized and taken account of, the larger problem cannot even be approached. Both autonomy and personal alienation are, after all, not only correlated but also relative terms.

All of us feel that we know what we mean when speaking of alienation: anomy, or emotional disturbance. But these words have no meaning unless we can speak of them in comparative terms; therefore, what concepts or terms do we oppose them to? Let me, for purposes of this discussion, suggest that personal integration is the opposite of both alienation and emotional disturbance, and that it is the necessary prior condition to autonomy. And let me further suggest that a justified self-respect, true self-determination, and the ability to form meaningful and lasting personal relations are in their combination tantamount to autonomy. Such definition suggests the Janus-like nature of alienation: it is an estrangement from the world we live in, and from our inner life; it is also an inability to establish harmony within ourselves, and between our inner self and our way of life in the world.

Seen this way, how high a degree of personal integration—and with it, of autonomy—a person needs to have achieved for it reliably to protect him against alienation depends on the severity of the impact of alienation he is subjected to, and how much he is threatened by emotional disturbance because of the conflicts existing within himself. Since our inner conflicts and our ability to integrate them both have their primary source in our early developmental experiences, how much ability we have to achieve and maintain personal integration will largely depend upon the alienating experiences we were subjected to during infancy and childhood within our family, and later, in society.

Psychoanalysis, for the most part, views earliest infancy as a time of utter passivity, when the infant's total wants are taken care of by others and he neither wishes nor needs to do anything on his own. Contrary to this, I believe that the infant is immensely active, especially in what to him are central events in his life, such as nursing. At such times he may not feel that he is moving mountains, but he certainly feels as if he were sucking them dry. To view such an experience as utterly passive contradicts the infant's experience, which is that his efforts are monumental. Fortunately, such ideas are slowly becoming more widely accepted both in psychoanalysis and in academic psychology.

No one is less autonomous, less integrated, or more alienated from himself and society than the child who is suffering from the disturbance known as infantile autism, such as some of the children with whom we work at the Orthogenic School. As we got to know these children well, we found that the cause of their disturbance was not primarily that they lacked passive satisfactions. Such satisfactions were very easy for us to provide; some autistic children accepted the offered satisfactions and remained as autistic as before. Others rejected them, but none moved out of the autistic position because of such satisfactions. The children did this only if we were able to activate them.

Many of these autistic children were reported to have developed more or less normally up to the age of about eighteen to twenty-four months. This is the age when the infant still has many needs he cannot fill himself, but when through walking and talking he is beginning to try to get what he wants on his own. Our findings suggest that these disturbed children had begun to develop normal speech and other skills in an effort to influence their environment, but gave them up when they failed to accomplish this.

The child does not withdraw simply because his needs are not adequately met, although this, too, will certainly scar his personality. He gives up living, so to say, when he is stymied in his active reaching-out because of too little response, or too many wrong responses. He withdraws when his own efforts to relate find him less able to affect the environment than before. If the trait of taking initiative is to be implanted in the child, it must prove its value by getting the desired results. That there is a critical age when this must happen is probably as true for human beings as it seems to have been proven to be for imprinting in some birds and mammals.

This is why artificial feeding times, arranged according to the clock, can dehumanize the infant. It is not so much that clock-feeding is contrary to the natural rhythm of the body, or that it stands for a mechanical ordering of time and of the mother-child relation. It is rather that for the infant to develop initiative, he has to experience that his cry for food brings about his satiation, according to his own timing. This is what makes feeding a social and humanizing experience. When the infant's smile evokes a parallel response in the mother, even that starts him on the road to autonomy, because it gives him the feeling "What I do makes a difference." Conversely, the frequent experience that his own actions—cries or smiles—make no difference at all is what starts him on the road toward alienation.

I mentioned that correct imprinting in animals is basically a matter of timing. An animal that doesn't have the right experience at the right time, but has it sooner or later than the correct moment in his early development, suffers severe consequences. The same is true for human beings although the latitudes are much wider: we all have to have the right experiences at roughly the right times. We are certainly aware of the adolescent's struggle for autonomy; of his turmoil, his conflicts, his fight for his own world against that of the adults. Much more dramatic and of far greater import is the small child's struggle to build his own world out of the meager pieces his reality provides. The parent's assurance to the frustrated child, "When you are older you will understand all the ramifications and then be master of your life," is of little help. The child's wish is not to become a self-directing person at some future date, but to be one right now. And his struggle is righteous: years of experience with life while lacking autonomy may destroy a person's trust in himself, which is even more basic a loss than one's trust in other people.

It was exactly this problem of early autonomy against views of the total dependence of the infant on his mother which motivated me to go to Israel in 1964 to study kibbutz child-rearing.[1] In the kibbutzim, infants are raised only in part by their mothers from the fourth day of life, and from the third month, the mother plays even less of a role in their lives. According to our theories, this would lead to extreme alienation; but it does not. The young kibbutz child develops autonomy in his interactions with others and in his mastery of his human and physical environment, and does so considerably earlier

---

[1] The findings of this study are reported in *Children of the Dream*. The following pages repeat some of the things said in this book. Since its publication, and in some measure because of what it reported, but mainly because of the changes which took place in Israel's economy, kibbutz child-rearing has changed in the direction of allowing young people considerably more autonomy in arranging their lives.

and to a greater degree than in our society. The kibbutz society is relatively free of alienation. There is no sexual acting-out or sex deviation there, almost no childhood psychosis, no delinquency whatsoever, no drug addiction, and marriage is remarkably stable.

Israeli society is very similar to ours. The children so reared in the kibbutzim grow up to be stable and competent adults. How this happens requires a lengthy explanation, so here I will only state that my experience in the kibbutz convinced me that every infant does need a "center" in his life—a star by which to navigate—but that this need not be his mother. To stick with the analogy, a constellation can replace the individual star, on the condition that what is lost in intensity is made up for by repeated definite directions as to how we expect the child to navigate.

It is true that the kibbutz child enjoys only limited leeway in adapting to these directions in his own individual way, but he is given ample gratification of his physical and other instinctual needs, with little pressure to control them at an early age. This, when combined with optimal conditions for autonomy in childhood, seems to go a long way toward supplementing deficiencies in even the earliest mothering of the child.

In its own way, kibbutz child-rearing seems to reflect many needs of modern man with regard to the relations of adults to children. It embodies one way of handling such relations, if tradition is disregarded and procedures chosen purely on pragmatic grounds. No restraints were imposed in the kibbutz against a child's going all the way to become what Riesman calls "other-directed" or peer-directed. And strangely enough, the kibbutz succeeds; these other-directed children are not alienated, but deeply integrated within their society—at a price, of course, which I shall soon name.

Living together in age groups from birth makes all kibbutz children feel like siblings. Emotionally, they relate most closely to their own age group and next, to all other kibbutz children. Together with all adults in the community, they form a single large family. Certainly there are exceptions; but a kibbutz child's positive and negative emotional responses to his parents are much less intense than those of an average middle-class American child. The emotional deficit in positive attachment to the parents, if there is such, is well compensated for by the less intense, more diluted, but nevertheless very real emotional ties to all members of the kibbutz. And since the kibbutz child is much less bound to his parents, there is much less cause for the child to reject them.

In the daily life of the kibbutz there is little alienation between child and adult because the worlds of the children and of the adults have much more in common than with us. Most of the community's income derives from the raising of food. This is eminently plain even to the very young child, both as to the work it entails, and as to why the work is needed and who must do it. Equally important and understood as such is the preparation of food in the communal kitchen, the proceedings in the laundry, the building of houses or furniture. Small children often raise animals at the children's house, and from grade-school age they cultivate their own farms. Thus, virtually all spheres of adult life are within the child's grasp. He understands all the things that are important in his world. This enhances beyond measure the child's feeling of being an integral part of his society, of making an important contribution to it; in turn, this creates a feeling of competence, security, and well being. So the shared daily activities prevent alienation, and enhance a limited autonomy, provided this does not conflict with group cohesion.

In this connection it is well to remember that the concept of alienation used here is derived from Marx's concept of proletarian alienation from the means of production, and the consequences this has for personality. Alienation from the means of production does not exist in the kibbutz, which is certainly one factor in the freedom from alienation. Conversely, where children are alienated from all that pertains to real work for survival, as they are widely here in the United States, this fact is certainly one source of their social as well as personal alienation. Oscar Lewis has spoken of a mystique of work that prevails in Castro's Cuba. It is not the mystique of work that is lacking in the life of the Puerto Rican families in New York who live in the "culture of poverty" he described. What is lacking is meaningful work, and it is their alienation from work that makes them feel so miserable, not the lack of a mystique.

Apart from this, what are the other essential differences in personality formation between the American system and the kibbutz system? In attempting to enumerate them, I shall use Erikson's revision of the psychoanalytic model, according to which human personalities form through having come to grips with, and mastered, a series of internal and interpersonal struggles or crises.[2]

The crucial problem posed in the first of these psycho-social and psycho-biological crises is that of trust versus mistrust. Depending on early life experiences and the child's reactions to them, the outcome of this crisis is that the child grows into a person who either trusts himself and others, or who is forever mistrustful of himself and others. Even at this earliest stage, things are very different for the kibbutz infant compared with his American middle-class counterpart, because trust in the kibbutz is derived not so much from the mother alone as from the several different persons who are responsible for a child's intimate care. So the kibbutz child is not simultaneously being cared for by and in the absolute power of a single person who can either be intensely attuned to him, a deadly enemy, or something in between. In our society, however, the child has to adjust himself to one particular person, and to that person's particular idiosyncrasies and personality type.

Differences seem even more marked in the second crisis, during the toddler stage or what is often called the age of "education to cleanliness." There the crisis centers on the striving for autonomy through self-discipline; if one fails to achieve it and soils oneself, one is shamed by one's parents, and this results in self-doubt. In the kibbutz, by contrast, toilet training occurs quite late and is very relaxed. Other aspects of the education to cleanliness, such as table manners or care of clothing, are much less emphasized than among us. With far less expected of the child in these areas, there is far less self-doubt among kibbutz children. At the same time, because they are left so much to their own devices, they achieve much greater autonomy much earlier in life.

While in American middle-class society the peer group does not become a significant formative influence until school age, in the kibbutz it is already very important during the second, or toddler, stage of development, if not even earlier. And because so much of the kibbutz child's education comes from his peers, what one must do and not do are enforced by the group, and not by the parents, as they are with us. With far fewer do's and don'ts and a much more lenient toilet

---

[2] Erik Erikson, *Identity and the Life Cycle* (New York: International Universities Press, 1959).

training, a child's superego is less rigid. But at the same time, the voice of the child's conscience is less the internalized voice of a parent, and much more the voice of the group that influences the child's behavior.

In the center of the third crisis encountered in growing up, roughly that of pre-schooler age, stand the issues of developing initiative and of avoiding guilt. But the nature of guilt is very different in the kibbutz. Again, it does not come from transgressing a law handed down by parents, but from going against the values of the group. Such an inner attitude is one that we would call other-directed, if not alienated. But in the kibbutz it means that the child is well integrated both within himself and within his society. Also, in the kibbutz physical initiative in work, in play, and in exploring is much more encouraged because the children largely fend for themselves in a community that is safe to move about in, and familiar.

The central conflict of the latency period is that one must become industrious or suffer from feelings of inferiority. About it Erikson says, "All children, at times, need to be left alone in solitary play, but they all, sooner or later, become dissatisfied and disgruntled without the sense of being useful, without the sense of being able to make things and make them well."

This statement illustrates once again how different matters are in our society when compared with the kibbutz situation. The kibbutz child is never alone. Even if he engages for moments in solitary activity, he is immediately interrupted by some other child or adult because throughout the kibbutz the prevalence of other-directedness and of group activities brings about a lack of respect for privacy which very much applies to the child, and he accepts interference with his privacy as justified and in line with the overwhelming mores of his society.

On the other hand, the kibbutz child's devotion to and high evaluation of industry, of making things working together with others, has made its appearance long before latency. From an early age he has learned to contribute to the kibbutz economy, and from the very beginning of school age he works on the children's farm, and works industriously. This is a prime example of how a relatively lower level of personal integration is compensated for by the higher degree of autonomy and self-respect which the child enjoys because of his meaningful work.

The same example shows how different the timetable is for the experiences which shape human development in the kibbutz, compared to American middle-class society. Solitude will not be available to the kibbutz youngster before he enters adolescence, and even then only rarely, for short periods and against heavy odds. On the other hand, while the American child's powerful desire to be useful is mainly frustrated, this need is fully satisfied for the kibbutz child by his constantly doing things which seem constructive to him, and which are appreciated by the entire community because they contribute directly to its well-being. This means accomplishing things which are of value right now, and not working at things which will prove of value only in the distant future like getting good grades or passing exams. The kibbutz child does not work for much-delayed rewards, but works at what is of immediate value; and it is exactly the same work which is done by his parents and all other adults.

Essentially, much greater mastery is expected of the kibbutz child rather early in life, and not much more later on. Psycho-social development seems in fact to have reached its goals as the kibbutz youngster becomes able to find his satisfaction in life through making useful things, working at it together with all other members of his kibbutz.

According to Erikson, Americans have at least four more crises to master to achieve complete personal and social integration as autonomous persons. Things are easier in the kibbutz. For example, the kibbutz-reared person is never confronted by the last and eighth of Erikson's crises: integrity versus despair. There is no place in the kibbutz for the existential despair that seems to haunt man in Western society. But such escape has a price. In terms of Erikson's model, the kibbutz member escapes anomie and alienation at the cost of a weakening of personal identity, emotional intimacy, and individual achievement, the place of which is taken by identification with the group, emotional relatedness to many others, and group achievement. As for autonomy and self-determination, in most important areas of life these are restricted to the decision of whether or not to remain a member of the kibbutz. If one decides to do so, most of the important decisions—at what kind of work to spend one's time, where to live, what to eat, how to spend what is earned through one's work—are made not by the individual but for him by the kibbutz; this is acceptable without interfering with his self-respect since as a member of the kibbutz he participates in all the decisions made by the community's general assembly.

The kibbutz example is relevant because it is a society which, though radically different from ours, consists of people very much like us. Its educational system secures for its members adequate integration, not by striving for the highest form of autonomy, but by preventing alienation—alienation both from the group and from work. And the kibbutz does achieve this by striving for only a relatively low level of what we would call personal autonomy. It can do this because it offers from a very early age an incredibly high degree of self-realization through work; because it integrates the child from birth into his group, where no competition for grades or achievement exists, and because this kibbutz system violates so little of the child's being in charge of his own body.

Coming back to my initial observation that autonomy and alienation are not opposite, but correlated concepts, I would like to add that they are not correlated only in regard to the individual versus society, but also in regard to man in relation to himself and to his body. Maybe the fascination with sex, violence, and madness, which I mentioned before, and which seems to haunt much of our alienated youth, speaks of their unconscious awareness that where they are most alienated and where they most lack autonomy is in relation to their own bodies. They prevent this from coming to awareness by insisting that the whole trouble comes from a society in which alienation is rampant, and that this society prevents them from gaining autonomy.

As the kibbutz example shows, the niceties of cleanliness, orderliness, and such things as table manners are only very small steps toward the socialization of the kibbutz child, who does nicely without them. But these niceties, when insisted upon, are very big steps toward the child's alienation from his body, since it is not he, but his parents, who are commanding what he should do and not do with his body. Control over our own elimination, for example, does not make us free so that we need never empty our bowels. Autonomy only requires that we, and nobody else, should decide when we empty them, and how, and where. It cannot possibly require that we shall not empty them when our body feels it must.

Our emotions too, like our bowels, must be free to assert their right for discharge and satisfaction of needs. Autonomy requires not that we have total, but only sufficient, control of them. Although other people may have an influence, we must certainly be in sufficient control of our emotions, most of all our aggressions, so that they do not lead us to damage ourselves or other persons.

Our bowels can be too much or too little controlled only within very narrow limits, but the same is not true of our emotions. Our desires can fairly easily be whipped up beyond a reasonable level, be they desires for physical possessions or for emotional and sexual experiences. Even our desires for intellectual and social achievement can be too much aroused. If so, then it becomes much more difficult to achieve a level of inner integration which will contain these desires sufficiently so that we may not be enslaved by them.

If we are so enslaved, emotional disturbance results; hence my earlier remarks about autonomy being the opposite of emotional disturbance. This is where the child of the kibbutz has a much easier time of maintaining personal integration, although his social autonomy may be considerably lower than ours. His desires for goods and possessions, for social success, and for sensual experiences are from our point of view understimulated. He does not develop them highly, but neither does he suffer as much from their being frustrated.

I am convinced that American youth will continue to suffer from an imbalance between autonomy and alienation, unless far-reaching changes occur, because presently we overstimulate their desires and at the same time frustrate them by restricting their autonomy over their own bodies. We keep our children alienated from work achievement where it counts, and frustrate them with the semblance of autonomy by letting them decide on their course of studies, only to rob them of autonomy where it counts by putting them into the straitjacket of an overly competitive educational and social system. We cannot successfully demand higher achievement and inner integration, and at the same time alienate them from their inner instinctual life. We cannot, at the same time, want them to read and enjoy books and also require them, while they are toddlers, not to soil and spoil these valuable books by, for example, building houses out of them.

Though Freud spoke little of man in society, on the rare occasions when he did he gave us important insights. When he wrote "The fateful question for the human species seems to me to be whether and to what extent our cultural development will succeed in mastering the disturbance of the communal life by the human instincts of aggression and self-destruction," he had in mind mastery of aggression, not its repression. Yet repression is what modern society seems to impose on its children, instead of guiding them to its mastery.

Why do I stress repression when, in many respects, most children in the past were brought up far more strictly, with far less autonomy than children are today? True, fifty years ago the child was not allowed to talk back to his mother. But this was a mother who had breast-fed him during the first years of his life; and she had not done it in the antiseptic manner in which infants are nursed today. Not so long ago, when a mother (or a wet nurse) breast-fed an infant, much of the child's nude body nestled against a commensurately extended area of the denuded body of the mother, so that there was considerable direct skin contact. The mother's body warmed the infant; her heartbeat was the rhythm—if not the music—to which he listened as he nourished his body directly from hers. Not so long ago a child was breast-fed not for some six months or less, as is typical today when supplementary feedings are started very early, but for some two years and longer. Thus during the first years of a child's life he was not only fed from his mother's body, but also had skin-to-skin contact with her for quite a while several times a day. In this connection one ought to remember that in breast-feeding, as the infant's hunger is satisfied from the mother's body, so his sucking provides her relief from the pressure of the accumulated milk in her breast. Body contact is thus made even more pleasurable by the experience of relief of tension—created in the infant's stomach due to his hunger, in the mother's breast due to the milk—which one partner provides for the other.[3] Subconscious memories of such intimacy experienced during the first years of life continue to shed a glow over interpersonal relations and can make later experiences with alienation bearable. Thus in past times prolonged instinctual satisfaction at the beginning of life anteceded all later restrictions of autonomy. Later, too, much of the child's time was spent working in the home and on the farm, or in the family shop, which offered the chance for closeness between parents and children and prevented alienation from work or family.

Now with all this changed, an entirely new balance is needed between the autonomy enjoyed and the alienation suffered—because

---

[3] Breast-feeding as the basis for the development of trust in oneself—and with it of autonomy—and for the ability to form positive relations is discussed in some more detail in *The Empty Fortress*.

in regard to this balance, the situation in the Western world has become radically altered in the last few generations. A homely example may illustrate this.

In a series of meetings with suburban mothers, one of them was very worried about the consequences later on of having spanked her child for soiling his pants. When I discussed with her why this worried her so much, she told me: "Maybe some of the anxiety comes from all that we hear about delinquency—all the terrible things youth is capable of doing in our day. It's gone way beyond the old days of turning over the outhouses. It's gotten a little bit more serious with the pep pills, and all that." What this mother said really fascinated me, because which child in suburbia today can turn over an outhouse? There are no outhouses left, and this mother in her unconscious connected this outlet, now gone, with the pep pills.

This takes us back to how she toilet-trains her son. What has changed is not that he got a slap on the bottom; this has happened traditionally, certainly also in earlier days. What is different now is that this child, when he is twelve, won't be able to get even for this by turning over the outhouse without being viewed as a delinquent. Now it's true that in the old days no parent went around suggesting to his child that he turn over the outhouse. But if he did, and his parents learned of it, there was nothing so terrible in having done it. Some such behavior was expected; "boys will be boys."

I understand that some teenagers in the suburbs now snap antennas off cars, and in other suburbs they string rolls of toilet paper from tree to tree. But there's a different attitude today about the antennas and such pranks. Now we are highly indignant; we worry about the future of children who play such pranks because we fear that they are going to be delinquents; we even call the police. We have closed up many avenues of response that existed only a couple of generations ago. Then a boy still spent many hours fishing and roaming the woods with his dog, or just sitting by the river. Now he's to stay in and just do his homework.

What I'm trying to suggest is that everything which happens to us has its consequences later on. But how it affects us depends very much on how these consequences can be expressed, or not, later on. When at adolescence the child could roam all day with his dog in the woods, you could afford even a very rigid type of toilet training. There were compensations, and they balanced each other out. Now that we have taken them away, and he no longer goes hunting with his dog, or turns over the outhouse, what happened in earlier childhood or infancy has a far deeper impact on his total experience of autonomy.

What is needed, I submit, is a reexamination of this new balance now set up between autonomy and alienation, if we are to function well in modern society. If a ready discharge is no longer possible or desirable, then the child needs, from the very beginning, much greater autonomy and a chance to develop true mastery of his body. He needs much less alienation from his own body and its function. He also needs much greater intimacy, which is the opposite of popularity, in his relations with those very few who, at different age levels, should be those closest to him.

Only then can the youth avoid feeling unduly cramped by the sense of alienation that a modern industrial society imposes on its citizens. Only then will he be able, at all ages, to enjoy fully the many advantages modern society can offer to those who have retained sufficient inner autonomy and freedom in using and satisfying the demands of their bodies. And only then will he achieve the ability to have intimate relations, because he will be a truly autonomous person, even in a modern mass society. To achieve this is quite possible, as I have tried to suggest; but it will take some doing.

Obsolete Youth

Certain things have changed radically since this essay was written; peace now reigns on our campuses. The article evokes the specter of bygone events, but the basic conflicts it deals with continue to pervade modern societies. Student revolts still occur in many parts of the world; and deviant adolescent psychology still results in acts of senseless terrorism by extreme left- (and right-) wing groups.

The quotation from Melville which begins this essay indicates that well over a century ago the causes underlying student revolt—the inner turmoil of adolescence—were recognized. Rebellion is not something peculiar to American students of the 1960s. Their revolt was not just the consequence of a specific political situation such as the Vietnam war, the draft, and student deferment, or due solely to the contradictions of an advanced technological mass society, although it fed on these. It is rather that the contradictions of the adolescent's position within society create problem situations with explosive potentialities (although these remain dormant most of the time) whenever and wherever there is a sizable adolescent group and society does not provide important functions for most of them. Adolescents need tasks and opportunities in accordance with their abilities and interests that allow them to play a significant role in society and permit their gaining personal satisfaction from their contributions to the world in which they live.

A decade before the sixties' destructive violence on American campuses I published a book on puberty rites (Symbolic Wounds, 1954). There I suggested that many primitive tribes found traditional ways to smooth the transition from puberty to adulthood. They did this through rituals and rites, while at the same time assigning pubertal youngsters very important age-specific functions in their youth societies which benefited all of society.

OBSOLETE YOUTH: Reprinted in considerably abridged form, and with some other changes, from *Encounter* 33 (September 1969), pp. 29–42.

Such puberty rites permitted young people about to enter adulthood to be confident that they mattered in the order of things, since they already performed unique services for all members of the tribe. It gave them a feeling of security and dignity which this age group, more than any other, needs for its psychological well-being. As if anticipating—and dismissing as fallacious—the so-called generation gap, in my conclusion I wrote, "Through the rites, young persons try to master not a man-made conflict between the old and the young, but conflict between man's instinctual desires and the role he wishes to play in society, or which society expects him to fulfill. They are efforts at self-realization."

The adolescent's striving for sexual, moral, intellectual, and social self-realization; his assertion of superiority to cover up deep insecurity; the tendency to externalize inner conflicts by projecting them onto society; the wish to see in the shortcomings of society the cause of one's personal difficulties—all this and much more is typical for the adolescent age whenever society fails to provide institutions suited to help the adolescent alleviate his suffering from deep inner struggles, and to solve his conflicts with adult society.

How the adolescent manages these conflicts depends on the personality of the individual and his relations to his parents, who often come to stand for the rest of the world, but also very much on the opportunities which society offers, and the attitudes the adult world takes toward his efforts—whether it encourages, supports, and condones him, or disapproves of him. The contradictions of adolescence can create an inescapable desire for confrontations—as witnessed on the campuses and on the streets, and as described by Melville in the wish to "[step] into the street, and methodically [knock] people's hats off"—or a wish to rely on acts of terrorism to assert one's own strength and that of one's convictions—Melville's "pistol and ball." Or the adolescent may strive for a more peaceful and constructive, but also more difficult, solution to the problem of discovering one's true self, through an inner process of integration symbolized by Ishmael's going to sea. It is the adolescent's past upbringing, and the relations that significant adults establish with him, which will be decisive in his unconscious choice of methods to solve both his conflicts with the world, and the contradictions within himself.

The following article was written in the heat of the battle for ensuring the survival of the university as the place for a scholarly search for knowledge, and to prevent its being made into the flotsam of the political fashions of the day. Thus this essay did not aspire to an Olympian objectivity.

But it tried to conform to what I view as the prime obligations of a member of a university, for the sake of which its continued existence ought to be protected: to understand causes; if there is conflict, to comprehend its nature; to warn against pseudo-solutions; and to suggest what might be more constructive ways to solve a crisis.

"Call me Ishmael," is how *Moby Dick* begins. So we know at once that Ishmael is not the hero's true name, and that his true name has no meaning because he has no true identity; and the stage is set for a novel about the struggle to gain an identity. But the pseudonym "Ishmael" told the reader even more in days when everyone was familiar with the Bible. For the Bible says of Ishmael that "his hand will be against every man and every man's hand against him." He is the outsider *par excellence*, and this is how Melville describes his state of mind:

> Whenever I find myself growing grim about the mouth; whenever it is a damp, drizzly November in my soul; whenever I find myself involuntarily pausing before coffin warehouses, and bringing up the rear of every funeral I meet; and especially whenever my hypos get such an upper hand of me, that it requires a strong moral principle to prevent me from deliberately stepping into the street and methodically knocking people's hats off—then, I account it high time to get to sea as soon as I can. This is my substitute for pistol and ball.

More than a hundred years ago, that is how Melville described the adolescent in crisis and his inner pressure to turn toward senseless violence and/or self-destruction. For Melville, the path to solutions was not to "drop out" or to attack—although the pressure to do one or the other was intense, then as now. His way was to leave the establishment temporarily and, in desperate struggle with the elements and moral issues, test his ability to be a man. In Melville's day this was still possible on many frontiers: one could go West, go to sea, even go native in the tropics. In any case, the goal was not to break up the established order but, having found one's true self, to eventually return from one's wanderings, find one's rightful place in society, and there improve it by virtue of the manhood one had gained.

The adolescent turmoil has not changed, nor have the social and psychological pressures that create it, but the great differences between Melville's time and our own are reflected in the ways of resolving this struggle. These differences constitute our problem today. So we must ask ourselves what social or psychological changes, what present-day constellations can explain these differences?

About the climate of student revolt, I can offer no deeper insight than Melville's description of Ishmael's state of mind. All too many of our late adolescents choose "pistol and ball" as an answer: with no frontiers left for flight or conquest, some try to evade and escape an inner conflict they find unbearable by dropping out—today, through the slow suicide of LSD, or "speed," or alcohol. Such persons, even if they escape killing themselves, destroy their autonomous selves through a delusional life of non-existence.

Others "step out into the street," in Melville's phrase, which perfectly expresses the adolescent itch to confront for the sake of confrontation. Such individuals are convinced that they are struggling actively for personal autonomy, but they are in fact destroying it as radically as those who withdraw into solipsistic isolation.

Nevertheless today, just as in pre-Hitler days, rebellious students are pictured by the mass media as the brave new generation, disgusted with the complacency of their parents, battling courageously for a better world. In 1968, leftist student activists burned books they disliked in the same manner and place (Berlin) in which Hitler's youthful followers burned them in 1933. If, however, I read the signs of our own times correctly, I do not think American student rebels, in and of themselves, are a serious political danger—although I do deem them a real threat to the integrity and true calling of the university, and to the intellectual life of our society.

What I do fear is that the provocative behavior of a very small group of students will arouse a dangerous counter-reaction: Student Fascism of the Left (particularly when, as in the U.S., it is combined with black Fascism such as that of the "Panthers") could bring on a right-wing backlash that would quite possibly strangle the democratic order. This is what I hold to be most menacing about student attempts to create chaos: the democratic process could prove ineffectual in containing them.

Destructive student violence that gets even limited results undermines trust in democratic institutions and tempts opponents of such uprisings toward extreme solutions of their own. This could swell the ranks of the still-insignificant number of Fascists on the Right, giving them a mass following that could constitute a very real danger. Even if this does not happen, in desperation, and in order to prevent chaos, repressive measures to squelch student unrest might be contemplated which, if carried out, would seriously threaten democracy.

The tactics of the New Left radicals, designed as they are to test and exhaust the patience of what they call the Establishment (or the System, or the Structure), do create desperation, particularly since the student movement has no comprehensive positive program of its own and since aimless revolution can only contribute to the creation of well-founded anxiety. Because of this ultimate danger, and the interim threat to our universities combined with radical mistrust expressed between generations, I believe we must deal with student rebellions. How else can we do this constructively except by dealing with the deep-seated causes of widespread unrest among academic youth?

In order to understand youth's discontent, one has to begin by asking: "What do the dissenting youth, all round the globe, have in common?" In the U.S., students point first to Vietnam and the Negro problem. Because of the first, they say, we have "no future" and no possibility of a "relevant" education; since society has failed to solve the problem of war and peace, it should be "destroyed." Even if some do not go quite so far, they distrust a society which (they say) does nothing to end violence, racial injustice, urban decay, air and water pollution, etc.

But in Germany there is no Negro problem; in Japan there is no Vietnam; in Italy and France no one threatens to make nuclear war. What, then, is common to so wide a cross-section of world youth? One thing they do share is that all are "against the Americans"— presumably because of the magnitude of our military establishment, and especially because of the Bomb. But Soviet Russia has an even larger standing army, relies just as much on atomic weapons, and not only represses small nations but grants her own population, including her young people, comparatively little freedom. Why, then, the concerted anger against the U.S.?

I am convinced that Vietnam and the Bomb serve youth as a screen for what really ails them. I refer to their feeling that "youth has no future" because modern technology has made them obsolete— they feel that they have become socially irrelevant and, as persons, insignificant. Their future looks bleak to them, not because of the prospect of a nuclear holocaust but because of their feeling that nobody needs them and that society can do nicely without them.

This is the anxiety behind students' expressed feeling that "youth has no future." Because if a young person does not feel that it is he who will be building the future, and that he is genuinely needed to bring it about, then he feels that he has no future. In hopes of denying such an anxious conviction, rebellious students insist that their mission is to build a "wholly new and different" future. Their anxiety is not (as they claim) about an impending atomic war; it is not that society has no future. Their existential anxiety is that *they* have no future in a society that does not need them to go on existing. Deep down, youth is fighting against a technology first developed in America, with which the U.S. is firmly identified, and that seems to rob all youth of any place in the real work of the world.

For it is modern technology—with its automation and computerization—that seems to make man and his work obsolete, seems to deprive him of his personal importance in the scheme of things. Since America's technology is the most advanced, it is Americans who have become the main target, whatever they do or do not do. This may also explain the lack of ire against Soviet Russia's imperialism and atomic weaponry. Young Russians may lack freedom of expression and thought, but there is no question in their minds or anyone else's that their society needs them for its future.

It makes sense, then, that so much of youth's battle is fought in and around institutions of higher learning, for it is these that prepare us for a specific place in the work of society. And if education today prepares us only to be replaceable items in the production machine, or to be program assistants in its computer systems, then it seems to prepare us not for a chance to emerge in importance as persons, but only to serve the machine better.

The vociferous outcry against the military-industrial complex serves to disguise how much it is based on a real hatred of modern technology altogether for seeming to dominate and endanger the whole of life. Essentially—as for the nineteenth-century Luddite—machinery, and what it appears to do to human beings, is seen as the true enemy. Since youth do not trust the human intellect to find ways out of this impasse to which modern technology has brought us, they become anti-intellectual. Even the outcry against basic research as failing to address itself to what seem like "relevant" issues at the moment bespeaks their conviction that intellectual labors are not the answer.

There are even more fundamental reasons why adolescent malaise grows so widespread. These begin to emerge, in my view, when we look in quite another direction: when we recognize that adolescent revolt is not a stage of development that follows automatically from our natural make-up. When a society keeps the next generation in a state of dependence for too long, this makes for adolescent revolt. This means it is too long before the adolescent is given mature responsibility and a sense of place that he has personally striven for and won—his independence. This, I believe, is the common denominator of the various new movements of student power and youthful revolution. These occur only where affluence exists, only in the modern industrial state; it is the common denominator when these problems are viewed from the outside.

Years ago when schooling ended for the vast majority at fourteen or fifteen, if not even earlier, and one immediately thereafter became part of the working force, if not also self-supporting, then got married and had children, there was no space for an adolescent age and hence no need for adolescent revolt. Puberty is a biological fact, but adolescence as we know it, with its special identity crises, is not. All children grow up and become pubertal, but they do not all become adolescents. To be adolescent means that one has reached (and even passed) the age of puberty, and is at the very height of one's physical development—healthier, stronger, even handsomer than one has been, or will be, for the rest of one's life—but that one must nevertheless postpone full adulthood till long beyond what was considered reasonable in any other period in history.

Unlike the situation in Melville's time, there are no more easily accessible open frontiers. With such escape routes now closed, our society has no special place for adolescence—with the single exception of our colleges and universities. To compound matters, nowadays we push our young people toward maturity even while overextending the years of their dependence. We start them sooner and sooner in school and make a farce of "graduations" (even from kindergarten now!) until school becomes a senseless rat race with never a home stretch in sight. And so, by the time they get to college, they've "had it." I, for my part, doubt whether life was ever less of a rat race than today. But it only became a *senseless* rat race when more and more people came to feel that they were racing after goals that were not really worthwhile or urgent, since survival seems assured by the affluent state.

At the same time, only a small minority of youth emerges from the educational experience today (whether in the home or the school) well prepared for such a prolonged waiting, for controlling their angry impatience. We should not overlook the symbolic meaning of the student invasions of the office of the president or dean. Big in size and age, those who "sit in" feel deep down small and unimportant, with a consequent need to "play big" by occupying papa's prestigious place. They want to sit in the driver's seat, and they want to have a say in how things are run, not because they feel competent to do so, but because they cannot bear to feel incompetent a single moment longer.

I think it is unnatural to keep a young person in dependence for some twenty years of school attendance. This may be bearable for that small elite devoted to a life of pure scholarly pursuits who have chosen it in the past and will do the same in the present and future. There were always those who could spend their entire life in academe, but they were never more than a very small percentage of the population—even of the university population, which now includes not only those attending as a matter of caste, or to enter a profession, but those who attend because it has become the required preparation for most occupations. The tremendous push for everyone to go to college has brought incredibly large numbers to the academic life who do *not* find their self-realization through study or the intellectual adventure—or not at that point in their lives. What they still want urgently, however, is to discover what is involved in gaining their autonomy; to achieve self-realization.

To make matters worse, our institutions of higher learning have expanded too fast. Under public pressure for more education for all, they have steadily increased enrollment without the means to make parallel adjustments in the learning and living situation. One result is classes that are far too large; another is the anonymity, the impersonal nature of student-faculty contacts against which students rightly complain. Too many classes in our large universities are taught by teaching assistants (some of whom share the students' dilemma, and hence tend to side with the rebellion). So, once again, the students feel cheated.

Professor Allan Silver of Columbia University has put his finger on what to me seems the real problem when he says, "Their attack on the university—whether as surrogate for society's sins, or for its own peculiar failings—has something to do with the desperate search for a livable home in America. . . ."[1] Most of all (one is tempted to add) they search for a home in which one is finally the master of his own domain. Such students want, essentially, those group therapeutic experiences which will help them feel they have at long last come of age. But colleges are simply not mass therapeutic institutions, and thus students are all too often disappointed just where their greatest need lies.

It is the waiting for things—waiting for the real life to come—that creates a climate where a sizable segment of students are chronically seduced into following the militant lead of a small group of zealots. In the words of Jerry Rubin, the Yippie organizer: "Who the hell wants to 'make it' in America any more? The American economy no longer needs young whites and blacks. We are waste material. We fulfill our destiny in life by rejecting a system which rejects us."[2]

Campus rebellion seems to offer youth a chance to short-cut the time of empty waiting and prove themselves real adults. This can be seen from the fact that most rebellious students, on both sides of the Atlantic as well as in Japan, are either undergraduates, or those studying the social sciences and humanities. There are precious few militants among students of medicine, chemistry, engineering, or the natural sciences. To dismiss this as solely due to self-selection would be oversimplifying. Those who come to the university already deeply dissatisfied with themselves and society tend to study psychology, political science, philosophy, sociology. Such students choose psychology in the hopes that studying it will add to self-knowledge (which it can) and will solve their psychological problems (which it cannot).

---

[1] Allan Silver, "Who Cares for Columbia?," *New York Review of Books*, January 30, 1969.
[2] Jerry Rubin, "An Emergency Letter to My Brothers and Sisters in the Movement," *New York Review of Books*, February 13, 1969. Rubin was project director for the March on the Pentagon in October 1967, and an organizer of Yippie activists at the 1968 Chicago Democratic Convention.

Feeling lost in themselves, these students also feel lost with others and come to think that by studying society, they will feel more at home in the world, and thus with themselves. But when the study of society and related subjects fails to solve their inner difficulties or the various problems they have in relating to others, the students come to hate the university whose teaching disappoints them. They become convinced that the teaching they are exposed to is "irrelevant"—as indeed it is when it comes to solving deep-seated emotional problems of long standing, because it was never designed to that end.

However, as Michael Beloff has pointed out, "Student power has no meaning in the laboratory; no one doubts the need for leadership by the more experienced of the less experienced. . . ."[3] While one can easily convince oneself that one knows precisely what's wrong with society, particularly if all one's friends agree, it is impossible to fool oneself about knowing what went wrong in the cancerous cell—or about how easy it would be to "create a new system" in the sciences. One has to try to test one's conviction about shortcomings in science through experiment; and if poorly thought-out experiments fail, one must study to see why they failed. It may seem easy to believe one can create "a better world" without working things out in detail, but it is impossible to claim a solution for a problem in chemistry without the experiment to prove it, and this takes real work.

Thus those who cannot find themselves in their studies or their work are the most vocal in finding the university irrelevant. Typically, the militant finds his largest following among newcomers, those with least time or chance as yet to find a place for themselves at the university. Some try to find this place instantly, by plunging into active, even violent battle against the existing order. Yet, if they should win the battle, they would be changing the university, which, despite all its shortcomings, is an institution serving inquiry and study, into something very different, namely a belligerent political workshop for the reshaping of society with unexamined and unpredictable results. That is exactly what the militant personality wants to be "part of"—not inquiry and study, but *la lutte finale*.

This is not to say that political change is not needed. It is merely

---

[3] Michael Beloff, "October for the Rebels," *Encounter* 31 (October 1968), pp. 48–56.

to insist that the campus is not the pertinent political arena, for the purpose of academic inquiry is to search for proper avenues of reform, not to drop the inquiry in order to carry the gun.

Another and even more widespread student disenchantment derives from the previously mentioned need of late adolescents to feel that their labors make a difference in the world, and the depressing conviction that they do not. It is hard to see how the average social science student or the student of humanities can get a sense of importance from his studies until such time as he is deeply immersed in them: this takes effort and concentration. Even then, the feeling may be somewhat esoteric. But what swifter and surer way to feel active than to become an activist?

Lacking the ability to arrange his own life, all the student activist can do to assert his independence is to reverse parental standards in his style of living, dress, and sexual behavior. Deep down the rebellious student knows these are empty postures, that he is only making a show of self-determination since he is sustained by his parents (or the taxpayers) while in college. All of his life, up to now, he has been told that he must learn to be a self-directing person. Now at last, when the pressures are overwhelming to be just that, he is told to go on being dependent and beholden to the grownups for his livelihood, to follow directions, to study hard, and to submit to examinations in which others will decide whether and what he has achieved.

The "scene" where this happens for millions of students is the university, and it is the university the student lashes out at—although the university can neither end a war, dismantle a military-industrial complex, or achieve for the student the personal independence he craves. Since he does not recognize the causes of his deepest longings and deepest rages, the student does not take them where they belong. He does not burn down his parents' home, or even the Capitol. What he threatens to burn down is the university. It is the university, he believes, that is keeping him from adulthood, and that must be revolutionized to serve youth.

This is not to say that established social orders are never due, and sometimes overdue, for reform. But despite high-sounding moral charges against the establishment's sins, I believe that the most offensive sin in the hearts and minds of youth is not so much "the destruction of youth in Vietnam" as the neglect of youth on the home front.

Today's youth think they have been classified as "waste material," and they feel compelled to "reject a system which rejects us."

The Germans called their own rebellious adolescents "the half-strong" (*die Halbstarken*). In German, the connotation is that such youth feel their weakness but wish to deny it through a show of great strength. Only this show does not "come off," because all their efforts (to continue in American slang) are only "half-assed"—which, in the *Dictionary of American Slang*, means: "Ignorant of a specific field of endeavor or pertinent facts; without full or proper plans, experience, knowledge or understanding. . . ."

The psychological make-up of the militant student leaders is very different indeed from that of serious students who are deeply concerned with what is wrong in our universities and in society. Many concerned students try for improved ways of doing things, but they know that violence only leads to destruction; they respect themselves and others too much to manipulate them, push them around, or prevent others from doing their own freely chosen work.

The small group of militant leaders have very different motives: most are consumed by a self-hatred from which they try to escape by fighting *any* establishment. Many of these extremists are highly intelligent and very verbal, so that their claims that they are acting out of high motives and their occasional on-target attacks against real evils have misled many well-meaning people into overlooking their true motivation: hate, not desire for a better world. This is not to say that much in our world is not itself hateful; but hatred and the lust for destruction have never led to an improvement of life. We should not overlook how many—and for how long!—were taken in by Hitler's emphasis on "the suffering of the people" as a mainspring of his actions; a great many Germans (and not a few other Europeans) hoped he would indeed create a new order, overlooking the fact that the real source of his passion for changes was an overwhelming *ressentiment*.

Recently a former extremist tried to explain to me why he became engaged in student rebellions:

> Instead of facing my true emptiness and hate, I could, in the Movement, claim that I loved man. I could think I was constructive and not destructive. Because I had no real self, did not feel any understanding for the individual, I had to have group beliefs. When I was able to take

my anger out on the system, screaming with others, "Hey, hey, LBJ, how many kids have you killed today?" it was both a release and a connection. . . .

After a few years of this existence he came to realize that "it was similar to Fascism and that I had gotten involved with an evil, power-hungry, manipulating, Fascist-type Left. . . . Then I was healthy enough to get out. . . ."

After such knowledge and parting of the ways, we should take very seriously what this formerly militant youth now has to say:

> I had and still have no respect for our schools because they always thought I was so good and bright [all through school he had been an outstanding student] when I was so sick. The rebelliousness of the extremists is caused by this emotionally starved and contact-denied infancy. I was attracted to Communism because they have communal nurseries, so that mothers cannot "murder" their infants [as he felt his mother had done]. . . . My leftist preoccupation was to change the world so that what had happened to me could not and would not happen to any other child.

What this youth meant was that his parents' narcissistic needs required that he should be an outstanding academic; that he concentrate on developing his intellect at the expense of satisfying his most urgent inner needs. Like many other extreme militants, who are often very bright, he was intellectually precocious but emotionally, terribly immature.

A young woman, also a former active militant, stated:

> One motivation in my politicalization wasn't in the least political. After having sat inactive, internally and externally—in school and outside—most of my life, I could picket, distribute leaflets, run off to Washington, work and talk with people all over the country, as if I had a connection to other people. . . .
>
> It was either doing that, or remaining what to me seemed an inept, selfish, bored, lifeless and friendless, in short, a lost child. I felt if I would stop fighting I would disappear, because my stake and claim to life would disappear with it. But in the movement there was always something new to get involved in, and I couldn't let my involvement stop and be faced with myself. . . .
>
> We had teach-ins. And in protest against the army draft we had a sit-in and a sleep-in. We all slept together in the president's office, on

his rugs. There I met a new boy-friend. Later that week I and a few other members of SDS went to confront the president in his office. I was aware of the fact that for me, and for many others on the Left, if we were granted what we said we wanted, we would no longer be happy—for then we could no longer protest. We would be useless, we would be nothing, we would have to face ourselves. . . .

My thesis is that more than anything else, it is the seeming vacuum into which we graduate so many of our young in this modern, technologically advanced state which convinces them that ours is a senseless society. This is the ground on which they make common cause with the activist leader; though for the activist, the emotionally barren world his essentially exploitative parents fashioned for him made "no sense" from the beginning. It is this common evaluation of present society that induces many to join ranks temporarily with the few who lead them against the existing order. But for the extremist, the overpowering motive is to uproot, not to reform—within him is an utter despair that anything can ever be right for him, an outlook bred into him during a lonely and desperate childhood when too much was asked of him and too little was given.

That is why student followers begin to look at things differently once the present becomes more rewarding—thanks either to a sexual relation which is also deeply satisfying personally, a reasonably good marriage, interesting work, or some other truly meaningful satisfaction.

The leaders remain committed to upheaval. The permanence of this commitment is again reflected in the lack of designs for a better world to come once the revolution is made. Their unhappy beginnings have been a prologue; the rest of their lives may turn out to be one long epilogue to the rage that overwhelmed them in childhood. They continue to feel helpless about building anything positive in the huge world outside them, the world of their parents. Just as the infant sees his elders as so forbidding that, while they are still around, he can do nothing to better his fate, so it is for these rebellious students who project their past onto present conditions. Until they can be rid of this "establishment," they feel they have no chance at all to live their own lives.

There are reasons why it is primarily the children of leftist parents who become hippies or student revolutionaries in American society. The emotional origin of adolescent revolt may always be the same, but its specific content, such as the political beliefs subscribed to, depends largely on the beliefs of the parents. In many ways such revolt is a subconscious attempt at doing better than the parent, especially when the parent seems weak at acting in line with his beliefs. The child has the desire to do and be better than his parent and also the desire to win the parent's admiration.

This is the unconscious dynamic force which powers many aspects of adolescent rebellion: the desire to defy the parent by showing off his weakness and by doing better than the parent, while at the same time still fearing the parent and desiring strongly to gain his admiration. Combined with all this is a desperate wish that the parent would be strong enough in convictions and actions to prevent his child from being projected into conflict.

Many of our radical students embrace Maoism, and chant "Ho Ho Ho Chi Minh" in their demonstrations (with the noise that other generations of students expended at football rallies). They chant about strong fathers with strong convictions, who have powerfully coerced their children to follow their commands. While consciously students demand freedom and participation, unconsciously their attraction to Mao and leaders like him suggests their desperate need for controls from the outside, since without them they fear being unable to bring order to their own inner chaos.

There is another reason why rebellious youth has put Castro, and particularly Che Guevara, in its pantheon of heroes. This is the romantic appeal of the man who leaves the city culture and goes out into the wilderness (as did Ishmael, and the early explorers and pioneers). It shows how little such adolescents have outgrown childhood identifications with archaic culture heroes. They have not yet accepted the ego ideals of maturity in our time—those of the scientist or the political and social reformer who attempts to ameliorate the imperfections of an advanced technological society, as opposed to those who try to escape or destroy it.

Both Castro and Guevara represent an image of individual man living a primitive life outside a despised society. The pre-industrial age is extolled, while modern technology is felt to rob man of the chance to be strong and independent. Like Che Guevara, these youth choose a quixotic battlefield and certain defeat alongside the destitute —to whom they romantically ascribe all the attributes of Rousseau's noble savage, although the poor want nothing more than to enjoy, at long last, all the material advantages which only a highly industrialized society can provide.

C. P. Snow's novel *The Sleep of Reason* deals with precisely this issue of adult abdication from the teaching of controls. Two young lesbians (one a leader raised in the new freedom, the other a follower) abduct a small boy. First they torture him, "to teach him obedience," and then they kill him, "to see how it feels." Both girls try to recapture through a sexual crime what they feel has been missing in their childhood: learning to obey, and being able to feel. Snow raises the problem of whether this is what comes of thinking we can raise our children in freedom. He asks: have we, in our desire for instinctual and political emancipation, so put our reason to sleep that we have brought forth monsters? A second and even deeper problem he broaches is the secret excitement provided for us by the violent and at times obscene behavior of these, our children.

From my own experience at faculty meetings, and while listening to intellectuals talking about the turbulent events of student rebellions, I have come to a sense of how much these movements feed on excitements secretly felt and hidden from oneself. There is abroad in society today a fascination with sex and violence, with drugs and "way-out" attitudes, that student militants exploit to the fullest. If students protest in an orderly fashion, they get little or no public attention. But if they shed all their clothes and walk around naked, this makes news across the nation, whatever the original cause or conflict may have been.

Universities in particular lend a prestige to the claims of revolutionary students which they would otherwise never enjoy. For example, there were days when no more than some twenty or thirty students occupied the administration building at the University of Chicago; but they got their daily headlines and were featured prominently in the newscasts of radio and TV. If some thirty people had demonstrated anywhere else, no such prominent coverage would have been devoted to their doings. The SDS knows this, so they concentrate on the universities. The contrast between an institution devoted to the highest achievements of reason, and the obscene and violent happenings perpetrated there, makes it all the more fascinating. On this fascination, student militants try to build their success.

Professor Erwin Scheuch has called this the technique of *parasitical publicity*.[4] An idea in itself, he says, may be next to nothing, but it becomes news by interfering with something else which is considered, for one reason or another, to be of public importance. Thus, in themselves, a couple of hundred demonstrators somewhere in New York or Chicago would mean very little. But "if you march into a large lecture hall, take control of the podium, and broadcast your own ideas to people who came to hear something quite different, then you have made news. . . . This is where the function of political phraseology becomes operative." If girls dress up as witches and put a curse on professors (as they did in Chicago), or undress in public and walk around naked (as they did on other campuses), but do this without reference to the "sickness of society," everyone may well get the impression that it is they, poor souls, who are sick. But if they

> do so as a condemnation of the Viet Nam war . . . they have the support of many of the older liberals and enlightened radicals, who will inevitably consider it all to be very socially significant. If you are a teen-ager wrestling with the police and you say you are doing it because of the moral superiority of a future social order, you cannot fail to get the sympathetic attention of the editors of all . . . radio- and TV-stations, rather than psychiatrists and youth welfare workers. The ritualistic invocation of ideology is thus both an alibi and a defence.

Absurd or not, however, these rebellions can and do paralyze universities. Not only because classes are interrupted and buildings occupied, not only because the faculty must devote all their energies to calming things down, but because all the time and effort that should go to more lasting achievements are diverted to forestalling the next confrontation.

In our universities today we see faculty members who strive to remain aloof from it all, while others try to anticipate even the most extreme student demands in order to avoid confrontations. Unfortunately, too little is done to activate more constructive attempts at reform or to mobilize alternative student groups. Yet what this age group needs and wants is to be active. Even if student representatives were to sit on all faculty committees and take part in all their ponder-

---

[4] E. K. Scheuch, "The Liberation from Right Reason," *Encounter*, 32 (April 1969), pp. 56–61.

ous deliberations, this is not the active life youth hankers for. Much as they now clamor for it, they would soon enough want "out."

Instead of searching for modes of bringing action into student life, however, university authorities seem to spend their time worrying about what the militants may do next or in anxious efforts to give them no offense. Worst of all, many are so intimidated that they cave in before the students have even begun to exert pressure. All this has been sapping the universities of their strength to the point of paralysis. This anxious avoidance of taking a firm stand gives militants—but also many non committed students—the feeling that they have the faculty on the run. What spectacle could be more irresistibly attractive?

If the colleges and universities felt sure of their values and took a determined stand against coercive intimidation—while remaining open to and inviting reasonable discussion of any and all constructive improvements and demonstrating a willingness to institute those which are feasible—I believe student rebellions would cease to be a threat. Here, I believe, lies the true challenge to our universities—the opportunity to give an additional impetus to intellectual life, and beyond that to society in general.

The liberals in America and elsewhere have made too much of a fetish out of formal democratism. They are so afraid that they may be thought "unpopulistic" that they have become helpless when faced by the threat of mob rule. True, no system of government is more vulnerable than a democratic framework of civil liberties. If it should ever lose its ability to right itself by adapting to emergencies without losing its democratic way, it will indeed perish: destroyed either by an authoritarianism of the Right or the Left, or by its own defensive recourse to repressions that would displace it just as decisively.

The alternative to being destroyed from without by revolution, or from within by suppression, is to win back the consensus that protects our democratic structures, without the need for repressive extremes. So far the universities have done a poor job of protecting themselves; they have been vacillating between repression and surrender.

But the day seems gone when we could rely on our institutions remaining unchallenged because those who formed them were once part of a broad consensus—part of the only establishment which counted and ran things. From now on, all institutions will be questioned—through force and intimidation, if the challengers can get away with it—through superior reasoning, if we are strong enough to permit nothing less. The more we invite and take advantage of sound reasons for and against change, and the more firmly we protect ourselves from coercion, the better off everyone will be.

After all, if proposed changes are bad, they should be rejected whether or not they are backed by violence. If they are better than what exists, why should they have to be dragged into being under duress, and thus legitimize the effectiveness of violence? On both counts it would seem the better part of valor for universities to recapture the vital thing they have lost: the initiative for change.

It should be obvious by now what I believe some of these much-needed changes might be. First, too many who go to university have little interest, ability, or use for what now constitutes higher education. They would be better off with a high-level education in the professions and the services, closely linked to a work program. This would give scope to their need to be active, and they could enjoy tangible achievement in the immediate present. Their complaint is that "nobody needs" them. Since they feel themselves to be parasites of society, they have come to hate the world that gives them such a feeling. But nothing so balances the uncertain sense of being an apprentice as to be already actively serving in the profession one wishes to make one's own.

Here we should not be above learning from those Communist countries where study is combined with work in the factory and field (particularly if we include the service occupations). I believe this to be a much better arrangement for those who feel no deep commitment to study and research—and those who do will always be a relatively small group. I would even suggest a youth service program of a few years' duration (something on the order of a civilian peace corps) in which young people could work on socially relevant projects while earning pay and getting higher occupational training. After this period, only those who really wanted to would go to universities. By that time most of them would probably have acquired a real stake in society because they had been helping to shape it. At the very least, they would be better prepared for permanent jobs because of the training received.

So long as the need for an army draft in the U.S. continues, civilian service could be an alternative choice. Only those young Americans who preferred to would serve in the armed forces, making it a voluntary army. I am convinced that if every able-bodied person had to serve two years in one program or the other, there would be no scarcity of those with a preference for two years of military service. This would further do away with the special draft exemption of college students which provokes so much unrest. Because if I am exempt from serving in Vietnam when others are not, I can live in peace with myself only by believing it an amoral war. (As if there were ever a moral war!)

As for the extreme elements in the *groupuscules* who lead the student rebellion, I have little to add here. Without the current widespread discontent among youth, they would find scant enough following, which might force them to do something more constructive for themselves. How could one assist in providing for them those emotional experiences that would help them out of their desperate dissatisfaction with themselves and the world?

For some, that could be provided most effectively by psychotherapy. If others did seriously break the law they could, without followers, readily be contained. It is the mass support they arouse among discontented youth which makes these people dangerous. I think it would be wrong to concentrate, in our thinking and planning for youth, in or out of college, on these very few. Our focus belongs on how to provide our young people with the real life experiences and emotional satisfactions they need, rather than those destructive ones they may find for want of better direction.

About the Sexual Revolution

While it seems somehow as though the battle for sexual freedom has been won, we are actually still in the midst of a revolution in sexual mores and practices, and utterly confused about how we may successfully arrange our lives and relationships based on the new approach to sexuality. Revolutions tend to be short-lived, and there is good reason to assume this current sexual revolution is no exception. Revolutions unfortunately often end in long periods of reaction, while their most favorable outcome seems to combine advances in limited areas with a return to some old attitudes temporarily rejected in the heat of revolutionary passion, but recognized as having lasting merit.

The great difficulties modern man encounters in arranging his personal and sexual life to his satisfaction suggest that the sexual revolution will turn out to have been a failure in some important respects unless a new sexual order actually comes about, one that would permit females and males to live more happily with each other and which, at the same time, would provide a better framework for raising their children. If the sexual revolution fails to bring about such improvements, it is to be feared that it may end in a sexual reaction, i.e., repression, as seems to have happened in China as a result of their political revolution.

There were good reasons for mankind to place sexual inhibitions on itself. It was the price we had to pay for the development of family, society, and culture. It is not likely that these institutions can continue if we cease imposing at least some appropriate restraints on our instinctual desires. The old restrictions were necessary because we had not yet learned to control nature; the ways in which our physiologies functioned were entirely natural events—the occurrence and sequence of pregnancies, for example. Thus many of these restraints on our sexuality had the purpose of permitting the

---

ABOUT THE SEXUAL REVOLUTION: This essay was published as a chapter in *Sexual Latitude: For and Against* (New York: Hart Publishing Co., 1971), pp. 227–43. It is here reprinted with considerable additions and some other changes.

creation of a social setting that would guarantee companionship in over-coming the hardships of living and with it prevent desertion and isolation when things became difficult, such as in sickness or old age.

At the same time these restraints served to provide children with what they needed to be well taken care of—protection and permanent attach-ment to adults who would educate them and, in turn, normally derive great satisfaction from doing this for the many years of their descendants' child-hood. In addition these restraints provided a framework within which blood-related adults formed the kind of permanent and permanently satisfying relation that provided them with the emotional security they craved.

On the other hand, the new-won freedom to manipulate our physiology to our liking, while freeing us from the hardship of being dominated by un-controlled pregnancies, does not free us from the need for controls over our sexuality. For example, when children were nursed from the breast as long as the mother's milk flowed, pregnancies were well spaced apart, since most women do not conceive while still nursing. With bottle feedings, and with breast-feeding time radically shortened since so many suitable substi-tute nutriments are readily available, we must take conscious measures to space pregnancies apart.

It would be naive to assume that we shall be able to create new, equally successful arrangements for all the purposes our former sexual restraints served. Thus the problem: since nature can now be controlled, will we be able through education of ourselves and our children to impose the nec-essary restraints on ourselves to achieve equally or more successful in-stitutions for the purposes of child-rearing and permanent, satisfying companionship? Or will it be necessary for society to continue to impose rigid checks on our sexuality? These are the questions to which this essay addresses itself directly.

By implication, the discussion that follows also raises the problem of autonomy versus complete freedom, here in the context of sexual matters. Personal autonomy is by no means identical with unrestricted freedom to act at all times as one desires at the moment; on the contrary, it often requires self-imposed restrictions. Personal autonomy is an ideal of ever more complete and meaningful self-realization. Such self-realization—with the exception of very rare and unusual situations—requires intimate, satis-fying, enriching relations to some other persons: one's spouse, for example, and one's children. Self-realization as a parent very much includes deep concern for the emotional well-being and security of one's child. This con-cern demands that one does not put the child's security into jeopardy through one's shifting sexual relations. Thus it makes necessary curbing one's sexual freedom to act as one is tempted at the moment to pay attention instead to the needs of others, such as one's children. The same is true in connection with the respect one holds for the emotional well-being of one's spouse, and the concern for her or his self-respect; in fact, all parts of one's self-realization within the context of a marital relation.

Autonomy thus does not require that no restrictions are put on one's freedom, be it in sexual or other matters. But it does demand that these restrictions be self-imposed, a matter of freely made choices; and not the consequence of submitting against one's will or without examination to the orders of an external authority, be it religion, state, or convention. Autonomy requires that I myself determine my actions. Therefore sexual autonomy does not imply the absence of sexual restrictions, but only that these must be self-imposed, within the context of the self-realization one strives for.

From the beginning of time, man has been subject to—even enslaved by—the necessities of his nature and his environment. He has had to accommodate himself to nature's realities, and refine his social institutions to ensure his survival as a distinctly human being. What differentiates man from all other beings is that his efforts to accommodate to nature involve his deliberate efforts to bend nature to his will.

Throughout the millennia, man's progress in freeing himself from the exigencies of nature has been very slow. However, within the last two centuries the pace has been noticeably quickened, and now we are witnessing an almost unbelievable acceleration of technological mastery. The changes in our relations with nature have been so rapid and bewildering that they seem almost to have overwhelmed us in the process. These changes have certainly had, and will continue to have, profound effects on our traditional style of life.

Nowhere is this more obvious than in the area of sex. Consider, for example, man's new standing in relation to the natural event of pregnancy. The changes regarding pregnancy are much more pervasive than those in any other sexual matter. In fact, many other changes in our sexual mores derive directly from the new relationship between sex and pregnancy.

My own lifetime spans the development from nearly complete

submission to nearly complete control over pregnancy. The older of my two grandmothers bore eleven children who lived to become adults; the other grandmother, born twenty-five years later, bore only five. The older grandmother also sustained some miscarriages. Thus, during the span of her life, she was pregnant about fifteen times—not an unusual number for that time, if both marital partners were healthy and enjoyed an active sex life. This grandmother's generation was indeed controlled by the inexorable realities of sex.

The degree to which Victorian sexual morality was the necessary consequence of a desire for a small family has not been sufficiently recognized. To have small families at that time required considerable control. Enduring a mostly celibate life required a strong moral conviction that sex was undesirable. Unless one *really* believed that, one could not be satisfied with a life that had to be sexually unsatisfactory. The large size of Victorian families attests to the fact that many people failed to convince themselves completely that sex was undesirable. When theory and practice clash in moral matters, hypocrisy is often used to bridge the gap.[1]

The Catholic Church has treated the question of pregnancy more consistently. Since the Church has traditionally maintained the sanctity of the body—witness its position on suicide—it could not sanction a woman's wish to decide consciously and on her own whether, when, and how often procreation would take place in her life. The only certain way for a Catholic woman to avoid a life of repeated pregnancies, without interfering with her natural processes, is to embrace permanent or temporary celibacy.

The Church supports its position by permitting the rhythm method of birth control, and by providing an institutional framework (religious orders) for lifelong celibacy. It is the Church's fear that any significant modification of these traditional postures would result in a severe dislocation of several of its most basic tenets.

For truly, once we say that a woman has the right to decide if procreation should take place, it seems only a small step to granting

---

[1] No one was more critical than Freud of the hypocrisy of Victorian sexual morality. One was virtually forced to hold that sex was certainly vulgar if not downright evil, while one enjoyed it on the sly. A child of his time, Freud could not conceive of a life not regulated by a Victorian rectitude, although he did more than anyone else to free man from the shackles of Victorian sexual morality and other crippling hypocrisies.

her the right to decide if a pregnancy should continue. In some states, only a few decades separate the legalizing of contraceptive devices and the legalizing of abortion. The threat of overpopulation has often been used as an argument for both contraception and abortion, probably in an unconscious attempt to justify these traditionally "immoral" procedures in terms of a higher social morality. But overpopulation has little to do with it. The most overpopulated countries lag far behind the less populated in the use of both contraceptives and abortions. The reason is that life in these countries is still, for the vast majority, much more bound to nature.

The new capacities—technical as well as personal—that permit today's woman to enjoy sex and yet control her pregnancies cannot help but have far-reaching implications for sex, both inside and outside marriage. The institution of marriage, with its censuring of premarital and extramarital sex, is another result of man's need to create social institutions to meet the necessities of nature. Here, the relevant aspect of nature is the helpless infant's long period of dependency, required not merely for his education, but for his very existence. While most animals not only feed, but also in all other respects successfully shift for themselves relatively soon after birth, the human infant cannot. Species survival requires that some adult provide a permanent protective setting for the child until he reaches physical maturity. At least for some ten to twelve years, the child must be sheltered, nourished, and in all ways protected while he also must learn from some adult those skills he will need to make it eventually on his own, and in due time care for his children as he was provided for. Particular arrangements vary from culture to culture, but the need for some sort of arrangement is invariable; nature necessitates some kind of family structure.

Since some form of marriage is the institution that best secures the survival of the species (in almost all societies), then children should be born only to married people, if survival is to be assured. As long as sex resulted in pregnancy, and as long as the resulting infant could survive only if some family structure existed, then premarital sex had to be prohibited or seriously restricted to protect the offspring; and extramarital sex on the part of women had to be outlawed in order to protect the family. This was so in the past; and even today, despite the commitment to sexual equality, a married woman's bearing a child by another man is much more destructive to the integrity of the family than a married man's having a child with another woman.

There have been and are societies in which the consequences of extramarital offspring were different. In the Middle Ages, for example, it was common practice for a feudal lord to bring bastard children into the family without their disrupting it. A woman's doing this was unthinkable. The historical basis for this is that it was thought that inheritance should be in the male line of descent, and not in that of the mother. As long as convention and often also fact held that the father provided the wherewithal of living through his labor, and as long as he was unwilling to provide it for a child who was not his, the double standard—that man can have extramarital sex and, with it, illegitimate offspring, and woman cannot—prevailed.

This double standard is historical rather than natural. Today, when woman is as able as man to provide for her offspring, extramarital sex—again facilitated through the use of contraceptives which prevent pregnancies—is equally available to both sexes, though the old tradition lingers on.

All this is immaterial if a society assumes responsibility for raising all the children born into it. Then sexual relations can take place without marital relations, since the child's survival is otherwise assured. In those countries, like Sweden, which assume full responsibility for raising illegitimate children, there is no longer a stigma attached to illegitimate birth. Since the state has assured survival, it is no longer necessary for children to be born only in wedlock.

Gradually, morality has shifted to reflect the view that it is a person's private affair what happens with his body, and that he should be the only one to make decisions about it. If that view becomes the moral precept, then sooner or later social inhibitions against premarital sex and extramarital sex will fall by the wayside, although psychological inhibitions may still remain.

Our more relaxed attitude toward unusual and deviate sexual behavior is another consequence of the fact that we can now arrange our lives with considerable control over our bodies. Once the idea is accepted that to do so is a person's right, legislation against pre- and extramarital sex, against abortion, or against a perversion such as homosexuality, becomes extremely difficult to enforce, just as prohibition laws were unenforceable and produced widespread defiance because the morality of the majority failed to support such laws. The popular belief in an individual's right to do what he pleases with his own body makes laws regulating sexual behavior among consenting adults practically unenforceable.

Once a solid majority of the population agrees that sexual intercourse need not always—indeed ought not always—to result in pregnancy, subject to our choice, then society will no longer have a basis for regulating any sexual behavior, always excepting those actions interfering with the rights or well-being of another person. We will still need laws designed primarily to protect those too young or otherwise unable to make reasonable decisions on their own, for example, but in general, legislation regarding any private behavior, including sexual behavior, that does not do damage to others is on the way out.

Changing patterns in life expectancy and other physiological factors have far-reaching consequences for sexual behavior and morality. I spoke of my grandmother who, like others of her generation, got married when she was about sixteen. Others married even younger, and an unmarried woman of twenty was considered an old maid. Such a pattern was necessary when a man's life expectancy was much shorter than it is today, and a woman's even shorter because so many died in childbirth. Under those conditions, sixteen was clearly a good age for a woman to marry if she was to raise her children.

In one of the great love stories of the Western world, *Romeo and Juliet*, Juliet, though not yet fourteen, is certainly considered marriageable. Her father even insists on her speedy engagement and marriage to Tybalt on the ground that Juliet is getting older. But Juliet loves Romeo, himself not yet sixteen, and marries him secretly. They then spend the night together. As they are in love, both healthy and of marriageable age, it does not require much imagination to draw conclusions as to how they spend the night. Given our current beliefs about proper behavior for fourteen-year-old girls, it is more than strange that modern American parents view Juliet as neither a child nor a sex delinquent. The reason is that everyone knows, deep down, that Juliet *is* marriageable. Unfortunately, this insight is rarely applied to our own youngsters of the same age.

Obviously, it was much easier for a girl to retain her virginity until marriage during an era when she married soon after the onset of her sexual maturity. When we consider changes in sexual morality, we need to remember that only very recently has there been introduced such a tremendous time gap between sexual maturity and marriage. To make matters more difficult, modern hygiene, modern medicine, modern nutrition, and all the other factors which have made us so much healthier and longer-lived have also had the effect of lowering the age of puberty's onset. Correct data are available only from about 1900 on; but they reveal that since the turn of the century, the first menses have occurred increasingly earlier; today, girls mature sexually about a year and a half younger on the average than they did in 1900.

Nor should we forget that at the turn of the century public free education stopped for a child when he was around thirteen or fourteen years old. (This is still the case in most parts of the world.) Free education stopped then because most youngsters of that age were expected to go out in the world and start working. If not fully adult in all respects, they were nevertheless able to begin an independent existence.

The last four decades have changed all that—at least in North America. In part because of technological improvements, and in greater part because of our unparalleled affluence, we can afford—and think it desirable—to keep youngsters in school until eighteen or until twenty-one or twenty-two if we add college.

As a matter of fact, we are tempted to think of and treat high school and college students as children, even calling them that, just because we are keeping them dependent. Most of them resent it deeply, because they know they are physically and sexually mature. But they accept living in a state of relative social immaturity, because they do not yet feel ready to make major decisions about their lives. Their unreadiness is, in part, the consequence of our educational system, which theoretically is supposed to help youngsters gain maturity; but in practice, it tends to unreasonably postpone reaching this goal. We cannot hope to understand what is happening on our streets, in our high schools, and on our campuses until the contradictory life of our young people is recognized as such: that while physically and sexually at the height of their potency, they live in a semi-dependency, socially and also often economically.

I wonder whether anyone in sixteenth-century Verona would have called Romeo a child because he was not yet sixteen; or whether anyone would have dared to call a child one of the greatest kings who ever ruled: Louis XIV of France, who ascended the throne of his fathers at the age of sixteen. The average age of present-day rulers of the world is probably at least three times that of Louis XIV when he began his reign. Comparing Louis's achievements to those of our present rulers, I am not convinced that we are so much better off as far as ruling the world is concerned. There have been many other political leaders who ruled well at an early age and who rose through their own efforts, such as the younger Pitt, who in his early twenties was prime minister.

The disparity between early physiological maturity and an ever-lengthening period of social and economical dependence, with the theoretical assumption of sexual inactivity, cannot help but produce severe pressures. A sexual morality that disapproved of premarital intercourse could easily be accepted when girls were married soon after reaching physiological maturity. But to expect our daughters to remain sexually inactive for eight or more years after reaching sexual maturity—that is, until they are twenty or older—is asking a sexual morality to work under conditions incredibly more demanding and prohibiting than those which originally supported it.

Changes in social structure tend to exacerbate the situation. Until fairly recently, an unmarried girl lived a sheltered life within the inner family circle and was only rarely exposed to unsupervised association with non-family members. In this respect, the story for the boy was quite different. He ran no risk of pregnancy, and hence could be permitted greater freedom in the world. The double standard, by the way, attests to the degree to which fear of pregnancy is a primary basis for traditional sexual morality. Sexual freedom for the boy, at either a tacit or an institutionalized level (ignoring or legalizing prostitution, for example), was in fact a way of protecting the sexual morality of girls.

Before contraception was readily available and psychologically acceptable, few halfway decent boys would risk sexual relations with a girl of whom they thought highly for fear of making her pregnant and hence ruining her life. It was not rare at that time for a young girl to commit suicide because she had gotten herself into trouble. The only honorable solution was for the boy to marry the girl. If the boy wasn't ready to assume family responsibilities, or if he wasn't sure that she was really the girl for him, the prospect of forced marriage became most unattractive. So the boy was, as often as not, as frightened of the girl's getting pregnant as she was herself. This made for a severe restriction of premarital sex, and interfered with its attractiveness because of the anxieties connected with it, short of the males' having recourse to prostitutes. This pattern of freedom for boys and severe restriction for girls still prevails in certain parts of the world, particularly in the Latin countries.

Our modern educational and social system, however, forces girls into frequent and close association with boys on an equal footing, and without any of the traditional modes of protection. Although girls now live with just as much exposure to the world and are just as unprotected by family as boys have always been, we somehow expect, or at least wish, that this fact should have no impact on girls' sexual behavior. Such an expectation is clearly unreasonable.

Many other inhibitory forces—one might say anxiety-creating factors—still powerfully reinforced Victorian sex morality in the early decades of this century. At that time, belief in hellfire had already begun to decline, but there still remained a great, if unsupported, fear of damnation. More importantly, there was widespread general disapproval of sex. Sex was treated as something secret and animal like, if not downright ugly. While we realized that our parents must have engaged in it, we found that fact hard to believe in the face of their attitudes toward sexual matters. Thus while we ourselves engaged in sexual activities, loudly asserting that it was all right to do so and viewing ourselves as the avant-garde of a new sexual morality, we had serious secret doubts. Girls in particular, whatever they might say to the contrary, and although quite a few were sexually active, deep down had the conviction that sex was truly all right only in marriage.

Fear of venereal disease was another anxiety-creating, inhibitory factor which, until very recently, produced powerful sexual anxiety. So that, too, made traditional sexual morality acceptable, because the anxiety made life safer. Although the disease itself was shrouded in secrecy, its irreversible and terrible consequences were well known and deeply dreaded. The anxiety which venereal disease aroused was deservedly great and inescapable: every sexually aware person had to cope with it. Indeed, the Victorian attitude that sex is ugly cannot be fully understood without reference to venereal disease. It is such an ugly and scary sickness that loathing of it extended back to the act through which it was transmitted.

But modern medicine, which has made possible sex without pregnancy and has rendered abortions relatively safe, has also produced a cure for venereal disease, and thus done away with most of the fear. Modern youth cannot really understand how their grandparents could have viewed sex as ugly, because they have never experienced the haunting fear of venereal infection. As a matter of fact, venereal disease has become such an unknown to young people that they fail to take the necessary, and now easily available, precautions. Thus venereal disease is again becoming a serious health problem, although fortunately it does not yet create great sexual anxiety.

When we were children, nobody told us what all children today are told about sex, if not at home or in school, at least by the mass media: that sex is healthy, sex is normal, sex is enjoyable, sex is beautiful, and that sex repression is damaging to our psyche. If sex is propagandized as attractive, why should one avoid it? Fifty years ago we were given the impression that most, if not all, sex practices—with the exception of "normal" intercourse—were dangerous and depraved, liable to destroy mind and health. Nowadays, children learn that *not* to engage in sex may be unhealthy, and that abstinence may eventually lead to severe neurosis, if not something worse.

Girls and boys now engage in sex at earlier ages than in recent generations; not because they enjoy it, although some do enjoy it momentarily. Some young girls do it out of a desperate desire to escape their loneliness and isolation. In fact, many teenagers refuse to take birth control measures, or to accept abortions when they get pregnant, because of a vain hope that the baby will provide a close companionship and a chance for a deep attachment, which they desperately desire.

Other adolescents engage in sex prematurely hoping that their partners will take care of them emotionally, that they will provide them with the tender, loving care which their parents, too much involved with themselves, have failed to give them. This hardly ever happens, of course. The loneliness and emotional deprivation of these children is usually the consequence of their parents' isolation, be they single parents or parents who have stayed together solely for convenience, or out of a sense of obligation to their children rather than deep emotional ties to each other.

The difficulties such parents have in relating to each other deprive their growing children of the chance to experience emotional closeness between two persons of different sex firsthand. This is an experience that children need in order not to feel emotionally deserted—an unbearable feeling many try to overcome through the temporary closeness that premature sex seems to offer—and later, to be able to form lasting and satisfyingly close relations to a person of the other sex.

Much of what on the surface looks like greater sexual freedom—earlier, more frequent, and more promiscuous engaging in sex (which is not the same as sexual relations because in most cases it is sex without a relation) and openly engaged-in homosexuality—is in fact most often the consequence of a sexual and also more general identity confusion.

In most instances, for example, homosexuality is not practiced for the satisfactions that a close emotional—and also sexual—attachment to another person provides. It is rather the consequence of an inability to relate closely to a person of the other sex because of a deep insecurity about one's own sexual identity, and a closely related anxiety about how destructive a heterosexual relation may be to a most shaky identity. All this is compounded by a vague hope that closeness to a person of the same sex will buttress one's tenuous sexual and personal identity.

That insecurity about one's sexual identity lies behind most homosexual attachments can be seen from the fact that homosexual tendencies typically flare up in early adolescence, when even the most normal youngsters experience deep insecurity about their identity. If these tendencies continue into a later age, and find open expression, this is the consequence of an inability to establish a secure sexual and social identity based on one's sex, and the connected anxiety that a heterosexual involvement would be destructive to oneself, the partner, or both. (I disregard here more pathological sources of homosexuality, such as the wish to dominate or debase a partner of the same sex; or the correlated masochistic need to submit to a person of the same sex, etc.)

Given the painful insecurity about who they are, it is understandable that youngsters would try to cut the Gordian knot of their tangled identity confusion by engaging in sex ever earlier, hoping that their heterosexual experience will reveal to them in one fell swoop the secret of their true identity, making it secure once and forever. Unfortunately, such premature sex experiences are in many ways more damaging in their consequences for a person's inner security and emotional well-being than were the sexual repressions of a previous age. I have observed more destructive consequences in teenagers, adolescents, and young women resulting from repression of a desire for chastity—the wish to keep their bodies inviolate, respectable to themselves and others, psychologically felt as their very own dominion—than I have observed as a result of sex repression. These girls who consciously believed in sexual freedom felt worthless, degraded, unloved, and unlovable, because they acted contrary to their unconscious but deep conviction that to live promiscuously was depraved, and that because of their sexual activities nobody could truly respect them, as they could not respect themselves. Even when their boy-friends loved and respected them at first, these girls found ways to be rejected by their boy-friends to prove their unconscious beliefs about themselves. Psychologically, it was certainly much easier to help undo the repression of sexual feelings and with it restore emotional well-being to those who had postponed sex experiences, than it was to try to free those who had openly flaunted their sexual freedom of their deep feelings of shame and worthlessness.

These early and, in a deeper sense, most unsatisfactory sexual experiences can lead to the opposite destructive consequences, also. Some youngsters seek more and more, or an ever-greater variety of sexual experiences, in the empty hope that frequency or variety will eventually reveal to them the secret of their sexual identity and make it secure. Others become permanently disappointed in sex, whether or not they give it up to some extent or entirely. Such youngsters can no longer believe that sex has much to offer them; and with such attitudes, although they may engage regularly in sex, most likely it will not provide much satisfaction, reinforcing the feeling that what they suspect is true.

Of course, while today's children are told how normal, enjoyable, and desirable sex is, there remains a widespread parental and societal expectation that sex should not be freely engaged in before marriage. Unfortunately for that expectation, it is much simpler to avoid activities when they are considered socially undesirable than to avoid them when public attitudes describe them as desirable. Traditional sexual restraint could never have been practiced had it not been supported at all times by virtually universal anti-sexual attitudes. With the removal of these anti-sexual attitudes, inhibitory factors have become so vastly mitigated that a very different sexual behavior had to emerge.

Let me now summarize the changes that have occurred in less than half a century in our sexual attitudes and behavior: we have overcome practically all the physiological and social reasons that forced sexual restraint on us. As a consequence, we have radically reduced the psychological anxieties which for centuries made an inhibitory sexual morality possible and livable. But even more important, the traditional sexual morality that used to bind anxieties inasmuch as it protected us against real dangers (such as undesired pregnancy and venereal disease) now creates anxiety. Today, fear of sex signifies much more serious neurosis than it did in the past. The results can be psychologically devastating when a person is caught up in a traditional morality that clashes with the prevailing one. Clearly, if a morality designed to protect against anxiety now engenders it, then such a morality has become unworkable and is in need of radical reform.

All of this hardly means that sex is now simple. As long as abortions were virtually unthinkable, there was little reason for concern about the psychological effects of an abortion. As long as premarital or extramarital sex was unspeakable (though not unthinkable), there was little place for worrying about the psychological consequences of sexual restraint—although one might suffer from them. There was also little worry about the psychological consequences of promiscuous extramarital or premarital sex, because one worried much more about the social and moral consequences if one's violation of the sexual mores became known. As long as homosexuality was outlawed, there was no reason to be concerned with its undesirable psychological effects. And so the evolution of our modern sexual morality, while doing away with many old hardships, has brought new problems, new difficulties; and these are much more elusive just because they are no longer societal or legal, but mainly psychological, or familial. It is simply not true that sex is no longer surrounded by anxieties, or that sex no longer leads to serious difficulties. It is just that the nature of these difficulties has changed from being dominantly social to being private and psychological.

It is my firm conviction, based on wide professional experience, that too early or too widely promiscuous sex, and particularly certain sexual practices (for example, homosexuality) can and do cause severe psychological damage, and this whether or not society disapproves. Such practices are detrimental to the person because of their psychic consequences to him and those closest to him. Unfortunately, public morality is not yet much concerned with the psychological damage people inflict on themselves or those closest to them.

Contrary to what some protagonists of sexual freedom wish to think, the mere breakdown of traditional sexual morality does not constitute a new sexual morality. It means as yet merely an *absence* of sexual morality—but man cannot live well without some sexual morality; nor can children be raised to be mentally healthy without being exposed in their formative years to a definite sexual morality.

If it is objected that some primitive tribes can do without a sexual morality, my rejoinder is that this may very well be one of the reasons they remain primitives. And if some want to return to Rousseau's image of the noble savage, the fact is that there is no reality to back up his fantasies. We must, therefore, protect our young against the real and potential dangers inherent in the absence of a definite sexual morality, and we must do this in a rational way. We must offer social and psychological protection—measures that are more effective than legalism and antiquated moral concepts. We shall have to steer clear of both the old tradition that sex is evil, and the playboy attitude that handling sex is easy and free of all problems. Neither is true.

Perhaps sex would be simple in utopia; but ours is not a utopian society, and it is a serious mistake to act as though it were. I have known girls and boys who engaged in sex not because they wanted to, but because they needed to prove to themselves or to others that they had no sexual problems. Thus their "free" sexual activities only increased the difficulties about sex they held within themselves.

What we need is a new morality freeing sex from the old anxieties, the old inhibitions, and from the social and sexual supremacy of one sex over the other, all of which are damaging to the full enjoyment of sex for both females and males. A new sexual ethic will have to be as definite as was the old one; but it ought to be a morality flowing from man's inner values, not one imposed on him by authority or tradition. Such morality will have to be based on respect for the body and its natural functions; and on concern for the psychological and sexual well-being of those we choose to live closely with, and whom we set into the world: our children.

In the past, all too often the price one sexual partner had to pay for his, or more often her, sexual, social, emotional security was to accept domination by the partner who provided them—and often even by a partner who failed to provide them. The new sexual morality will have to be of such a nature as to enhance greatly the emotional and social protection the partners derive from the permanence of their sexual relation and the satisfaction it provides because it is free of any domination of one partner by the other. In short, it will have to be a sexual morality which results in a secure bond, free of any bondage. It will have to be a morality that facilitates sexual, emotional, and social relationships in which each partner finds deep satisfaction of his dependent needs; but within which he can also afford to develop his individuality to the fullest, due to the pleasure each partner finds in watching the other achieve his self-realization. Such self-realization will be more readily available because each sexual partner will know that whatever weaknesses may come in the wake of his greater strengths will not be taken advantage of, but will be compensated for with loving care. Such a new morality will permit sexual relations to be fully satisfying in both their active and their passive aspects; strength in the partner will be admired without being resented; dependent needs of the partner will not be taken advantage of, but experienced as an opportunity to deepen the bond and to enrich the relation. To make these and many more satisfactions possible within a permanent sexual and caring relationship the new sexual morality must embody what ought to be by now a self-evident truth: that neither the desire to assert nor the desire to yield is peculiar to one sex or the other; both exist in each sex, as both are very much part of the make-up of every human being, albeit to different degrees at various moments in one's life, and in a relationship. Both sexes have deep-seated and pressing needs for receiving dependent gratifications, and there can be no sexual or emotional well-being as long as these remain unsatisfied, although the nature of these dependent needs, as much as that of the need for self-assertion, may take on different forms in the two sexes; these certainly vary over time, and with the vicissitudes of the relationship within which these needs seek —and for the sexual and emotional well-being of the partners must find—satisfaction.

That pregnancies are now much more due to conscious decision than to chance has, if anything, increased our obligation to be concerned not only with our own and our sexual partner's sexual, physical, emotional, and moral well-being, but very much also with that of our children. As far as sexual morality is concerned, this means they must be exposed during their formative years to a constructive sexual morality that enriches the unique personal and social importance of sex in the life of the individual. Thus the new sex morality must be permanent and secure, and increase man's well-being by making sex not only freer and more enjoyable, but also more meaningful by dignifying all sexual relations, and with this the individual himself and his sexual partner as well. Only if we achieve such a new sexual morality for ourselves, and hand it over to our children, will the sexual revolution be a success.

Portnoy Psychoanalyzed

THERAPY NOTES FOUND IN THE FILES OF DR. O. SPIELVOGEL,
A NEW YORK PSYCHOANALYST

Asked to write a review of Philip Roth's Portnoy's Complaint, I attempted a satire instead. Only an interesting work of fiction permits and deserves to be made the substance of a satire—which suggests my evaluation of this book. I proceeded as if Roth's novel were what it artfully pretends to be: the account of what the hero told his psychoanalyst at the beginning of his treatment. This permitted me to intimate how a psychoanalyst may react to what his patient tells him; a subject that may be of some interest, particularly to psychoanalytic patients, but which is hardly ever touched upon in the literature. I also took this opportunity to suggest that uncontrolled sexual acting-out, which is all too often mistaken for sexual freedom, is actually a bondage to sex that destroys it, for the hero ends up impotent.

The novel describes the hero's confusion about who he is and wishes to be—the consequence of his entire life not being ordered, enlightened, or enriched by a definite morality in regard to human, and with this also sexual, relations. Writing about the novel this way permitted stressing that the goal of psychoanalysis is the internalization of experiences as a step toward their integration, and then the achievement of a consistent morality in sexual as well as personal relations, since the two are closely interwoven in any intimate male-female relation.

For those who might not be aware of it, I would like to add that the name or central topic assigned by Dr. Spielvogel to each of the sessions at its end is the title Roth gave to that chapter of his book. It concludes with the hero's realization that engaging in sex any which way, and at completely disregarded expense to others, is not "living big," but a vacuous boast that can no longer serve to hide the emptiness of his life. This is the consequence of his having made sex a substitute for meaningful human relations. With this realization psychoanalysis becomes possible, and this is the author's

PORTNOY PSYCHOANALYZED: Reprinted with slight editorial changes from Midstream 15 (June/July 1969), pp. 3–10.

conclusion—to which I fully subscribe. So the book ends with a last chapter, "Punch Line," consisting in its entirety of "So [said the doctor]. Now vee may perhaps to begin. Yes?"

Monday, the first hour: A troublesome—aren't they all?—new patient, thirty-three years old, raised in Newark, New Jersey. Typical petty bourgeois Jewish Orthodox background. He is highly intelligent, a compulsive talker, extremely narcissistic and exhibitionistic. He hides his intellectual arrogance behind ironic self-deprecation. He cannot stop the diarrhea of talk, because it is his way of denying his essential constipation—his total inability to give of himself. His working for the underdog (some kind of public relations work for the poor) is not only a denial of his own exploitativeness, but reflects his inner feeling that only the lowest and most miserable could possibly accept him.

He gave me no chance to explain what psychoanalysis is all about, claimed to be very familiar with it, and proceeded to show that he lacks even the slightest understanding. He seems to think psychoanalysis is a self-serving rattling-off of complaints and accusations leveled at others and oneself, instead of recognizing the serious introspection and contemplation it ought to evoke. He is capable of neither of the latter, because he feels he is so worthless that he cannot be serious about anything that touches him—not his own self, nor his parents, nor those he cohabits with.

He wants to do everything himself without any relation to, or contribution by, another person, in a typical masturbatory phallic fixation. He permits no one, including me, to make any contribution to his life. Obviously he has spent years at his self-justifying ruminations, where even his self-criticism is meant only to show how shrewd and honest he is about himself. Mainly the self-criticism serves to let him go on exactly as before without internalizing his guilt to the degree that he would need to do something about it; it serves him to avoid any need to change. He is convinced that to rattle off in this way becomes psychoanalysis when he does it aloud with me listening.

Despite his long account of all that went wrong in his life beginning with infancy, there is absolutely no realization of his sickness—his complete inability to relate to other persons. How can he, when all he sees of the world is his own projections, which he is certain are true pictures of reality?

He sees psychoanalysis as one vast catharsis, without the need for any deeper insight or internalization. Everything is just one huge ejaculation. I doubt if he can establish even the minimal transference that would enable him to analyze. Probably his selecting me for an analyst typifies his unwillingness to give up his bondage to his Jewish past. I wonder if I should have insisted that he go to a gentile, American-born analyst. I may still have to transfer him to one.

In our brief talk before treatment began, I asked him why, given his feeling that his troubles originate with his Orthodox Jewish background, he selected me, not only Jewish, but European-born, as his analyst. He could not understand my point, saying that no gentile analyst could ever understand him. He speaks as if the issue were finding an analyst whose sympathy and understanding are endless, as were his parents'—not his own coming to understand himself. His selection of me for an analyst suggests that deep down he does not want to transcend his own background, and so chose an analyst who will not alienate him from what he pretends to hate, but without which he feels there would be nothing left for him or his life. It remains to be seen whether we can overcome this handicap.

Since he thinks his need is to spill out, uninterruptedly, I shall let him, for a full week. Then we shall see if he can stop the spilling long enough for analysis to be possible.

He carries on as if to convince me that all the clichés of a spoiled Jewish boyhood are indeed valid: the overpowering, overindulgent, overprotective mother and the ineffectual father. Essentially the hour was one long alibi. I am to understand that if he cannot meet life, cannot relate to another human being, it's not because of how he construes things, but because of his parents and their ritual background, along with two specific traumata.

He is a master of the alibi, and like the clever lawyer he is, he plays both sides of the street. He blames his misery on both kinds of trauma: the physical (an undescended testicle) and the psychological (his mother's threat of desertion, and her scaring him by holding a knife in her hand to make him eat). He must be certain I will see him as the suffering victim, no matter what kind of theories I hold about physical or emotional trauma as causing behavior like his. Actually, it is not traumata, but only his disgust with himself, that forces him to defeat all those who love him (his parents, his sexual partners, etc.).

The tirade against his parents, especially his mother, is uninterruptable. A few times I indicated the wish to say something, but he only talked on more furiously. His spiel was like a satire on the complaints of most of my patients, and on the tenets of psychoanalysis: a satire on the dominating and castrating father, and a mother too involved in herself and her own life to pay much attention to her son. This extremely intelligent young Jew does not recognize what he is trying to do—by reversing the oedipal situation, he is trying to make fun of me as he does of everyone, thus asserting his superiority over me and psychoanalysis itself. His overpowering love for his mother is turned into a negative projection, so that what becomes overpowering is the mother's love for him. Overtly he complains that she would never let him alone, was all-intrusive—behind which lies an incredibly deep disappointment that she was not even more exclusively preoccupied with him. While consciously he experienced everything she did as destructive, behind this claim is an incredible wish for more, more, more. His is an insatiable orality which is denied and turned into the opposite by his continuous scream of its being much too much.

Even the most ordinary, everyday request from his mother, such as her reminding him to send a card on his father's sixty-sixth birthday, is experienced by him as the most unreasonable demand, forcing on him a life of guilt and indebtedness to his parents. Whatever the mother did for him was always too little; the smallest thing she requested was always too much.

After listening all day to the endless complaints of patients about mothers who were never interested in whether they did or did not eat, whether or not they defecated, whether or not they succeeded in school, it should have been refreshing to listen to an hour of complaints about a mother who did exactly all that—but it was not. It was so obvious that he felt cheated at not being given enough. No doubt he is tortured by memories of his past, and by his present inability to be a man and enjoy normal sex. But he certainly makes the most of it, and nowhere do I see any effort on his part to free himself of this bondage to the past. Obviously he expects my magic and that of psychoanalysis to do this for him.

An important clue, to be followed up later: he is fascinated by his father's constipation, which is so stark a contrast with his excessive masturbation and incessant, diarrhea-like talk. This seems like an

interesting fixation at the phallic level, as though the father's constipation has made him so anxious about his own ability to produce that to
compensate, he produces without interruption—whether by masturbating, talking, or intellectual achievement. If he does not learn to
hold in and store, but continues this indiscriminate discharge, analysis
will certainly fail.

If I were to give a name to this patient after this first hour, I
would call him *The most unforgettable character I've met.* This is not
because the patient thinks this designation is true of his mother, as he
sees her (as is so of everyone and his mother) but because, while he
wishes to believe the foregoing, his major effort is to impress me with
himself as "the most unforgettable character I've ever met." Poor
soul. Instead of trying to get from me the help he so desperately
needs, he tries to impress me with his uniqueness. Everything he accuses his mother of, he is himself, in the extreme. She exploited him
because she loved him so much. He exploits everyone because he
loves no one.

Tuesday, the second hour: Despite the same incessant stream of talk,
little new material. Speculations arrived at by the end of the last hour
seem borne out today. As a child, he masturbated, preferably on the
toilet, in line with the father's constipation which emerges ever more
as a central experience leading to a negative identification. The father
cannot let go. The son cannot hold anything in, or hold onto anyone.
The father, out of incessant fear for the future, chose and stuck to his
job of life insurance salesman. This influence is internalized by the
son as fear about his masculinity. For this he finds only one defense:
the excessive masturbation which seems to prove his body is working,
but at the price of self-disgust. Because this patient wants not a penis
that gives pleasure, but an instrument that expels its contents; he
seeks a self-assurance which his masturbation cannot give him.

Otherwise it was a repetition of the first hour's contents. In the
deliberately vulgar language of the patient, I would entitle this session
Whacking off. He uses much obscenity to impress others and fools
himself into thinking he is liberated, while actually he is expressing his
loathing for himself.

Wednesday, the third hour: It becomes increasingly clear that this patient has read too much about psychoanalysis while understanding nothing—for example, about castration anxiety and the effect of seeing menstrual blood. What he does not see is how desperately he wishes he *had* a castrating father, and how deeply disappointed he is because what he encounters instead is only what he experiences as a castrating mother. But even as he complains of how castrating she is, he cannot help admiring her inner strength, which alone seems to sustain the entire family. One gets the feeling that he has to see her as castrating, because he needs to see her as being strong enough to protect him. It becomes also more clear that his true sickness is the refusal to recognize his parents' deep love for him, because that would mean the obligation to love them back, and later, other human beings. Instead, he clings to his vision of all human relations as exploitative power plays.

A characteristic memory: an athletic cousin, Heshie, got in a physical fight with his father. Although considerably the stronger, Heshie had let his father pin him down and then defeat him in physical combat. My patient wonders a great deal about this. He cannot understand why his cousin deliberately lost the fight. He cannot recognize what he unconsciously knows: that while the father was keeping his son from marrying the gentile girl he loved, which had led to the fight, the father's motive was deep love for his son. The cousin realized, consciously or unconsciously, that to be overpowered by the deep love of another for oneself is the greatest victory possible in human relations, even if outwardly it seems like defeat. My patient, unfortunately, is unable to consciously accept such concepts about love, and I fear he never will. If he could, it would mean his problems were over and his analysis done.

The fact that he never had the closeness that exists between Heshie and his father, that he can neither let go of nor enjoy the specific Jewishness of his background, that he denies what he craves —all this gives my patient the particular *Jewish Blues* that formed the leitmotif of this session.

Thursday, the fourth hour: The patient connects an incident of his exhibitionary masturbation on the bus to his having eaten un-kosher food (lobster) for the first time. In his unconscious he thus recognizes the connection between oral and phallic anxiety, and how much of his sexual acting-out is based on oral anxiety, like the baby who shows off his phallus. From here, his associations moved to reveal what an anxious person his mother really is—but he refuses to recognize it. He even mentioned her endless stories of how she tries everything once only to find that any venturing out into the world leads to immediate punishment, if not destruction. An explicit memory—the mother's first attempt to drive, which led to an accident and so much anxiety that she never drove again—still brings no realization of how anxiety-ridden she is. Such an insight would destroy his image of her as the all-powerful, castrating woman. He does not realize that what he identifies with in his mother is not her strength, but her abysmal fear of life.

From talking of his resentment at the feeling that he owes his parents something—to get married and provide them with grandchildren, or to be a success in life so that they can brag about their son, as their friends and relatives do about theirs—he moves to his sexual desire for gentile girls. This association seems to indicate that he can have sex only if it is sex that his parents disapprove of. He is so tied to them that he cannot feel he has a separate existence unless he does something to hurt them. Of course this does not work out, and even in the midst of having intercourse he is already dissatisfied, already longing anxiously for the next girl to have sex with.

Clearly his promiscuity is one big effort to keep satisfaction from his parents—and he makes certain he is punished for this by getting nothing that is meaningful to him. For all his reading of psychoanalytic literature, he does not see that his promiscuity, particularly with gentiles, is one big reassurance that he is not having incestuous relations with his mother. By keeping his women ever-changing and meaningless to him, he remains faithful to his mother—not because she won't let him go, but because he won't let go of her. Having enslaved himself to her, he projects the relation to see it as if she, or both parents, had enslaved him to them.

Another crucial memory: a fifteen-year-old boy was pushed too hard by his ambitious mother to perform, and he hanged himself. Pinned to his shirt was a telephone message he had taken for his mother: that she is to take the mah-jongg rules along when she goes out that night. My patient can see in it only the boy's obedience, and not the boy's lethal venom at his mother who dares to enjoy a game with her friends instead of doing nothing all day and night except cater to her son.

As is typical for patients totally unable to form any human relations, who complain endlessly of the deficiency of human relations in their childhood, he tries to provide for others what is, in fact, totally absent in his own life. This patient, it turns out, is assistant commissioner of the New York Commission on Human Opportunity, concerned in his work with improving the lives of others. In his professional life he tries to prevent the poor from being exploited, while all he chases in his personal life is the chance to sexually exploit others.

The worst part of it is that he, who is so lacking in ego and the capacity to give, who is so driven to act out his uncontrolled instinctual tendencies, thinks he is suffering from a deficiency of the id. At one point he tells me what he wants from me: to put the id back into this particular Yid. That is, he does not really want to analyze himself; he does not want to have to develop ego control over superego and id. All he wants of me is to rid him of all the pangs of conscience he still feels about his selfish and asocial behavior. This is how he conceives of the purpose of psychoanalysis. Indeed, he offers to pay me an even higher fee if only I could do that for him.

He recalls masturbating once into a piece of liver which was then eaten at the family dinner. He has no inkling that this shows an extreme sexualization of the oral stage. But most of his seemingly phallic sexuality is really nothing but a screen for his fixation at the oral stage—this shows in his incessant demand to be given to. All the giving by both parents was not enough to fill him up. At least the girl he calls "The Monkey" understood him well. According to him she cried out against him, this great humanitarian whose job it is to protect the poor from their landlords, while his own sexual enjoyment comes from sexually degrading this girl who really seems to have fallen in love with him. She seems to have hoped their relationship might help her out of her own sexual, moral, human morass.

How wise Freud was to impose the sexual abstinence rule, and the rule against patients' reading in psychoanalysis. This patient uses his reading of Freud to masturbate with. Having no intention of analyzing himself, he wants me to do everything for him, as he expected and actually received from his mother, without his having to do anything for himself.

The only enjoyment he seems to get out of sex is in cunnilingus.

Like his incessant talking and his pleasure in four-letter words, so with his preference for this perversion—all indicate that he was so intensely satisfied by the oral pleasure his mother provided, that he cannot conceive of its coming from anything else. He is, I am tempted to say, crazy in his efforts to wring oral satisfaction out of sex. In the language of the patient, this session exemplifies his *Cunt craziness.*

Friday, the fifth hour: He begins the session by referring to Freud's paper on the misuse of sex to degrade the partner; this leads to memories of his sexual relations with some upper-class gentiles. He recognizes that his feelings of Jewish inferiority and his resentment of anti-Semitism are why he cannot find sexual satisfaction except through seducing his gentile partners into practices which to him are degrading. He induced "The Monkey," who did not mind fellatio or even enjoyed it, to have lesbian sex with a prostitute—at which point, he was through with her. His excuse for setting that up is that "The Monkey" had hinted at it, and she had—since she really loved him, she tried to please him in every way. She had felt unworthy of him, felt that though she gave all she had, tried everything she knew, it never seemed to be enough. So she tried to suggest her readiness to do whatever else might satisfy him. Her offer to do anything he might want of her was then used by him to exculpate himself to me, to convince me and himself that it is really her fault that he so degraded her that she wants to kill herself. All his life it is always the same desperate story: unable to love anybody, including himself, he cannot believe that anybody—his parents, "The Monkey"—could do anything out of love for him.

Since he has never known true empathy for anyone, he cannot see that those "nice" gentile girls had sex with him precisely because he lived up to their stereotyped notions of the dirty, sex-crazed Jew. His forcing them into what they view as perverted sex proves to them that they were right about Jews in the first place. They selected this highly intelligent, thus seemingly very worthwhile, Jew because being specially admirable, he threatened their image of Jews as inferior beings. But if even this very bright, nice, concerned Jew wants nothing so much as to degrade them in sex, then their initial image of the "dirty" Jew is again confirmed.

And my patient does his best to oblige. Still thinking he degrades only them, he degrades himself even more. This mutual exploitation extends also to what the pair use each other for: to defeat their parents. For my patient the worst thing he can do to his parents is live with a gentile girl. Sleeping with a Jew is probably the worst thing these girls can do to their parents. How these neurotics always find each other! How they help each other act out their neurosis so there is no need to face it! His sex experiences certainly seem like an illustration to Freud's *The most prevalent form of degradation in erotic life.*

Saturday, the sixth hour: Were I to see my patients only four or five times a week, as do my American colleagues, and not six times as I learned it in Vienna, this patient's story might have developed very differently. Last night, going over the notes taken up to now, I came close to deciding that this patient's narcissistic self-involvement, his deep oral fixation, his inability to relate, etc., all would make analysis impossible, and I had pretty much decided to tell him so at the end of today's hour. I hoped that the shock might, later on, permit him to seek out another analyst; I planned to suggest a gentile one. With a gentile it's possible this patient might begin to analyze, instead of misusing the psychoanalyst as a prop to get rid of his guilt, while continuing to destroy all who have positive feelings for him.

If this session had taken place on Monday, probably nothing would have changed. Maybe the fact that this was a Saturday, *the Sabbath*, had something to do with it; this I shall find out later. Anyway, today was entirely different. Instead of regaling me with his sexual successes—in masturbation, cunnilingus, and fellatio—the patient finally became a bit more human in recounting his sexual defeats, all by Jewish girls. This began with the patient's recalling how he admired Jewish men like his father, with his Sunday morning ball game, and how he wished to identify with such men but could not, because he wanted even more then to possess his mother. He had to run from his girl friend "The Monkey" because as soon as he had gotten a girl to the point where no further degradation was likely to occur, all her attraction was gone for him. Unable, as always, to respond when the love of others for him was so obvious he could no longer deny it, the patient's only solution was to run away. Blaming women for trying to put him in bondage—though all he really wishes is to see them in bondage to him, with his having no return obligation —the patient fled to Israel, the mother country.

There unconsciously (but so close to consciousness that I feel analysis may begin after all) he realized that if he was no longer a Jew in a gentile world, if he could no longer use that excuse to justify his whole pattern of demanding and receiving without ever giving, then he was nothing—and he could not even manage an erection.

In desperation he tried to seduce a kibbutz girl by reversing the methods he had used with his gentile girls. He had degraded gentiles, and their debasement had made them extremely attractive to him, but also useless. Here instead it was he who submitted to debasement, particularly when the girl told him what should have long been obvious: that his self-degradation is the more despicable because he is a man of such high intelligence. He reacted to this by inviting her to have intercourse with him. Then, blaming others as always, he tried to pin his sudden impotence on his mother, claiming the kibbutz girl reminded him of her. He believed it to be the oedipal (but genital) attachment which made him impotent, while it was really his oral attachment, his wish to remain the suckling infant forever.

The long-suffering Jewish mother who lets herself be blamed for everything is willing to thus serve her son. He will never have to feel guilty about anything he might do, because he can always blame it on her. And in a way he can; but not as he thinks. He can blame his mother for letting him believe that whatever he wants, he must immediately be given. This—the central theme of his life—he screamed out at the kibbutz girl: "I HAVE TO HAVE." It was she who finally told him that this belief of his—that he has to have what he wants, whatever it may cost the other—is not valid.

In a fantasy of being judged for his crimes, he realized, at least for a moment, that blaming his mother will not get him off, cannot justify his behavior to others. This raised the hope that analysis might just succeed. So, instead of dismissing him, as I had planned, I said, "Now we may perhaps begin." Only the future will tell if I was not too optimistic.

One more thought: He is very clever at presenting himself, and right after the first session I had the uneasy feeling that he wants to impress me as the most unforgettable patient I ever had. What if all he said so far was carefully prepared and selected? His determination not to permit me to interrupt with questions or interpretations suggests the possibility that he was afraid that any interference might throw him off his apparently stream-of-consciousness-like talk, because actually it was a carefully prepared story, designed to impress me. What if all he presented as the outpourings of his unconscious and preconscious, of his id and superego (the self-criticism, the fantasy about his being judged) were conscious ego productions? Was he trying to test me in order to find out whether I am smart enough not to mistake an essentially literary production for an effort at analysis?

If all this was so, did I do the right thing not to insist on interrupting him, or on directing his associations, and not to tell him at the end of the last session that it is time to stop being a man of letters so that, through analyzing himself, he might finally become a man? Again, we shall see.

But even if what has happened so far was not more than an effort to tell a good story, it is significant that it is "The Monkey" who emerges as having the greatest dignity. Though born desperately poor, social success means nothing to her. Having been married to one of the richest men of France meant nothing to her. When she felt used by him, she left him without another thought. Though aspiring to culture, she is not at all impressed by its trappings, nor by being invited to the mayor's mansion, because what is important to her is to be with the patient, not to attend a formal dinner. This she made clear by having sex with him within view of the mayor's house, not caring what others might think of her or what she did there, while he was deathly afraid of how all this might look to others. He, as always, involved only in himself, did not recognize that she was not motivated by any hedonist impulsiveness, but by the anxious question: "Are you taking me to the mayor's reception because you love me and want me near you, or because I am ornamental and therefore useful in your social climbing?"

What view can he have of himself as a person and as a Jew if social and sexual honesty, that is, if true humanity—in his eyes—resides only in the poor "Monkey"? Is it just another case then of the self-hating Jew living *in exile*?

Some Comments on Privacy

When contemplating the issues raised by an ever more frequent, pervasive, and intrusive invasion of privacy by governmental agencies, private organizations, and the mass media—aggravated by requests from researchers for all kinds of detailed information on one's activities, opinions, and preferences—I am motivated by my considerable personal need and liking for privacy, and my resentment when it is infringed upon. I even dislike intensely what appear to be quite innocuous invasions of my private domain, unless I happen to be momentarily in the mood where it makes no difference to me. For example, there are times when I am quite annoyed if I have to listen to some music in an elevator or airplane, because it may jar with my mood of the moment, stop me from pursuing private thoughts, or interfere with a conversation. While petty, such incidents are indicative of a much larger issue: the usurpation of my right to decide whether, and if so, where I should listen to music, and what kind of music this should be. The fact that it is an anonymous organization which has made these decisions for me only makes it worse; while I am involved as an individual, there is no other individual to whom I can complain about the music, or ask for redress.

What I resent is not the music per se; even as I am disturbed by it, I recognize that it was arranged with the good intention of entertaining me while I am forced to spend time in a dull place. What bothers me is the tacit assumption either that I have no private thoughts I wish to pursue without interruption, or that these thoughts can easily be fitted to the mood of the music, or most offensive of all, that my wish to engage in thoughts of my own need not be respected.

I cite a trivial example because I believe privacy to be an unqual-

SOME COMMENTS ON PRIVACY: This previously unpublished paper was presented in 1966 on the occasion of a University of Chicago symposium on privacy and its protection.

ified right. The same principle that one's privacy should be respected and inviolate should apply in minor areas like elevators as well as in major ones such as one's professional life. As a psychoanalyst I am the recipient of highly confidential information about people's most intimate affairs, and not just from patients suffering from severe psychological disturbances. I am frequently subjected to the demand that I divulge this information. Although I reject such requests, to do so is often made very difficult. With all this, I would make a forceful case that privacy must be safeguarded under all circumstances, especially against any infringements by the power of the state. This conviction has been strengthened by my experiences with totalitarian systems.

However, I recognize how much my attitudes were formed in a particular era—the late- and post-Victorian one—and how much things have changed since that time. Reflecting on how things are now, I began to feel not just old, but outright archaic. I have had to accept that privacy is not universally desired, nor an absolute good, as I wished to believe. Instead, its high valuation belongs very much to a particular style of life and historical period, is further characteristic of certain social classes, and thus is culture-bound.

The troublesome nature of this divergence of attitudes began to dawn upon me as I was typing the first draft of these remarks, in solitude, the door of my room closed, in the stillness of the night—the time when I prefer working and when I work best, because no unexpected interruptions interfere with my concentration. As I was typing away, my eyes strayed to a favorite picture hung on the wall over the desk, and I had to laugh at myself. The picture was a copy of a famous painting by Pieter Breughel the Elder, a master I greatly admire. I particularly like this painting of his because it seems to me to be a celebration of life as it really is, not as it pretends to be, as is often rendered in pictures. It shows a world teeming with people, doing all sorts of things. A crowd is depicted who, singly or in groups, are unconcernedly, even happily, going about in public what I, from my very different perspective, would have called their private business. Only for them, such affairs were not at all private—on the contrary. They were fully aware that they transacted their interactions in public; they wanted all to be seen and known by neighbors and strangers; and they did things with more gusto because they did them in the presence of others who reacted to the events being carried on in their presence. I had enjoyed and admired this and other paintings of the Dutch masters, many of which depicted the most "private" aspects of life as being transacted in the public domain, without recognizing that my admiration was incompatible with my feelings about the desirability of privacy. These paintings and many others from later periods indicate how recently our need for privacy has developed; and as I reflected on it, I also realized that this need may already be passing out of our life.

When I studied as a youngster, the door to my room had to be closed; all had to be quiet, and was quiet. Only then could I concentrate on my thoughts and my work, to the exclusion of all other distractions. But my own children—the generation born during and after World War II—studied best with the door open and the record player or the radio going full blast; in this radically different setting they learned as much and as well as I had. Why then do I still need a high degree of privacy and have to work—or at least much prefer to work—only in quiet concentration; and why do they—like the people in the Breughel painting—need to be in continuous close touch with their age-mates, or at least symbolically through a shared musical interest, when they want to concentrate on a mentally demanding task?

Maybe the answer is that we all function best when we feel in communion with what seems to symbolize our highest personal value. I, as a child of the Victorian age, had to create for myself a setting that emphasized privacy, personal uniqueness, and individual development before I could concentrate on a learning task whose ultimate goal—whether or not I was consciously aware of it—was to attain the highest possible degree of individuation. My children, in order to work best, needed to feel that they had not lost touch with their peer group. Nothing and nobody forced them to accept the intrusion of the music into the privacy of their thoughts. If anything, their parents, who were the "authorities" in the home, were most dubious about their studying with the songs of the Beatles distracting them—or at least we thought that this loud music must distract them.

Actually, far from distracting, the music helped my children to concentrate by comforting and reassuring them that they had not lost contact with what they needed most. It gave them the feeling that even when immersed in their studies, they were still somehow in touch with what counted for much in their lives: the connection to their age group. This connection heightened life for them in all of their doings, including the effort to study.

The more lonely they felt, the more these children needed to deny their isolation, to drown it out by the loudness of the music. It expressed for them their angers, their longings, even their loneliness. In doing so, the loud music did for them what they felt unable to do for themselves: to bring their emotions into some semblance of order, put them into a frame which would make them manageable enough to be expressed; emotions which otherwise would be much too chaotic to be coped with in any way. This vicarious expression of their feelings by the music permitted the children—who hardly listened to it but let themselves be enveloped by it—to continue with their studies; otherwise the pressure of these feelings might have prevented them from doing so. The music did this for them because they knew their age-mates who suffered from overpowering parallel emotions listened to the same music. Thus even in their anger, their alienation, their loneliness, it established an invisible—I am tempted to say, an audible—imaginary bond between them and those others with whom, alas, no real bonds existed.

When I came to this country about thirty years ago, among the many customs which struck me as different and thus strange was having the window shades pulled down halfway, more or less all the time. The lowered shade signified a wish for privacy, while leaving half of the window unobstructed expressed that there was no desire, nor any need, to hide from inspection what went on in the room behind the window. This seemed to me to bespeak a strange ambivalence about the wish for privacy. Now the picture window, which exposes so much more of what goes on in the inside to outside scrutiny, while at the same time permitting insiders to observe so much of what is going on in front of the window, has more or less done away with half-pulled-down shades.

In comparison, I remembered how the same problem of seeing and being seen through a window was often dealt with in my native Vienna, and in many other European countries. In the generation of my grandparents, many homes had one window of the living room fitted with an outside mirror that was angled so that a person sitting inside, in a window seat specially fitted for this purpose, could spy on all the comings and goings in the street by watching the mirror without being observed.

I could not help reflecting that a situation where one person would sit hidden in semi-obscurity while observing the behavior of others had its similarities with the psychoanalytic setting, where things go on in utter privacy and confidentiality. If so, the semi-private and semi-public nature of the partly pulled-down shade, and the more public exposure inherent in the picture window, might then be likened to group therapeutic settings or encounter groups, where a mixed group of patients and therapist are equally exposed to each other and things can barely be kept private or confidential. Maybe there were some deeper reasons why a setting that was typically Victorian in its insistence on maintaining total privacy and confidentiality was conducive to the invention of psychoanalysis, and with this to the liberation from Victorian hypocrisy.

How things have changed since Freud explained his reasons for developing the particular psychoanalytic setting! He created it because people, he felt, could not be expected to talk about sexual or other "private" matters while they were aware that somebody was observing their face. But the setting protected the analyst equally: sitting behind the couch where the patient could not observe him was absolutely necessary for the analyst, if he was to be able to concentrate on the patient and what he was saying without worrying about any expressions which might appear on *his* face as he listened to the patient's revelations.

But since Freud's time, and to a considerable degree because of his influence, what used to be eminently private has become quite public—often, I feel defensively, with a vengeance. Feelings and actions a patient could talk about only to the trusted analyst in the carefully guarded privacy of the treatment room are now freely discussed in public, with relative strangers and in the most casual settings. Questions which once a patient broached to his analyst only with great anxiety are now asked in widely and indiscriminately disseminated questionnaires and are readily answered, although they pertain to matters which I still believe ought best to be kept private. What used to be considered most intimate matters are now discussed in great detail in family magazines or shown on the TV or movie screen.

This greater openness, as concerning sexual matters for example, has not altered the fact that today, as in Freud's time, there is much a person will not disclose unless he is absolutely certain that his confidences will be kept secret; but the content of what needs to be kept private has changed. For example, it used to be that the revelation of a person's sexual predilections—ordinary or deviant—had to be protected by complete confidentiality before he dared open up about them. Today many people speak freely about such matters in public. What now is kept secret is often a person's true feelings about behavior which he openly flaunts; feelings which may be the opposite of those he claims to have, for he may secretly be ashamed of what he so openly admits to, or, contrary to his assertions, he may not be able to feel at all.

Thus today, as much as in Freud's time, people insist on confidentiality and on keeping things private, whenever they are ashamed of what they have to reveal. What people may be ashamed of can and does change radically from place to place, and over time. This poses the psychological problem of whether such shame—and with it the demand for confidentiality and privacy—is desirable and beneficial, or rather lessens our well-being as individuals, or that of man in society. Do we benefit more when we are able to hide, keep private and secret, that of which we are ashamed, or is it preferable that this should be made public and openly accepted?

Here the psychoanalyst is caught in his own contradictions, like the rest of us. He tells his patients that there is nothing to be ashamed of in fantasies and feelings, not to mention dreams and daydreams. All these flow of necessity from one's total life history, from the vagaries of experiences and one's reactions to them. Most of all, they reflect early childhood events and reactions, and how one then immaturely interpreted the world; there is no reason for anybody to feel shame about such things. Yet when the same patient behaves in society too openly by acting on the basis of these fantasies, when he thus makes public things he has been told not to shrink from, then as likely as not, the psychoanalyst will consider such openness as acting-out on the part of the patient, viewing it as irresponsible and self-destructive behavior—which indeed it may be.

We all seem caught between our own morality and society's clamor about what should be kept private, and what not. So we all end up functioning by a double standard of morality. But as Freud has shown, keeping a double moral standard—maintaining one for public show and another for private and somehow shameful action— leads only to neurosis and hysteria. Maybe our present dilemma regarding what belongs in the private domain and what in the public, although different from the double standard of Freud's day, is caused by equally severe unresolved inner conflicts about what is right and what wrong.

As a Freudian psychoanalyst I cannot help one further reflection: that the genitals are called a person's private parts, and that the place where one defecates is called a privy. Behind these two "private" designations lies a discomfort with natural functions, a distrust concerning basic parts of oneself, and an uneasiness about how others feel about such things—in short, a deep inner conflict.[1] Maybe these are the emotions behind many demands for privacy.

Lewis Mumford writes: "Today the degradation of the inner life is symbolized by the fact that the only place sacred from intrusion is the private toilet."[2] In this connection it might be mentioned that organizations which wish to de-individualize the individual insist on the use of common toilets, such as in the army, or in summer camps, where the desire is to make everybody feel like "one of the boys." This underlines the relation between individualism and privacy on the one hand, and on the other that between feelings of communality and absence of privacy. (Deliberate deprivation of all privacy can be used not only for purposes of de-individualization, but also of degradation and depersonalization, as happened in the concentration camps.)

Now the degradation Mumford talks of can be interpreted in two ways. One is the thought Mumford had in mind: that unfortunately too little in our lives is as private, as safe from intrusion, as we are while we are on the toilet. But is it not also degrading that functions so natural to our bodies, eliminatory functions we cannot live without, are considered so shameful that they have to be carefully hidden from others, and avoided through lingual circumlocution even with ourselves?

---

[1] As openly as many people now talk about sexual matters, when it comes to elimination we still talk about "going to the bathroom," or washroom. Elimination is still "dirty." The shame about this finds expression in our circumlocution as we refer not to elimination, but instead to that which will free us from having been engaged in something we consider "dirty"—washing and cleaning ourselves.

[2] Lewis Mumford, *The City in History* (New York: Harcourt, Brace & World, 1961).

It is precisely the feelings we experience around toilet training, or what is called anality, that often become the greatest source of neurotic anxieties; our inherited shame about elimination sometimes forces us to keep shameful and guilty feelings private and hidden from others, causing tremendous unhappiness. At the same time, this very shame is one of the foundations on which our Western civilization rests, although along with it came the discomfort Freud wrote about which bedevils modern man.

Nevertheless in other areas, when and where we crave privacy has undergone great change. My Victorian parents, when they went out to dinner, preferred a spacious restaurant with their table set off by an ample distance from the next one. Conversation would then not be overheard, nor their attention imposed on or distracted by too immediate an awareness of others. Nowadays our young people seem to prefer to crowd together in small discotheques, not to speak of the hippies who sleep many to a room. Many of the latter feel so desperately alone and out of contact with others that bodily closeness is sought avidly to bridge the gap. This raises the problem of whether parents have not gone too far in their demand for and in their imposition of privacy.

One need not go as far back as when whole families lived in one room. Nobody had privacy then. One couldn't effectively hide certain skeletons in the closet then because there were no closets. Reconstructions of what life was like in colonial days, even among the affluent, show that parents and children alike lived not only physically close, but with hardly any privacy. A family had to be quite well off to afford separate bedrooms—that is, one for the parents, and one for all the children together. Nowadays the ideal seems to be for each child to have his own room and own bathroom. But the children raised in this spacious isolation are often those who, when they finally come into their own, crowd together into one tiny room.

Our Western society has gone far in seeking privacy and avoiding the pains of closeness; at least as an ideal, although many poor people cannot afford the luxury of privacy, which they desire. On the other hand, many who can afford privacy in consequence suffer from too much distance, from isolation. Maybe what we view as the infringement of privacy today has to do with human efforts at rectifying the balance.

Mumford writes that

the first radical change which was to alter the form of the Medieval house, was the development of a sense of privacy. This means in effect withdrawal at will from the common life and the common interests of one's fellows. Privacy in sleep, privacy in eating, privacy in religious and social rituals, finally privacy in thought. . . . The desire for privacy marked the beginning of that new alignment of classes which was to usher in the merciless class competition and individual self-assertion of a later day. . . . In the castles of the thirteenth century, one notes the existence of a private bedroom for the noble owners; and one also finds, not far from it, perched over the moat, a private toilet. . . . Privacy in bed came first in Italy among the upper classes only, but the desire for it seems to have developed almost as slowly as the means. Michelangelo, for example, on occasion slept with his workmen four to a bed.

From these remarks it seems obvious that an absence of privacy in living conditions did not and need not interfere with creative achievements, which even we moderns regard as the reflection of rarest uniqueness. But it also appears that as long as all the bodily functions, including sex and elimination, were more or less public, no great shame attached to them. Only as they became more and more relegated to a private room which became the privy, did we learn to feel shame about our bodies and bodily functions. The tragedy is that alienation from one's body leads to alienation from oneself and from others. And once we no longer feel comfortable with others, we crave privacy. Maybe what is missing is the right balance between closeness and distance, between public and private.

When we think about privacy we think of the wish for privacy in thought, feeling, and experience; these should be exclusively our own. No one should have the right to intrude on these inner processes; they should be open to others only when we wish to give of them. Otherwise they should be and remain our private "business."

The desire for privacy is closely linked to the increased insistence on private property in ever-larger aspects of life. My home ought to be the castle where I am protected from anyone's intruding on my privacy. But my home is my castle only when it is my private possession. Understandably, it was the lord of the castle who first claimed privacy for himself and his doings. Thus from the very beginning, demands for privacy were closely connected with private property.

Whoever owned no place of his own, owned no privacy either, and he has very little even today. And private property is virtually inseparable from class structure.

Only in the seventeenth century, for example, did the common dinner table stop being common to all members of the household, servants and masters alike; no private conversations were held at the dinner table then. In short, the more class-structured a society becomes, the more privacy do its privileged members demand. How understandable, then, that a society which tries to do away with class structure should also try to do away with privacy, and demand that ever larger areas of life should be public.

What comes as harder to realize is that as long as everyone knew everything about everyone else there was no need for informers, for elaborate spy systems, or for bugging in order to know what people did, said, and thought. This brings to mind the absence of crime, delinquency, and other asocial behavior in the Israeli kibbutzim. There are no police there, because there is no need for policing. Everyone lives much more collectively and openly with everyone else than among us, and with this, in essence everybody polices everybody else. There is very little privacy and everyone knows just about everything about everyone else. I personally felt suffocated by the lack of privacy, when I lived there for a time. But I could not blind myself to what to me was an astonishing absence of all asocial behavior in this society, as follows from the absence of privacy—or from having everything in the public domain.

Servan-Schreiber, in comparing Americans to the French, remarks that "France is a country where distrust of one's neighbor still prevails. This is due to the conviction that men are by nature hostile and egotistical. Therefore each protects himself from the other through a complex network of laws, which complexity conforms to the French tendency of carefully limiting and defining all aspects of human existence. The straitjacket which results, quite naturally, prevents all change."[3] And it is true that the demand for privacy implies a distrust of others.

·   ·   ·

---

[3] J. J. Servan-Schreiber, *Le Défi américain* (Paris: Denoel, 1967).

Where does all this leave me? Despite all of my realizations I do not cherish privacy less, and I still resent deeply any intrusion upon it.

I recognize that modern anomy and alienation, even much of modern *tedium vitae*, result from how distantly people live from each other. Most of our social problems, whether distrust by one group in the population of the other—call it racial discrimination, or class hatred—or the prevalence of crime and delinquency, merely reflect this alienation. The best way to do away with them, perhaps the only one, would be to create true communities. But one cannot live in true communality and also keep much of life private to oneself. Many of our laws telling us what to do and what not to do, which even invade our private lives, are intended to make our society more equitable.

If consensus does not arise from communal living, from everyone's sharing the same values and having much the same concerns, then it has to be imposed from the outside. But what suffers then is the individualism my own rearing forces me to cherish so highly. So I am caught in my own contradictions, truly a child of our age of transition. At present I see no way to achieve all these good things together: a true community of living, and an individualism safeguarded by privacy. So let me close with some thoughts on the psychological dimensions of the problem.

Professionally I am confronted daily with the suffering of emotionally disturbed children who were raised in situations where great privacy deteriorated into complete isolation from others, and with it from themselves. As a result they became desperately fearful and ashamed of any relations with others, or any familiarity with their bodies. It remains for the next generation to see if it can design a model of privacy which is not founded on repression—on feelings of shame about one's body, its function in elimination, its desire for various forms of sexual satisfaction. Maybe the solution is in a much better balance between those areas that should remain private and those we are better off assigning to the public domain. What is certainly needed is a privacy which does not dwarf but enhances our capacity for true intimacy with those who ought to be closest to us.

Among the unresolved problems of modern city life today is the prevalence of fear in our streets. I would like to suggest something far removed from reconstructing our cities, or an incredible enlarging of the police force and law-enforcing agents within them. What we need, in my opinion, is a return to much smaller, more self-contained communities where a great deal of what is now private can become public; where we would share and know much more about each other, and care about each other, even to the degree of protecting each other's well-being and property. After all, much crime is prevented, and criminals apprehended, when neighbors pay attention and report their observations to the police. In short, what we need is a desire for privacy that is based not on shame or the fear of what others might do to or think of us, but solely on a wish for simple solitude.

Maybe what we must strive for is a way of life where we would wish to share far more with each other because we can trust others more than we presently can, but without the community imposing any rules on how one must think, feel, and shape one's life, as was typical before the anonymity of big city life offered protection against such restraints on the individual's chance to find self-realization in his own ways. What would then be kept private would be kept that way not because it was shameful, but because it was valuable. And if there were less emphasis on private property, as in the kibbutz, there would be less need to protect private property, but only private emotions and experiences. If private property were less valued, it would require less protection and would arouse less desire to grab it away on the part of those who do not own it; and then we might come to value the private experience much more highly. Out of the high value we would then place on our own private experience we would come to respect the privacy of others.

While the millennium is not about to arrive, there is at least reasonable hope that modern technology will make the necessary types of property so readily available that they will no longer need to be anxiously guarded. Certainly our attitudes toward our bodies and what is shameful about them, needing to be hidden, are changing. We are a long way from accepting the body and its functions freely, but there is hope that the time may come when the desire for privacy will no longer be based on the need to hide what is experienced as the shameful functions of the body. The less we feel ashamed of, the less we feel curiosity about the private life of others. After all, it is the Peeping Tom who knows so little about his own body and emotions, is so afraid and confused about his own sexuality that he is sneakily trying to find out about that of others; it is he who is so embarrassed about his own instinctual desires that he tries to gain satisfaction from embarrassing others.

If we all became more secure about our own bodies, more secure economically, socially, and sexually, we would be able to grant others great individual freedom both out of a desire for such freedom for ourselves, and out of a lack of interest in their private lives, because any morbid interest in the other is always the consequence of a felt inadequacy in ourselves. That is why we are dying to know how others manage things. If we all were able to manage our own lives, we would have little reason to try to manage the lives of others.

Neither a medieval absence of privacy, nor a big brother's spying that makes all of our life public, will do. What we must strive for, as so often and in so many other matters, is the right balance between what should be respected and protected as private in our life, and what should be part of our more or less public communal life. Then the home will be just that—neither a castle, nor a public place.

Art and Art Education:
A Personal Vision

Art and aesthetics—the nature and history of art, the study of its place in human life—were my first avocation. Changing interests and the vagaries of life have taken me far afield, and during the last thirty-five years I have devoted myself to the healing of sick minds. Yet as the French like to remind us, we are always returning to our first love, as I am doing here. I am only too aware of how far I have removed myself from what stood once at the center of my interests. At the same time, having remained an educator, I have also remained aware that creativity ought to stand at the center of all education. So in a way, my work has bridged the worlds of creative endeavors and therapeutics.

Exposed as I have been every day to the often fantastic productions of schizophrenic minds and to the outpourings of the unconscious, I have become convinced that while psychoanalysis can enlighten us about the motives for such originality, it can tell us little of importance about the nature of creativity or the artistic achievement. My daily experiences with the unexpected and often most unusual productions of emotionally disturbed children were of deep interest to me for what they revealed about the delusional images dwelling in their minds and pressing for expression—that is, for relief. And these outpourings also led me, in turn, to an important insight: such children create images, but they are not creative; they create fantastically interesting pictures, but not works of art.

The most fascinating dream, expressing the deepest layers of the unconscious, is at best clinical raw material. It will not make a good poem, short story, or novel. If one recalls the dream sequence which

ART AND ART EDUCATION: A PERSONAL VISION: This paper was originally presented as the Charles Francis Cook Memorial Lecture at the Annual Conference of the National Committee on Art Education, 1962. It is here reprinted in revised form from *Art* (New York: The Museum of Modern Art, 1964), pp. 41–64.

introduces Ingmar Bergman's movie *Wild Strawberries*, one realizes that in itself, the sequence is totally meaningless. At best it creates an emotional climate for the aesthetic experience to follow. It is a windup that remains an empty, misleading gesture, if no pitched ball is to follow. I am afraid that much of what we accept from students in our art classes is of this ineffectual nature; it simply expresses, and fails to communicate.

To the psychoanalyst it is appalling how progressive education, and art teaching in particular, have responded to the insights of psychoanalysis. It is a response showing equal confusion about art teaching and about psychoanalysis. It is especially hard to see how art teachers came to harbor the notion that giving the unconscious "free rein" can be of value, either as education, aesthetics, or therapy. (To those interested in so-called art therapy, I might add that there is hardly a human interaction that cannot lend itself to therapeutic use: some priests serve as therapists for troubled people, but this hardly makes religion therapeutic. Some art teachers endowed with personal skill have had a great therapeutic impact on this or that student while teaching him art; but so have some football coaches, and we do not class football as a therapeutic activity.)

It might seem obvious that if artistic efforts could cure emotional disturbance, then the greater the artistic achievement, the more likely should be the cure. However, I need only refer to van Gogh, whose artistic accomplishments were certainly great but who, as he reached the height of his artistic achievement, first cut off his ear, and then committed suicide. His artistic progress neither led to a schizophrenic break nor did it prevent one. Beethoven, as he wrote his later compositions, perhaps the greatest masterworks of all music, was at the same time becoming beset by delusions of persecution.

It is not the outpouring of the unconscious but rather the mastery of unconscious tendencies, the subjection of creative ability to the greatest aesthetic discipline which alone makes for works of art. Art teachers should know from their own creative efforts what tremendous discipline is necessary to achieve a significant work of art. How then can undisciplined outpourings of the unconscious be accepted as true creation, or as leading to it?

It is true that "artistic" outpourings can be useful for diagnostic purposes. As a matter of fact, there are several tests in the field of visual representation which have proven vastly superior as diagnostic instruments to all more structured, more systemized artistic efforts. They are, for example, the Goodenough Draw-A-Man test, Rorschach's ink blots, and Murray's TAT. All three are characterized by mediocrity as far as aesthetic merits are concerned. The ink blots, which have no structure and no artistic merit whatsoever, are the best of the three, probably because they come closest to the chaotic, wholly unstructured nature of the unconscious. TAT pictures have little or no artistic merit, yet as diagnostic instruments they are far superior to the Goodenough Draw-A-Man test, though the Draw-A-Man gives artistic talent the widest scope.

Again, what makes for creativity is not any unconscious outpouring, but the process whereby carefully selected and arranged elements of such fantasies are rigidly worked over by a critical mind in a most disciplined way within the framework of a well-understood tradition. It is immaterial whether the artist accepts, modifies, or rejects a specific tradition, that is, how in his works he relates to it; but to communicate meaning the work of art in some way must be positively or negatively connected with its tradition. Psychoanalytically speaking, this implies that while the contents of the unconscious serve as the substratum for the work of art, to become one they must be molded and socialized by the forces of the ego and the superego. If I were to express my thinking in a somewhat pedestrian way, I would say that when the importance of the unconscious in art education was recognized, it gave art a unique role, because so much of all other education is designed to repress the unconscious. But to therefore conclude that the remedy is simply to let the unconscious reign in art teaching is erroneous—it is to combat the devil with the devil's grandmother.

Art teaching should indeed show the student that the unconscious is not to be repressed, that it can become a source of great vitality— but only when it has been controlled by the forces of the ego and enriched by its content. What is needed is a disciplined working-over of chaotic unconscious material, a casting of it into forms that are meaningful to others as well as to oneself. Our students must learn that an unconscious used as a natural resource can tremendously vitalize the total personality, while an unrestrained open expression of the unconscious is a step in the direction of personality disintegration.

Perhaps a simple analogy will make the point more graphically. Freud, for good reasons, was fond of illustrating his thinking about the dynamic forces of the unconscious by drawing on parallels from the science of hydrodynamics. Sometimes he compared the mechanics of repression to a huge dam erected to store water.

Unfortunately, this is also an accurate representation of much of our educational system. By erecting a huge dam of repressive measures, we close up behind it all the instinctual pressures, and further channel into the reservoir so created added pressures from our societal demands. But by and large our educational system fails to build sluice-gates into the dam. So the land below it lies fallow and remains arid, because the dam has stopped up the river (of the unconscious) which used to flow through the land. The result of this educational storing-up and repression is, in the majority of cases, a dried-up personality, and in a minority, an explosive spilling of water over the dam that destroys it—as in dropping out, delinquency, violence, and addiction. In my example these may be likened to a breaking-down of the dam, unleashing flood waters that drain away all its accumulated energy as they devastate the land.

Art educators using this simplified example should be aware of the power locked up in this tremendous amount of energy. If they neither dam it up beyond what is best for a person nor allow it to spill wastefully over and away, they can channel and guide it to carefully laid-out beds, so that a valley will blossom in a continued renewal of abundance and creation.

Much damage was done when Freud, in the interest of showing how wide was the application of his psychoanalytic insights, undertook to analyze artists and their works. But, as if to warn us unconsciously that psychoanalysis has nothing to say about aesthetics, he chose for his first full-length study of an artistic creation an extremely poor novel. This was Jensen's *Gradiva*; I do not suggest that you read it, because it would be a waste of time. But even in Freud's famous study of Leonardo, which, as Meyer Schapiro points out, is based on erroneous translations and unjustified extrapolations, Freud had to conclude that while his analysis tells us something about Leonardo the man, it fails entirely to explain why he was a great artist.[1]

---

[1] Freud's most interesting and valuable excursion into the field of art appreciation is his study of the *Moses* of Michelangelo. In it Freud uses introspection—of which he was and remains the supreme master—based on assiduous observation of the work of art to conclude why this work of art is so deeply moving

The same is true for all psychoanalytic studies of great artists. Thousands of people with the same life history and the same emotional disturbance roam the earth and create nothing, or at best empty scribbling. Again and again Freud stated that he had no answer as to why certain psychological constellations, which he deduced to exist in great artists, enabled them to create works of art. Psychoanalysis simply cannot explain creativity.

What happened in the wake of the eager and all too uncritical adoption of psychoanalysis by art education is best expressed by Edith Kramer: "It seems as if the discovery of the role of unconscious processes and primitive instinctual drives in artistic creation has led to a lack of distinction between cause and effect, a confusion of the source of energy with its end results, based on the misunderstanding and over-simplification of psychoanalytic theory."[2]

Art educators, in trying to apply psychology's findings to art, have been led to accept the primitive, unstructured, or playful use of art materials, and to mistake regression for creativity or sublimation. But the value of teaching art to the child, and of all creative activity, does not lie in a freedom of expression that is often little more than regression, but rather in the chance, through art, to integrate unconscious and preconscious material into ego-controlled, creative work. This is doubly important because, as noted earlier, most of the pupil's other classes inhibit the unconscious and preconscious material from any access to the educational process.

Mistaken notions of psychoanalysis have led art to change from the sublime and generally valid statement of a very meaningful personal experience to a humdrum expression of a highly personalized, extremely individual experience that has no general validity. This is a perversion of art. Because true art, in a strange dialectical process unique to it—just because it stands for the deepest personal statement made universal by disciplined effort—becomes one of the greatest

and meaningful to him, and to those who experience it as he does. Thus psychoanalysis can teach us more than other disciplines why a work of art is significant to a person, and in what ways. But this is an entirely different dimension of aesthetics from that which is concerned with what makes a work of art great, or what talents are needed to make it possible for an artist to create it.

[2] Edith Kramer, "Art and Emptiness: New Problems in Art Education and Art Therapy," *Bulletin of Art Therapy* 1:1 (1961).

forces binding people together without lessening what is uniquely personal to them. Art permits them to share with others what all consider something higher—something that lifts them out of the everyday experience to a vision greater than themselves. It is an experience that sheds new meaning on the tribulations of the daily round of existence. It binds the artist to his creation, and the person who experiences art to the very same creation. An aesthetic experience permits the spectator to participate vicariously in the awakening of what is very best in man.

Differing from other experiences that bind people together in something bigger than they are, the aesthetic experience does not ask them to forfeit anything of their personal uniqueness, but leaves it enriched. It is a transpersonal experience that does not infringe on, or reduce, the personal. Need I add that such a view of the creative experience has nothing to do with a view of art as the outpouring of the unconscious? That view perverts art into the opposite, a solipsistic experience that is meaningless to others, cannot be shared by them, and prevents all access to any suprapersonal meaning.

My title for this essay was meant to suggest that it contains one man's opinion about the place of art in education and the life of human beings. But I also wanted to indicate what I believe art's unique role to be: that of guiding the individual to a personal vision of the world, and of his place in it.

Contrary to theories held by some who have disdained art, such as Plato and his followers, art is not an imitation of reality, either external reality or the inner reality of the unconscious. Art is always a vision, an attempt to express visibly—I am tempted to add: and tangibly—what a particular age, a particular society, a particular person has viewed as the true nature and essence of reality, the essence of both man and his relations to significant aspects of the world.

If art educators can make available to future generations the chance to create order out of the chaos of their unconscious, to create a visual image of the hidden aspirations of man—as we are told the Lord created order out of the Chaos—then perhaps man will be able to shape reality in the image of his inner artistic vision.

This has already happened in history; human progress was achieved when reality began to imitate art. The Greeks, in their inner attitudes toward life and themselves, tried to emulate what the sculptors and poets had created from their vision of what man ought to be.

The Renaissance and Reformation, above and beyond the religious struggle, represented a parallel effort. Each tried to free man from being beholden to a world of the beyond. They tried to show him a vision of the world as here and now, and of how to live in it with dignity; a vision we have still to translate fully into reality. The artists of the Renaissance and Reformation, much more than the philosophers, helped man to throw off the burden of original sin, to free himself of his sense of guilt and eternal inadequacy. Man, forming his reality in the image of the artist's vision, slow step by slow step came to feel himself a son of this earth, came to feel that this was a good world in which to live, a world not to be negated but enjoyed in its fullness.

Similarly, Dutch genre painting of the sixteenth and seventeenth centuries was by no means chiefly an authentic image of a fragment of that time's external reality. We are badly mistaken when we consider such paintings "realistic" because they seem so to us. For we view them from the distance of centuries, and we have been living in a world that was created in the image of these paintings.

At the time of their creation, such paintings were only in the most incidental sense re-creations of external reality. They were actually statements of defiance against a religious teaching which looked upon this world as a sham without merit. Far from being "realistic" or imitative, these paintings are a happy vision of this world, as opposed to the next. They present a vision of the sanctity, the beauty, and the vitality of the material world; a vision of how good life can and should be for man here and now. Their vision was in stark opposition to the official view of the world as a vale of tears, one to be quit—the sooner the better—for a life of asceticism, or preferably for Heaven, which passed as the real world.[3]

That we have now come to see these Dutch visions as realism in art, to interpret as mere representation what was actually a statement of revolutionary daring, a new vision of the world, and a call to reexamine every known reigning value shows how successful these artists were in their guidance. For what followed the Renaissance and Reformation was a radical transformation of man's inner attitude toward life. Eventually this transformation led to the rise of the nat-

---

[3] Similar ideas were expressed by Erich Neumann, in *Art and the Creative Unconscious* (New York: Pantheon Books, 1959).

ural sciences, as the scientist began to study nature as carefully in his way as the painter had in his, devoting minute attention to depicting every detail of it.

While the Renaissance rediscovered the dignity of man by creating him in a somewhat idealistic image, it was the painting of the Reformation that discovered him as an individual not in passage to Heaven, but firmly rooted in this time and this place. In a way, such paintings even gave us a vision of the future social sciences. Paintings by Breughel, for example, are also statements of the relation of man to man and to nature; no longer are they statements of his relation to God or to ideals toward which man should strive.

This, in my opinion, is the calling of art: to create for each period a vision of higher integration to come. If the art educator can convey to his students the excitement which such a vision confers, the student, in turn, should find it easier to commit himself to a view of human uniqueness that will prevent him from embracing the narrowness and conformity of a mass society. It should also protect students from being seduced, as some of the best are, into seeking personal salvation by trying to escape from twentieth-century society, whether in the pretend rural settings of exurbia or in the inner retreat of the esoteric circle. Instead the young artist must set his inner artistic vision of a transpersonal meaning against the blinders of self-advancement, to which the rest of his educational experience seems to guide him. Through such a vision this world of mass living might be changed, while there is still time, into a human society where people work successfully together to translate their unique personal visions of the good life into reality by helping to create a social setting which encourages people to integrate themselves and facilitates their living autonomously.

The visions of the great artists have, each in its own time and its own society, transcended person and place, leading fellow-men or the next generations out of their confinements toward the not yet existent, not yet realized age and society. For it is this struggle alone that dignifies our existence on earth. Artists express it through painting and sculptures. I lack the gift of translating their visions into words. Fortunately the poets do paint with words, and I would like to quote one of them on his vision of beauty, of its nature and place in our world.

Rilke, in what he jotted down on the writing-pad which contains the draft of the last two of the *Duino Elegies* to be written, comments on what separates art from therapy, or from social engineering. "Art cannot be helpful through our trying to keep and especially concerning ourselves with the distresses of others, but in so far as we bear our own distresses more passionately, give, now and then, a perhaps clearer meaning to endurance, and develop for ourselves the means of expressing the suffering within us and its conquest more precisely and clearly than is possible to those who have to apply their powers to something else."[4] And as if he had foreseen where we should find ourselves standing today, he also wrote: "Only through one of the greatest and innermost renovations it has ever gone through will the world be able to save and maintain itself." As for the artist's task in this our world, it was: "To prepare in men's hearts the way for those gentle, mysterious, trembling transformations, from which alone the understandings and harmonies of a serener future will proceed." And here in essence is Rilke's vision, from the first of the *Duino Elegies*:

> For Beauty's nothing
> but beginning of Terror we're still just able to bear,
> and why we adore it so is because it serenely
> disdains to destroy us.

Beauty, he knew, takes us to the very brink of our existence, forces on us the harsh knowing of limitations, but at the same time opens up visions of a world where we shall transcend our limitations and win out over terror.

This is an experience that only a few of the greatest artists are able to make universal through form, give objective existence in their work. But it can be shared by many, perhaps all of us, if we are taught to keep ourselves open. In this sense, great art is a learning experience. To the art teacher falls the glory of educating his students to be able to experience within themselves subjectively what the artist has given life to in objective form.

With this as a point of departure, I would like to mention at least one further misconception rampant at present about the role of art in life. It is one that has a negative influence on the art educator, be-

---

[4] This and the following quotations are from Rainer Maria Rilke, *Duino Elegies* (New York: W. W. Norton & Co., 1939).

cause his views of contemporary life and the role of art in society are affected by it.

To quote Arthur J. Goldberg as secretary of labor: "In a complex, modern society like our own, art of all kinds is called to one of the essential services of freedom—to free man from the mass. Art—whether on the stage, in a gallery or in a concert hall—asserts the supremacy of the individual. The insight of the artist leads to a cultural discovery for all of the people."[5] If he is correct, and I believe that he is, in asserting that the great significance art can have in our own time and society is to free man from the mass, then we must beware of making art merely one more aspect of mass living.

The number of people who paint means very little compared to what they paint and how they paint it. Yet all too often I find the correct notion—that the insight of the artist leads to a cultural discovery for all of the people—perverted to mean that all people can, by their dabbling in paint, transform their insights into art. The slogan that everybody can paint, which everybody certainly can, should never be taken to mean that everybody is an artist. But unfortunately, the conviction that art has something of great import to say to everybody who is ready and able to respond appropriately to its message is often taken to mean that everybody who has learned to dip his brush into paint has something of importance to add to man's understanding of himself and the world.

An example from the field of music may illustrate this point: hundreds of thousands of people can only fumblingly play a piece by Bach on the piano. But through these fumbling efforts, they achieve a far greater understanding of Bach and his achievement than they would had they never struggled to re-create his music on their own. Apart from the very few great musicians, and a few others who may delude themselves into believing they are great musicians, the overwhelming majority know perfectly well that they are not artists, and that while they try to play great music, the sounds they produce are a far cry from great, or from being creative. But they also realize that their own efforts, non-creative and non-artistic as they are, provide them with a deeper appreciation of the achievement of the great art-

---

[5] Arthur J. Goldberg, "To Come to the Aid of the Arts," *New York Times Magazine*, March 11, 1962, pp. 26, 110–11.

ist, and a heightened trust in their own aesthetic experience of the great work of art.

In learning music, a student is often asked to write some music, perhaps a chorale. He usually is able to write a perfectly correct musical score. But his score is almost always so unmusical that it teaches the student an unforgettable lesson in what good music is really all about. Thus his own effort reveals, rather than bridges, the abyss between what he can do and what Bach achieved.

Applying this to painting, the fumbling efforts of the student are perfectly legitimate exercises, as scales are in music, and in some cases these efforts are of great value, if they lead the student to a better understanding of great art. But such efforts must be correctly viewed by the student as exercises, showing him the tremendous gap between creative art and non-creative exercises in the same medium. His own painting is a harmless and enjoyable pastime, and may offer him access to a better appreciation of great art, but with very rare exceptions it is neither art nor creative.

Therefore art educators will have to make up their minds whether painting as a leisure-time activity for the masses is a price worth paying if it reduces art to a diversion from humdrum mass living rather than what lifts us out of it and challenges us to strive for a higher integration of ourselves and of our society. I fear that art cannot be both a leisure-time activity for the masses that is yet given most serious acceptance as such, and the realization in form, the embodiment, of what in a religious age might have been called the divine spirit.

Related to this, I find that art educators, in writing for their colleagues, make fervent assertions of how practical art is—that it is rational and that it contributes to a more comfortable and better life. The pyramids were neither practical nor did they make for a better life for the pharaohs; nor did Leonardo make life more practical or better for Mona Lisa. If we are after practicality, rationality, and comfort, it would seem to me that almost any human endeavor except art has a better claim to our attention. We shall have to give up the notion that art can be everything to everybody, because if it is, then it adds up to being nothing of real importance to anyone.

I believe that the whole of our education has grown much too practical and rational in a narrow sense, being far too concerned with what seems useful at the moment, as against a long-range view of life, art, and humanity. I am personally in great sympathy with the humanistic tradition. This is not because of the veneration usually accorded its subject matter, often by those who have no use for it in their own lives, but because of its insistence that the educational process deal with subjects that are not necessarily practical, do not necessarily yield monetary returns or spell success in our present-day society. My sympathy rests not with those who insist on the learning of Latin, Greek, or ancient history because of the "importance" of these subjects—for as subjects they are not preferable to many others —but with those who insist on a philosophy of education which asserts that a human being must be concerned with things that don't necessarily have practical application; with matters that far transcend what might be useful at the moment, or a particular political end. Subjects such as Latin or ancient history—but also many others, such as physics—when taught well, however impractical, offer wide vistas to the imagination of the human being, transcending not only the self, but also the immediate, the practical, the necessary or advantageous.

Now, I do not believe that Latin or Greek is necessarily the best way to offer future generations of Americans a chance for transpersonal, transpractical experiences. I believe that other subjects, such as the arts, can be far more effective in leading students toward a truly personal view of life and man, full of richness, imagination, and comprehension, going beyond what is useful.

Whatever the chosen medium of a student, I believe that the main purpose of his efforts in the arts should be to accept the importance, first of listening carefully and trying to understand what is moving man from the inside, and then of making disciplined efforts to express it in external form, both to understand it better and for others to see. But even if a student succeeds in his efforts, that does not make him an artist. It cannot make him an artist, because he is much too young for that. It takes a mature mind and a great deal of living to bear in oneself a vision of the better world which the real artist strives for and then embodies in aesthetic form. Students can barely be taken to the threshold of a new freedom of life and experience.

The task of a student at a young age is to try to bring order and comprehension to the chaos that reigns within him. In all his other classes he is asked to deny his chaos, to repress it and consider it invalid and unimportant. Only in art teaching can one show him that from a child, expected to take in and learn what others tell him to, he can grow into a free person struggling with and expressing his vision of himself and of life.

Here again, the paths of the psychoanalyst and the art educator cross. Like true philosophers and healers of the mind, art educators must be good midwives, trying to bring into being the personal visions which have not yet seen the light of the world. For an infinitely small number, this midwifery will bring into being a great or perhaps only a middling-great artist. For the overwhelming majority of students, such midwifery may well be the only chance they encounter in their lives to come close to the visions of the great artists. That chance is enough for most of us, and will have to be enough for most of them.

But this is no easy task, because of the inimical institutional framework within which most art teachers work. Our educational system per se exposes the art educator to heavy stresses, because it is basically contrary to the needs of the developing individual seeking to realize himself. Official well-meant statements to the contrary, art teaching still has to proceed within a basically closed system. Within it our children and adolescents continue to be the victims of a cultural heritage of domination and bias, of fears and anxieties on the part of parents and teachers. Despite loud assertions to the contrary, these adults remain afraid of permitting children to think and act for themselves. The outcome of such domination is familiar to all of us: on the one hand we find a lack of motivation or else revolt, and on the other hand an empty conformity, submission, or, in fact, atrophy.

While most American high school curricula are possibly adequate to teach biology or math or American history—though I doubt it— they give the student little chance for rising above the level of a cultural wasteland. Nearly the whole of the student's school experience relates uniquely and exclusively to the recorded experience of others. Most of the problems have ready-made answers in the back of the book or, more up to date, in the preset teaching machines. Our educational system is not concerned with originality or creativity; it is concerned mainly with acquiring a body of knowledge narrowly defined; with the memorization of facts, the finding of ready answers to problems, answers that are already known to somebody—or the test could not be scored.

Art, on the other hand, should eternally pose new problems of freedom and higher integration, despite our being beholden to nature and our inherent weakness. To these new problems of creative freedom each person can find his own unique solution, because no general answers are possible. I would remind you of Kant's *Critique of Judgment,* where he makes an all-important point: that the essential value of the aesthetic experience resides in this uniqueness, that only about this single human experience can no true-or-false statements be made. This is the realm of imaginative freedom, where all questions, including ones about the meaning of life and of beauty, can be discussed but not solved, because their permanent solution leaves nothing to live for, spells death.

That is why I question courses that tell us how to look at pictures or what to see in them. That can only lead to teaching machines in art. Such courses are at best crutches, at worst blinders preventing an aesthetic experience. I recall how the great poets were for decades ruined for me because I was taught what made them great and how to enjoy and understand them. It was hard work for me later to unearth their greatness, their tremendous personal message, from under the rubble of teaching which had buried them for me. That was bad teaching, and though we all know it, continuous watchfulness is still necessary so that a better way to create or appreciate art can reign in our art classes.

This, then, is my thesis: the teaching of art is the only subject in his educational experience where a member of the future generation can be offered the chance to truly find himself as a unique person; because only here are there no ready-made answers telling him what he ought to see, feel, and think or in which way he ought to find his self-realization. But too often in practice either the art teacher insists that he knows what is good art and bad; or else there is an uncritical acceptance of any outpouring as being imbued with the artistic spirit. Neither the right-or-wrong approach which prevails in all other subjects, nor an uncritical acceptance of any outpouring, will give art a chance to rectify the deadening impact much of the rest of the educational experience has on children.

Art education, more than any other subject taught, presents the student with the rare opportunity to free himself at least temporarily from the falseness, the pretensions, the trappings of our culture. But it can do so only if those trappings are not introduced in the art class, as concern either with prestige, with success in the practical sphere, or with culture as a social adornment. Art must remain free of those features of the educational system that are contrary to the aesthetic experience, such as assignments, competition for grades, or other expedient routines. Only then will art education leave the student open to a personal encounter with art. And by this I mean what he learns from his own inadequate efforts, and from measuring those efforts against the achievement of the great artists. This process is what gives him a chance to open the totality of his own experience to a true encounter with great art. In this manner his own chaotic unconscious and its derivatives will be formed and aesthetically mastered, both by the conscious demands of his medium and through the head-on encounter with the visions of the masters.

Here I would like again to refer back to my own past. Another of my early interests lay with what might be called Jewish tradition. Although an atheist, I was deeply impressed by the poetic view of the world that some Hasidic rabbis expressed in their enigmatic sayings. Like us, they were teachers; and what they were trying to teach was a religious experience freed of the shackles of institutional religion. (Since art and religion have a common origin, perhaps art is destined, in our secular society, to take the place which religion once held.) In any case, Rabbi Nachman taught that: "Just as the hand held before the eyes conceals the greatest mountain, so this petty earthly life conceals from view the vast light and mysteries of which the world is full, and he who can withdraw it from his eyes, as one withdraws the hand, will behold the great light of the innermost world."

This is the book of a survivor; hence its title. In it I assembled themes which have occupied my mind since I became a survivor. I can best adumbrate my purpose for doing so by quoting from the preface to *The Nigger of the Narcissus*, which originally was printed as its afterword. In it Joseph Conrad writes: "My task which I am trying to achieve is, by power of the written word to make you hear, to make you feel—it is, before all, to make you *see*. That—and no more, and it is everything. If I succeed, you shall find there according to your deserts: encouragement, consolation, fear, . . . and, perhaps, also that glimpse of truth for which you have forgotten to ask."

Index

"The Ignored Lesson of Anne Frank" and "Growing Up Female" originally appeared in *Harper's* magazine.

"Portnoy Psychoanalyzed" originally appeared in *Midstream* magazine.

A review of Hannah Arendt's "Eichmann In Jerusalem: A report on the Banality of Evil" originally appeared in *The New Republic* magazine.

The essay "Surviving" appeared originally in *The New Yorker*.

Grateful acknowledgment is made to the following for permission to reprint previously published material:

The American Academy of Political and Social Science: for the article "Violence: A Neglected Mode of Behavior," reprinted from Vol. 364 (March 1966) of *The Annals of The American Academy of Political and Social Science,* © 1966 by The American Academy of Political and Social Science. All rights reserved. Philadelphia.

American Orthopsychiatric Association, Inc.: for "Schizophrenia as a Reaction to Extreme Situations," reprinted, with permission, from *The American Journal of Orthopsychiatry,* copyright © 1956 by The American Orthopsychiatric Association, Inc.

Hart Publishing Company, Inc.: "About the Sexual Revolution" was published as a chapter in *Sexual Latitude: For and Against* by Bruno Bettelheim, New York: Hart Publishing Company, Inc., 1971, pp. 227-243. Reprinted with additions and changes by permission of Hart Publishing Company, Inc. "About Summerhill" was published as a chapter in *Summerhill: For and Against,* by Bruno Bettelheim, Hart Publishing Company, Inc., New York, 1970. Reprinted with some changes by permission of Hart Publishing Company, Inc.

Harvard University Press: "Education and the Reality Principle", copyright © 1970 by the President and Fellows of Harvard College.

The Museum of Modern Art: for "A Personal Vision, the Charles Francis Memorial Lecture," first published in *Art: As the Measure of Man* by George D. Stoddard; *As Education* by Irwin Edman; *A Personal Vision* by Bruno Bettelheim. Copyright © 1964 by the Museum of Modern Art, New York. All rights reserved. Reprinted by permission of the publisher.

Quadrangle/Times Books, Inc.: Excerpt from *The Third Reich of Dreams* by Charlotte Beradt. Copyright © 1966 by Nymphenburger Verlagshandlung GmbH, Munich. First published 1966 as *Das Dritte Reich des Traums.* English translation copyright © 1968 by Quadrangle/Times Books, Inc. from *The Third Reich of Dreams* by Charlotte Beradt.

University of Chicago: for "Alienation and Autonomy," published in *Changing Perspectives On Man,* ed. Ben Rothblatt, by University of Chicago Press, © 1968 by the University of Chicago; "The Decision to Fail," reprinted, with minor changes and deletions, from *The School Review* copyright © 1961 by the University of Chicago; "Mental Health in the Slums," reprinted from *The Social Impact of Urban Design* copyright © 1971 by the University of Chicago. "The Ultimate Limit" incorporates part of a different essay with the same title that appeared originally in *Midway,* IX, 2, Autumn 1968, copyright © 1968 by the University of Chicago. All articles reprinted by permission of the University of Chicago.

ABOUT THE AUTHOR

Bruno Bettelheim, recognized throughout the world as one of the greatest living child psychologists, and honored especially for his work with autistic children, was born in Vienna in 1903. He received his doctorate at the University of Vienna, and came to America in 1939, after a year in the concentration camps of Dachau and Buchenwald. He is Distinguished Professor of Education Emeritus and Professor Emeritus of both psychology and psychiatry at the University of Chicago. His previous books include *Children of the Dream, The Informed Heart, Love Is Not Enough,* and *A Home for the Heart.* In 1977 he won both the National Book Award and the National Book Critics' Circle Award for *The Uses of Enchantment.*